I NEVER KNEW
I HAD A CHOICE

3rd Edition

Other books by Gerald Corey:

Case Approach to Counseling and Psychotherapy,
2nd Edition (1986)

Theory and Practice of Counseling and Psychotherapy,
3rd Edition (and *Manual*) (1986)

Theory and Practice of Group Counseling,
2nd Edition (and *Manual*) (1985)

By Gerald Corey and Marianne Schneider Corey:

Groups: Process and Practice,
2nd Edition (1982)

Issues and Ethics in the Helping Professions,
2nd Edition (1984, with Patrick Callanan)

Casebook of Ethical Guidelines for Group Leaders
(1982, with Patrick Callanan)

Group Techniques
(1982, with Patrick Callanan and J. Michael Russell)

I NEVER KNEW
I HAD A CHOICE

3rd Edition

Gerald Corey

California State University, Fullerton
Diplomate in Counseling Psychology,
American Board of Professional Psychology

in collaboration with
Marianne Schneider Corey

Brooks/Cole Publishing Company
Monterey, California

Brooks/Cole Publishing Company
A Division of Wadsworth, Inc.

Printed in the United States of America

10 9 8 7 6 5 4 3 2 1

Library of Congress Cataloging in Publication Data

Corey, Gerald F.
   I never knew I had a choice.

   Bibliography; p.
   Includes index.
   1. Self-perception.   2. Choice (Psychology)
3. Emotions.   4. Success.   I. Corey, Marianne
Schneider, 1942–   . II. Title.
BF697.C67   1985   158   85-11306
ISBN 0 534 05418 8

Sponsoring Editor: *Claire Verduin*
Project Development Editor: *John Bergez*
Production Coordinator: *Fiorella Ljunggren*
Manuscript Editor: *William Waller*
Permissions Editor: *Carline Haga*
Cover and Interior Design: *Sharon Kinghan*
Cover Illustration: *Sharon Kinghan, Neil Oatley*
Back-Cover Photo: *Olan Mills*
Art Coordinator: *Michèle Judge*
Interior Illustrations: *Ron Grauer*
Photo Editor: *Judy K. Blamer*
Photo Researcher: *Marquita Flemming*
Typesetting: *Donnelley/Rocappi, Inc., Cherry Hill, New Jersey*
Printing and Binding: *R. R. Donnelley & Sons Company, Crawfordsville, Indiana*
(Credits continue on p. 411)

In memory of my friend Jim Morelock,
a searcher who lived and died with dignity
and self-respect,
who struggled and questioned,
who made the choice to live his days fully
until time ran out on him at age 25.

I Never Knew I Had a Choice is intended for college students of any age and for all others who wish to expand their self-awareness and explore the choices available to them in significant areas of their life. The topics discussed include choosing a personal style of learning; reviewing childhood and adolescence; the challenges of adulthood and autonomy; the body; the significance of sex roles, sexuality, love, intimacy, solitude, and work in our life; the meaning of death and loss; and the ways in which we choose our values and philosophy of life.

This is a personal book, because I encourage readers to examine the choices they have made and how these choices affect their present level of satisfaction. (It is also a personal book in another sense, inasmuch as I describe my own concerns, struggles, decisions, and values with regard to many of the issues raised.) The book is designed to be a personal workbook as well as a classroom text. Each chapter begins with a self-inventory that gives readers the chance to focus on their present beliefs and attitudes. Within the chapters, sections called Time Out for Personal Reflection offer an opportunity to pause and reflect on the issues raised. Additional activities and exercises are provided at the end of each chapter for classroom participation or activity outside of class. Each chapter also contains a list of suggested readings, most of which are available in paperback. I wish to stress that this is an *unfinished book*, since readers are encouraged to become the co-authors in their own personal way through the many opportunities for active involvement.

What are the changes from the second to this third edition? The introductory chapter now emphasizes the importance of self-exploration and invites students to consider the values and excitement, as well as the commitment and work, involved in learning about oneself, others, and personal growth. Chapters 2 and 3 provide theoretical material on personality development within a life-span perspective, as well as practical tools for helping readers modify the design of their present and future existence in their struggle toward autonomy. Chapter 4, "Your Body," has been largely rewritten to expand on topics such as body image, touch and sensuality, self-expression, body-oriented psychotherapies, and the body and stress. Sex roles and sexuality are now covered in separate chapters (Chapters 5 and 6), which include more material on challenging traditional sex roles, learning to appreciate ourselves as sexual beings, and viewing sex in the context of intimacy.

Fewer major changes are evident in Chapter 7, "Love," and Chapter 8, "Intimate Relationships," but there is new material on effective interpersonal communications and choosing the single life-style. Chapter 9, "Loneliness and Solitude," focuses on the creative dimensions of solitude, and it also contains a new section on shyness. Chapter 10, "Work," has been largely rewritten, and several important issues have been introduced, such as college education as work, trends in the world of work, specific factors in vocational decision making, the role of leisure in providing a balance to work, and active career planning. The remaining chapters, "Death and Loss" and "Meaning and Values: Putting Life in Perspective" (Chapters 11 and 12), have been updated and expanded as needed, with new coverage of the following topics: fears of death, the interdependence of life and death, the importance of grieving, meaning in life and the threat of nuclear annihilation, and choosing experiences for personal growth.

Another new feature of the third edition is the Resource Guide at the end of the book. It provides practical tools to help students carry out the attitudinal and behavioral changes they are challenged to make throughout the chapters. These how-to resources include study hints; a model for self-directed change; a scale for monitoring stress; relaxation methods; suggestions for weight control; an alcoholism inventory; strategies for vocational choice; consumer guidelines for counseling services; and other inventories and self-assessment scales.

Fundamentally, my approach in *I Never Knew I Had a Choice* is humanistic and personal; that is, I stress the healthy and effective personality and the common struggles that most of us experience in becoming autonomous. I especially emphasize accepting personal responsibility for the choices we make and consciously deciding whether and how we want to change our life.

Although my own approach can be broadly characterized as humanistic and existential, my aim has been to challenge readers to recognize and assess their own choices, beliefs, and values, rather than to convert them to a particular point of view. My basic premise is that a commitment of self-exploration can create new potentials for a choice. Many of my clients are relatively well-functioning people who desire more from life and who want to recognize and remove blocks to their personal creativity and freedom. It is for people like these that I've written this book.

In developing the various chapters, I talked with both students and instructors in courses such as Psychology of Personal Growth at many community colleges. A frequent theme was that students selected such a course because of their interest in discovering more about themselves and their relationships with others. Most of them were looking for a *practical* course, one that dealt with real issues in everyday living and that would provide an impetus for their own personal growth. Accordingly, I have focused on helping readers recognize blocks to their creative and productive energies, to find ways of removing these obstructions, and to make conscious choices to modify their attitudes and behavior.

The experiences of those who have read and used the earlier editions of *I Never Knew I Had a Choice* reveal that the themes explored have application to a diversity of ages and backgrounds. Readers who have taken the time to write us about their reactions say that the book encouraged them to take an honest look at their life and challenge themselves to make certain changes. Although the book was written primarily for a college market, some readers have shared it with friends and relatives.

I wrote this book for use in college courses dealing with the psychology of adjustment, personality development, applied psychology, educational psychology, personal growth, and self-awareness. It has also been adopted in courses ranging from the training of teachers and counselors to introductory psychology. My experience has been that active, open, and personal participation in these courses can lead to expanded self-awareness and greater autonomy in living.

An updated and expanded *Instructor's Resource Manual* accompanies this textbook. It includes sections on test items, both multiple-choice and essay, for every chapter; a student's study guide covering all chapters; questions for thought and discussion; numerous activities and exercises for classroom participation; guidelines for using the book and teaching the course; examples of various formats of personal-growth classes; guidelines for maximizing personal learning and for reviewing and integrating the course; and a student evaluation instrument to assess the impact of the course on readers.

Acknowledgments

I wish to acknowledge the contributions of a number of people to this book. Most significant is my wife, Marianne Schneider Corey, who has collaborated with me on this project. Although I did most of the actual writing, Marianne and I discussed at length each of the issues explored, and many of the ideas and illustrative examples in these pages are hers. Some of our friends have commented that I have provided the body and Marianne has given the book its soul!

I also wish to express my deep appreciation for the insightful suggestions given to me by friends, associates, reviewers, readers, and students. The following people provided helpful reviews for this revision: John H. Brennecke, Mount San Antonio College; Kenneth E. Coffield, University of Alabama, Huntsville; Helene Goodwin, Merritt Community College; Michael Levine, Bloomsburg University; Joan Matthews, Coordinating Board, Texas College and University System; and Margaret C. Park, St. Louis Community College. Allan Abbott and his wife, Katherine, provided much help in connection with Chapter 4, as did James M. Morrow, Western Carolina University, with Chapter 10.

Friends and former students who provided many valuable ideas and who reviewed the manuscript are Joanna Doland, who also prepared the index for the book, Carl Johnson, Andrea Mark, and Jane Sipe.

I am indebted to my close friends and colleagues J. Michael Russell, California State University, Fullerton, and Patrick Callanan, in private practice in Santa Ana, California, for many provocative discussions concerning the ideas raised in this book.

Finally, I want to acknowledge the contributions and exceptionally fine support of the Brooks/Cole staff, especially Claire Verduin and John Bergez. They arranged for and participated in a weekend seminar with the reviewers of this third edition, held in September 1984. As a result of the lively exchanges that took place that weekend, this edition has been substantially improved. Finally, Bill Waller, manuscript editor, Fiorella Ljunggren, production coordinator, and Sharon Kinghan, designer, deserve congratulations for their special contributions to the quality of this book.

Gerald Corey

C O N T E N T S

3   ADULTHOOD AND AUTONOMY   63

4   YOUR BODY   99

5   SEX ROLES   132

12 MEANING AND VALUES: PUTTING LIFE IN PERSPECTIVE   338

RESOURCE GUIDE   369

I NEVER KNEW
I HAD A CHOICE

3rd Edition

INVITATION TO PERSONAL LEARNING AND GROWTH

INTRODUCTION: CHOICE AND CHANGE

This book is for anyone who seriously wants to examine his or her life and live by free choice rather than by past conditioning. By *conditioning* I mean the shaping of our attitudes and behaviors by outside influences. Here are a few ways in which your life may be restricted by conditioning: You may be clinging to old decisions you made under the influence of your parents or others. You may be avoiding asking yourself what the meaning of your life really is. You may be allowing society to dictate what it means to be a woman or a man, rather than choosing your own sex-role identity. And you may be letting others tell you what you should value, rather than carving out your own meanings and values. You might say: "Well, obviously nobody wants to be restricted by conditioning. We're all interested in growing, learning more about ourselves, and being the master of our own fate rather than being directed and shaped by others." Yet to varying degrees most of us are living in ways that are not fully satisfying. In large ways or in small ones we complain of feeling powerless, of living by the expectations and designs of others, and of believing that external circumstances prohibit any real change on our part. Statements such as the following reflect this attitude of being convinced that our destiny is determined: "If only my wife were more affectionate, I'd feel more worthwhile." "I'd like to say what I feel, but I'm afraid I'll lose my friends if I do." "I know I'm shy, but it's too late for me to change because I've been this way since I was a child."

Are You Ready to Change?

One way to begin focusing on the quality of your life is by reflecting on these questions: Are you comfortable with yourself now? Or are there some things you'd like to change? Do you see any risks in making a personal commitment to explore various aspects of your life? Are you reluctant to recognize problem areas, for fear that you'll feel overwhelmed if you begin to question your life?

It is not uncommon to hear someone say: "I don't know if I want to rock the boat. Things aren't all that bad in my life. I'm fairly secure, and I don't want to take the chance of losing this security. I'm afraid that if I start probing around I may uncover things I can't handle." I don't see it as a sign of cowardice to have doubts and fears over changing your stance in the world. In fact, it is a mark of bravery to acknowledge your resistance to change and your anxiety over taking increased control of your life. Furthermore, there are outer as well as inner obstacles when you take significant steps to live differently. Those who are close to you may not support your changes and may even put up barriers to your designing a new life. Your culture may have taboos against your assuming a new role

and modifying certain values. All of these factors are likely to cause some anxiety as you contemplate making your own choices rather than allowing others to choose for you. Exploring yourself, being honest with yourself and others, thinking for yourself, and making a commitment to live by your choices entail hard work.

I encourage you to challenge your fears rather than being stopped by them. This book is intended to inspire you to reflect on the quality of your life and to help you decide for yourself on some ways in which you want to improve it. Socrates said "The unexamined life is not worth living." As you examine your values and typical behavior in this course, fresh and exciting options are likely to open up to you. As one of my clients put it: "One thing I can see now that I didn't see before is that I can change my life if I want to. *I never knew I had a choice!*" This remark captures the central message of this book: we are *not* passive victims of life, we *do* make choices, and we *do* have the power to change major aspects of our life as we struggle toward a more authentic existence.

What about Other People?

In his book *How I Found Freedom in an Unfree World* Harry Browne (1973) argues that it is a great mistake to assume that we cannot change or become free until other people give us permission to. Instead, Browne insists, we must retain final "permission rights" for ourselves. By the same token, we should not expect that others will necessarily change because we do. The focus for change needs to be on ourselves, *not* others. For one thing, we don't have the power to change other people unless they want to change. Moreover, we can easily encounter an impasse by focusing on all the ways we wish they would change. If we wait for others to become different or if we blame them for the fact that we're not as happy as we'd like, we diminish our power to take full control of our own life. For example, if you want a closer relationship with your father and insist that he talk to you more and approve of you, you are likely to experience frustration. He may never approach you the way you want him to. You will increase your chances of success if *you* do what you want *him* to do.

As this example shows, the idea of personal choice does not imply doing whatever we want without regard for others. Making a commitment to examine our life does not mean becoming wrapped up in ourselves to the exclusion of everyone else. But I believe that, unless we know and care about ourselves, we cannot develop genuinely caring relationships. As we enrich our own life by making constructive choices, we can also improve our interpersonal relationships.

Throughout this book I've made disclosures about my own life. It seemed fitting to use a personal style and to openly share with you how I arrived at some of the beliefs and values I write about. I hope that knowing my assumptions, biases, and struggles helps you evaluate your own position with more clarity. I'm not suggesting that you adopt my philosophy of life but rather that you ask how the issues I raise concern *you*. What are *your* answers? What are the choices *you've* made for yourself? What choices do you want to make now?

SELF-ACTUALIZATION: A MODEL FOR PERSONAL GROWTH

One of the obvious benefits of choosing to change our life is that we will grow by exposing ourselves to new experiences. It's time we looked more closely at just what personal growth entails. This section contrasts the idea of *growth* with that of *adjustment* and offers a humanistic model of what ideal growth can be.

Adjustment or Growth?

Although this book deals with questions in what is often called "the psychology of adjustment," I have an uneasy feeling about this common phrase. The term *adjustment* is frequently taken to mean that there is an ideal norm that people should be measured by. This notion raises many problems. You may ask, for example: What is the desired norm of adjustment? Who determines the standards of "good" adjustment? Is it possible that the same person could be considered well adjusted in our culture and poorly adjusted in some other culture?

A further bias I have against the "adjustment" concept of human behavior is that those who claim to be well-adjusted have often settled for a complacent and dead existence, one that has neither challenge nor excitement. My hope is that we can create our own definitions of ourselves as persons, rather than being primarily ruled by other people's norms or expectations.

Instead of talking about *adjustment*, then, I prefer to talk about *growth*. A psychology of growth rests on the assumption that growth is a lifelong adventure, not some fixed point at which we arrive. Personal growth is best viewed as a *process* rather than as a goal or an end. A growth-oriented perspective assumes that we will face numerous crises at the various stages of our development. These crises can be challenges to give our lives new meaning. In order to continue to grow, we have to be willing to let go of some of our old ways of thinking and being in order to make room for new behavior. During your reading and studying, think about the ways in which you've stopped growing and the degree to which you're willing to invest in personal growth.

A Humanistic Approach to Personal Growth

I Never Knew I Had a Choice is based on a humanistic view of people. A central concept of this approach to personal growth is that of *self-actualization*. Striving for self-actualization means working toward fulfilling our potential, toward becoming all that we are capable of becoming. Humanistic psychology is based on the premise that we have such a "growth urge," but you should not think that this is an automatic process. Since we realize that growth can be painful, we experience a constant struggle between our desire for security, or dependence, and our desire to experience the delights of growth.

Self-actualization was a central theme in the work of Abraham Maslow (1968, 1970, 1971). Maslow used the phrase "the psychopathology of the average" to highlight his contention that merely "normal" people may never extend themselves to become what they are capable of becoming. Further, he criticized Freudian psychology for its preoccupation with the sick and crippled side of human nature; if we base our findings on a sick population, Maslow reasoned, we will have a sick psychology. Thus, he believed that too much research was being conducted into anxiety, hostility, and neuroses and too little into joy, creativity, and self-fulfillment.

In his quest to create a humanistic psychology that would focus on our potential, Maslow studied what he believed were self-actualizing people and found that they differed in important ways from so-called "normals." Some of the characteristics that Maslow found in these people were a capacity to tolerate and even welcome uncertainty in their life, an acceptance of themselves and others, spontaneity and creativity, a need for privacy and solitude, autonomy, a capacity for deep and intense interpersonal relationships, a genuine caring for others, a sense of humor, an inner-directedness (as opposed to the tendency to live by others' expectations), and the absence of artificial dichotomies within themselves (such as work/play, love/hate, weak/strong).

Carl Rogers (1961, 1980), a major figure in the development of humanistic psychology, has built his entire theory and practice of psychotherapy on the concept of the "fully functioning person," which is much like Maslow's notion of the "self-actualizing" person. According to Rogers, most people ask the basic questions "Who am I? How can I discover my real self? How can I become what I deeply wish to become? How can I get behind my facade and become myself?" Rogers found that, when people give up their facade and accept themselves, they move in the direction of being open to experience (that is, they begin to see reality without distorting it), they trust themselves and look to themselves for the answers to their problems, and they no longer attempt to become fixed entities or products, realizing instead that growth is a continual process. Such fully functioning people, Rogers writes, are in a fluid process of challenging and revising their perceptions and beliefs as they open themselves to new experiences.

Rogers, in contrast to those who assume that we are by nature irrational and destructive unless we are socialized, exhibits a deep faith in human beings. He sees people as naturally social and forward-moving, as striving to become fully functioning, and as having at their deepest core a positive goodness. In short, people are to be trusted; and, as they are basically cooperative and constructive, there is no need to control their aggressive impulses.

Overview of Maslow's Self-Actualization Theory

We can summarize some of the basic ideas of the humanistic approach by means of Maslow's model of the self-actualizing person. Maslow describes self-actualization in his book *Motivation and Personality* (1970), and he also treats the concept in his other books (1968, 1971).

Self-Awareness.   Self-actualizing people are more aware of themselves, of others, and of reality than are nonactualizing people. Specifically, they demonstrate the following behavior and traits:

1. *Efficient perception of reality*
   a. Self-actualizing people see reality as it is.
   b. They have an ability to detect phoniness.
   c. They avoid seeing things in preconceived categories.
2. *Ethical awareness*
   a. Self-actualizing people display a knowledge of what is right and wrong for them.
   b. They have a sense of inner direction.
   c. They avoid being pressured by others and living by others' standards.
3. *Freshness of appreciation.* Like children, self-actualizing people have an ability to perceive life in a fresh way.
4. *Peak moments*
   a. Self-actualizing people experience times of being one with the universe; they experience moments of joy.
   b. They have the ability to be changed by such moments.

Freedom.   Self-actualizing people are willing to make choices for themselves, and they are free to reach their potential. This freedom entails a sense of detachment and a need for privacy, a creativity and spontaneity, and an ability to accept responsibility for choices.

1. *Detachment*
   a. For self-actualizing people, the need for privacy is crucial.
   b. They have a need for solitude in order to put things in perspective.
   c. They have an ability to be objective—to see life as it is.
2. *Creativity*
   a. Creativity is a universal characteristic of self-actualizing people.
   b. Creativity may be expressed in any area of life; it shows itself as inventiveness.
3. *Spontaneity*
   a. Self-actualizing people don't need to show off.
   b. They display a naturalness and lack of pretentiousness.
   c. They act with ease and grace.

Basic Honesty and Caring.   Self-actualizing people show a deep caring for and honesty with themselves and others. These qualities are reflected in their interest in humankind and in their interpersonal relationships.

1. *Sense of social interest*
   a. Self-actualizing people have a concern for the welfare of others.
   b. They have a sense of communality with all other people.
   c. They have an interest in bettering the world.
2. *Interpersonal relationships*
   a. Self-actualizing people have a capacity for real love and fusion with another.

   b. They are able to love and respect themselves.
   c. They are able to go outside themselves in a mature love.
   d. They are motivated by the urge to grow in their relationships.
3. *Sense of humor*
   a. Self-actualizing people can laugh at themselves.
   b. They can laugh at the human condition.
   c. Their humor is not hostile.

Trust and Autonomy.   Self-actualizing people exhibit faith in themselves and others; they are independent; they accept themselves as valuable persons; and their lives have meaning.

1. *Search for purpose and meaning*
   a. Self-actualizing people have a sense of mission, of a calling in which their potential can be fulfilled.
   b. They are engaged in a search for identity, often through work that is a deeply significant part of their lives.
2. *Autonomy and independence*
   a. Self-actualizing people have the ability to be independent.
   b. They resist blind conformity.
   c. They are not tradition-bound in making decisions.
3. *Acceptance of self and others*
   a. Self-actualizing people avoid fighting reality.
   b. They accept nature as it is.
   c. They are comfortable with the world.[1]

The above profile is best thought of as an ideal rather than a final state that we reach once and for all. Thus, it is more appropriate to speak about the self-actualizing process rather than becoming a self-actualized person.

How do we achieve self-actualization? There is no set of techniques for reaching this goal, but in a sense the rest of this book, including the activities and Time Out sections, is about ways of beginning this lifelong quest. As you read about the struggles we face in trying to become all we are capable of becoming, I hope you will begin to see some options for living a fuller life.

TIME OUT FOR PERSONAL REFLECTION

The Time Out sections in this book are an opportunity for you to pause and reflect on your own experiences as they relate to the topic being discussed. Unlike most quizzes and tests you have taken, these inventories have no right and wrong answers. Taking them will probably be a differ-

[1]Adapted from *Motivation and Personality*, by A. H. Maslow. Copyright © 1970 by Harper & Row, Publishers, Inc. Used by permission.

ent experience for you, and you may have to make a conscious effort to look within yourself for the response or answer that makes sense to you, rather than searching for the expected response that is external to you.

To what degree do you have a healthy and positive view of yourself? Are you able to appreciate yourself, or do you discount your own worth? Take this self-inventory by rating yourself with the following code: 4 = this statement is true of me most of the time; 3 = this statement is true of me much of the time; 2 = this statement is true of me some of the time; 1 = this statement is true of me almost none of the time.

_____ 1. I generally think and choose for myself.
_____ 2. I usually like myself.
_____ 3. I know what I want.
_____ 4. I am able to ask for what I want.
_____ 5. I feel a sense of personal power.
_____ 6. I am open to change.
_____ 7. I feel equal to others.
_____ 8. I am sensitive to the needs of others.
_____ 9. I care about others.
_____ 10. I can act in accordance with my own judgment without feeling guilty if others disapprove of me.
_____ 11. I do not expect others to make me feel alive.
_____ 12. I can accept responsibility for my own actions.
_____ 13. I am able to accept compliments.
_____ 14. I can give affection.
_____ 15. I can receive affection.
_____ 16. I do not live by a long list of "shoulds," "oughts," and "musts."
_____ 17. I am not so security-bound that I will not explore new things.
_____ 18. I am generally accepted by others.
_____ 19. I can give myself credit for what I do well.
_____ 20. I am able to enjoy my own company.
_____ 21. I am capable of forming intimate and meaningful relationships.
_____ 22. I live in the here and now and do not get stuck in dwelling on the past or the future.
_____ 23. I feel a sense of significance.
_____ 24. I am not diminished when I am with those I respect.
_____ 25. I believe in my ability to succeed in projects that are meaningful to me.

Now go back over this inventory and identify not more than five areas that keep you from being as self-accepting as you might be. What can you do to increase your awareness of situations in which you do not fully accept yourself? For example, if you have trouble giving yourself credit for things you do well, how can you become aware of times when you discount *yourself? When you do become conscious of situations in which you put yourself down, think of alternatives.*

Take a few minutes to review Maslow's theory of self-actualization and then consider the following questions as they apply to you:

- *Which of these qualities do you find most appealing? Why?*
- *Which would you like to cultivate in yourself?*
- *Which of Maslow's ideal qualities do you most associate with living a full and meaningful life?*
- *Who in your life comes closest to meeting Maslow's criteria for self-actualizing people?*

ARE YOU AN ACTIVE LEARNER?

As we have seen, an important aspect of growth as it is viewed by Maslow and Rogers is our ability to be open to new experiences and to look to ourselves for the answers to our problems. This process implies that we will be *active learners*, assuming responsibility for our education, questioning what is presented to us, and applying what we learn to ourselves in a

personally meaningful way. Unfortunately, our schooling experiences often fail to encourage us to learn actively. Instead of questioning and learning to think for ourselves, we can easily assume a passive stance by doing what is expected of us, memorizing facts, and giving back information on tests. Unfortunately, what we are learning often does not make a significant impact on our life. This section asks you to review your school experiences and assess whether you are an active learner.

During my own childhood and adolescence, school was a meaningless and sometimes painful experience. In addition, my educational experiences from grammar school through graduate school often taught me to be a passive learner. I learned that pleasing the teacher was more important than pleasing myself; that accepting the opinions of an authority was more valuable than becoming a questioner; that learning facts and information was more valuable than learning about myself; that learning was motivated by external factors; that there was a right answer to every problem; that school life and everyday life were separate; that the sharing of personal feelings and concerns had no place in the classroom; and that the purpose of school was mainly to cultivate the intellect and acquire basic skills, not to encourage me to understand myself more fully and make choices based on this self-awareness. I do think that it is essential to learn basic skills, but I also think that academic learning of content is

most fruitful when it is combined with the personal concerns of the learners.

You can get the most out of your courses if you develop an active style of learning in which you raise questions and search for answers within yourself. Since this kind of active learning be may be different from most of your previous experiences in school, the Time Out below will help you review your own experiences as a learner and think about the effects your education has had on you.

I hope that you'll try to determine how some of your present values and beliefs are related to these experiences. If you like the kind of learner you now are or if you have had mostly good experiences with school, then you can build on this positive framework as you approach this course. You can continue to find ways of involving yourself with the material you will read, study, and discuss. If you feel cheated by a negative educational experience, you can begin to change it. *You* can make this class different by applying some of the ideas provided in this chapter. Once you become aware of those aspects of your education that you don't like, *you* can decide to change your style of learning.

TIME OUT FOR PERSONAL REFLECTION

How do you rate your education? In taking this inventory, respond quickly by giving your initial reaction. Indicate your response by circling the corresponding letter. You may choose more than one response for each item, or, if none of the responses fits you, you may write your own response on the blank line.

1. *How would you evaluate your experience in elementary school?*
   a. *It was a pleasant time for me.*
   b. *I dreaded going to school.*
   c. *It taught me a lot about life.*
   d. *Although I learned facts and information, I learned little about myself.*

   e. _____

2. *How would you evaluate your high school experience?*
   a. *I have mostly favorable memories of this time.*
   b. *I got more from the social aspects of high school than I did in terms of learning.*
   c. *I remember it as a lonely time.*
   d. *I was very involved in my classes.*

   e. _____

3. *How do you evaluate your present college experience?*
   a. *I like what I'm getting from my college education.*
   b. *I see college as an extension of my earlier schooling experiences.*
   c. *I'm learning more about myself as a result of attending college.*
   d. *I'm here mainly to get a degree; learning is secondary.*

   e. _____

4. *To what degree do you see yourself as a "teacher pleaser"?*
   a. *In the past I worked very hard to gain the approval of my teachers.*
   b. *I'm now more concerned with pleasing myself than I am with pleasing my teachers.*
   c. *It's very important to me to please those who are in authority.*
   d. *Good grades are more important than what I learn.*

   e. _____

5. *To what degree have you been a questioner?*
   a. *I generally haven't questioned authority.*
   b. *I've been an active learner, and I've raised many questions.*
   c. *Basically, I see myself as a passive learner.*
   d. *I didn't raise questions earlier in my schooling, but now I'm willing to question the meaning of what I do in school.*

   e. _____

6. *Have you been motivated externally or internally?*
   a. *I've been motivated primarily by competition and other forms of external motivation.*
   b. *I've learned things mainly because of the satisfaction I get from learning.*
   c. *I see myself as having a lot of curiosity and a need to explore.*
   d. *I've generally learned what I think will be on a test or what will help me get a job.*

   e. _____

7. *To what degree are you a confident learner?*
   a. *I'm afraid of making mistakes and looking foolish.*
   b. *I often look for the "correct way" or the "one right answer."*
   c. *I trust my own judgment, and I live by my values.*
   d. *I think there can be many right answers to a problem.*

   e. _____

8. *To what degree has your learning been real and meaningful?*
   a. *School has been a place where I learn things that are personally meaningful.*

b. *School has been a place where I mostly perform meaningless tasks and pursue meaningless goals.*

c. *I've learned how to apply what I learn in school to my life outside of school.*

d. *I've tended to see school learning and real life as separate.*

e. _____

9. *To what degree have feelings been a part of your schooling?*
   a. *School has dealt with issues that relate to my personal concerns.*
   b. *I've believed that what I feel has no place in school.*
   c. *The emphasis has been on the intellect, not on feelings.*
   d. *I've learned to distrust my feelings.*

   e. _____

10. *How much freedom have you experienced in your schooling?*
    a. *Schooling has taught me how to handle freedom in my own learning.*
    b. *I've found it difficult to accept freedom in school.*
    c. *I've experienced schools as places that restrict my freedom and do not encourage me to make my own choices.*
    d. *I've experienced schools as sources of encouragement to make and accept my own choices.*

    e. _____

Now that you've taken this inventory, I have some suggestions for applying the results to yourself. Look over your responses and then decide which of the following questions might be meaningful follow-up activities for you.

1. *How would you describe yourself as a learner during elementary school? during your high school years? as a college student?*

2. *What effects do you think your schooling has had on you as a person?*

3. *If you don't like the kind of learner you've been up until now, what can you do about it? What changes would you like to make?*

4. *What important things (both positive and negative) did you learn about yourself as a result of your schooling?*

When you've completed your review of your school experience, you might consider (a) bringing your responses to class and sharing them, and/or (b) using a journal to write down memories of school experiences that have had an impact on you and to keep an ongoing account of significant events in your present learning. Many students find that keeping a journal helps them personalize the topics addressed in this book, and they value looking back over what they wrote earlier. Further suggestions for journal writing are given in this chapter under the section on Suggestions for Using This Book.

CHOOSING AN ACTIVE LEARNING STYLE

If you became aware in the preceding section that you are not exercising your full power as a learner, you can decide now to be a more active learner. To be challenged to think for oneself and to reflect and to search within for direction is a new experience for many students. It is unsettling to them when they do not get definite answers to their questions. Such students may have a high need for structure and little tolerance for ambiguity. They have been conditioned to find the "one correct answer" to a problem and have been trained to support whatever statements they make with some authoritative source. My experience with university students repeatedly shows me how timid many of them are when it comes to formulating and expressing their position on an issue. They are often apologetic for using the word *I* in a paper, even if their viewpoint is backed up with reasoning and material from other sources.

Even many passive learners, however, are excited over the prospect of identifying and expressing their views on the topics they are exploring. They are disenchanted with mechanical and impersonal learning, and they truly want to learn how to think through issues and to find meaning in the courses they take. One of the ways to do this involves employing what is known as divergent thinking.

Using Divergent Thinking

You can use two styles in approaching a problem—convergent thinking or divergent thinking. In *convergent thinking* the task is to sort out alternatives and arrive at the best solution to the problem. A multiple-choice test taps convergent thinking, for you must select the one best answer from a list of alternatives given. *Divergent thinking*, in contrast, involves coming up with many acceptable answers to the problem. Essay tests have the potential to tap divergent thinking. Your education should value divergent thinking as much as it values convergent thinking. For many subjects there are often multiple routes that lead to a number of correct answers. Part of being an active learner means that you have the capacity to raise questions, to brainstorm, and to generate multiple answers to your questions. This process implies a personal involvement with the material to be learned. This book is based on divergent thinking, because the themes it addresses do not have simple solutions. It is designed to engage you in exploring how these themes apply to you and to help you find your own answers.

Taking Responsibility for Learning

What is most important is that you take responsibility for your own learning. Students who fail to see their own role in the learning process may blame the system to support their stance of helplessness. I have little sympathy with those who maintain an apathetic attitude toward their own learning while doing nothing but complaining about their boring teachers and their irrelevant classes. If you're dissatisfied with your education, I hope you'll look at yourself and see how much you're willing to invest in order to make it more vital. Are you just waiting for others to make your learning meaningful? How much are you willing to do to change the things you don't like? Are you accepting your share of responsibility for putting something into the learning process?

Many students who complain among themselves seem unwilling to risk approaching their instructors to talk about their feelings. Consequently, I encourage my students not to make excuses why they "can't" approach their instructors but instead to have the courage to express their views directly. I encourage you to do the same.

I'm sure that you can think of other ways to assume responsibility for changing those aspects of your education that you don't like. Regardless of the format or structure of a course, you can actively search for ways of becoming personally involved in the issues it deals with. For example, this book discusses personal topics that have a direct bearing on your life. Whatever the limits set by your instructor, you will have many opportunities to decide how involved to become in these issues. Whether the class is conducted primarily as a lecture, a lecture/discussion, an experiential group with some structure, or an open-ended group, you can decide to be only marginally involved or to actively apply these topics to yourself. During a lecture, you can raise many of your own unanswered questions and think about your daily behavior.

Developing Effective Study Habits

At the beginning of a new semester some college students are typically overwhelmed by how much they are expected to do in all their courses while maintaining a life outside of school. One reaction to this feeling of being swamped by demands is to put things off, which typically leads to discouragement. Quite simply, many students have not mastered basic time-management and study techniques. Although acquiring these skills alone does not guarantee successful learning, knowing how to organize time and how to study can contribute significantly to assuming an active and efficient style of learning. In the Resource Guide at the end of this book you will find the five-step SQ3R technique for studying, reading, and reviewing (Resource 1). There are also some specific suggestions for organizing and managing time (Resource 2). These practical suggestions can be applied to all of your courses. I suggest that you take a few minutes now to look at these guidelines for study.

One way to begin to become an active learner is to think about your reasons for taking this course and your expectations concerning what you will learn. The following Time Out will help you focus on these issues.

TIME OUT FOR PERSONAL REFLECTION

1. What are your main reasons for taking this course?

_____

_____

_____

_____

2. *What do you expect this course to be like? Check all the comments that fit you.*

—————— *I expect to talk openly about issues that matter to me.*
—————— *I expect to get answers to certain problems in my life.*
—————— *I hope that I will become a more fulfilled person.*
—————— *I hope that I will have less fear of expressing my feelings and ideas.*
—————— *I expect to be challenged on why I am the way I am.*
—————— *I expect to learn more about how other people function.*
—————— *I expect that I will understand myself more fully by the end of the course than I do now.*

List other specific expectations:

_____

_____

_____

_____

3. *What do you most want to accomplish in this course?*

_____

_____

_____

_____

4. *What are you willing to do in order to become actively involved in your learning? Check the appropriate comments.*

—————— *I'm willing to participate in class discussions.*
—————— *I'm willing to read the material and think about how it applies to me.*
—————— *I'm willing to question my assumptions and look at my values.*
—————— *I'm willing to spend some time most days in reflecting on the issues raised in this course.*
—————— *I'm willing to keep a journal and to record my reactions to what I read and experience.*

Mention any other things you're willing to do in order to be actively involved:

_____

_____

_____

_____

GETTING THE MOST FROM THIS COURSE: SUGGESTIONS FOR PERSONAL LEARNING

Few of your courses deal primarily with *you* as the subject matter. Most of us spend years in acquiring information about the world around us, and we may even equate learning with absorbing facts that are external to us. Although such learning is essential, it is equally important to learn about oneself. To a large degree, what you get from this course will depend on what you're willing to invest of yourself; so it's important that you clarify your goals and the steps you can take to reach them. The following guidelines may help you become active and involved in personal learning as you read the book and participate in your class.

1. *Preparing.* Reading and writing, of course, are excellent devices for getting the most from this class. Many students have been conditioned to view reading as an unpleasant assignment, and they tolerate textbooks as something to plow through for an examination. As an active learner, however, you can selectively read this book—and the books that interest you in the Suggested Readings at the end of each chapter—in a personal way that will stimulate you intellectually and emotionally. Read this book for your personal benefit, and make use of the Time Outs and exercises to help you apply the material to your own life. Writing can also give you a focus. In addition to completing the Time Outs you can take personal notes, keep a log or journal, and write brief reactions about the personal impact of the topics. This can be done in the margins as you read and as you feel touched personally. It is helpful to simply write in a free-flowing and unedited style, rather than attempting to analyze what you write. The idea is simply to keep some record of personally significant issues.

2. *Dealing with fears.* Personal learning entails experiencing some common fears. Some of these are the fear of taking an honest look at yourself and discovering terrible things; the fear of the unknown; the fear of looking foolish in front of others, especially your instructor; the fear of being criticized or ridiculed; and the fear of speaking out and expressing your values. It's natural to experience some fear about participating personally and actively in the class, especially since this kind of participation may involve taking risks you don't usually take in your courses. What is critical is how you deal with any fears you experience. You have the choice of remaining a passive observer or recognizing your fears and dealing with them openly, even though you might experience some degree of discomfort. Facing your fears takes both courage and a genuine desire to increase your awareness of yourself, but by doing so you take a first big step toward expanding the range of your choices.

3. *Deciding what you want for yourself.* If you do make the decision to invest yourself in the course, I cannot overemphasize the importance of deciding on your own concrete goals. If you come to class with only vague

ideas of what you want, the chances are that you'll be disappointed. You can increase your chances of having a profitable experience by taking the time and effort to think about what problems and personal concerns you're willing to explore.

4. *Taking risks.* If you make the choice to invest yourself fully in the course, you should be prepared for the possibility of some disruption in your life. You may find yourself changing. It can be a shock to discover that those who are close to you do not appreciate your changes. They may prefer that you remain as you are. Thus, instead of receiving their support, you may encounter their resistance.

5. *Establishing trust.* You can choose to take the initiative in establishing the trust necessary for you to participate in this course in a meaningful way, or you can wait for others to create a climate of trust. Often students have feelings of mistrust or other negative feelings toward an instructor yet avoid doing anything. One way to establish trust is to seek out your instructor and discuss any feelings you have that might prevent you from participating fully in the course. The same applies to any feelings of mistrust you have toward other class members. By expressing your feelings, you can actively help establish a higher level of trust.

6. *Practicing self-disclosure.* Disclosing yourself to others is one way to come to know yourself more fully. Sometimes participants in self-awareness courses or experiential groups fear that they must relinquish their privacy in order to be active participants. However, you can be open and

at the same time retain your need for privacy by deciding how much you will disclose and when it is appropriate to do so. Although it may be new and uncomfortable for you to talk in personal ways to people whom you don't know that well, I encourage you to say a bit more than you typically would in most social situations. You will need patience in learning this new communication skill.

7. *Being direct.* You can adopt a direct style in your communication. You'll be more direct if you make "I" statements than if you say "you" when you really mean "I." For example, instead of saying "You can't trust people with what you feel, because they will let you down if you make yourself vulnerable," substitute "I" for "you." In this way, you take responsibility for your own statement. Similarly, it will help your communication if you make eye contact and speak directly *to* a person, rather than speaking *at* or *about* the person.

8. *Avoiding asking questions.* If you want to get the most from your interactions in class, don't adopt a style of asking questions of others. Continually asking questions can lead to a never-ending chain of "whys" and "becauses." Moreover, questioning can be a way of avoiding personal involvement. I have seen people in a class or group push others to be personal, yet never say anything significant about themselves. A question keeps the questioner safe, unknown, and hidden. Instead, I often urge people to reveal the feelings that led to their question. For example, behind "Why are you so quiet?" may lie any of the following statements: "I'm afraid of you, and I'd like to know what you think of me." "I don't know what's going on with you, and I'm interested." "I notice that you're not saying much, and I suspect that you're judging me." "I'm aware that you've been quiet. When I'm quiet I'm usually afraid, and I wonder what you're thinking and feeling."

9. *Listening.* You can work on developing the skill of really listening to what others are saying without thinking of what you will say in reply. The first step in understanding what others say about you is to listen carefully, neither accepting what they say wholesale nor rejecting it outright. *Active listening* (really hearing the full message another is sending) requires remaining open and carefully considering what others say, instead of rushing to give reasons and explanations.

10. *Thinking for yourself.* Only you can make the choice whether to do your own thinking or to let others do your thinking and deciding for you. Many people seek counseling because they have lost the ability to find their own way and have become dependent on others to direct their life and take responsibility for their decisions. If you value thinking and deciding for yourself, it is important for you to realize that neither your fellow students nor your instructor can give you answers.

11. *Avoiding self-fulfilling prophecies.* You can increase your ability to change by letting go of ways in which you've categorized yourself or been categorized by others. If *you* start off with the assumption that you're

stupid, helpless, or boring, you'll probably convince others as well. For example, if you see yourself as boring, you'll probably present yourself in such a way that others will respond to you as a boring person. If you like the idea of changing some of the ways in which you see yourself and present yourself to others, you can experiment with going beyond some of your self-limiting labels. Allowing yourself to believe that a particular change is possible is a large part of experiencing that change. And once you experience *yourself* differently, others might experience you differently too.

12. *Practicing outside of class.* One important way of getting the maximum benefit from a class dealing with personal learning is to think about ways of applying what you learn in class to your everyday life. As I mentioned at the beginning of this list, you can do this by keeping a journal and by writing personal reactions to your experiences in and out of class. You can make specific contracts with yourself (or with others) detailing what you're willing to do to experiment with new behavior and work toward the changes you want to make.

CHANGE THE WAY YOU SEE YOURSELF.

At this point, it would be worthwhile to pause and assess your readiness for taking an honest look at yourself. Right now you may or may not feel motivated to examine the issues explored in the following chapters. You may feel that you don't need to explore these topics, or you may see yourself as being not quite ready. If you do feel some hesitation, I hope that you'll leave the door open and give yourself and the course a chance. I've had many students who entered a self-development and experiential course mainly for the units, only to leave feeling very excited and committed to go further. If you open yourself to change and try the techniques I've suggested, you may well experience a similar sense of excitement and promise.

SUGGESTIONS FOR USING THIS BOOK

This book is not written to tell you how you should be; rather, its purpose is to challenge you to think of how you want to be. Once you become aware of the ways in which you function, you will be in a position to make a decision about what you want to do about yourself.

Many of the exercises, questions, and suggested activities will appeal differently to different readers. Considerations such as your age, life experiences, and cultural background will have a bearing on the meaning and importance of certain topics to you. Most of these topics, however, do seem to be personally significant to most readers, regardless of their background. I hope you'll treat this book in a personal way. Rather than merely reading it as you do any other text, attempt to apply it to yourself. With this in mind, I'd like to make some suggestions.

1. At the beginning of the subsequent chapters is a self-inventory. These inventories are designed to involve you personally with each subject. For the most part, they consist of personal statements intended to stimulate your thinking about the topics of discussion. I have resisted providing methods of rigidly diagnosing and neatly interpreting the meaning of your responses. There are no "universal norms" that you can compare yourself to on these inventories. Instead, I hope that you will simply assess your attitudes and beliefs and think about aspects of your life that you might otherwise ignore. You may want to bring your responses to class and discuss your views or compare them with those of others. If you're reading this book alone, you may want to have a close friend or your mate answer some of the questions and react to the statements in the inventories. Doing this is a good way to stimulate meaningful dialogue with a person close to you. It could also be interesting for you to quickly take all of the prechapter self-inventories now and record your responses on a separate sheet. This is a useful means of assessing your current thinking

on the topics to be covered. Then retake these inventories as you work through each chapter and compare your answers with your previous responses. At the end of the semester you can look over the inventories and determine the degree to which you have changed your thinking on selected topics.

2. In one sense this is an *unfinished book*. You are challenged to become a co-author by completing the writing of this book in ways that are meaningful to you. In many of the chapters, examples are drawn from everyday life. You can extend the impact of these examples by thinking and writing about how they apply to you. Rather than reading simply to learn facts, take your own position on the issues I raise. As much as possible, put yourself into what you read.

3. As you have seen, Time Out sections are inserted from time to time. Since these sections are designed to help you focus on specific topics, it will be most valuable if you do these exercises as you read. Actually writing down your responses in the text will help you begin to think about how each topic applies to you. Then you can look for common themes, go back to review your comments, or share them with a few friends or others in class. The process of reflecting and writing can help you get actively involved with the topics. Here again you have many opportunities to become a co-author in finishing this book.

4. At the end of each chapter are additional activities and exercises suggested for practice, both in class and out of class. Although I encourage you to take risks in disclosing yourself, ultimately you will be the one to decide which activities and exercises you are willing to do. You may find some of the suggested exercises too threatening to do in a class with 50 other students, yet exploring the same activities in a small group in your class could be easier. If small discussion groups are not a part of the structure of your class, consider doing the exercises alone or sharing them with a friend. Don't feel compelled to complete all the activities; select those that have the most meaning for you at this time in your life.

5. One activity I suggest throughout the book is keeping a journal. You might purchase a separate notebook in which to write your reactions to each topic or to do more extensive writing on some of the exercises. Later, you can look for patterns in your journal; doing so can help you identify some of your critical choices and areas of conflict. Frequently, I give concrete suggestions concerning things you might include in your journal, but the important thing is for you to decide what to put in and how to use it. Consider writing about some of the following topics:

- what I learned about others and myself through today's class session
- the topics that were of most interest to me (and why)
- the topics that held the least interest for me (and why)
- the topics I wanted to talk about
- the topics I avoided talking about

- particular sections (or issues) in the chapter that had the greatest impact on me (and why)
- some of the things I am learning about myself in reading the book
- some specific things I am doing in everyday life as a result of this class
- some concrete changes in my attitudes, values, and behavior that I find myself most wanting to make
- what I am willing to do to make these changes
- some barriers I encounter in making the changes I want to make

It is best to write what first comes to your consciousness. Spontaneous reactions tend to tell you more about yourself than well-thought-out comments.

6. It is a good idea to read the final chapter, on meaning and values, early in the course. Chapter 12 puts the entire book in perspective, and it serves as an excellent preview of the topics as well as a review. As you first read the chapter, try to identify your own values as they pertain to each issue raised.

7. After the final chapter is the Resource Guide, which contains a variety of techniques for personal exploration. Students and professors who used earlier editions of this book commented that, although the topics discussed often led to a revised outlook on a particular issue, making life changes did not automatically follow the gaining of these new insights. I agree with them that insight alone is not sufficient to bring about behavioral change, and therefore I offer some resources to encourage you to take an active path that can lead to change. For example, readers often become more aware of the many ways in which they are experiencing stress in daily life. They may then say: "So now I know I'm under a great deal more stress than I admitted to myself, but I'm still at a loss to know where to begin in actually coping with stress more effectively. I know how I'd like to be different, but bringing about these changes is a different matter." Resource 5 is a relaxation exercise that will at least give you a start in learning some practical steps that you can take by yourself. This exercise is not the last word in relaxation. As a caution, I must emphasize that making changes in your behavior is hard work, takes time, and is not the result of following a simplistic formula. These resources may often work best if you use them in conjunction with other programs. In the example given, you might read a book on relaxation and meditation techniques, take a class, or attend a workshop. The resources should be the *beginning* of any struggle to bring about change. The Resource Guide is not to be read at one time as you might a chapter; rather, as you work through the chapters, references will be made to a specific resource. It is intended that you'll make frequent use of the guide as you read each of the chapters.

8. Resource 12 is an outline entitled Writing Your Philosophy of Life. Consider addressing some of these issues as you begin this book and this course. Then, toward the end of the semester, you can revise and expand

on your essay. Writing your philosophy will assist you in evaluating changes in your attitudes and beliefs and will help you to put your values in perspective.

9. Apply the study methods mentioned earlier (Resource 1) to getting acquainted with this book. Look over all the major headings in the chapters. At least take a glance at some of the Time Out sections to get an idea of ways that you can become actively involved in your learning. As you skim the chapters, raise questions that are of most interest to you. Taking the time now to get acquainted with this book will help you see how all of these topics are interconnected, and it will prepare you to assume an active learning stance.

CHAPTER SUMMARY

We do not have to passively live out the plans that others have designed for us, but with awareness we can begin to make significant choices. Taking a stand in life by making choices entails both potential gains and risks. Changing long-standing patterns is not easy, and there are many obstacles to overcome, yet a free life has many rewards.

One of these benefits is personal growth. Growth is a lifelong process of expanding our awareness and accepting new challenges. It does *not* mean total disregard for others but rather implies fulfilling more of our potentials, including our ability to care for others. Perhaps the best way to conceptualize personal growth is by considering Maslow's ideal of *self-actualization*. Striving for self-actualization does not cease at a particular age but is an ongoing process. Four basic characteristics of self-actualizing people are self-awareness, freedom, basic honesty and caring, and trust and autonomy.

This course can be a first step on the journey toward achieving your personal goals and living a self-actualizing existence. Growing obviously entails learning. I've encouraged you to review your school experiences and to make an inventory of the ways in which your present attitudes toward learning have been influenced. Becoming aware of the effects schooling has had on you gives you the power to choose a new learning style.

A major purpose of this chapter has been to challenge you to examine your own responsibility for making your learning meaningful. It's easy to lash out at impersonal institutions if you feel apathetic about your learning. It's more difficult and more honest to look at *yourself* and ask such questions as: When I find myself in an exciting class, do I get fully involved and take advantage of the opportunity for learning? Do I expect instructors to entertain and *teach* me while I sit back passively? If I'm bored, what am I doing about it?

Even if your earlier educational experiences have taught you to be a passive learner and to fear taking risks in your classes, once you become aware of this influence, you acquire the power to change your learning style. In this chapter I've asked you to decide how personal you want your learning to be in the course you're about to experience, and I've suggested several guidelines to help you personalize your own learning.

List some of the major ideas in this chapter that had the greatest impact on you. You might write down statements that captured your own experience and also some that you disagreed with.

ACTIVITIES AND EXERCISES

1. The following are exercises that you can do at home. They are intended to help you focus on specific ways in which you behave. I've drawn the examples from typical fears and concerns often expressed by college students. Study the situations by putting yourself in each one and deciding how you might typically respond. Then keep an account in your journal of actual instances you encounter in your classes.

   a. *Situation.* You'd like to ask a question in class, but you're afraid that your question will sound dumb and that others will laugh.
   Issues. Will you simply refrain from asking questions? If so, is this a pattern you're willing to continue? Are you willing to practice asking questions, even though you might experience some anxiety? What do you imagine will happen if you ask questions? What would you like to have happen?

   b. *Situation.* You feel that you have a problem concerning authority figures. You feel intimidated, afraid to venture your opinions, and even more afraid to register a point of view opposed to your instructor's.
   Issues. Does this description fit you? If it does, do you want to change? Do you ever examine where you picked up your attitudes toward yourself in relation to authority? Do you think they're still appropriate for you?

c. *Situation.* You and most of the other students think that your instructor is very boring. He goes strictly by an outline and lectures from your textbook. It isn't worth it to you to change to another instructor, however, because the change would disrupt your schedule.

Issues. What options do you have if you stay in the class? Are you condemned to tolerating boredom for a semester? Are you content to tell yourself that there's really nothing you can do, since all the power belongs to the instructor? Are you willing to go to your instructor during office hours and tell him how you experience the class? Do you have any ideas or suggestions for making the class more lively?

d. *Situation.* In your psychology class a few students dominate the discussion time. They go on with long-winded stories, continually make their own points, and are irritating you and most of the class. The instructor doesn't deal with the situation.

Issues. Have you experienced this kind of situation? What alternatives do you see yourself as having? Might you openly tell these persons in class that you would appreciate it if others had a chance to express themselves? Would you confront them privately?

e. *Situation.* There is a great deal of hostility in your class; the class members show little respect for one another. You feel somewhat overwhelmed by this tension.

Issues. Would you tend to withdraw, or would you deal openly with your feelings about this hostility? What can you do when you're aware that somebody treats another class member with disrespect? What fears do you have about confronting the tensions you sense in the room? What steps might you take to confront them?

f. *Situation.* Your instructor seems genuinely interested in the students and the course, and she has extended herself by inviting you to come to her office if you have any problems with the course. You're having real difficulty grasping the material, and you're falling behind and doing poorly on the tests and assignments. Nevertheless, you keep putting off going to see the instructor to talk about your problems in the class.

Issues. Have you been in this situation before? If so, what kept you from talking with your instructor? If you find yourself in this kind of situation, are you willing to seek help before it's too late?

2. Review Maslow's characteristics of self-actualizing people. Then consider the following questions:

   a. To what degree are these characteristics a part of your personality?
   b. How self-actualizing do you see your closest friends as being?
   c. Do you think that Maslow's ideal of self-actualization fits for individuals of all cultural and ethnic groups? Are there any characteristics that are not appropriate for certain cultures?

SUGGESTED READINGS

At the end of each chapter I list several books that are relevant to its topic. The following are some books that deal with many of the general themes discussed in *I Never Knew I Had a Choice*. You might want to select several of them for supplementary reading.

Brennecke, J., & Amick, R. (1980). *The Struggle for Significance* (3rd ed.). Encino, Calif.: Glencoe. Deals with most of the topics covered in this book. Written in a thought-provoking style.

Daniels, V., & Horowitz, L. (1984). *Being and Caring: A Psychology for Living* (2nd ed.). Palo Alto, Calif.: Mayfield. A very well-written self-development book. The authors maintain that we are responsible for finding our own way and that with awareness we can create our own world. They discuss awareness, acceptance, self-honesty, living with feeling, being and sharing, and centeredness.

Maslow, A. (1970). *Motivation and Personality* (2nd ed.). New York: Harper & Row. Of particular interest are Chapters 11 and 12, which deal with self-actualizing people. This is considered a classic.

Rainwater, J. (1979). *You're in Charge! A Guide to Becoming Your Own Therapist*. Los Angeles: Guild of Tutors Press. A very informative book on ways to achieve self-understanding, including journal writing, autobiography, working with dreams, meditation, being in charge of one's physical health and one's death, and learning how to choose for oneself. The many exercises make this an excellent self-help book.

Rogers, C. (1983). *Freedom to Learn for the 80's*. Columbus, Ohio: Charles E. Merrill. Rogers calls for free learning instead of stifling, authoritarian approaches to education. Methods for creating a climate of responsible freedom in the classroom, the philosophical aspects of person-centered teaching, and the difficulties and opportunities of this approach to learning are explored.

2

REVIEWING YOUR
CHILDHOOD AND ADOLESCENCE

PRECHAPTER SELF-INVENTORY

Use the following scale to respond: 4 = this statement is true of me *most* of the time; 3 = this statement is true of me *much* of the time; 2 = this statement is true of me *some* of the time; 1 = this statement is true of me *almost none* of the time.

————— 1. I'm capable of looking at my past decisions and then making new decisions that will significantly change the course of my life.

————— 2. "Shoulds" and "oughts" often get in the way of my living my life the way I want.

————— 3. To a large degree I've been shaped by the events of my childhood and adolescent years.

————— 4. When I think of my early childhood years, I remember feeling secure, accepted, and loved.

————— 5. As a child I was taught not to express negative feelings such as rage, anger, hatred, jealousy, and aggression.

————— 6. I had desirable models to pattern my behavior after when I was a child and an adolescent.

————— 7. In looking back at my early school-age years, I think that I had a positive self-concept and that I experienced more successes than failures.

————— 8. I went through a stage of rebellion during my adolescent years.

————— 9. My adolescent years were lonely ones.

————— 10. I remember being significantly influenced by peer-group pressure during my adolescence.

Here are a few suggestions for using this self-inventory:

• Retake the inventory after reading the chapter and again at the end of the course, and compare your answers.
• Have someone who knows you well take the inventory for you, giving the responses he or she thinks actually describe you. Then you can discuss any discrepancies between your sets of responses.
• In your class, compare your responses with those of the other members, and discuss the similarities and differences between your attitudes and theirs.

INTRODUCTION

This chapter and the next one lay the groundwork for much of the rest of the book by focusing on our lifelong struggle to achieve psychological emancipation, or autonomy. The term *autonomy* refers to a mature type of independence. The autonomous person is able to function without constant approval and reassurance, can effectively meet the demands of daily living, is willing to ask for help when it is needed, and can provide support and give to others. In essence, autonomy is the ability to stand alone *and* to stand by another person. An autonomous individual can take care of his or her own needs without imposing on or detracting from the needs of others and without requiring undue direction and support (Okun, 1984). The achievement of personal autonomy is a continuing process of growth and learning, not something we arrive at once and for all.

Our attitudes toward our body, sex-role identity, sexuality, love, intimacy, loneliness, work, death, meaning, and values—the themes I'll be discussing in future chapters—are largely shaped by our experiences and decisions during our early years. Each period of life has its own challenges and meanings, however, and we continue to develop and change, ideally in the direction of autonomy. Before going on to discuss these specific themes, therefore, I want to look at the developmental stages that make up a complete human life, from infancy through old age.

STAGES OF PERSONALITY DEVELOPMENT: A PREVIEW

By getting a picture of the challenges at each period of life, we will be able to understand how earlier stages of personality development influence choices we make later in life. These stages are not precise categories that people neatly fall into. In reality there is great variability among individuals within a given developmental phase. Although there are general developmental tasks and problems associated with adolescence, for example, each adolescent reacts to the challenges of this period uniquely. The same is true for middle-aged people. It may be difficult to describe a "typical middle-aged woman," since some women are making a new life for themselves as a student or entering a new career. The important point is that there is continuity in our life. Our childhood experiences have a direct impact on how we approach the adolescent years. How well we master the tasks of adolescence has a bearing on our ability to cope with the critical turning points of adulthood. If we do not develop a clear sense of identity during adolescence, for example, then finding meaning in adult life becomes extremely difficult. As we progress from one stage of life to the next, we at times meet with roadblocks and detours. These barriers are often the result of failing to master basic psychological competencies of an earlier period.

The father of psychoanalysis, Sigmund Freud, is credited with developing one of the most comprehensive theories of personality. Freud emphasized unconscious psychological processes and stressed the importance of early childhood experiences. According to his viewpoint, our sexual and social development is largely based on the first five years of life. During this time, he maintained, we go through three stages (*oral*, *anal*, and *phallic*), and our later personality development hinges on how well we have resolved the demands and conflicts of each stage. My own professional experience has taught me that most of the problems that people wrestle with in adulthood seem to have some relationship to unresolved conflicts dating from their early childhood. Those who wish to read further into the Freudian psychoanalytic perspective are referred to Freud's *An Outline of Psychoanalysis* (1949), his *The Interpretation of Dreams* (1955), and Hall's *A Primer of Freudian Psychology* (1954).

My discussion of the tasks of the entire life span incorporates ideas from Erik Erikson's (1963, 1982) *psychosocial* view as well as from Freud's *psychosexual* perspective. As you will see, Freud developed a model for understanding early development, especially its psychosexual aspects. Erikson built on and extended Freud's ideas by stressing the psychosocial aspects of development and by carrying his own developmental theory beyond childhood. Although he is intellectually indebted to Freud, Erikson suggests that we should view human development in a more positive light, emphasizing health and growth.

Erikson's theory of development holds that psychosexual and psychoso-

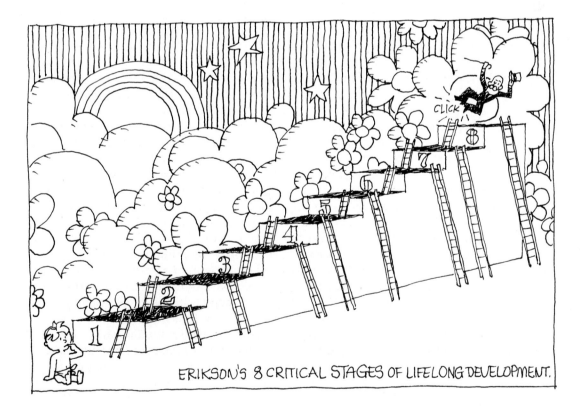

ERIKSON'S 8 CRITICAL STAGES OF LIFELONG DEVELOPMENT.

cial growth occur together and that at each stage of life we face the task of establishing an equilibrium between ourselves and our social world. Erikson describes human development over the entire life span in terms of eight stages, each marked by a particular crisis to be resolved. You may think of a crisis as a gigantic problem or catastrophic happening. But for Erikson, *crisis* means a *turning point* in life, a moment of transition characterized by the potential to go either forward or backward in development. At these turning points we can achieve successful resolution of our conflicts and move ahead, or we can fail to resolve the conflicts and regress. To a large extent our life is the result of the choices we make at each stage.

Although the life-span perspective presented in these two chapters relies heavily on concepts borrowed from Freud's and Erikson's perspectives, I have also drawn on ideas from other writers who describe crises as we progress to new stages of life. Some of these writers are Berne (1975), Gould (1978), the Gouldings (1978, 1979), Havighurst (1972), Sheehy (1976, 1981), and Steiner (1975). Table 2–1 gives you an overview of the major turning points in the life-span perspective of human development.

INFANCY

Developmental psychologists contend that a child's basic task in the first year of life is to develop a sense of trust in self, others, and the environment. Infants need to count on others; they need to sense that they are cared for and loved and that the world is a secure place. They learn this sense of trust by being held, caressed, and taken care of.

Erikson asserts that infants form a basic conception of the social world. He sees their core struggle as *trust* versus *mistrust*. If the significant other persons in an infant's life provide the needed warmth, cuddling, and attention, the child develops a sense of trust. When these conditions are *not* present, the child becomes suspicious about interacting with others and acquires a general sense of mistrust toward human relationships. Although neither orientation is fixed to one's personality for life, it is clear that well-nurtured infants are in a more favorable position with respect to future personal growth than are their more neglected peers.

A sense of being loved is also the best safeguard against fear, insecurity, and inadequacy. Children who receive love from parents or parental substitutes generally have little difficulty accepting themselves, whereas children who feel unloved and unwanted may find it very hard to accept themselves. In addition, rejected children learn to mistrust the world and to view it primarily in terms of its ability to do them harm. Some of the effects of rejection in infancy include tendencies in later childhood to be fearful, insecure, jealous, aggressive, hostile, and isolated.

Table 2-1 Overview of Developmental Stages

Life Stage	Freud's Psychosexual View	Erikson's Psychosocial View	Potential Problems
Infancy (1st year of life)	*Oral stage.* Most critical stage in terms of later development. Failure to get one's need for basic nurturing met may lead to greediness later on. Material things may become a substitute for love. Infant's nursing satisfies the need for both food and pleasure.	*Infancy.* Basic task is to develop a sense of trust in self, others, and the environment. Infants need a sense of being cared for and loved. Absence of a sense of security may lead to suspiciousness and a general sense of mistrust toward human relationships. Core struggle: *trust* versus *mistrust*.	Later personality problems that stem from infancy can include greediness and acquisitiveness, the development of a view of the world based on mistrust, fear of reaching out to others, rejection of affection, fear of loving and trusting, low self-esteem, isolation and withdrawal, and inability to form or maintain intimate relationships.
Early childhood (ages 1–3)	*Anal stage.* Child experiences parental demands and faces frustration. Toilet training is first experience with discipline. Attitudes toward body and bodily functions are direct results of this period. Problems in adulthood such as compulsive orderliness or messiness may stem from parental disciplinary practice.	*Early childhood.* A time for developing autonomy. Failure to master self-control tasks may lead to shame and doubt about oneself and one's adequacy. Core struggle: *self-reliance* versus *self-doubt*.	Children experience many negative feelings such as hostility, rage, destructiveness, anger, and hatred. If these feelings are not accepted, individuals may not be able to accept their feelings later on.
Preschool age (ages 3–6)	*Phallic stage.* Sex-role identity is a key issue. Child's interest in sexual matters increases; sexual attitudes are formed. Sexual dysfunctions in adulthood often have their roots in early conditioning and experiences.	*Preschool age.* Characterized by play and by anticipation of roles; a time to establish a sense of competence and initiative. Children who are not allowed to make decisions tend to develop a sense of guilt. Core struggle: *initiative* versus *guilt*.	Parental attitudes can be communicated verbally and nonverbally. Negative learning experiences tend to lead to feelings of guilt about natural impulses. Strict parental indoctrination can lead to rigidity, severe conflicts, remorse, and self-condemnation.

Table 2-1   Overview of Developmental Stages *(continued)*

Life Stage	Freud's Psychosexual View	Erikson's Psychosocial View	Potential Problems
Middle childhood (ages 6–12)	*Latency stage.* Socialization takes place as children turn outward toward relationships with others. New interests emerge: school, playmates, sports, books. The sexual impulses are relatively quiescent, and social interests become prominent.	*School age.* Central task is to achieve a sense of industry; failure to do so results in a sense of inadequacy. Child needs to expand understanding of the world and continue to develop appropriate sex-role identity. Learning basic skills is essential for school success. Core struggle: *industry* versus *inferiority*.	Problems that can originate during middle childhood include negative self-concept, feelings of inferiority in establishing social relationships, conflicts over values, confused sex-role identity, dependency, fear of new challenges, and lack of initiative.
Adolescence (ages 12–18)	*Genital stage.* Old themes of phallic stage are revived. Interest develops in opposite sex, with some sexual experimentation. Genital stage is the longest, beginning at puberty and lasting until later adulthood. In face of social restrictions and taboos, adolescents can redirect sexual energy by engaging in socially acceptable activities.	*Adolescence.* A critical time for forming a personal identity. Major conflicts center on clarification of self-identity, life goals, and life's meaning. Struggle is over integrating physical and social changes. Pressures include succeeding in school, choosing a job, forming relationships, and preparing for future. Core struggle: *identity* versus *role confusion*.	A time when individual may anticipate an *identity crisis*. Caught in midst of pressures, demands, and turmoil, adolescent often loses sense of self. If *role confusion* results, individual may lack sense of purpose in later years. Absence of a stable set of values can prevent mature development of a philosophy to guide one's life.
Early adulthood (ages 18–35)	*Genital stage* (continues). Core characteristic of mature adult is the freedom "to love and to work." The move toward adulthood involves developing intimacy, freedom from parental influence, and capacity to care for others.	*Young adulthood.* Sense of identity is again tested by the challenge of achieving intimacy. Ability to form close relationships depends on having a clear sense of self. Core struggle: *intimacy* versus *isolation*.	The challenge of this period is to maintain one's separateness while becoming attached to others. Failing to strike a balance leads to self-centeredness or to exclusive focus on needs of others. Failure to achieve intimacy can lead to alienation and isolation. *(continued)*

Table 2–1   Overview of Developmental Stages *(continued)*

Life Stage	Freud's Psychosexual View	Erikson's Psychosocial View	Potential Problems
Middle adulthood (ages 35–60)	*Genital stage* (continues).	*Middle age.* Individuals become more aware of their eventual death and begin to question whether they are living well. The crossroads of life; a time for re-evaluation. Core struggle: *generativity* versus *stagnation.*	Failure to achieve a sense of productivity can lead to stagnation. Pain can result when individuals recognize the gap between their dreams and what they have achieved.
Late adulthood (age 60 onward)	*Genital stage* (continues).	*Later life.* Ego integrity is achieved by those who have few regrets, who see themselves as living a productive life, and who have coped with both successes and failures. Key tasks are to adjust to losses, death of others, maintaining outside interests, and adjusting to retirement. Core struggle: *integrity* versus *despair.*	Failure to achieve ego integrity often leads to feelings of hopelessness, guilt, resentment, and self-rejection. Unfinished business from earlier years can lead to fears of death stemming from sense that life has been wasted.

According to the Freudian psychoanalytic view, the events of the first year of life are extremely important for later development and adjustment. Infants who do not get the basic nurturing needs met during this time (known as the *oral stage*) may develop greediness and acquisitiveness in later life. Material things thus become substitutes for what the children really want—love and attention from parents. For instance, a person whose oral needs are unmet may become a compulsive eater, in which case food becomes a symbol for love. Other personality problems that might stem from this period include a mistrustful and suspicious view of the world, a tendency to reject affection from others, an inability to form intimate relationships, a fear of loving and trusting, and feelings of isolation.

According to psychoanalytic theorists, we experience a number of critical conflicts before we begin school, and we are presented with several developmental tasks. One task is to develop a sense of trust in the world, which requires that we feel loved and accepted. If love is absent, we will suffer during later years from an inability to trust ourselves and others, a fear of loving and becoming intimate, and low self-esteem. Let me hasten to add that I don't take a fatalistic view that we're doomed if we didn't get our quota of love. Many people reexperience their childhood feelings of hurt and rejection through some form of counseling; in this way, they come to understand that the fact that they didn't feel loved by their parents doesn't mean that they are unlovable or that others find them unlovable now. With awareness, we can open ourselves up and begin to trust.

The case of 9–year-old Joey, the "mechanical boy" described by Bettelheim (1967) in *The Empty Fortress*, is a dramatic illustration of how the pain of extreme rejection during infancy can affect us later on. When Joey first went to Bettelheim's school, he seemed devoid of any feeling. He thought of himself as functioning by remote control, with the help of an elaborate system of machines. He had to have his "carburetor" to breathe, "exhaust pipes" to exhale from, and a complex system of wires and motors in order to move. His delusion was so convincing that the staff members at the school sometimes found themselves taking care to be sure that Joey was plugged in properly and that they didn't step on any of his wires.

Neither Joey's father nor his mother had been prepared for his birth, and they had related to him as a thing, not a person. His mother simply ignored him; she reported that she had no feeling of dislike toward Joey but that "I simply did not want to take care of him." He was a difficult baby who cried most of the time, and he was kept on a rigid schedule. He wasn't touched unless necessary, and he wasn't cuddled or played with. Joey developed more and more unusual symptoms, such as head banging, rocking, and a morbid fascination with machines. Evidently, Joey discovered that machines were better than people; they didn't hurt you, and they could be shut off. During years of intense treatment with Bettelheim, Joey gradually learned how to trust, and he also learned that feelings are real and that it can be worth it to feel.

Another case that illustrates the possible effects of severe deprivation during the early developmental years is that of Sally, who is now in her early forties. Sally was given up by her natural parents and spent the first decade of her life in orphanages and foster homes. She recalls pleading with one set of foster parents who had kept her for over a year and then said that they had to send her away. As a child Sally came to the conclusion that she was at fault; if her own parents didn't want her, who could? She spent years trying to figure out what she had done wrong and why so many people always "sent her away."

As an adult Sally still yearns for what she missed during infancy and childhood. Thus, she has never really attained maturity; socially and emotionally, she is much like a child. Sally has never allowed herself to get close to anyone, for she fears that they will leave if she does. As a child she learned to isolate herself emotionally in order to survive; now, even though she is 42, she still operates on the assumptions that she had as a child. Because of her fear of being deserted, she won't allow herself to venture out and take even minimal risks.

Sally is not unusual. I have worked with a number of women and men who suffer from the effects of early psychological deprivation, and I have observed that, in most cases, such deprivation has lingering adverse effects on a person's ability to form meaningful relationships later in life. Many people I encounter—of all ages—struggle with the issue of trusting others in a loving relationship. They are unable to trust that another can or will love them, they fear being rejected, and they fear even more the possibility of closeness and being accepted and loved. Many of these people don't trust themselves or others sufficiently to make themselves vulnerable enough to experience love.

At this point, you might pause to ask yourself these questions:

- Am I able to trust others? myself?
- Am I willing to open myself—to make myself known to a few selected people in my life?
- Do I basically accept myself as being OK, or do I seek confirmation outside of myself? Am I hungry for approval from others? How far will I go in my attempt to be liked? Do I need to be liked and approved of by everyone? Do I dare make enemies, or must I be "nice" to everyone?
- Am I in any way like Sally? Do I know of anyone who has had experiences similar to hers?

EARLY CHILDHOOD

Freud called ages 1–3 the *anal stage*. The tasks children must master at this time include learning independence, accepting personal power, and learning skills to cope with negative feelings such as rage and aggression. Their most critical task is to begin the journey toward autonomy by progressing from being taken care of by others to being able to care for their own physical needs.

In this second stage, children take their first steps toward becoming self-supporting. They assume a more active role in taking care of their own needs, and they begin to communicate what they want from others. During this time children also face continual parental demands. For instance, they are restricted from physically exploring their environment, they begin to be disciplined, and they have toilet training imposed on them. According to the Freudian view, parental feelings and attitudes associated with toilet training are highly significant for their children's later personality development. Thus, problems in adulthood such as compulsive orderliness or messiness may be due to parental attitudes during this time. For instance, a father who insists that his son be unrealistically clean may find that the son develops into a sloppy person as a reaction against overly strict training—or that he becomes even more compulsively clean.

Erikson identifies this period as the time for developing a sense of autonomy. The core struggle of early childhood is *autonomy* versus *shame* and *doubt*. Children who fail to master the task of establishing some control over themselves and coping with the world around them develop a sense of shame and feelings of doubt about their capabilities. Erikson emphasizes that during this time children become aware of their emerging skills and have a drive to try them out. Parents who do too much for their children hamper their proper development. They are saying, however indirectly, "Let us do this for you, because you're too clumsy, too slow, or too incapable of doing things for yourself." Young children need to experiment; they need to be allowed to make mistakes and still feel that they are basically worthwhile. If parents insist on keeping their children dependent on them, the children will begin to doubt the value of their own abilities. If parents don't appreciate their children's efforts, the children may feel ashamed of themselves.

Young children also must learn to accept their negative feelings. They will surely experience rage, hatred, hostility, destructiveness, and ambivalence, and they need to feel that such feelings are permissible and that they aren't evil for having them. Of course, they also need to learn how to express their feelings in constructive ways.

In many ways, then, early childhood is a time when we struggle between a sense of self-reliance and a sense of self-doubt. Many people I work with in counseling seek professional help precisely because they have a low level of autonomy. They doubt their ability to stand alone, so they depend on others to do for them things they could do for themselves. This applies particularly to some marriages; some people marry so that they will have a mother figure or a father figure to protect them and take care of their needs. Similarly, many of us have grave difficulty in recognizing our negative feelings, even when they are fully justified. We swallow our anger and rationalize away other feelings, because we learned when we were 2 or 3 years old that we were unacceptable when we had such feelings. As children, we might have shouted at our parents: "I hate you! I never want to see you again!" Then we may have heard an equally enraged parent reply: "How dare you say such a thing—after all I've done for you! I don't ever want to hear that from you again!" We soon take these messages to mean: "Don't be angry! Never hate those you love! Keep control of yourself!" And we do just that—keeping many of our feelings to ourselves, stuffing them in the pit of our stomach and pretending we didn't experience them. Is it any wonder that so many of us suffer from migraine headaches, peptic ulcers, hypertension, or heart disease?

Again, take time out to reflect in a personal way on some of your current struggles in the area of autonomy and self-worth. You might ask yourself:

- Am I able to recognize my own feelings, particularly if they are "unacceptable" to others? How do I express my anger to those I love? Can I tolerate the ambivalence of feeling love and hate toward the same person?
- Do I take care of myself, or do I lean on others to support me? Do I keep myself a psychological cripple by encouraging others to do for me what I can do for myself?
- How assertive am I? Do I let others know what I want, without becoming aggressive? Or do I let myself be manipulated and pushed by others?

PRESCHOOL AGE

The preschool years (ages 3–6) are characterized by play and by anticipation of roles. During this time children seek to find out how much they can do. They imitate others; they begin to develop a sense of right and wrong; they widen their circle of significant other persons; they take more initiative; they learn to give and receive love and affection; they identify with their own sex; they begin to learn more complex social skills; they learn basic attitudes regarding sexuality; and they increase their capacity to understand and use language.

According to Erikson, the basic task of the preschool years is to establish a sense of competence and initiative. The core struggle of ages 3–6 is between *initiative* and *guilt*. Preschool children begin to initiate many of their own activities as they become physically and psychologically ready to engage in pursuits of their own choosing. If they are allowed realistic freedom to choose their own activities and to make some of their own decisions, they tend to develop a positive orientation characterized by confidence in their ability to initiate and follow through. If they are unduly restricted or if their choices are ridiculed, however, they tend to experience a sense of guilt and ultimately to withdraw from taking an active and initiating stance.

In Freudian theory this is the *phallic stage*, during which children become increasingly interested in sexual matters and begin to acquire a clearer sense of sex-role identity. Before children enter school, they begin to decide how they feel about themselves in their roles as boys and girls. Children exhibit a natural curiosity about sexual matters, and very early in life they form attitudes toward their sexuality and sexual feelings, their bodies, and what they think is right and wrong. Many adults suffer from deep feelings of guilt concerning sexual pleasure or feelings. Some have learned that their sexual organs are disgusting; others have traumatic memories associated with sexual intercourse. Much sexual dysfunctioning in adulthood has its roots in early conditioning and experiences. Preschool children begin to pay attention to their genitals and experience pleasure from genital stimulation. They typically engage in both masturbatory and sex-play activities. They begin to show considerable curiosity about the differences between the sexes and the differences between adults and children. This is the time for questions such as "Where do babies come from?" and "Why are boys and girls different?" Parental attitudes toward these questions, which can be communicated nonverbally as well as verbally, are critical in helping children form a positive attitude toward their own sexuality. Since this is a time of conscience formation, one danger is that parents may instill rigid and unrealistic moral standards, which can lead to an overdeveloped conscience. Children who learn that their bodies and their impulses are evil soon begin to feel guilty about their natural impulses and feelings. Carried into adult life, these attitudes can prevent people from appreciating and enjoying sexual intimacy. Another danger is that strict parental indoctrination, which can be accomplished in subtle, nonverbal ways, will lead to an infantile conscience. Children may thus develop a fear of questioning and thinking for themselves, instead blindly accepting the dictates of their parents. Other effects of such indoctrination include rigidity, severe conflicts, guilt, remorse, and self-condemnation.

Children need adequate models if they are to accept their sexual feelings as natural and develop a healthy concept of their body and their sex-role identity. In addition to forming attitudes toward their body and sexuality, they begin to formulate their conceptions of what it means to be feminine or masculine. By simply being with their parents, they are getting some perspective on the way men and women relate to one another, and they are acquiring basic attitudes toward such relationships. They are also deciding how they feel about themselves in their roles as boys and girls.

Our learning and decisions during the phallic stage pave the way for our ability to accept ourselves as men or women in adulthood. Many people seek counseling because of problems they experience in regard to their sexual identities. Some men are very confused about what it means to be a man in this society. Some are stuck in a stereotype of the masculine role, which for them means never being tender or passionate, never feeling intensely (*thinking* their way through life instead), never crying, and, above all, *always* being "strong." Because they fear that they might not be manly enough, these men often have a desperate drive to succeed financially or to prove their "manhood," or else they measure themselves against some yardstick of what they think constitutes the normal male. On the other side, there are some biological men who have tried to convince themselves and others that there are simply no differences between themselves and women. Some of these men resist doing anything that might be labeled "masculine," and they hold up as ideal the concept of unisex. And there are men who look to consciousness-raising groups to tell them how they should behave as men.

Of course, such problems are not limited to men. Many women seek some form of therapy because of a sex-role identity crisis. There are women who have submerged their identity totally in the roles of mother and housewife, because they feel they have no other choice. Others, who want to be wives and mothers, have become aware that they also want something more. Unfortunately, some women have identified themselves completely with some type of women's movement, to the point of following blindly. I don't mean to suggest that consciousness-raising groups for both women and men cannot be useful, but I do believe that some people can use a "movement" to find answers outside of themselves, instead of struggling and deciding on their own direction.

Again, pause and reflect on some of your own current struggles with these issues.

- Do you have a clear picture of who you are as a woman or man? What are your standards of femininity or masculinity? Where did you get them?
- Are you comfortable with your own sexuality? with your body? with giving and receiving sensual and sexual pleasure? Are there any unresolved conflicts from your childhood that get in the way of your enjoyment? Do your present behavior and current conflicts indicate areas of unfinished business?

Impact of the First Six Years of Life

In describing the events of the first six years of life, I have relied rather heavily on the psychoanalytic view of psychosexual and psychosocial development, as originally formulated by Freud and later extended and modified by Erikson. This approach emphasizes the critical nature of the early developmental years in the formation of our personalities. In my work with clients in individual counseling and with relatively well-functioning people in therapeutic groups, I have come to see these early years as a strong influence on our levels of integration and functioning as adults.

When I think of the most typical problems and conflicts I encounter in my counseling work and in my college classes, the following areas come to mind: inability to trust oneself and others; inability to freely accept and give love; difficulty in recognizing and expressing negative feelings; guilt over feelings of anger or hatred toward those one loves; inability or unwillingness to control one's own life; difficulties in fully accepting one's sexuality or in finding meaning in sexual intimacy; difficulty in accepting oneself as a woman or a man; and problems concerning a lack of meaning or purpose in life or a clear sense of personal identity and aspirations. Notice that most of these adult problems are directly related to the turning points and tasks of the early developmental years. I don't think the effects of early learning are irreversible in most cases, but these experiences, whether favorable or unfavorable, clearly influence how we relate to future critical periods in our lives.

Many people learn new values, come to accept new feelings and attitudes, and overcome much of their past negative conditioning. In contrast, many people steadfastly hang on to the past as an excuse for not taking any action to change in the present. We can't change in a positive direction unless we stop blaming others for the way we are now. Statements that begin "If it hadn't been for . . . " are too often used to justify an immobile position. For example: "If it hadn't been for the fact that I was adopted and had several foster parents, I'd be able to feel loved now, and I wouldn't be stuck with feelings of abandonment." "If only my parents had done more for me, I could feel a sense of security and trust." "If only my parents had done less for me, I could have grown up independent." "If only my parents had given me a healthy outlook on sex, I wouldn't feel so guilty now about my sexual feelings."

I remember one client who used to blame his mother for everything. Because she had dominated his father, he felt that he could not trust any woman now. If he couldn't trust his own mother, he reasoned, then whom could he trust? At 25 he saw himself as fearing independence, and he blamed his mother for his fear. He refused to date, and he tried to convince himself that he did so because his mother had "messed up my life by making me afraid." He continually wanted to use his therapy sessions to dwell on the past and blame his present problems on what his parents had and hadn't done. Through counseling he became aware that his dwelling on his past and his focusing on others were ways in which he was avoiding assuming responsibility for his own life. After actively questioning some of his beliefs about women and about himself, he decided that not all women were like his mother, that he didn't have to respond to women in the way his father had, and that he could change his life now if he was willing to accept the responsibility for doing so.

It may often be important to go through a stage of experiencing feelings of anger and hurt for having been cheated in the past, but I think it is imperative that we eventually claim for ourselves the power we have been giving to the people who were once significant in our life. Unless we recognize and exercise the power we now have to take care of ourselves, we close the door to new choices and new growth.

If you still wonder about the extent to which normal children really experience the crises I've described, I suggest reading Dorothy Baruch's very moving book, *One Little Boy* (1964). Baruch vividly describes the evolution of a boy named Ken through play therapy, and she makes a strong case that his feelings are typical of most children. In her work with Ken, she drew on a psychoanalytic perspective and had him relive many of the unresolved conflicts of his early childhood. Almost immediately he crawled onto her lap and allowed himself to be loved and cared for. During the early stages of play therapy Baruch created a climate in which he could freely give vent to all his feelings. As he felt increasingly safe, he began to express pent-up feelings of hostility and rage directed toward both his brother and his father. He built things of clay, and then he destroyed them. He took delight in making bombs and then "destroying" his father. Before his therapy, he had hardly been able to breathe because of severe asthma attacks. As he let go of many of the bottled-up feelings that he had been afraid to experience, he was able to breathe more freely, and many other crippling psychosomatic symptoms decreased.

Ken had developed many fears surrounding sexual matters, and during his play therapy he expressed in symbolic ways his guilt over masturbation, his castration anxiety, and his preoccupation with sex differences. Through the medium of play therapy, he was able to work through much of the unfinished business that presented so many problems in his later childhood. He grew to trust more; he became able to accept love and to express negative feelings without being destructive or feeling guilty; and he began to accept his sexual feelings as natural. He learned the difference between having feelings and acting out all of them. My students have gained a much deeper knowledge of the events of early childhood by reading *One Little Boy*, and almost all of them report that the book provided a rich and moving experience.

Another book that I highly recommend is Virginia Axline's *Dibs: In Search of Self* (1976). Most of my students say they are moved to tears as they read how Dibs struggles and finds himself in his play therapy. Although Axline used a client-centered approach in her play therapy (as opposed to Baruch's psychoanalytic approach), we see similar results as Dibs learns to trust and as he expresses his fears. I like the way Axline puts it:

> Dibs experienced profoundly the complex process of growing up, of reaching out for the precious gifts of life, of drenching himself in the sunshine of his hopes and in the rain of his sorrows. Slowly, tentatively, he discovered that the security of his world was not wholly outside of himself, but that the stabilizing center he searched for with such intensity was deep down inside that self [p. ix].

Think about Dibs and Ken in the context of your own life. Have you known children like them?

TIME OUT FOR PERSONAL REFLECTION

1. *Close your eyes and reflect for a moment on your memories of your first six years. Attempt to identify your earliest concrete single memory—something that you actually remember that happened to you, not something that you were told about. Spend a few minutes recalling the details and reexperiencing the feelings associated with this early event.*

   a. *Write down your earliest recollection:* _____

   _____

   _____

   _____

   _____

   b. *Do you have any hunches about how this early memory may still be having an impact on the way you think, feel, and behave today?*

   _____

   _____

   _____

   _____

2. *Reflect on the events that most stand out for you during your first six years of life. In particular, think about your place in your family, your family's reaction to you, and your reactions to each person in your family. What connections do you see between how it felt to be in your family as a child and how you now feel in various social situations? What speculations do you have concerning the impact your family had then and the effect that these experiences continue to have on your current personality?*

   _____

   _____

   _____

   _____

   _____

3. *Take the following self-inventory. Respond quickly, marking "T" if you believe the statement is more true than false for you as a young child and "F" if it tends not to fit your early childhood experiences.*

_____   *As a young child I felt loved and accepted.*
_____   *I basically trusted the world.*
_____   *I felt that I was an acceptable and valuable person.*
_____   *I didn't need to work for others' approval.*
_____   *I didn't experience a great deal of shame and self-doubt as a child.*
_____   *I felt that it was OK for me to express negative feelings.*
_____   *My parents trusted my ability to do things for myself.*
_____   *I believe that I developed a natural and healthy concept of my body and my sex-role identity.*
_____   *I had friends as a young child.*
_____   *I felt that I could talk to my parents about my problems.*

Look over your responses. What do they tell you about the person you now are? If you could live your childhood over again, how would you like it to be? Record some of your impressions in your journal.

MIDDLE CHILDHOOD

During middle childhood (ages 6–12), children face the following key developmental tasks: to engage in social tasks; to expand their knowledge and understanding of the physical and social worlds; to continue to learn and expand their concepts of an appropriate feminine or masculine role; to develop a sense of values; to learn new communication skills; to learn how to read, write, and calculate; to learn to give and take; to learn how to accept people who are culturally different; to learn to tolerate ambiguity; and to learn physical skills.

For Freudians this period is the *latency stage*, characterized by a relative decline in sexual interests and the emergence of new interests, activities, and attitudes. With the events of the hectic phallic period behind them, children take a long breathing spell and consolidate their positions. Their attention turns to new fields, such as school, playmates, books, and other features of the real world. Their hostile reactions tend to diminish, and they begin to reach out for friendly relationships with others in the environment.

Erikson, however, disagrees with the Freudian view of this period as a time of latency and neutrality. He argues that the middle-childhood years present unique psychosocial demands that children must meet successfully if their development is to proceed. According to Erikson, the major struggle of middle childhood is between *industry* and *inferiority*. The central task of this period is to achieve a sense of industry; failure to do so results in a sense of inadequacy and inferiority. The development of a sense of industry includes focusing on creating and producing and on attaining goals. Of course, starting school is a critical event of this time. Children who encounter failure during the early grades may experience severe handicaps later on. A child with early learning problems may begin to feel worthless as a person. Such a feeling may, in turn, drastically affect his or her relationships with peers, which are also vital at this time.

Helen's case illustrates some of the common conflicts of the elementary-school years. When Helen started kindergarten—a bit too early—she was smaller than most of the other children. Although she had looked forward to beginning school and tried to succeed, for the most part she felt overwhelmed. She began to fail at many of the tasks her peers were enjoying and mastering. School-age children are in the process of developing their self-concept, whether positive or negative, and Helen's view of her capacity to succeed was growing dimmer. Gradually, she began to avoid even simple tasks and to find many excuses to rationalize away her failures. She wanted to hide the fact that she was not keeping up with the other children. She was fearful of learning and trying new things, so she clung to secure, familiar ways. She grew increasingly afraid of making mistakes, for she believed that everything she did had to be perfect. If she did some art work, for instance, she would soon become frustrated and rip up the piece of paper because her picture wasn't coming out exactly as she wanted it to. Basically, Helen was afraid of putting her potential to the test, and she would generally freeze up when she had to be accountable for anything she produced. Her teachers' consistent evaluation of her was, "Helen is a sensitive child who needs a lot of encouragement and direction. She could do much more than she does, but she quits too soon, because she feels that what she does isn't good enough."

Helen grew to resent the fact that some of her teachers were not demanding much of her because they didn't want to push her. She then felt even more different from her peers, completing the vicious circle. Despite her will to try and her desire to succeed, she was prevented from venturing out by her fears of gambling and making mistakes. When she was in the third grade, she was at least a grade level behind in reading, despite the fact that she had repeated kindergarten. As she began to feel stupid and embarrassed because she couldn't read as well as the other children, she shied away from reading aloud. Eventually, she received instruction in remedial reading in a clinic, and this attention seemed to help. She was also given an intelligence test at the clinic, and the results were "low average." The reading staff and those who tested Helen were surprised, for they saw her as creative, insightful, and much brighter than the results showed. Again, Helen froze up when she felt that she had to perform on a test.

Helen's case indicates that the first few years of school can have a powerful impact on a child's life and future adjustment to school. Her school experiences colored her view of her self-worth and affected her relationships with other children. At this point ask yourself: Can I identify in any ways with Helen's case? What struggles did I experience in forming my self-concept? Does Helen remind me of anyone I know?

Developing a Self-Concept

Your self-concept is essentially how you see yourself and how you feel about that self-perception. This picture of yourself includes your view of your worth, value, and possibilities. It includes the way you see yourself in relation to others, the way you'd ideally like to be, and the degree to which you accept yourself as you are. From ages 6–12 the view you have of yourself is influenced greatly by the quality of your school experiences, by contact with your peer group and with teachers, and by your interactions with your family.

To a large extent your self-concept is formed by what others tell you about yourself, especially during the formative years of childhood. Whether you develop a basically positive or negative outlook on yourself has a good deal to do with what people close to you have expected of you.

This view of yourself has a significant impact on how you present yourself to others and how you act and feel when you are with others. For example, you may feel inadequate around authority figures. Perhaps you tell yourself that you have nothing to say or that whatever you might say would be stupid. Since you have this view of yourself, you behave in ways that persuade people to adopt your view of yourself. More often than not, others will see and respond to you in the way you "tell" them that you are. It is difficult for those who are close to you to treat you in a positive way when you consistently discount yourself. Why should others treat you better than you treat yourself? In contrast, people with a positive self-concept are likely to behave confidently, which causes others to react to them positively.

Protecting Our Self-Concept: The Ego-Defense Mechanisms

Freud conceived of ego-defense mechanisms as involving an unconscious process that prevents a person from becoming consciously aware of threatening feelings, thoughts, and impulses. For our purposes, defense mechanisms can be thought of as psychological strategies we use to protect our self-concept against unpleasant emotions through self-deception and distorting of reality. These protective devices are used at various stages of life to soften the blows of harsh reality to our self-concept. These ego defenses typically originate during our childhood years, and later ex-

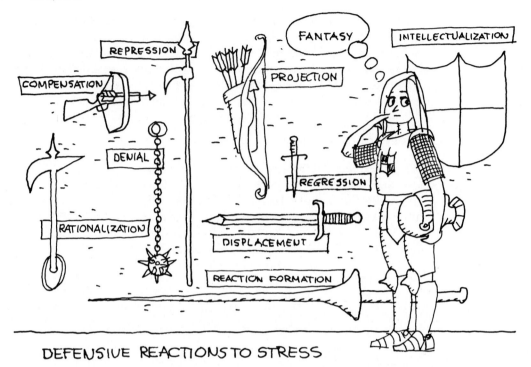

DEFENSIVE REACTIONS TO STRESS

periences during adolescence and adulthood reinforce some of these styles of self-defense. Although this concept of ego defense is rooted in the psychoanalytic tradition, psychologists regardless of their theoretical orientation are interested in the nature and functioning of defensive behavior. Building on Freud's original ideas of the functioning of unconscious psychological processes, contemporary psychologists have broadened the scope and added to the list of ego-defense mechanisms.

To illustrate the nature and functioning of these ego defenses, I will use the case of Helen discussed earlier. Helen is now in the sixth grade, and for the most part she has made poor adjustments to her school and social life. Other children stay away from her because of her aggressive and unfriendly behavior. She says that she hates school, that her teachers don't like her, and that others are to blame for the fact that she is falling so far behind in her schoolwork. In the face of these failures in life, she might make use of any one or a combination of the following ego-defense mechanisms.

Repression.   The mechanism of repression is one of the most important Freudian processes, and it is the basis of many other ego defenses. It is a means of defense through which threatening or painful thoughts and feelings are excluded from awareness. Repression may block out stressful experiences that could be met by realistically facing and working through a situation.

In Helen's case, she is unaware of her dependence/independence struggles with her parents; she is also unaware of how her painful experiences of failure are contributing to her present feelings of inferiority and her insecurity with other children. She has unconsciously excluded most of her failure experiences and does not allow them to come to the surface of awareness.

Denial.   Denial plays a defensive role similar to that of repression, yet it generally operates at conscious levels. It is a way of distorting what the individual thinks, feels, or perceives to be a stressful situation. Helen simply "closes her eyes" to her present failures in school. Even though she has evidence that she is not performing well academically, she refuses to acknowledge this reality.

Displacement.   Displacement involves redirecting emotional impulses (usually hostility) from the real source to a substitute person or object. In essence, anxiety is coped with by discharging impulses to a "safer target." For example, Helen's sister Joan is baffled by the hostility that she is getting from her. Joan does not understand why Helen is critical of her every action. Helen is probably using Joan as the target of her aggression, especially in light of the fact that Joan is doing exceptionally well at school and is very popular.

Projection.   Another mechanism of self-deception is projection, which consists of attributing to others our own unacceptable desires and impulses. Typically, projection involves seeing clearly in others actions that would lead to guilt feelings in ourselves. Helen is blaming everyone but herself for her difficulties in school and with others. She complains that her teachers unfairly pick on her, that she can never do anything right for them, and that all of the other children are mean to her for no reason.

Reaction Formation.   One defense against a threatening impulse is to actively express the opposite impulse. This involves behaving in a manner that is contrary to one's real feelings. A characteristic of this defense is the excessive quality of a particular attitude or behavior. For example, Helen bristles when her teachers or parents offer to give her help. She is convinced that she does not need anyone's help. Accepting their offers would indicate that she really *is* stupid.

Rationalization.   Rationalization involves manufacturing a false but "good" excuse to justify unacceptable behavior and explain away failures or losses. Helen is quick to find many reasons for the difficulties she is having, a few of which are sickness, which causes her to fall behind in her classes; teachers who go over the lessons too fast; other children who won't let her play with them; and brothers and sisters who keep her awake at night.

Compensation. Another defensive reaction is compensation, which consists of masking perceived weaknesses or developing certain positive traits to make up for limitations. The adjustive value in this mechanism lies in keeping one's self-esteem intact by excelling in one area to distract attention from an area in which the person is inferior. The more Helen experiences difficulties at school and with her peers, the more she withdraws from others and becomes absorbed in art work that she does by herself at home.

Regression.   Faced with stress, some people revert to a form of immature behavior that they have outgrown. In regression, they attempt to cope with their anxiety by clinging to such inappropriate behaviors. Faced with failure in both her social and school life, Helen goes on emotional tirades, crying a lot, storming into her room, and refusing to come out for hours.

Fantasy.   Fantasy involves gratifying frustrated desires by imaginary achievements. When achievement in the real world seems remote, some people resort to screening out unpleasant aspects of reality and living in their world of dreams. Helen develops a rich fantasy in which she imagines herself to be an actress. She plays with her dolls for hours and talks to herself. In her daydreams she sees herself in the movies, surrounded by famous people.

Summary of Defensive Reactions.   As you were reading about Helen's defensive behavior in response to her personal problems, you may have seen yourself in some of her reactions to her difficulties. From time to time we all use some of the ego-defense mechanisms to soften failure, to alleviate anxiety, to repair our wounded pride, and to maintain feelings of adequacy. Although using these defensive behaviors involves deceiving ourselves and distorting reality, they can be considered normal coping mechanisms that have some adjustive value. The major problem in relying on defensive strategies is that they rarely provide a long-term solution to our problems. Further, they often preclude constructive approaches to dealing with stressful events. In order to cope effectively, we must first face up to the causes of problems, and then we must recognize our own part in creating them. Thus, the ego-defense mechanisms can be considered unhealthy reactions when they are used to the extent of interfering with our ability to directly and realistically meet the demands of living. When we develop various defensive strategies as children, we often feel helpless, and these mechanisms seem like the only way to cope with the

demands of reality. As we go through adolescence and young adulthood, a major task is to learn to recognize our problems and find direct ways to deal with them. In this way we can develop a positive self-concept as we mature.

Becoming aware of *how* you've formed your view of yourself is basic to any efforts to change. One way to acquire this awareness is to spend time reviewing some of the significant experiences of your childhood. In particular, you can reflect on how these experiences have affected the way you feel about your competence and worth. It is helpful to recall specific instances in which you have made certain decisions. For example, as a child you might have decided that you were "stupid" and therefore have engaged in withdrawal behavior. Now, as an adult, you may still be acting in many ways like that scared child. As you come to realize that you accepted an inaccurate view of yourself, you can begin to challenge that early decision and start to behave in new, more rewarding ways.

ADOLESCENCE

The years from 12 to 18 constitute a stage of transition between childhood and adulthood. For most people this is a particularly difficult period. It is a paradoxical time: adolescents are not treated as mature adults, yet they are often expected to act as though they had gained complete maturity;

they are typically highly self-centered and preoccupied with their subjective world, yet they are expected to cope with the demands of reality and to go outside of themselves by expanding their horizon.

Adolescence is a time for continually testing limits, and there is usually a strong urge to break away from dependent ties that restrict one's freedom. It is not uncommon for adolescents to be frightened and lonely, but they may mask their fears with rebellion and cover up their need to be dependent by exaggerating their degree of independence. Although young people are becoming increasingly aware of the extent to which they are the products of their own family, it seems extremely important for them to declare their uniqueness and establish a separate identity. Much of adolescents' rebellion, then, is an attempt to determine the course of their own life and to assert that they are who and what *they* want to be, not what others expect them to be.

In this quest to define themselves, adolescents may tend to dismiss completely anything their parents stand for, because they are insecure about not achieving their own sense of uniqueness unless they do. It would be better to recognize that our parents, our family, and our history are a part of us, and that it's unrealistic to think that anyone can completely erase this influence. Instead of totally rejecting parental influences, young people could learn how to incorporate those values that could give their life meaning, to modify those values that they deem in need of change, and to reject the ones that they choose not to live by. Those who go to the extreme of attempting to be totally different from their parents are really not free, because they are investing a great deal of energy in proving themselves and, by their overreaction, are continuing to give their parents undue importance in their life.

Adolescence is a time for integrating the various dimensions of one's identity that have been achieved in the past. As infants we must learn to trust ourselves and others; as adolescents we need to find a meaning in life and models in whom we believe. As toddlers we begin to assert our rights as independent people by struggling for autonomy; as adolescents we make choices that will shape our future. As preschoolers we engage in play and fantasize different roles; as adolescents we commit ourselves by assuming new roles and identities. As schoolchildren we try to achieve a sense of competence; as adolescents we explore choices concerning what we want from life, what we can succeed in, what kind of education we want, and what career may suit us.

Adolescence is a critical period in the development of personal identity. For Erikson, adolescents' major developmental conflicts center on the clarification of who they are, where they are going, and how they are going to get there. He sees the core struggle of adolescence as *identity* versus *role confusion*. A failure to achieve a sense of identity results in role confusion. Adolescents may feel overwhelmed by the pressures placed on them; if so, they may find the development of a clear identity a difficult task. They may feel pressured to make an occupational choice, to compete in the job market or in college, to become financially independent, and to commit themselves to physically and emotionally intimate relationships. In addition, they may feel pressured to live up to the standards of their peer group. Peer-group pressure is such a potent force that there is a danger that adolescents will lose their focus on their own identities and conform to the expectations of their friends and classmates. If the need to be accepted and liked is stronger than the need for self-respect, adolescents will most likely find themselves behaving in nongenuine ways, selling themselves out, and increasingly looking to others to tell them what and who they should be.

During adolescence a crucial part of the identity-formation process requires *individuation*. This term refers to the separation from our family system and the establishing of our identity based on our own experiences, rather than merely following our parents' dreams. This process of psychological separation from parental ties is the most agonizing part of the adolescent struggle and lays the foundation for future development. Although adolescents may accept many of their parents' values, to genuinely individuate they must choose these values freely rather than automatically incorporating them into their personality (Okun, 1984).

A strain on adolescents' sense of identity is imposed by the conflict between their awareness of expanding possibilities and society's narrow-

ing of their options for action. Adolescents confront dilemmas similar to those faced by old people in our society. Both age groups must deal with finding a meaning in living and must cope with feelings of uselessness. Just as older people may be forced to retire and may encounter difficulty in replacing work activities, young people frequently feel that they are useless to society. They have not completed the education that will give them entry to many careers, and they generally haven't had the chance to acquire the skills necessary for many occupations. Instead, they are in a constant process of preparation for the future. Even in their family they may feel unneeded. Although they may be given chores to do, many adolescents do not experience much opportunity to be productive.

The question of options is made even more urgent by the myth that the choices we make during adolescence bind us for the rest of our life. Adolescents who believe this myth will be hesitant to experiment and test out many options. Too many young people yield to pressures to decide too early what they will be and what serious commitments they will make. Thus, they may never realize the range of possibilities open to them. To deal with this problem, Erikson suggests a *psychological moratorium*—a period during which society would give permission to adolescents to experiment with different roles and values so that they could sample life before making major commitments.

Adolescents are also faced with choices concerning what beliefs and values will guide their actions; indeed, forming a philosophy of life is a central task of adolescence. In meeting this challenge young people need adequate models, for a sense of moral living is largely learned by example. Adolescents are especially sensitive to duplicity, and they are quick to spot phony people who tell them how they *ought* to live while they themselves live in very different ways. They learn values by observing and interacting with adults who are positive examples, rather than by being preached to.

A particular problem adolescents face in the area of values concerns sexual behavior. Adolescents are easily aroused sexually, and everywhere they turn, whether in the media or in real life, they are saturated with sexual stimuli. At the same time, our society formally frowns on engaging in most types of sexual behavior before marriage. The resulting conflict can produce much frustration, anxiety, and guilt. Even apart from moral values with regard to sexuality, adolescents need to assess anew issues related to their sex-role identities. What is a woman? What is a man? What is feminine? What is masculine? What are the expectations we must live up to, and where do they originate? Wrestling with these difficult questions is part of the struggle of being an adolescent.

With all of these tasks and conflicts it isn't surprising that adolescence is typically a turbulent and fast-moving period of life, and one that is often marked by loneliness. It is a time for making choices in almost every area of life—choices that, to a large extent, define our identity. The identity that we develop during adolescence, although not necessarily final, has a profound effect on how we relate to future turning points throughout adult life.

TIME OUT FOR PERSONAL REFLECTION

At this point it could be useful to review the choices open to adolescents, and especially to think of the choices that you remember having made at this time in your life. How do you think those choices have influenced the person you are today?

A few of the choices adolescents are faced with include:

What kind of identity will I choose, a positive or a negative one?

Will I choose to remain self-centered, or will I go beyond myself by developing an interest in the world and in others?

There is the choice to use drugs and alcohol excessively, to the point of escaping from reality, or to face reality.

There is the choice to follow the crowd (to the extent of losing any sense of uniqueness), or to dare to be different (even if it means not being universally accepted).

How will I find meaning in the world? What will I look to for a sense of direction in life? Will religion be a part of this framework, and if so, what kind of religion will I embrace?

Will I merely accept the values I've been taught, or will I question them and eventually find values to live by that I've thought out? Will I let someone else decide how I should live, or will I draw my own blueprints and follow them?

1. *What major choices did you struggle with during your adolescent years?*

   _____

   _____

   _____

   _____

2. *If you could live your adolescent years again, what would you most like to change?*

   _____

   _____

   _____

   _____

3. How do you think your adolescence affected the person you are today?

_____

_____

_____

_____

CHAPTER SUMMARY

A road map giving a general overview of the developmental tasks of the life span reveals that each stage presents certain dangers and opportunities. In a positive sense, crises can be seen as challenges to be met rather than catastrophic events that happen to us. In normal development there are critical turning points and choices for each phase. There is continuity in life, for our early experiences influence the choices we make at a later time in our development. There are no neat marks to delineate one stage of development from another. There is a great deal of overlap between stages; moreover, we all experience each period of life in our own unique ways.

The struggle toward autonomy, or psychological independence, begins in early childhood, takes on major proportions during adolescence and young adulthood, and extends into later adulthood. Actualizing our full potential as a person and learning to stand alone in life, as well as stand beside others, is a task that is never really finished. Although major life events during childhood and adolescence have an impact on the ways that we think, feel, and behave in adult life, we are not helplessly molded and hopelessly determined by such events. Instead, we do choose our attitudes toward these events, which in turn affects how we behave today.

Freud's psychoanalytic view of human development during the first six years of life emphasizes the importance of acquiring a sense of trust toward the world, of learning how to recognize and express the full range of feelings, and of acquiring a healthy attitude toward sexuality and a clear sense of our sex-role identity. His psychosexual perspective shows how our later personality development hinges on the degree to which we have successfully met the demands and conflicts during early childhood.

Erikson built on Freud's basic ideas, and his psychosocial theory offers a more complete and comprehensive perspective of the unique tasks of the entire life span. In his eight stages of development Erikson emphasizes the critical turning points facing us at each transition in our life. At these points we can either successfully resolve the basic conflict (such as trust versus mistrust during infancy) or get stuck on the road to development. Again, early choices affect the range of choices open to us later in life.

From infancy through adolescence we are faced with developmental challenges at each stage of life. The basic task of *infancy* is to develop a sense of trust in others and our environment, so we can trust ourselves. Later personality problems that can stem from failure to develop this trust include fearing intimate relationships, low self-esteem, and isolation. *Early childhood* presents the challenge of beginning to function independently and acquiring a sense of self-control. If we do not master this task, becoming autonomous is extremely difficult. During the *preschool age* we are forming our sex-role identity, and ideally we experience a sense of competence that comes with making some decisions for ourselves. Parental attitudes during this period are very powerful, and these attitudes are communicated both verbally and nonverbally. Our school experiences during *middle childhood* play a significant role in our socialization. At this time the world is opening up to us, and we are expanding our interests outside of the home. Problems that typically begin at this phase include a negative self-concept, conflicts over values, a confused sex-role identity, a fear of new challenges, and disturbed interpersonal relationships. *Adolescence* is the period when we are forming an identity as well as establishing goals and values that give our life meaning. A danger of this time of life is that we can follow the crowd out of fear of being rejected. If that happens, we fail to listen to ourselves and discover what it is that we want for ourselves.

Each of these developmental phases lays the foundation on which we build our adult personality. As we will see in the next chapter, mastery of these earlier challenges is essential in learning to cope with the problems of adult living.

ACTIVITIES AND EXERCISES

1. In your journal, write an account of the first five years of your life. Although you may think that you can't remember much about this time, the following guidelines should help in your recall:
   a. Write down a few key questions that you would like answered about your early years.
   b. Seek out your relatives, and ask them some of these questions.
   c. Collect any reminders of your early years, particularly pictures.
   d. If possible, visit the place or places where you lived and went to school.
2. Rewrite your past the way you *wish* it had been. Think of the things you wanted (and allow yourself to have them in fantasy), and remember situations that you wish had been different. After you reconstruct your past the way you'd like it to have been, write a brief account of

how you think your life would be different today if you had experienced *that* past instead of your real one.

3. Choose from among the many exercises in this chapter any that you'd be willing to integrate into a self-help program during your time in this course. What things are you willing to do to bring about some of the changes you want in your life?

4. Pictures often say more about you than words. What do your pictures tell about you? Look through any pictures of yourself as a child and as an adolescent, and see if there are any themes. What do most of your pictures reveal about the way you felt about yourself? Bring some of these pictures to class. Have other members look at them and tell you what they think you were like then. Pictures can also be used to tap forgotten memories.

SUGGESTED READINGS

Axline, V. (1976). *Dibs: In Search of Self*. New York: Ballantine. This book gives a touching account of a boy's journey from isolation toward self-awareness and self-expression and emphasizes the crucial effects of the parent/child relationship on the development of a child's personality. It also describes how play therapy can be a tool for developing an autonomous individual.

Baruch, D. (1964). *One Little Boy*. New York: Dell (Delta). This is a fascinating account of one boy's feelings and problems and of how his personal conflicts originated in the family dynamics, as revealed through play therapy. The book gives the reader a sense of appreciation for the struggles most children experience during early childhood in relationship with their parents.

Erikson, E. (1963). *Childhood and Society* (2nd ed.). New York: Norton. Using a modified and extended version of psychoanalytic thought, Erikson describes a psychosocial theory of development. He delineates eight stages and their critical tasks.

Erikson, E. (1982). *The Life Cycle Completed*. New York: Norton. In his latest book Erikson updates his psychosocial theory of life-span development.

Twiford, R., & Carson, P. (1980). *The Adolescent Passage: Transitions from Child to Adult*. Englewood Cliffs, N.J.: Prentice-Hall (Spectrum). The authors explain the critical factors that shape the life of the adolescent, and they give practical strategies for relating to youth. Both normal and abnormal psychological development are discussed, as well as sexual interests and behaviors, drug abuse, and adolescent traumas.

ADULTHOOD AND AUTONOMY

PRECHAPTER SELF-INVENTORY

Use the following scale to respond: 4 = this statement is true of me *most* of the time; 3 = this statement is true of me *much* of the time; 2 = this statement is true of me *some* of the time; 1 = this statement is true of me *almost none* of the time.

_____   1. For the most part, my values and beliefs are very much like my parents'.

_____   2. I'm an independent person more than I'm a dependent person.

_____   3. I think about early messages I received from my parents.

_____   4. I would say that I have psychologically divorced my parents and become my own parent.

_____   5. As I get older, I feel an urgency about living.

_____   6. Much of my life is spent in doing things that I do *not* enjoy.

_____   7. I look forward with optimism and enthusiasm to the challenges that lie ahead of me.

_____   8. I expect to experience a meaningful and rich life when I reach old age.

_____   9. There are many things I can't do now that I expect to do when I retire.

_____ 10. I have fears of aging.

INTRODUCTION

This chapter continues our discussion of the life-span perspective by focusing on the transitions and turning points in adulthood. As we saw in the last chapter, childhood and adolescent experiences lay the foundation for our ability to meet the developmental challenges of the various phases of adulthood. Whatever stage of adulthood you are now in, I hope that you will continue your struggle for autonomy. Before taking up early, middle, and late adulthood, this chapter examines how you can become more autonomous. One facet of this struggle involves recognizing the early life decisions you made and realizing that you can change them if they're not working. This entails challenging your inner "parent" and becoming your own parent. You can also learn to dispute your irrational, negative thinking and develop a positive, constructive self-image.

Although this chapter addresses some typical developmental patterns, I don't want to give the impression that everybody goes through these stages in the same way at the same time. But we will all eventually pass through them. If you are a young adult, you may wonder why you should be concerned about middle age and later life. I invite you to look at the choices you are making now that will have a direct influence on the quality of a later adulthood phase. As you read this chapter, reflect on what you hope to be able to say in regards to how you have lived when you reach later adulthood.

THE STRUGGLE TOWARD AUTONOMY

As we leave adolescence and approach young adulthood, our central task is to assume increased responsibility and independence. Although most of us have moved away from our parents physically, we have not always done so in a psychological sense. To a greater or lesser degree our parents will have a continuing influence on our life. The challenge we face as mature adults is to be aware of the ways in which our parents still have an influence on us. Having reviewed your own childhood and adolescent years in the last chapter, you can probably recognize more clearly the impact of your parents on your life. With this self-awareness comes the capacity to make new decisions. The struggle toward autonomy entails choosing for yourself and working for your own approval, rather than living your life primarily by your parents' designs and their approval. This struggle begins in early childhood and does not really end until we do.

Recognizing Early Learning and Decisions

Transactional analysis offers a useful framework for understanding how our learning during childhood extends into adulthood. TA is a theory of personality and a method of counseling that was originally developed by Eric Berne and later extended by practitioners such as Claude Steiner and Mary and Robert Goulding. The theory is based on the assumption that adults make decisions based on past premises, premises that were at one time appropriate to their survival needs but may no longer be valid. It stresses the capacity of the person to change early decisions and is oriented toward increasing awareness with the goal of enabling people to alter the course of their life. TA teaches people how to recognize the three ego states (Parent, Adult, and Child) in which they function. Through TA, people learn how their current behavior is affected by the rules and regulations they received and incorporated as children and how they can identify the "life script" that determines their actions. Ultimately, they come to realize that they can now change what is *not* working while retaining what serves them well.

Ego States: Parent, Adult, and Child.   TA identifies three ego states that encompass important facets of personality. According to TA, people are constantly shifting from one ego state to another, and their behavior at any one time is related to the state of the moment.

The *Parent* part of personality represents that which has been incorporated from one's parents and parental substitutes. When we are in the Parent ego state, we react to situations as we imagine our parents might have reacted, or we act toward others the way our parents acted toward us. The Parent contains all the "shoulds" and "oughts" and other rules for

living. When we are in that ego state, we may act in ways that are strikingly similar to those of our parents. We are likely to use some of their very words and phrases, and our posture, gestures, tone and quality of voice, and mannerisms may replicate theirs. Such behavior occurs whether the Parent in us is a positive ego state (a Nurturing Parent) or a negative one (a Critical Parent).

The *Adult* ego state is our processor of data. It is the objective part of our personality and gathers information about what is going on. It is not emotional or judgmental but works with the facts and with external reality.

The *Child* ego state consists of feelings, impulses, and spontaneous acts. The Child in each of us is either the "Natural Child," the "Little Professor," or the "Adapted Child." The Natural Child is the spontaneous, impulsive, open, alive, expressive, often charming but untrained being within each of us. The Little Professor is the unschooled wisdom of a child. It is manipulative, egocentric, and creative. The Adapted Child is the tamed version of the Natural Child, the part of us that learns to accommodate to the expectations of others in order to gain acceptance and approval.

People who participate in TA counseling are taught how to recognize what ego state they are functioning in when they are faced with a problem. In this way they can make conscious decisions about the particular ego state in which they want to function. For example, if Betty becomes aware that she is treating her children in the same critical way in which her own mother responded to her, she is in a position to change her behavior. As Betty becomes more aware of her ego states in various situations, she also becomes more aware of her adaptive behavior (both to her internal Parent and to the outside world). With this awareness she can knowingly choose other options.

Life Scripts.   The concept of the life script is an important contribution of TA. A life script is made up of both parental teachings and the early decisions we make as children. Often, we continue to follow our script as an adult.

Scripting begins in infancy with subtle, nonverbal messages from our parents. During our earliest years, we learn much about our worth as a person and our place in life. Later, scripting occurs in both subtle and direct ways. Some of the messages we might "hear" include: "Always listen to authority." "Don't act like a child." "We know that you can perform well, and we expect the best from you, so be sure you don't let us down." "Never trust people; rely on yourself." "You're really stupid, and we're convinced that you'll never amount to much." Often these messages are sent in disguised ways. For example, our parents may never have told us directly that sexual feelings are bad or that touching is inappropriate. However, their behavior with each other and with us may have taught us to think in this way. Moreover, what parents *don't* say or do is just as important as what they say directly. If no mention is ever made of sexuality, for instance, that very fact communicates significant attitudes.

According to TA theory, our life script forms the core of our personal identity. Our experiences may lead us to such conclusions as: "I really don't have any right to exist." "I can only be loved if I'm productive and successful." "I'd better not trust my feelings, because they'll only get me in trouble." These basic themes running through our life tend to determine our behavior, and very often they are difficult to unlearn. In many subtle ways these early decisions about ourselves can come back to haunt us in later life.

A couple of examples may help to clarify how early messages and the decisions we make about them influence us in day-to-day living. In my own case, even though I now experience myself as successful, for many years of my life I felt unsuccessful and unworthy. I haven't erased my old script completely, and I still experience self-doubts and sometimes question my worth. I don't think that I can change such long-lasting feelings by simply telling myself "OK, now that I'm meeting with some success, I'm a successful person." It may be necessary to deal again and again with feelings of being insecure and unworthy. In fact, even striving for and attaining success can be a compulsive way of denying basic feelings of inadequacy. In short, although I believe that I can change some of my basic attitudes about myself, I don't think I can ever get rid of all vestiges of my early learning. In general, although we need not be determined by old decisions, it's wise to be continually aware of manifestations of our old ways that interfere with our attempts to develop new ways of thinking and being.

A second illustration of how we can be affected by early decisions concerns a woman I'll call Pamela. Pamela is 38 years old, and she has been divorced three times. She finds it very difficult to take anything for herself or to experience needing anything from anyone. Instead, she has continually sought ways of being a "giver." She has told herself that she must be strong, that she mustn't allow herself to depend on others, and that she mustn't cry or experience grief. Yet Pamela isn't satisfied to continue living in this way, for she has felt lonely and resentful much of the time. She has typically picked men whom she views as weak—men who can give her nothing but whom she can take care of, thereby satisfying her "giving" needs. She sees the dishonesty in believing that she has been unselfish; she is aware that she has been motivated more by her own need to *be needed* than by her concerns for others. Gradually, she has also become aware that her parents used to "tell" her such things as: "Always be strong. Don't let yourself need anything from anyone, and in that way you'll never get let down." "Keep your feelings to yourself; if you feel like crying, don't do it in front of others." "Remember that the way to win approval and affection is to do things for others. Always put others before yourself." Pamela's behavior was determined by these values until she realized that she could change her early decisions if she so chose.

Ask yourself at this point if there are any ways in which you identify with Pamela. Can you detect any of your current behavior that has been determined by basic decisions you made earlier in life?

Injunctions.   Let's look more closely at the nature of the early messages (often called injunctions) that we incorporate into our life-style. First of all, I want to stress that these injunctions aren't just planted in our heads while we sit by passively. By making decisions in response to real or imagined injunctions, we assume some of the responsibility for indoctrinating ourselves. Thus, if we hope to free ourselves, we must become aware of what these "oughts" and "shoulds" are and of how we allow them to operate in our lives.

Robert and Mary Goulding, the directors of the Western Institute for Group and Family Therapy in Watsonville, California, are among the leaders in the field of transactional analysis. The following list, based on the Gouldings' works (1978, 1979), includes common injunctions and some possible decisions that could be made in response to them.

1. *Don't:* Children who hear and accept this message will believe that they cannot do anything right, and they will look to others to make their decisions for them.
   - *Possible decisions:* "I'm scared of making the wrong decision, so I

simply won't decide." "Because I made a dumb choice, I won't decide on anything important again!"

2. *Don't be:* This lethal message is often given nonverbally by the way parents hold (or don't hold) the child. The basic message is "I wish you hadn't been born."
   - *Possible decisions:* "I'll keep trying until I get you to love me." "If things get terrible, I'll kill myself."

3. *Don't be close:* Related to this injunction are the messages *Don't trust* and *Don't love.*
   - *Possible decisions:* "I let myself love once, and it backfired. Never again!" "Because it's scary to get close, I'll keep myself distant."

4. *Don't be important:* If you are constantly discounted when you speak, it is not surprising that you will get the message that *you* are unimportant.
   - *Possible decisions:* "If, by chance, I ever do become important, I'll never let anyone know it." "I'll keep a low profile."

5. *Don't be a child:* This message says: "Always act adult! Don't be childish and make a fool of yourself. Keep control of yourself."
   - *Possible decisions:* "I'll take care of others and won't ask for much myself." "I won't let myself have fun."

6. *Don't grow:* This message is given by the frightened parent who discourages the child from growing up in many ways.
   - *Possible decisions:* "I'll stay a child, and that way I'll get my parents to approve of me." "I won't be sexual, and that way my father won't push me away."

7. *Don't succeed:* If children are positively reinforced for failing, they may accept the message not to seek success.
   - *Possible decisions:* "I'll never do anything perfect enough, so why try." "I'll succeed, even if it kills me."

8. *Don't be you:* This involves suggesting to children that they are the wrong sex.
   - *Possible decisions:* "They'd love me only if I were a boy (girl), so it's impossible to get their love." "I'll pretend I'm a boy (girl)."

9. *Don't be sane* and *don't be well:* Some children get attention only when they are physically sick or acting crazy.
   - *Possible decisions:* "I'll get sick, and then I'll be included." "I am crazy."

10. *Don't belong:* This injunction may indicate that the family feels that the child does not belong anywhere.
    - *Possible decisions:* "I'll be a loner forever." "I'll never belong anywhere."

At this point, think about some of the childhood conclusions that you made about yourself and about life. For example, you might have made any one of the following early decisions:

- "I will be loved only when I live up to what others expect of me."
- "I'd better listen to authorities outside of myself, because I can't trust myself to make decent decisions."
- "I won't let myself trust people, and that way they won't ever let me down again."

Themes like these run through your life to determine not only your self-image but also your behavior. It is a difficult matter to unlearn some of these self-defeating assumptions and learn new and constructive ones in their place. This is one reason for learning how to critically evaluate questions such as:

- What messages have I listened to and "bought"?
- How valid are the sources of these messages?
- In what ways do I now continue to tell myself self-defeating sentences?
- How can I challenge some of the decisions I made about myself and make new ones that will lead to a positive orientation?

Although some of our early decisions may have been made to ensure physical and psychological survival—and thus have been appropriate at the time—many of them are both archaic and inappropriate as they are carried into our adult life. Through the process of increased self-awareness, we are able to critically examine early decisions to determine if we will continue to live by them.

One avenue of increasing your self-awareness and changing early decisions is individual and group counseling. Guidelines for assessing when you might profit from professional counseling are found in Resource 13.

Learning to Challenge Your Inner Parents

I'd like to expand a bit on the general concepts of TA and discuss some related ideas about challenging early messages and working toward autonomy. I use the term *inner parent* to refer to the attitudes and beliefs we have about ourselves and others that are a direct result of things we've learned from our parents or parental substitutes. I see the willingness to challenge this inner parent as a mark of autonomy. Since being autonomous means that we are in control of the direction of our life, it implies that we have discovered an identity that is separate and distinct from the identities of our parents and of others. We haven't really achieved autonomy if our actions are dictated by an unquestioned inner parent.

Many of us, however, are reluctant to give up our inner parent, and we keep it alive and functioning in many ways. By doing so, we become incapable of directing ourselves. Some of the ways in which we can cling to our parents and other significant figures are:

- choosing to live at home because it's more secure than having to leave and establish our own way of life

- making decisions that are primarily motivated by a need to please our parents rather than by a need to please ourselves
- attaching ourselves to a substitute parent, such as some hero, guru, or model
- marrying a person who is an extension of our father or mother in the hope that he or she will take care of our unmet needs
- striving to become perfect parents, thus making up for all that we never had as children
- clinging to the irrational notion that we haven't exhausted all the possible ways of pleasing our parents, and continuing to search and search in the hope that someday we will find a way to make them proud of us

Although becoming autonomous involves challenging our inner parent, it doesn't necessarily involve rejecting all or most of our parents' values. Some of our early decisions may have stimulated growth, and many of the values we incorporated from our parents may be healthy standards for guiding our behavior. No doubt our past has contributed in many respects to the good qualities we possess, and many of the things that we like about ourselves may be largely due to the influence of the people who were important to us in our early years. What is essential is that we look for the subtle ways in which we have psychologically incorporated our parents' values in our life without a deliberate choice.

How do we learn to recognize the influence that our parents continue to have on us? One way to begin is by talking back and engaging in dialogue with our inner parent. In other words, we can begin to notice some of the things we do and some of the things we avoid doing, and then ask ourselves why. For instance, suppose you avoided enrolling in a college course because you'd long ago branded yourself "stupid." You might tell

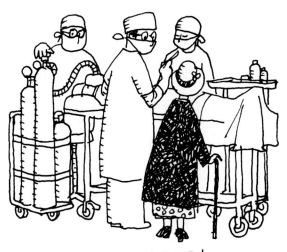

PLEASE, MOTHER!

yourself that you'd never be able to pass that class, so why even try? In this case an early decision that you'd made about your intellectual capabilities would prevent you from branching out to new endeavors. Rather than stopping at this first obstacle, however, you could challenge yourself by asking: "Who says that I'm too stupid? Even if my father or my teachers have told me that I'm slow, is this really true? Why have I bought this view of myself uncritically? Let me check it out and see for myself whether it's really true."

In carrying out this kind of dialogue, we can talk to the different selves we have within us. For example, you may be struggling to open yourself to people and trust them, while at the same time you hear the inner injunction "Never trust anybody." In this case you can carry on a two-way discussion between your trusting side and your suspicious side. The important point is that we don't have to passively accept as truth the messages we learned when we were children. As adults we can now put these messages to the test.

In his excellent book *Making Peace with Your Parents* the psychiatrist Harold Bloomfield (1983) makes the point that many of us suffer from psychological wounds as a result of unfinished business with our parents. According to Bloomfield, before we can resolve any conflicts with our actual parents, we first must make peace with our inner parent—the messages we bought from our parents, the feelings and conflicts we still carry with us, and the memories and hidden resentments we cling to from childhood.

Becoming Your Own Parent

Achieving emotional maturity involves divorcing ourselves from our inner parent and becoming our own "parent." But maturity is not some fixed destination at which we finally arrive; it is rather a direction in which we can choose to travel. What are some of the characteristics of the person who is moving toward becoming his or her own parent? There is no authoritative list of the qualities of an autonomous person, but the following characteristics may stimulate you to come up with your own view of what kind of parent you want to be for yourself and what criteria make sense to you in evaluating your own degree of psychological maturity. For each of these characteristics, ask yourself whether it applies to you and whether you agree that it is a mark of one who is becoming independent. I encourage you to add to or modify this list as you see fit.

1. People moving in the direction of autonomy recognize the ways in which their inner parent controls them. They see how they are controlled by guilt or by the promise of love and how they have cooperated in giving parents and parent substitutes undue power in their life.
2. People moving in the direction of autonomy have a desire to become

free and responsible, living on their own and doing for themselves what they are capable of doing.

3. People moving in the direction of autonomy have a sense of identity and uniqueness. Rather than looking outside of themselves, they find answers within. Instead of asking: "What do you expect of me? What will it take for me to win your approval? What should I be and do?" they ask: "What can I do that will make me pleased with myself? Who is it that I want to become? What seems right for me? What do I expect of myself?"

4. People moving in the direction of autonomy have a sense of commitment and responsibility. They are committed to some ideals and personal goals that make sense to them. Their sense of commitment includes the willingness to accept responsibility for their actions rather than blaming circumstances or other people for the way their life is going.

5. The discovery of a meaning or purpose in life is an important mark of independent people. Although this meaning can be derived from many sources, an independent life is characterized by purpose and direction.

In order to become our own parent, Gould (1978) says, it is essential that we deal with the unfinished business from childhood that periodically intrudes in our adult relationships. Referring to this unfinished business as the "angry demons of childhood consciousness," he asserts that our central developmental task consists of striving for a fuller and more independent *adult consciousness*. We accomplish this transformation from childhood to adult consciousness by reformulating our definition of self, which is a risky and continuing process. Thus, developing a mature personality involves eliminating the distortions of childhood demons and the protective devices we've developed to cope with these demons. Gould captures the essence of this struggle toward autonomy when he says: "As our life experience builds, ideally we abandon unwarranted expectations, rigid rules and inflexible roles. We come to be the owners of our own selves, with a fuller, more independent adult consciousness" (pp. 37–38).

In writing about "becoming your own best parent," Bloomfield (1983) challenges us *as adults* to recognize that we are responsible for satisfying our psychological needs for maintenance, encouragement, and affection. His message is that, rather than getting stuck in whining about all the ways our parents did not live up to our expectations, we can learn to give to ourselves what we missed from our parents:

> Becoming your own best parent is not a final destination but a new beginning. You can live your life with more inner peace instead of being controlled by unresolved conflicts from your upbringing. Taking charge of your life will give you more energy and vitality to express your own special talents more effectively [p. 214].

TIME OUT FOR PERSONAL REFLECTION

The following self-inventory is designed to increase your awareness of the injunctions that you have incorporated as a part of your self-system and to help you challenge the validity of messages that you may not have critically examined.

1. *Place a check (✔) in the space provided for each of the following "don't" injunctions that you think applies to you.*

_____   *Don't be (or don't exist).*
_____   *Don't be you.*
_____   *Don't think.*
_____   *Don't feel.*
_____   *Don't be close.*
_____   *Don't trust.*
_____   *Don't be sexy.*
_____   *Don't fail.*
_____   *Don't make it.*
_____   *Don't be foolish.*
_____   *Don't be important.*
_____   *Don't brag.*
_____   *Don't let us down.*
_____   *Don't grow or change.*
_____   *Don't be rude.*

List any other "don't" messages you heard frequently:

_____

_____

_____

_____

_____

2. *Check the following ways that you sometimes badger yourself with "do" messages.*

_____   *Be perfect.*
_____   *Say only kind things.*
_____   *Be more than you are.*
_____   *Be obedient.*
_____   *Work up to your potential.*
_____   *Be practical at all times.*
_____   *Listen to authority figures.*
_____   *Always put your best foot forward.*

_____   *Put others before yourself.*
_____   *Be seen but not heard.*

List any other injunctions that you can think of that apply to you:

_____

_____

_____

_____

_____

3. *What are some messages you've received concerning:*

   your self-worth? _____

   your potential to succeed? _____

   your sex role? _____

   your intelligence? _____

   your trust in yourself? _____

   trusting others? _____

   making yourself vulnerable? _____

   your security? _____

   your aliveness as a person? _____

   your creativity? _____

   your ability to be loved? _____

   your capacity to give love? _____

4. *Because your view of yourself has a great influence on the quality of your interpersonal relationships, I invite you to look carefully at some of the views you have of yourself and also to consider how you arrived at these views. To do this, reflect on these questions:*

   a. *How do you see yourself now? To what degree do you see yourself as confident? secure? worthwhile? accomplished? caring? open? accepting?*

b. How do you feel about the way you see yourself now? How would you describe this to a close friend in one concise sentence?

_____

_____

_____

_____

c. What is the difference between the way you see yourself now and the way you'd like to be? Do you feel hopeful about closing this gap?

_____

_____

_____

_____

d. Do others generally see you as you see yourself? What are some ways that others view you differently than you view yourself?

_____

_____

_____

_____

e. Who in your life has been most influential in shaping your self-concept, and how has he or she (they) affected your view of yourself? (father? mother? friend? teacher? grandparents?)

_____

_____

_____

_____

Learning to Dispute Irrational Thinking

As children and adolescents we uncritically incorporate certain assumptions about life and about our worth as a person. Rational-emotive therapy (RET) contends that feelings of anxiety, depression, rejection, anger, and alienation are initiated and perpetuated by a self-defeating belief system based on irrational ideas that we embraced at this time. These self-defeating beliefs are supported and maintained by negative, absolutistic, and illogical statements that we make to ourselves over and over again: "If I don't win universal love and approval, then I'll never be happy"; "If I make a mistake, that would be horrible"; and so forth.

Albert Ellis (1984), the developer of RET, has devised an A-B-C theory of personality that explains how people develop negative evaluations of themselves. According to Ellis, it is our faulty thinking, not actual events that happen in our lives, that creates emotional upsets.

An example will clarify this A-B-C concept. Assume that Sally's parents abandoned her when she was a child ("A," the activating event). Sally's emotional reaction may be feelings of depression, worthlessness, rejection, and unlovability ("C," the emotional consequence). However, Ellis asserts, it is not "A" (her parents' abandonment of her) that caused her feelings of rejection and unlovability; rather it is at point "B" (her belief system) that the cause of her low self-esteem lies. Sally made her mistake when she told herself that there must have been something terrible about herself for her parents not to want her. Sally's irrational beliefs are involved in the sentences she continues to tell herself: "I am to blame for what my parents did." "If I were more lovable, they would have wanted to keep me."

According to Ellis (1984), most of our irrational ideas can be reduced to three main forms of what he refers to as *must*urbation: (1) "I *must* be competent, and I *must* win the approval of all the significant people in my life"; (2) "Others *must* treat me fairly and considerately"; and (3) "My life *must* be easy and pleasant. I need and *must* have the things I want."

RET is designed to teach people how to *dispute* irrational beliefs such as those listed above. Let's apply RET to Sally's example. She does not need

SALLY, THE TROUBLE WITH YOU IS...

to continue believing that she is basically unlovable. Instead of clinging to the belief that something must have been wrong with *her* for her parents to have rejected her, she can begin to dispute this self-defeating statement and think along different lines: "It hurts that my parents didn't want me, but perhaps *they* had certain problems that kept them from being good parents." "Maybe my parents didn't love me, but it's a large world, and I'd be foolish to assume that nobody could love me." "While it's unfortunate that I didn't have parents in growing up, it's not devastating, and I no longer have to be a little girl waiting for their protection."

Ellis stresses that we feel about ourselves the way we think. Thus, if you hope to change a negative self-image, it is essential to learn how to dispute the illogical sentences you now continue to feed yourself and to challenge irrational premises that you have accepted uncritically. Further, you also need to work and practice at replacing these self-sabotaging beliefs with constructive ones. If you wish to study common ways of combating this self-indoctrination process, I refer you to Ellis and Harper (1975), *A New Guide to Rational Living.*

EARLY ADULTHOOD

In the previous chapter I focused the discussion of the developmental process from infancy through adolescence on Freud's psychosexual stages and Erikson's psychosocial stages. Inasmuch as Freud deemphasized development in adulthood, this chapter will rely on Erikson's perspective on the core struggles and choices from early adulthood through late adulthood.

The period of early adulthood is ages 18–35. According to Erikson, we enter adulthood after we master the adolescent conflicts over *identity* versus *role confusion.* Our sense of identity is tested anew in adulthood, however, by the challenge of *intimacy* versus *isolation.*

One characteristic of the psychologically mature person is the ability to form intimate relationships. Before we can form such relationships, we must be sure of our own identity. Intimacy involves a sharing, a giving of ourselves, a relating to another out of strength, and a desire to grow with the other person. Failure to achieve intimacy can result in isolation from others and a sense of alienation. The fact that alienation is a problem for many people in our society is evidenced by the widespread use of drugs and by other ways in which we try to numb our sense of isolation. If we attempt to escape isolation by clinging to another person, however, we rarely find success in the relationship.

Erikson's concept of intimacy can be applied to any kind of close relationship between two adults. Relationships involving emotional commitments may be between close friends of the same or the opposite sex, and they may or may not have a sexual dimension. Identifying characteristics of intimate relationships include sharing, individuation, mutuality, commitment, emotional support, caring, trust, responsibility, and mutual understanding (Okun, 1984).

Entering the Twenties

Whereas adolescence is a time of extreme preoccupation with internal conflicts and with the search for identity, your adulthood is a time for beginning to focus on external tasks, such as developing intimate relationships, getting established in an occupation, carving out a life-style, and perhaps marrying and starting a family. In *Passages*, Sheehy (1976) says that the tasks of this period are both enormous and exhilarating. During this time we create a dream, and this vision of ourselves generates tremendous energy and vitality. She writes that the "trying twenties" are characterized by an effort to do what we "should." Our "shoulds" are defined mainly by the media, by our family models, and by peer-group pressures. Some of these "shoulds" might be: "I should get married." "I should have children." "I should better myself by completing college." "I should be working to get ahead in the organization." "I should be saving money for a house."

During the twenties young people are faced with a variety of profound choices. If you are in this age group, you are no doubt facing decisions about how you will live. Your choices probably include questions such as: Will I choose the security of staying at home, or will I struggle financially and psychologically to live on my own? Will I stay single, or will I get involved in some committed relationship? Will I stay in college full time, or will I begin a career? If I choose a career, what will it be, and how will I go about deciding what I might do in the work world? If I marry, will I be a parent or not? What are some of my dreams, and how might I make them become a reality? What do I most want to do with my life at this time, and how might I find meaning?

Choices pertaining to work, education, marriage, family life, and a life-style are complex and deeply personal, and it is common to struggle over what it is we really want. There is the temptation to let others decide for us or to be overly influenced by the standards of others. But if we choose that path, we remain psychological adolescents at best.

We have the choice to live by parental rules, or we can leave home psychologically and decide for ourselves what our future will be. The following personal statements of individuals in their twenties illustrate the struggles of this period. A young man says:

> I want to live on my own, but it's very difficult to support myself and go to college at the same time. The support and approval of my parents is surely something I want, yet I am working hard at finding a balance between how much I am willing to do to get their approval and how much I will live by my values. When I look at my parents, it scares me to see how limited their lives are, and I want my life to be different. I love my parents, yet at the same time I resent them for the hold they have on me due to my dependency needs. When I live differently than they think I should, I feel guilty.

Another person in her twenties expresses her desire for intimacy, along with her reservations and doubts:

> While I realize that I want to be in a close relationship with a man, I know that I am also afraid of getting involved. I wonder if I want to spend the rest of my life with the same person. One thing that worries me is that if I allow myself to get close, he might leave, and I don't know if I'm ready for that hurt again. At other times I'm afraid I'll never find someone I can love who really loves me. I just don't want to give up my freedom, nor do I want to be dependent on someone.

Sheehy stresses that one of the terrifying aspects of the twenties is the conviction that the choices we make at this time are cast in cement. For instance, we might choose to "do nothing" for a time, or to go to graduate school, or to get married, or to get established in a career. Whatever we choose, we often fear that we will have to live with our choice for the rest of our life. According to Sheehy, this fear is largely unjustified, for major changes are almost inevitable. As she puts it: "But since in our twenties we're new at making major life choices, we cannot imagine that possibilities for a better integration will occur to us later on, when some inner growth has taken place" (p. 86). However, she does indicate that, although our choices aren't irrevocable, they do set the stage for the choices we'll make later on.

Martha, age 23, typifies young people who are willing to allow themselves to dream and remain open about what they want in life. She is also a good example of Sheehy's conviction that the choices made during the twenties aren't irrevocable. Martha works for a savings and loan association, and she is about to begin full-time graduate study toward a counseling degree. Here is what she is looking forward to:

> At this time in my life I think I have a thousand choices open to me. I don't like my job as a loan officer that much, but it does provide me with security. I never want to stop learning, and I'm sure I want to be a vital person. At some time, though not yet, I'd like to be married. Eventually I'd like kids. I'd like to publish someday, as well as having a counseling practice.

When I asked Martha what she'd like to be able to say in her old age, she replied:

I have a friend whose grandmother was 63 and she rode a pogo stick. I'd like to be as energetic in my old age as I am now. I never want to get bogged down with old ideas. Some people get set in their values, and they just won't change. I always want to evaluate and to be in the process of integrating new values in my life.

When I asked Martha if she saw herself as typical of those her age, her answer was:

Most people between 18 and 23 don't look inward that much. I think they look to other people to make choices for them. I hope I can do what feels right to me at the time. I'm uncertain now about many of my specific goals. I like taking life as it comes, but by that I'm not talking about being passive. I hope to be open to the possibilities that might eventually open up to me. I don't want to lose myself in someone else, but I would like to share my life with someone else.

Transition from the Twenties to the Thirties

According to Gould (1978), the transition from the late twenties to the early thirties is sometimes characterized by depression. It is a time of changing values and beliefs. For example, men who are switching careers or making changes within a career may be assuming that they will find a new direction in life. When their visions do not materialize, they may lapse into depression. Women who are married and have children may decide to work full time, and they may not find that this choice was what they were looking for. Gould talks about the thirties as a time for making a new contract—making basic changes in life-style, priorities, and commitments. It is during this period of unrest, disillusionment, depression, and questioning that people modify some of the rigid rules of their twenties. They also realize other facts: that their dreams do not materialize if they simply wish for things to happen; that there is no magic in the world; that life is not simple but, in fact, is complicated and bewildering; and that we can get what we want not by waiting and wishing passively but by working actively to attain our goals. As we open up in our thirties, a crisis can be precipitated when we discover that life is not as uncomplicated as we had envisioned it to be. The major challenge open to us as we realize these truths is put well by Gould (1978):

Our disappointment at this information can send us into a tailspin, or we can discard our disillusion and gain a realistic view of what we must do to live as adults. That is, we must become responsible for our own growth and learn to shape our future based on a realistic view of what is inside us and the world around us [pp. 182–183].

Sheehy (1976) contends that we become impatient with a life based on "shoulds" when we enter our thirties. Both men and women speak of feeling restricted at this time and may complain that life is narrow and

dull. Sheehy asserts that these restrictions are related to the outcomes of the life-style choices we made during our twenties. Even if these personal and career choices have served us well during our twenties, in our thirties we become ready for some changes. This is a time for making new choices and perhaps for modifying or deepening old commitments. We are likely to review our commitments to career, marriage, children, friends, and life's priorities. Because we realize that time is passing, we make a major reappraisal of how we are spending our time and energy. This process, which may involve considerable turmoil and crisis, relates to our desire for more out of life. We may find ourselves asking: "Is this all there is to life? What do I want for the rest of my life? What is missing from my life now?" Thus, a woman who has primarily been engaged in a career may now want to spend more time at home and with the children. A woman who has devoted most of her life to being a homemaker may now yearn to extend her horizon by getting established in a career. Men may do a lot of questioning about their work and wonder how they can make it more meaningful. If a man has been an "organization man" for a number of years, he may now consider breaking out of this mold by establishing his own business or changing careers. Single people may consider finding a partner, and those who are married may experience a real crisis in their marriage, which may be a sign that they cannot continue with old patterns.

TIME OUT FOR PERSONAL REFLECTION

1. *Think about a few of the major turning points in your young adult-hood. Write down not more than three turning points, and then state how you think they were important in your life. What difference did your decisions at these critical times make in your life?*

   Turning point: _____

   Impact of the decision on my life: _____

   _____

   _____

   _____

   _____

   Turning point: _____

   Impact of the decision on my life: _____

   _____

   _____

   _____

   _____

   Turning point: _____

   Impact of the decision on my life: _____

   _____

   _____

   _____

   _____

2. *Complete the following sentences by giving the first response that comes to mind.*

   a. *To me, being an independent person means* _____

   _____

   b. *The things I received from my parents that I most value are* _____

   _____

c. *The things I received from my parents that I least like and most want to change are* _____

_____

d. *If I could change one thing about my past, it would be* _____

_____

e. *My fears of being independent are these:* _____

_____

f. *One thing I most want for my children is* _____

_____

g. *I find it difficult to be my own person when* _____

_____

h. *I feel the freest when* _____

_____

MIDDLE ADULTHOOD

The time between the ages of 35 and 60 is characterized by a "going outside of ourselves." It is a time for learning how to live creatively with ourselves and with others, and it can be the time of greatest productivity in our life. For most of us it is also the period when we reach the top of the mountain yet at the same time become aware that we must begin the downhill journey. In addition, we may painfully experience the discrepancy between the dreams of our twenties and thirties and the hard reality of what we have achieved.

According to Erikson, the stimulus for continued growth in middle age is the core struggle between *generativity* and *stagnation*. By generativity, Erikson means not just fostering children but being productive in a broad sense—for example, through creative pursuits in a career, in leisure-time activities, in teaching or caring for others, or in some meaningful volunteer work. Two basic qualities of the productive adult are the ability to love well and the ability to work well. Adults who fail to achieve a sense of productivity begin to stagnate, which is a form of psychological death.

The Late Thirties and the Forties

When we reach middle age, we come to a crossroads. We reach the midpoint of our life's journey, and, even though we are in our prime, we begin to realize more acutely that life has a finishing point and that we are moving toward it. Between the ages of 35 and 45 our physical powers may begin to falter, and the roles that we have used to identify ourselves may lose their meaning. We may begin to question what else is left to life and to reexamine or renew our commitments. We face both dangers and opportunities. There are many dangers of slipping into deadening ruts and failing to make changes to enrich our life. There are also opportunities for choosing to rework the narrow identity of the first half of our life.

During middle age we realize the uncertainty of life, and we discover more clearly that we are alone. We stumble on masculine and feminine aspects of ourselves that had been masked. We may also go through a grieving process, because many parts of our old self are dying. This process does allow us to reevaluate and reintegrate an identity that is new and emerging, as opposed to an identity that is the sum of others' expectations. A few of the events that might contribute to the mid-life crisis are:

- We may come to realize that some of our youthful dreams will never materialize.
- We may begin to experience the pressure of time, realizing that now is the time to accomplish our mission.
- Coping with the aging process is difficult for many; the loss of some of our youthful qualities can be hard to face.
- The death of our parents drives home a truth that is difficult for many to accept: ultimately, we are alone in this life.
- There is the realization that life is not necessarily just and fair and that we often do not get what we had expected.
- There are marital crises and challenges to old patterns. A spouse may have an affair or seek a divorce.
- Our children grow up and leave home at this time. People who have lived largely for their children now may face emptiness.
- We may lose our job or be demoted, or we may grow increasingly disenchanted with our work.
- A woman may leave the home to enter the world of work and make this her primary interest.

Along with these factors that can precipitate a crisis, we may have the following choices available to us at this time:

- We can decide to go back for further schooling and gear up for a new career.
- We can choose to develop new talents and embark on novel hobbies, and we can even take steps to change our life-style.
- We can look increasingly inward to find out what we most want to do with the rest of our life and begin doing what we say we want to do.

You may be some distance away from middle age, but I hope you don't stop reading at this point, determined that this will never happen to you! Now may be a good time for you to reflect on the way your life is shaping up and to think about the person you'd like to be when you reach middle age. To help you in making this projection, it could be useful to consider the lives of people you know who are over 40. Do you have any models available in determining what direction you pursue? Are there some ways you'd not want to live? Also, consider the following brief first-person accounts, all statements made by middle-aged people:

A man says that it's difficult to always be striving for success, and he shares some of his loneliness:

> So much of my life has been bound up in becoming a success. While I am successful, I continually demand more of myself. I'm never quite satisfied with anything I accomplish, and I continually look ahead and see what has to be done. It's lonely when I think of always swimming against the tide, and I fear getting dragged into deep water that I can't get out of. At the same time, I don't seem to be able to slow down.

A woman says that she has stayed in a miserable marriage for 23 years. She finally recognizes that she has run out of excuses for staying. She must decide whether to maintain a marriage that is not likely to change much or decide on ending it.

> I'm petrified by the idea that I have to support myself and that I'm responsible for my own happiness—totally. All these years I've told myself that if *he* were different, I'd feel much more fulfilled than I do in life. I also had many reasons that prevented me from taking action, even when it became very clear to me that he wasn't even slightly interested in seeing things change. I'm not afraid to go out and meet people on a social basis, but I'm terrified of getting intimately involved with a man on a sexual or emotional basis. When I think of all those years in an oppressive marriage, I want to scream. I know I've kept most of these screams inside of me, for I feared that if I allowed myself to scream I'd never stop—that I might go crazy. Yet keeping my pain and tears inside of me has made my whole body ache, and I'm tired of hurting all the time. I want something else from life besides hurt!

The Fifties

The fifties are years in which many adults enjoy the benefits of years of struggle and dedication. Adults at this stage often do a lot of reflecting, contemplating, and evaluating of themselves. Many are at their peak in terms of status and personal power.

In her popular book *Pathfinders,* Sheehy (1981) conducted extensive interviews around the United States. She found that the fifties can be a very satisfying period of adulthood provided the earlier developmental tasks have been resolved. Some of the new potentials listed by Sheehy (p. 228) are:

- a relaxation of roles
- increased assertiveness in women

- freedom to express one's opinions
- an increase of leisure and money
- a greater tolerance for others
- greater opportunities for companionship with one's mate
- opportunities to develop new relationships with children
- chances to contribute to the community

In the fifties people often begin the process of preparing for older age. This can be a satisfying time of life, because now they do not have to work as hard as they did in the past, nor do they have to meet others' expectations. They are often able to savor their accomplishments rather than striving to continually prove themselves.

Changing Careers in Mid-Life

The awareness of options can be an important asset at this time in life. Most of the people I know have changed their job several times; you might think about whether this pattern fits any people you know. And, whether or not you've reached middle age, you might ask yourself about your own beliefs and attitudes toward changing careers. Although making large changes in our life is rarely easy, it can be a good deal harder if our own attitudes and fears are left unquestioned and unexamined.

A common example of mid-life change is the woman who decides to return to college or the job market after her children reach high school age. Many community colleges and state universities are enrolling women who realize that they want more fulfillment at this time in their life. They may still value their work at home, but they are looking forward to developing new facets of themselves.

This phenomenon is not unique to women. I know of many men who are deciding in middle age to quit a job they've had for years, even if they're successful, because they want new challenges. Men often define themselves by the work they do, and work thus becomes a major source of the purpose in their life. If they feel successful in their work, they may feel successful as persons; if they become stagnant in work, they may feel that they are ineffectual in other areas.

Such is the case with John, a 52-year-old aerospace engineer who finally decided that too much of his identity was wrapped up in his profession. He decided to keep his job in industry as a consultant to various engineering firms while at the same time starting a master's-degree program in counseling. His interest in counseling stemmed from some marriage counseling he and his wife had received. He had experienced a new realm of feelings, and he decided that he didn't always have to be detached, thing-oriented, logical, and unemotional. Eventually, John received his degree in counseling, and even though he hasn't switched from engineering to counseling as a profession, it has been important for him to know that he has the qualifications to assume a new career if he so chooses. In this way he experiences more freedom in the world of work, because he knows that he is in engineering because he *wants* to be now, not because he *has* to be.

People such as John are finding new directions and new dimensions of meaning in their life because they're willing to question long-standing assumptions about themselves and about work. Although such self-aware-ness is always relevant and helpful, it is particularly so during mid-life, when we can either renew ourselves or set the stage for a life of doing a job simply to survive.

TIME OUT FOR PERSONAL REFLECTION

If you have reached middle age, think about how the following questions apply to you. In your journal you might write down your reactions to a few of the questions that have the most meaning for you. If you haven't reached middle age, think about how you'd like to be able to answer these questions when you reach that stage in your life. What do you need to do now in order to have your expectations met?

1. *Is this a time of "generativity" or of "stagnation" for you? Think about some of the things you've done during this time of life that you feel the best about.*
2. *Do you feel productive? If so, in what ways?*
3. *Are there some things that you'd definitely like to change in your life right now? What prevents you from making these changes?*
4. *What questions have you raised about your life during this time?*
5. *Have you experienced a mid-life crisis? If so, how has it affected you?*
6. *What losses have you experienced?*
7. *What are some of the most important decisions that you have made during this time of your life?*
8. *Are you developing new interests and talents?*
9. *What do you look forward to in the remaining years?*
10. *If you were to review the major successes of your life to this point, what would they be?*

LATE ADULTHOOD

After about the age of 60 our central developmental tasks include the following: adjusting to decreased physical and sensory capacities, adjust-ing to retirement, finding a meaning in life, being able to relate to the past without regrets, adjusting to the death of a spouse or friends, accepting inevitable losses, maintaining outside interests, and enjoying grandchildren.

Late adulthood is a time for reflection and integration. Many physical and psychological changes occur as we approach older age. How we adapt to such changes is influenced by past experiences, coping skills, beliefs about changing, and personality traits. At this time, work, leisure, and family relationships are major dimensions of life.

According to Erikson, the central issue of this age period is *integrity* versus *despair*. Persons who succeed in achieving ego integrity feel that their life has been productive and worthwhile and that they have managed to cope with failures as well as successes. They can accept the course of their life and are not obsessed with thoughts of what might have been and what they could or should have done. They can look back without resentment and regret and can see their life in a perspective of completeness and satisfaction. Finally, they can view death as natural, even while living a rich and meaningful life to the day they die.

Unfortunately, some elderly people fail to achieve ego integration. Typically, such people fear death. They may develop a sense of hopelessness and feelings of self-disgust. They cannot accept their life's cycle, for they see whatever they have done as "not enough" and feel that they have a lot of unfinished business. They yearn for another chance, even though they realize that they cannot have it. They feel inadequate, for they think that they have wasted their life and let valuable time slip by. These are the people who die unhappy and unfulfilled.

Old age does not have to be something that we look forward to with horror or resignation; nor must it be associated with bitterness. However, many elderly people in our society do feel resentment, because we have generally neglected them. Many of them are treated as members of an undesirable minority and are merely tolerated or put out to pasture in a convalescent home. Their loss is doubly sad, because the elderly can make definite contributions to society. Many elderly persons are still very capable, yet the prejudice of younger adults keeps them from fully using their resources. Perhaps we are afraid of aging (and death) and "put away" the elderly so that they won't remind us of our future.

Stereotypes of Aging

In their book *Ageism*, Levin and Levin (1980) describe the various forms of prejudice and discrimination against the elderly. They define ageism as a negative evaluation of old people in general. More specifically, ageism predisposes us to discriminate against old people by avoiding them or in some way victimizing them because of their age alone. The authors discuss the images of the aged by looking at common stereotypes. Asserting that the images of the aged are based more on myth than reality, they point out several fictions relating to growing old.

- The elderly are viewed as sexually inactive. Sex is typically thought of as unimportant for them.
- The public image of the elderly is generally associated with reduced job performance. Thus, old people are frequently discriminated against in the world of work and are often forced to retire while they are still capable of productive work.
- There is the view that, as one grows old, intelligence takes a downward trend. Childlike qualities are often attributed to the elderly.
- A pervasive stereotype is that the elderly are "set in their ways" and are highly conservative.
- The elderly are viewed as resisting change and welcoming a withdrawal from society.

Levin and Levin present research evidence that contradicts each of these stereotypes. These images are based on half-truths or outright fallacies, yet they are often used to justify the mistreatment of the elderly.

In addition to the stereotypes mentioned above, there are some other commonly held myths about the elderly, a few of which are:

- Most people who retire become depressed.
- Retirement is just a step away from death.
- It's disgraceful for an old person to remarry.
- Old people are not creative.
- An elderly person will die soon after his or her mate dies.
- Old people are no longer beautiful.

These are only a few of the myths that can render older people helpless if they accept them. I believe that the attitude an older person has about aging is extremely important. Like adolescents, the aged may feel a sense of uselessness because of others' views of them. Then it is easy for them to accept the myths of others and turn them into self-fulfilling prophecies.

Again, although you may not have reached old age, I hope that you won't brush aside thinking about your eventual aging. Your observations of old people whom you know can provide you with information about what it is like to grow older. From these observations, you can begin to formulate some picture of the life you'd like to have as you get older.

Retirement

Retirement is arriving earlier for many people, and it is not uncommon for people to retire in their fifties. Some look forward to this time so that they can take up new projects; others fear this prospect, for they wonder how they will spend their time if they are not working.

Retirement can be traumatic for many people. How can people who have relied largely on their job for meaning or structure in their lives deal with being idle? Must they lose their sense of self-worth when they are forced to retire? Can they find a sense of purpose and value apart from their occupation?

I remember talking to a woman who was close to 65 and who was feeling abandoned because she was being forced to retire as a teacher in junior high school. She loved interacting with the students, and her principal made it clear that she was still a fine teacher. Deeply saddened by what she described as "being put out to pasture," she gradually assumed a hopeless stance and became depressed. Of course, she did have some choice in regard to her response to this situation; instead of remaining depressed, she could have gone on to search for other ways to give of herself, perhaps through some form of volunteer work. The difficulty she had in envisioning any other possibilities for herself illustrates how difficult retirement can be for people who have had a meaningful and fulfilling career. Still, it was unquestionably sad that, because of the school district's policy, her age alone deprived her of the chance to do what she loved doing. As a result, both she and the students were cheated by her forced retirement.

Of course, there are people who initiate retirement for themselves and continue to find meaning in their life by involving themselves in substitute activities. Lester is an example of this kind of person. Although he is formally retired, he says that he continues to work by doing household repairs and remodeling, because he "couldn't stand to do nothing." Although the income he derives from this work is small, he takes satisfaction in the feeling of being needed.

Lester had originally managed a resort before changing jobs during his middle years. Although he had found the work at the resort exciting, he decided to quit because of his disenchantment with the commercial aspects of the job. He then took the risk of accepting a job as chief maintenance man at a hospital. As it turned out, he liked that job immensely. Lester's job change perhaps made it easier for him to refuse to be idle once he did retire. Now he actively creates jobs that not only help people but at the same time give him a sense of being a productive member of the community.

What happens to us when we retire depends to a great extent on how well we've resolved the conflicts and issues of the previous stages in our life. I think it's very unfortunate that so many of us live for the future, deluding ourselves into thinking that we will find what we want once we retire. We may find that, if we haven't achieved a sense of creativity, identity, and purpose in our earlier years, we'll feel a sense of inadequacy, emptiness, and confusion once retirement arrives. If we haven't defined for ourselves during our years on the job the place work has in our life and the meaning we find away from the job, we'll be poorly equipped to deal with the questions of meaning and purpose in later life.

Lester's case shows that there *is* life after retirement. Just because people no longer work at a job does not mean that they have to cease being active. There are many options open to retired people who would like to stay active in meaningful ways. This is the time for them to get involved with the projects that they have so often put on the back burner due to their busy schedules. What is essential is for retirees to keep themselves vital as physical, psychological, and social beings. Following are some of the ways in which retired people I know have stayed involved:

- going back to school to take classes simply for interest or to prepare themselves for a new career
- joining organizations and becoming an integral part in the community
- sharing their expertise, experiences, and wisdom with others, either on a paid or voluntary basis
- becoming more interested in and caring for their grandchildren
- taking trips to places that they have wanted to see
- visiting relatives and friends
- taking time for more physical activity
- cultivating hobbies that they have neglected
- joining a senior citizens' center

This list is not exhaustive, and you can probably add to it. Retirees do have choices to create meaning in their life. They may discover that retirement is not an end but rather a new beginning. Let me conclude this chapter with a brief example of a person who is leading a simple and meaningful life in her old age. This woman, who is 82 years old, has lived alone since her husband died. She has a routine that involves keeping up her garden, talking with friends, watching her favorite shows on television, and doing chores. At times she takes care of her grandchildren for a few days, but then she is eager to get back to her routine. When her grandchildren asked her if she didn't get lonely, she quickly responded by letting them know that she enjoys her solitude and that her days are full. She likes not having to answer to anyone but herself, and she looks forward to each day. She doesn't brood over the past, nor does she wish that things had been different. Instead, she accepts both her accomplishments and her mistakes, and she still derives pleasure in being alone as well as in being with those she loves.

TIME OUT FOR PERSONAL REFLECTION

1. *If you haven't yet reached old age, imagine yourself doing so. Think about your fears and about what you'd like to be able to say about your life—your joys, your accomplishments, and your regrets. To facilitate this reflection, you might consider the following questions:*

   - *What do you most hope to accomplish by the time you reach old age?*
   - *What are some of your greatest fears of growing old?*
   - *What kind of old age do you expect? What are you doing now that might have an effect on the kind of person you'll be as you grow older?*
   - *What are some things you hope to do during the later years of your life? How do you expect that you will adjust to retirement? What meaning do you expect your life to have when you reach old age?*
   - *How would you like to be able to respond to your body's aging? How do you think you'll respond to failing health or to physical limitations on your life-style?*
   - *Assume that you will have enough money to live comfortably and to do many of the things that you haven't had time for earlier. What do you think you'd most like to do? With whom?*
   - *What would you most want to be able to say about yourself and your life when you become elderly?*

   In your journal you might write down some impressions of the kind of old age you hope for, as well as the fears you have about growing older.

2. *What can you do at this time in your life to anticipate and prepare for retirement?*

_____

_____

_____

_____

3. *Do you know any retired people? If so, do you think they are leading happy lives? In what ways have they found or failed to find fulfillment in this stage of life?*

_____

_____

_____

_____

4. *What are your present attitudes about retirement? Check each statement with which you find yourself more in agreement than disagreement.*

_____ *People shouldn't be forced to retire against their will.*
_____ *Most people are lost without work.*
_____ *We need to be educated to make the optimum use of leisure time.*
_____ *Most people look forward to their retirement.*
_____ *I believe in saving money during the earlier stages of life so that I'll be secure after I retire.*
_____ *I see myself as preparing emotionally for the time when I'll retire.*
_____ *I see myself as preparing financially for the time when I'll retire.*
_____ *When I retire, I'd like to travel to various parts of the world and experience different ways of life.*
_____ *I expect retirement to be a lonely and frustrating experience more than a creative and meaningful one.*

CHAPTER SUMMARY

Adulthood involves the struggle for autonomy. One part of this quest is learning to challenge our inner parent and doing what is necessary to become our own parent in a psychological sense.

Transactional analysis can help us recognize early learning and decisions. Our life script is made up of both parental messages and decisions we make in response to these injunctions. The events of childhood and, to some extent, adolescence contribute to the formation of our life script, which we tend to continue to follow into adulthood. By becoming increasingly aware of our life script, we are in a position to revise it. If we determine that earlier decisions are archaic, we can then redecide. Instead of being hopelessly "scripted" by childhood influences, we can use our past to change our future. In short, we can shape our destiny rather than being passively shaped by earlier events.

Our quest for autonomy and maturity is truly a lifelong endeavor. Each stage of adulthood presents us with different tasks to be resolved; meeting the developmental tasks of later life hinges on successfully working through earlier issues.

During early adulthood, it is important to learn how to form intimate relationships. To develop intimacy we must move beyond the self-preoccupation that is characteristic of adolescence. This is also a time when we are at our peak in terms of physical and psychological powers and can direct these resources establishing ourselves in all dimensions of life. Choices that we make pertaining to education, work, and life-style will have a profound impact later in life.

As we approach middle age, we come to a crossroads. The mid-life crisis is filled with potential for danger and for new opportunities. At this phase we can assume a stance that "it's too late to change," or we can make significant revisions. There are opportunities to change careers, to find new ways to spend leisure time, and to find other ways of making a new life.

Later life can be a time of real enjoyment, or it can be a time of looking back in regret to all that we have not accomplished and experienced. It is important to recognize that the quality of life in later years often depends on the choices we made at earlier turning points in life.

To review the tasks and the choices of each period of the entire life span, I recommend that you go back to the overview table presented in Chapter 2 and think about the continuity of the life cycle. Now that you have studied each stage of life, reflect on the meaning of these stages to you. If you have not yet arrived at a particular stage, think about what you can do at this time to assure the quality of life you'd like in a future phase.

The experiences and events that occur during each developmental stage are crucial in helping to determine our attitudes, beliefs, values, and actions regarding the important areas of our life that will be discussed in the chapters to come: the body, sex-role identity, sexuality, love, intimate relationships, loneliness and solitude, work, death and loss, and meaning and values. For this reason, I've devoted considerable attention to the foundations of our life choices. Understanding how we got where we are now is a critical first step in deciding where we want to go from here.

Now write down some of the ideas in this chapter that you most want to remember.

_____

_____

_____

_____

_____

ACTIVITIES AND EXERCISES

1. Do you believe that you're able to make new decisions? Do you think that you're in control of your destiny? In your journal, write down some examples of new decisions—or renewals of old decisions—that have made a significant difference in your life.

2. Mention some critical turning points in your life. In your journal, draw a chart showing the age periods you've experienced so far and indicate your key successes, failures, conflicts, and memories for each age period.

3. After you've described some of the significant events in your life, list some of the decisions that you have made in response to these events. How were you affected by some of these milestones in your life? Then think about what you've learned about yourself from doing these exercises. What does all of this tell you about the person you are today?

4. Many students readily assert that they are psychologically independent. If this applies to you, think about some specific examples that show that you have questioned and challenged your parents' values and that you have modified your own value system.

5. Summarize the main injunctions you received as a child. Bring your list to class, and in a small group explore the injunctions that have had the *greatest* impact on you. What are the circumstances surrounding these injunctions? In what ways have you helped to keep these injunctions alive through a self-indoctrination process? How do you think they have negatively influenced your self-concept? Elect a recorder in your group to summarize the most commonly mentioned injunctions and their effects.

6. To broaden your perspective on human development in various cultural or ethnic groups, talk to someone you know who grew up in a very different environment from the one you knew as a child. You could find out how his or her life experiences have differed from yours by sharing some aspects of your own life. Try to discover whether there are signif-

icant differences in values that seem to be related to the differences in your life experiences. This could help you to reassess many of your own values.

7. Talk with some people who are significantly older than yourself. For instance, if you're in your twenties, you could interview a middle-aged person and an elderly person. Try to get them to take the lead and tell you about their lives. What do they like about their lives? What have been some key turning points for them? What do they most remember of the past? You might even suggest that they read the section of the chapter that pertains to their present age group and react to the ideas presented there.

SUGGESTED READINGS

Berne, E. (1975). *What Do You Say after You Say Hello?* New York: Bantam. Based on transactional analysis, this book demonstrates how we learn certain scripts that determine our present behavior. It discusses how we write our life script and how we can change it.

Bloomfield, H. H., with Felder, L. (1983). *Making Peace with Your Parents.* New York: Ballantine. A timely book aimed at helping people release the emotional pains of growing up. Deals with coming to terms with our parents by working through resentment and achieving forgiveness. Also discusses how to become our own best parent.

Bridges, W. (1980). *Transitions: Making Sense of Life's Changes.* Reading, Mass.: Addison-Wesley. A readable book designed to help people identify and cope with critical changes in their life. The author describes the transition process and offers skills and suggestions for creatively dealing with each of the perilous passages of life.

Ellis, A., & Harper, R. A. (1975). *A New Guide to Rational Living.* Englewood Cliffs, N.J.: Prentice-Hall. A self-help book that presents a straightforward approach to rational-emotive therapy, stressing homework assignments aimed at bringing about change in a person's ways of thinking, feeling, and acting. It is an easy-reading and useful book for challenging self-defeating beliefs.

Gould, R. L. (1978). *Transformations: Growth and Change in Adult Life.* New York: Simon & Schuster (Touchstone). A well-written book on the life span, with descriptions of key tasks to be accomplished at the various stages, along with case examples. The author develops the theme that, as we grow, we take steps away from childhood and toward adulthood. At the same time, unfinished business from our past intrudes in the present and demands psychological work.

James, M., & Jongeward, D. (1971). *Born to Win: Transactional Analysis with Gestalt Experiments.* Reading, Mass.: Addison-Wesley. This is a very readable guide to understanding how we develop a sense of whether we are "winners" or "losers." An overview of the principles of TA and a description of Gestalt experiments make up the core of the book, which deals with "stroking," life scripts, injunctions, early decisions, parenting, childhood, personal and sexual identity, "game playing," adulthood, and autonomy. It is an excellent source for under-standing parenting and learning how we are presently influenced by earlier childhood conditioning.

Levinson, D. J. (1978). *The Seasons of a Man's Life*. New York: Knopf. The author describes growth patterns from the viewpoint of the entire life span.

Sheehy, G. (1981). *Pathfinders*. New York: Morrow. This is a popular book that describes developmental tasks and choices of stages of adulthood. Some topics explored include the capacity for loving, friendship and support systems, male and female strengths, life's purpose, coping and mourning, and the view from the top of the mountain.

Steiner, C. (1975). *Scripts People Live: Transactional Analysis of Life Scripts*. New York: Bantam. One of the best accounts of life scripts is given in this very useful and interesting book.

4

YOUR BODY

PRECHAPTER SELF-INVENTORY

Use the following scale to respond: 4 = this statement is true of me *most* of the time; 3 = this statement is true of me *much* of the time; 2 = this statement is true of me *some* of the time; 1 = this statement is true of me *almost none* of the time.

_____   1. Touching and being touched are important to me.

_____   2. It is important for me to keep my body in good shape.

_____   3. Being upset or under stress can make me feel physically ill.

_____   4. The way I take care of my body expresses the way I feel about myself.

_____   5. I'd characterize my life-style as a stressful one.

_____   6. It is relatively easy for me to be able to fully relax.

_____   7. When I look in the mirror, I feel comfortable with my physical appearance.

_____   8. To be honest, there probably are many ways in which I could take better care of my body.

_____   9. Making basic changes in my life-style to improve my health isn't really a priority for me.

_____   10. The way I live, I worry at times about having a heart attack.

INTRODUCTION

Your body—the physical you—is the subject of this chapter.[1] We will begin by exploring the topic of bodily identity, which includes the way you experience yourself and express yourself through your body. It also involves your view of your body and the decisions you have made about it. If you look at your body inside and out, you'll see that it reflects some significant choices. Do you take care of the physical you? How comfortable are you with your body? How do your feelings and attitudes about your body affect your choices in areas such as self-worth, sexuality, and love?

Stress and its effects on your body are another central topic of this chapter. Living in contemporary society means that we cannot eliminate stress from our life, yet we can monitor the impact that stress has on us physically and psychologically. We can become aware of destructive reactions to stress and learn constructive ways to deal with it.

The goal of "wellness" is explored as a life-style choice that enhances our body and also our mind. As a part of this choice I take up subjects such as making decisions about diet and exercise and ultimately accepting responsibility for our body.

[1]I would like to acknowledge the contributions to this chapter of our friends Dr. Allan Abbott and his wife, Katherine, who consulted with Marianne and me and brainstormed many of the issues and ideas discussed.

An honest examination of the choices you are making about your body can reveal a great deal concerning your feelings about your life. If you aren't taking care of your body, what beliefs and attitudes might be getting in the way? What resources do you require to begin modifying those parts of your life-style that affect your bodily well-being?

YOUR BODILY IDENTITY

One of my colleagues tells his students that we have the body we deserve. Of course, we are limited in how much we can actually change our body, but there is much we can do to work with the material we have. First, however, we must pay attention to what we are expressing about ourselves through our body, so that we can determine whether we *want* to change our bodily identity. This involves increasing our awareness of how we experience our body through, for instance, touch and movement. As you read this section, reflect on how well you know your body and how comfortable you are with it. Then you can decide about changing your body image—for example, by losing weight.

Experiencing and Expressing Yourself through Your Body

Some of us are divorced from our body; it is simply a vehicle that carries us around. If someone asks us what we are thinking, we are likely to come up with a quick answer. If asked what we are experiencing and sensing in

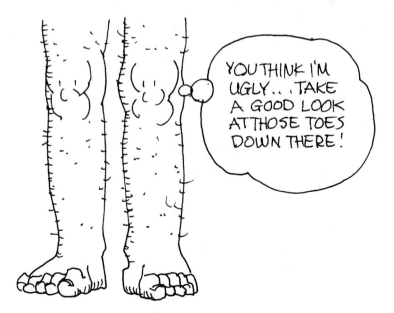

our body, however, we may be at a loss for words. Yet our body can be eloquent in its expression of who we are. Much of our life history is revealed through our body. By looking at some people's faces we are able to see evidence of stress and strain. There are those who speak with a tight jaw and who seem to literally choke off feelings. Others typically walk with a slouch and shuffle their feet, expressing their hesitation in presenting themselves to the world. Their bodies are communicating their low self-esteem and their fear of interacting with others. As you look at your body, what feelings do you have? What story does your body tell about you?

Character Armor and Body-Oriented Psychotherapy.   Wilhelm Reich pioneered body-oriented psychotherapy. He put the body at the center of psychology by studying how bodily blockages prevent people from experiencing and expressing certain emotions. His central idea was that emotions are an expression of the movement of bodily energy and that chronic muscle tensions block this flow of energy and thus block emotions. Reichian therapy stresses the importance of loosening and dissolving what is known as "muscular armor" so that bottled-up emotions can be released. According to Reich, *character armor* includes certain defenses that are manifested in some form of bodily expression. It was his contention that attitudes and personality traits have a corresponding physical attribute. Thus, an individual expresses his or her personality in terms of muscular rigidity.

Reichian and other body-oriented therapies are aimed at loosening the muscular armor. Part of the therapy consists of teaching clients how to breathe properly. Body-oriented therapists have found that restricted breathing results in a restriction of emotional expression. These therapists use methods that deepen the client's breathing, which also has the effect of opening up the feelings. Body therapies focus on working with muscular tensions, such as a tight jaw or mouth, a frown, and so forth. In working with a person who shows any of the above symptoms, body-oriented therapists pay particular attention to where there is a blockage of energy. For example, by direct manipulation of a tight jaw they release certain feelings. People are frequently surprised by the outpouring of emotions. After such a bodily and emotional release people typically describe a deep sense of relaxation and peace. Only now are they really aware of the difference between a very tense body and a relaxed body. They also become aware of how many emotions they have been locking up.

The following are some other ways that our bodies express ourselves:

- The eyes can express life or emptiness.
- The mouth can be tight or too loose.
- The neck can hold back expressions of anger or crying, as well as holding onto tensions.

- The chest can develop armor that inhibits the free flowing of crying, laughing, and breathing.
- The diaphragm can restrict the expression of rage and pain.
- The abdomen can develop armor that is related to fear of attack.
- The pelvis can be rigid and asexual, or it can become a source of experiencing intense pleasure.

Unexpressed emotions do not simply disappear. The chronic practice of "swallowing" emotions can take a physical toll on our body and manifest itself in physical symptoms such as severe headaches, ulcers, digestive problems, and a range of other bodily dysfunctions. In counseling clients I often see a direct relationship between a person's physical constipation and his or her emotional constipation. When people are successful in expressing feelings of hurt and anger, they often comment that they are finally no longer physically constipated. Later in this chapter I address in greater detail how emotions and stress are related to heart disease.

In summary, then, the aim of the body-oriented therapies is to open up the channels of intense emotional expression such as pleasure, rage, fear, grief, pain, and anxiety. These therapies have taught us that, if we seal off certain emotions (such as grief and anger), we also keep ourselves from experiencing intense joy.

Experiencing Your Body.   In looking at one woman we may be impressed with how rigid her body appears. She walks around very stiffly. It is as if she feels disassociated from various bodily parts. She is rarely conscious of how different parts of her body feel. By contrast, we can look

at another person and notice that she moves about with ease, her movements express a harmony, and she appears to be comfortable with her body. We would say that she owns her body.

One way of becoming more aware of experiencing our body is by paying attention to our senses of touch, taste, smell, seeing, and hearing. Simply pausing and taking a few moments to be aware of how our body is interacting with the environment is a helpful way of learning to make better contact. For example, how often do you allow yourself to really taste and smell your food? How often are you aware of the tension in your body? How many times do you pause to smell and touch a flower? How often do you listen to the chirping of birds or the other sounds of nature? If these simple pleasures are important to us, we can increase our sensory experience by pausing more frequently to fully use all of our senses.

Enjoying our physical self is something that we often fail to make time for. Treating ourselves to a massage, for example, can be exhilarating and can give us clues to how alive we are physically. Dancing is yet another avenue through which we can enjoy our physical self and can express ourselves spontaneously. Dance therapy is a popular approach to teach people through movement to own all parts of their body and to express themselves more harmoniously. These are a few paths to becoming more of a friend and less of a stranger to our body. We can express our feelings through our body if we allow ourselves to be in tune with our physical self.

The Importance of Touch.   Some people are very comfortable with touching themselves, with touching others, and with being touched by others. They require a degree of touching to maintain a sense of physical and emotional well-being. Other people show a great deal of discomfort in touching themselves or allowing others to be physical with them. They may bristle and quickly move away if they are touched accidentally. If such people are embraced by another, they are likely to become rigid and not to respond. For instance, in my own family of origin there was very little touching among members. I found that I had to recondition myself to feel comfortable with being touched by others and in touching others. In contrast, my wife, Marianne, grew up in a German family characterized by much more spontaneous touching. Between the two of us there were differences in the amount of touching that we seek and require. There are times when I seem to forget about my need for physical contact and can get along without missing it very much. Marianne tells me that her tolerance level for not being touched is much lower, and she is quicker to point out when she misses touching.

The culture in which people grow up also has a lot to do with their attitude toward touching. For many cultures, touching is a natural mode of expression; for other cultures, touching is minimal and regulated by clearly defined boundaries. Some cultures have taboos against touching strangers, against touching people of the same sex, against touching people of the opposite sex, and against touching in certain social situations. In spite of these individual and cultural differences, numerous studies have demonstrated that physical contact is essential for healthy development of body and mind.

Your Body Image

Your view of your body and the decisions you have made about it have much to do with the choices that we are about to study in the rest of this book. In my view, people are affected in a very fundamental way by how they perceive their body and how they think others perceive it.

If you feel basically unattractive, unappealing, or in some other way physically inferior, these self-perceptions are likely to have a powerful effect on other areas of your life. For example, you may be very critical of some of your physical characteristics. You may think that your ears are too big, that your nose is ill-shaped, that you have an ugly complexion, that you're too short, or that you're not muscular enough. Perhaps some part of you believes that others will not want to approach you because of your appearance. If you *feel* that you are basically unattractive, you may well tell yourself that others will see your defects and will not want to be with you. Because of this feeling, you may contribute to the reactions that others have toward you by the messages you send them. You may be perceived by others as aloof, distant, or judgmental. Even though you may want to get close to people, you may also be frightened of the possibility of meeting with their rejection.

If something like this is true of you, I challenge you to look at the part you may be playing in contributing to the reactions you get from others. How does your state of mind influence both your view of yourself and the view others have of you? Do you take even less care of your body because you're unhappy with it? Why should others approach you, if you continue to tell them that you are not worth approaching? Will others think more of you than you think of yourself?

You may say that there is little you can do to change certain aspects of your physical being, such as your height or basic build. Yet you *can* look at the attitudes you have formed about these physical characteristics. How important are they to who you are?

As children and, even more so, as adolescents many of us learn to associate parts of our body with shame. Small children may be oblivious to nudity and to their body, but as they run around nude and are made the objects of laughter and jokes by other children and by adults, they gradually become more self-conscious. Sometimes the sense of shame remains with people into adulthood. The following brief cases represent some typical difficulties:

- A woman painfully recalls the onset of menstruation. Since no one had really taken the time to prepare her for this event, she became mildly frantic the first time it happened. Her immediate reaction was that she was being punished for having evil thoughts.
- A man finally shares his concern over the size of his penis, which he thinks is small. His anxiety about this has caused him extreme embarrassment when he has showered with other men, and it has inhibited him in his sexual relations with women. He is convinced that women will laugh at him and find him sexually inadequate.
- A young, attractive woman relates that she walked stoop-shouldered as an adolescent, trying to conceal her large breasts. She actually felt a sense of shame over being, as she put it, so "well built." Now, as an adult, she frequently feels that men are interested in her only for her physical qualities. She doubts their sincerity in finding her interesting apart from her body.
- A man is convinced that his body is dirty and his impulses vile. He is preoccupied with fears of sinning. He learned early in life to associate shame with his sexual and sensual feelings, and now this attitude prevents him from experiencing his body.

Consider also whether you made some decisions about your body early in life, or during adolescence, that still affect you. Did you feel embarrassed about certain of your physical characteristics? As you matured physically, these characteristics might have changed—or become less important to others—yet you may still be stuck with some old perceptions and feelings. Even though others may think of you as an attractive person, you may react with suspicion and disbelief, for you continue to tell yourself that you are in some way inferior. By examining where you picked up some of your attitudes about your body, you can begin to challenge yourself with respect to the evidence that justifies your current self-perception.

Your Weight and Your Body Image.   How often do you come across people who are really satisfied with their physical appearance? Chances are that you'll hear more about their dissatisfaction with their body than what they like about it. As a matter of fact, most people would be embarrassed to say that they like the way they look. They find it much easier to tell someone how they don't like themselves rather than making positive self-statements. We spend much time in thinking about how we look, and, as I've mentioned earlier, our self-perceptions influence the way we feel about ourselves and how we project ourselves to others. Because of certain conclusions that we make about our physical attractiveness, we are likely to shy away from certain social situations and activities.

From years of experience in reading student journals and counseling people, I have concluded that many people are preoccupied with maintaining their vision of their "ideal weight." Although there are people who view themselves as too skinny and who are striving to gain weight, there is

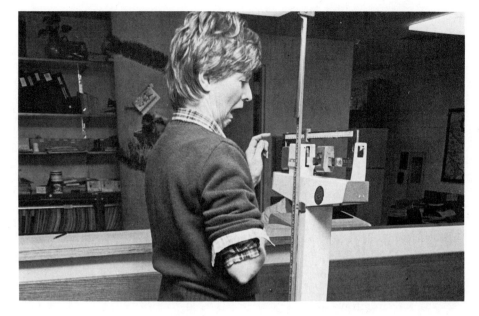

more concern over finding effective ways to lose weight. You may be one of these people who thinks that your weight significantly affects the way you feel about your body. In this section and in Resource 3 you will find material that can help you make an assessment of your present weight and provide you with some strategies for weight control. Perhaps you have said:

- "I've tried every program there is, and I just can't seem to stick to one."
- "I've lost extra pounds many times, only to put them on again."
- "I'm too occupied with school to think about losing weight."
- "I love to eat and I hate to exercise, but I get disgusted with the shape of my body."

Can you think of other such statements that you've made about the condition and appearance of your body? Even if you are interested in taking off extra pounds, you might well encounter difficulty in regulating your eating habits and keeping yourself motivated to follow a regular exercise program. You might be lured into thinking that there is an easy solution to the problem of being overweight and thus be easy prey for a succession of diet plans that promise quick and painless weight loss.

The chances are that you will not be able to eat all you want when you want and expect to effortlessly maintain an ideal weight for your body structure. Consequently, you'll need some degree of motivation for taking off excess weight and keeping it off. And you'll need to examine what stops you from following your plan.

In their excellent self-help book, *Toward a Self-Managed Life Style*, Williams and Long (1983) describe a behavioral approach to weight reduction that involves taking systematic steps to attain realistic goals. Cautioning that people are often lured by diet plans that promise quick, painless, and dramatic results, they emphatically make the point that such plans seldom produce long-lasting results and that weight reduction involves personal effort and a long-term commitment. I fully agree with the spirit of their message to those of us who are serious about weight control: "In a word, your style of eating must be changed. Any plan that fails to seek a permanent change in life style—a change you and your body can accept indefinitely—will produce, at best, only temporary results" (p. 89).

Thus, a basic change in attitudes and life-style seems important in successfully dealing with a weight problem. Fat people do not eat simply because they are hungry. They are typically more responsive to external cues in their environment. One of these is the acquiescence of well-meaning friends, who may joke with them by saying: "Oh, don't worry about those extra pounds. What's life without enjoyment of eating? Besides, there's more of you to love this way!" This kind of "friendship" can make it even more difficult to discipline ourselves by watching what and how much we eat.

One good way to determine if you want to change is to look at yourself standing naked before a full-length mirror. If you are overweight, pretend that your body could speak. Could your body be saying any of the following?

- "I don't like myself."
- "My weight will keep me at a distance."
- "I am killing myself slowly."
- "I am burdened."
- "I don't get around much any more!"
- "I'm basically lazy and self-indulging."

Whatever condition your body happens to be in, let it "speak," and respect what it is "saying" by listening with care. If you determine that you are heavier than you'd like to be, it could prove useful to devote some time to thinking about why you are in the shape that you are in. While you are likely to say that you love to eat and hate to exercise, the truth of the matter may not be quite so obvious. You could begin by thinking about what you actually get from being overweight. Like it or not, there are certain "payoffs" to being overweight, even if they are negative. Here are some possible reasons why people get and stay overweight:

- An overweight son or daughter may keep weight on as a way of getting constant parental attention, even if that attention consists of nagging to watch what he or she is eating.
- A girl may gain weight during adolescence because her father is threatened by her physical attractiveness.
- Overweight persons may convince themselves that they are being re-

jected for their obesity, and thus not have to look at other dimensions of themselves.

- Some who are afraid of getting close to others may use their weight as a barrier.
- Those who are afraid of their sexuality and where it might lead them often gain weight as a way to keep themselves safe from becoming sexually involved.
- Some think that being overweight is beautiful or is a sign of their identity.

Review the above list of reasons for remaining overweight. Are there any people you know, including yourself, who give reasons such as these? Others may nag you about doing something about your weight. They may be well-intentioned, yet you may resist their efforts. Ultimately, it is you who must decide what you want to do about your body. Only then can you begin to change it. To assist you in assessing your current weight and in taking actions to control it, refer to Resource 3 for specific suggestions.

TIME OUT FOR PERSONAL REFLECTION

1. *What are your attitudes toward your body? Take some time to study your body, and become aware of how you look to yourself and what your body feels like to you. Try standing naked in front of a full-length mirror, and reflect on some of these questions:*

   - *Is your body generally tight or relaxed? What parts tend to be the most unrelaxed?*
   - *What does your face tell you about yourself? What kind of expression do you convey through your eyes? Are there lines on your face? What parts are tight? Do you force a smile?*
   - *Are there any parts of your body that you feel ashamed of or try to hide? What aspects of your body would you most like to change? What are the parts of your body that you like the best? The least?*

2. *After you've done the exercise just described (perhaps several times over a period of a few days), record a few of your impressions below, or keep an extended account of your reactions in your journal.*

   a. *How do you view your body, and how do you feel about it?*

   _____

   _____

   _____

   _____

b. *What messages do you convey to others about yourself through your body?*

_____

_____

_____

_____

c. *Are there any decisions you are now willing to make about changing your body?*

_____

_____

_____

_____

3. *If you decide to stand naked in front of a mirror, go through each of your body parts and "become each part," letting it "speak." For example, give your nose a personality, and pretend that your nose could speak. What might it say? If your legs were to speak, what do you imagine they'd say? (Do this for every part of your body, even if you find yourself wanting to bypass certain parts. In that case you might say: "I'm an ugly nose that doesn't want any recognition. I'd just like to hide, but I'm too big to be inconspicuous!")*

4. *If you are overweight, is your weight a barrier and a burden? For example, consider whether your fat is keeping you from doing what you want to do. Does it keep certain people away from you? You might pick up some object that is equivalent to the extra pounds you carry with you, letting yourself hold this object and begin to experience the excess weight.*

5. *Imagine yourself as looking more the way you'd like to. Let yourself think about how you might be different, as well as how your life would be different.*

THE BODY AND STRESS

Stress is an event or series of events that leads to strain, both bodily and psychological. Everyday living involves dealing with frustrations, conflicts, pressures, and change. At certain times in our life, moreover, most of us are confronted with severely stressful situations that are difficult to cope with, such as the death of a family member or a close friend, the loss of a job, a personal failure, or an injury. If the stress is severe enough, it will take its toll on us physically and psychologically.

A *Time* cover story ("Stress," 1983) reported that the medical profession was becoming increasingly aware of the price we pay for a high-stress lifestyle. Leaders of industry expressed concern about the costs of stress, which manifests itself in symptoms such as absenteeism, alcoholism, and a wide range of physical dysfunctions. These costs have been estimated at $50 billion to $75 billion a year, or more than $750 for each worker in the United States. Stress is now recognized as one of the major contributors to the six leading causes of death in the United States—heart disease, cancer, lung ailments, accidental injuries, cirrhosis of the liver, and suicide.

In most places in the modern world, stress is an inevitable part of life. Perhaps we cannot eliminate stress, but we can learn how to manage it. We don't have to allow ourselves to be victimized by the psychological and physiological effects of stress. It is true that there are external sources of stress, yet how we perceive and react to them is subjective and internal. By interpreting the events in our lives, we define what is and is not stressful, and thus we determine our levels of stress adaptation. Therefore, the real challenge is to learn how to recognize and deal constructively with the sources of stress, rather than trying to eliminate them.

At this point, I suggest you pause for a bit and take time to assess how stress is affecting you. To help you, refer to Resource 4, Monitoring Stress in Your Life.

Sources of Stress

Environmental Sources. Many of the stresses of daily life come from external sources. Consider for a moment some of the environmentally related stresses that you face at the beginning of a semester. You are likely to encounter problems just in finding a parking place on campus. Perhaps you must stand in long lines and cope with many other delays and frustrations. Some of the courses you need may be closed; simply putting together a decent schedule of classes may be next to impossible. There may be difficulties in arranging your work schedule to fit your school schedule, and these difficulties can be compounded by the external demands of friends and family and other social commitments. Financial problems and the pressure to work so that you can support yourself (and perhaps your family, too) make being a full-time student a demanding task.

Our mind and body are also profoundly affected by more directly physiological sources of stress. Illnesses, exposure to environmental pollutants, improper diet, lack of exercise, poor sleeping habits, and abusing our bodies in any number of other ways—all of these take a toll on us.

Psychological Sources.   Stress is a subjective phenomenon, in that how we label, interpret, think about, and react to those events that impinge on us has a lot to do with determining it. In discussing the psychological sources of stress, Coleman and Glaros (1983) identify frustration, conflict, and pressure as the key elements. Consider each of these sources of stress by applying them to yourself and your situation.

Frustration results from a blocking of your needs and goals. External sources of frustration, all of which have psychological components, include accidents, delays, hurtful interpersonal relationships, loneliness, and isolation. Additionally, internal factors can hinder you in attaining your goals. These include a lack of basic skills, physical handicaps, and a lack of belief in yourself. What are some of the major frustrations you experience, and how do you typically deal with them?

Conflict, another source of stress, occurs when there are two or more incompatible motives. Conflicts can be classified in terms of the reward or punishment values the alternatives have for the person. These conflicts can be classified as approach-approach, avoidance-avoidance, and approach-avoidance (Coleman & Glaros, 1983).

Approach-approach conflicts occur when a choice must be made between two or more attractive or desirable alternatives. Such conflicts are inevitable because we have a limited time to do all the things we would like to do and be all the places we'd like to be. An example of this type of conflict is being forced to choose between two or more job offers, all of which have attractive features.

Avoidance-avoidance conflicts arise when a choice must be made between two or more unattractive or undesirable goals. At times you may feel "caught between a rock and a hard place." You may have to choose between being unemployed and accepting a job that you do not like, neither of which appeals to you.

Approach-avoidance conflicts are produced when a choice must be made between two or more goals, each of which has positive and negative elements. For example, you might be offered a challenging job that appeals to you, yet it entails much traveling over the country, which you consider a real drawback.

How many times have you been faced with two or more desirable choices and been forced to choose one path? And how many times have you had to choose between unpleasant realities? Perhaps your major conflicts involve your choice of a life-style. For example, have you wrestled with the issue of being independent or blindly following the crowd? Of living a self-directed life or living by what others expect of you? Consider for a few minutes some of the major conflicts you've recently faced. How have these conflicts affected you? How do you typically deal with the stress you experience over value conflicts?

Pressure is part of the "hurry-sickness" of modern living. We may respond to the pressures placed on us by others at home, school, and work and in our social lives. Also, we continually place internally created pressures on ourselves. Many people are extremely demanding of themselves, driving themselves and never quite feeling satisfied that they've done all they could or should have. If you find yourself in this situation, consider some of the irrational and unrealistic beliefs that you might be living by. Are you overloading your circuits and heading for certain burn-out? How do you experience and deal with the pressure in your daily life?

Effects of Stress

Stress produces adverse physical effects, for in our attempt to cope with everyday living our body experiences what is known as the "fight-or-flight" response. Our body goes on constant alert status, ready for aggressive action to combat the many "enemies" we face. If we subject it to too many stresses, the biochemical changes that occur during the fight-or-flight response may lead to a situation of chronic stress and anxiety. This causes bodily wear and tear, which can lead to a variety of what are known as *psychosomatic*, or *psychophysiological*, disorders. These are real bodily disorders, manifested in disabling physical symptoms yet caused by emotional factors and the prolonged effects of stress. These symptoms range from minor discomfort to life-threatening conditions; most commonly they take the form of peptic ulcers, migraine and tension headaches, asthma and other respiratory disorders, high blood pressure, skin disorders, arthritis, digestive disorders, disturbed sleeping patterns, poor circulation, strokes, and heart disease.

Dr. Allan Abbott and his wife, Katherine, spent some time treating primitive people in Peru. This experience stimulated their interest in the ways in which stress affects our body. The Abbotts became especially interested in coronary-prone behavior, which is so characteristic of the North American way of life, when they observed that stress was not a part of the lives of these people. While the leading causes of death in North America are cardiovascular diseases and cancer (diseases the Abbotts relate to stress), they rarely cause the death of Peruvian Indians.

In Allan Abbott's view, our bodies are paying a high price for the materialistic and stressful manner in which we live. As a family-practice specialist, Abbott has come to believe that about 75% of the physical ailments he treats are psychologically induced or related to stress. As an aside, he asserts that 90% of what he does as a physician that makes a significant difference is psychological in nature, rather than medical. According to him, belief in the doctor and in the process and procedures a doctor employs has a great deal to do with curing patients. Taking a blood test, having an X ray done, getting a shot, and simple conversation with the physician are factors that appear to make patients improve. Indeed, faith healers work on this very principle of the role of belief and its effect on the body.

In agreement with Abbott is Albrecht (1979), who writes that many physicians have commented that 80% of their patients have emotionally induced disorders. A number of physicians treat their patients with medications such as tranquilizers, stomach remedies, sleeping pills, and pain killers. Instead of dealing with those factors that are producing the disorders, namely the life-styles of the patients, they treat the symptoms.

High-Stress Life-Style and Your Heart. I, too, am guilty at times of not listening to signals my body is sending. A few years ago I was confronted with some heart pains. Tests showed irregular heart beats, and my cardiologist tried to give me a subtle message that I should look at my life-style and slow down a bit. Knowing that I was a psychologist, he did not give me a lecture on the relationship between stress and heart attacks, but he did ask me to read a book by Friedman and Rosenman (1974), *Type A Behavior and Your Heart.* At the very least, that incident taught me that I am not an indestructible machine.

Traditionally, medical experts have considered diet, hereditary factors, being overweight, smoking cigarettes, and a lack of exercise as the primary causes of heart disease. There is increasing evidence, however, that a high-stress life-style is causally linked to heart disease.

Studying the relationship of life-styles and personality behavioral patterns to heart attacks, Friedman and Rosenman concluded that the major cause of coronary disease is a complex of emotional reactions they call "Type A" behavior. Key characteristics of the Type A personality are a *time urgency,* a preoccupation with *productivity and achievement,* and a *competitive drive.* These people are aggressively involved in a chronic and incessant struggle to achieve more and more in less and less time. Possessed by a "hurry sickness," they strive to make more money and to produce as much as possible as fast as possible. Type A personalities do not accept the fact that they can become exhausted. Friedman and Rosenman (1974) write: "It is the Type A man's ceaseless striving, his everlasting *struggle* with time, that we believe so very frequently leads to his early demise from coronary heart disease" (p. 87).

Other behaviors of Type A personalities are as follows: Creating deadlines that they try to beat; assuming too many responsibilities and therefore becoming trapped in several stressful situations at once; being unable to really relax or to have fun; experiencing chronic stress; passively accepting high-stress situations and pressures; perceiving life as serious; being preoccupied with work and productivity, with little balance for solitude and meaningful social relationships; and being driven.

Thus, although all the evidence is not yet in, it appears that chronic, unrelieved stress is a primary cause of heart attacks. The contributions of

Friedman and Rosenman challenge us to think about concrete ways to reduce stress, to learn to manage it better, and to make some basic changes in living that will lead to a low-stress life-style—becoming what they call the "Type B" person. Considering that each year over a million people in the United States suffer heart attacks (about two every minute), it is imperative that we learn to cope more successfully with stress.

Destructive Reactions to Stress

Our reactions to stress can be viewed on a continuum from being effective and adaptive, on one end, to being ineffective and maladaptive, on the other. If our reactions to stress are ineffective over a long period of time, we suffer harm to our physical and psychological well-being.

Defensive Behavior. If we experience stress associated with failure in school or work, we may react by attempting to defend our self-concept by denying or distorting reality. Although we may feel better for a short time, in the long run we are compounding our problems by not dealing directly with those factors associated with our failure. Faced with the stress of everyday life, many of us resort to defensive reactions as a way of maintaining our self-esteem. Although defensive behavior does at times have adjustive value and does result in reducing the impact of stress, such behavior can actually increase levels of stress in the long run. If we are more concerned with defending our bruised ego than we are in constructively coping with reality, we are not taking the steps necessary to reduce the source of stress. (I suggest you review the various ego defenses that were described in Chapter 2.)

Drugs and Alcohol. We are conditioned to take an aspirin for a headache, to take a tranquilizer when we are anxious, to rely on stimulants to keep us up all night at the end of a term, and to use a variety of drugs to reduce other physical symptoms and emotional stresses. The *Time* story ("Stress," 1983) reported that the three best-selling drugs in the United States were an ulcer medication (Tagamet), a drug for high blood pressure (Inderal), and a tranquilizer (Valium). Americans obviously rely heavily on drugs to alleviate symptoms of stress, rather than looking at the life-style that produces this stress.

We all use drugs in some form or another. We are especially vulnerable to relying on drugs when we feel out of control, for drugs offer the promise of helping us gain control of our life. Consider some of the ways that we attempt to control problems by relying on both legal and illegal drugs. If we are troubled with shyness, boredom, anxiety, depression, or stress, we may become chemically dependent to relieve these symptoms. A drawback to depending on these substances to gain control of our life is that through them we numb ourselves physically and psychologically. Instead of paying attention to our bodily signals that all is not well in our life, we deceive ourselves by believing that we are something that we are not. When drugs are used excessively as a way to escape from painful reality, this use compounds our problems rather than solving them. As tolerance is built up for these substances, there is a tendency to become increasingly dependent on them to anesthetize both physical and psychological pain. Yet once the effects of the drugs wear off, we are still confronted by the painful reality that we sought to avoid. According to the psychiatrist William Glasser (1984), if we continue to use any addicting drug, no matter how good we feel, we will always lose more and more control of our life. In his book *Take Effective Control of Your Life*, Glasser develops the thesis that we cannot gain effective control of our life through the use of drugs and alcohol. For him, chemical dependency gets in the way of satisfying basic human needs for love, power, fun, and freedom.

What is critical is that we be aware of our motivations and that we know the effects that alcohol and drugs are having on our life. When our patterns of using drugs and alcohol serve the function of distorting reality, we are preventing ourselves from finding direct and effective means of coping with stress. The problem here is that stress is now controlling us, instead of our controlling stress.

Alcohol is perhaps the most widely used and abused drug of all. It is also the most dangerous and debilitating of drugs. This is true not only because of its effects on us physically and psychologically but also because it is legal, accessible, and socially acceptable. Glasser (1984) asserts that alcohol is an integral and glorified aspect of our culture. "Alcohol is the get-things-done, take-control drug, and to deal with it well is a sign of strength and maturity. Because it enhances the sense of control, we welcome it instead of fearing it as we should" (p. 132).

As you read this section, you may be asking yourself whether you have a problem with using substances as a way of coping with stress. For example, you may be worried about the ways you use alcohol or the effects that drinking has on you. Perhaps the most difficult aspect of making this self-assessment is simply being honest with yourself. Resource 6 is a questionnaire designed to help you determine the degree to which drinking is a problem for you. In the final analysis, people who use any drug must honestly consider what they are getting from it as well as the price they are paying for their decision. They must determine for themselves whether the toll on their physical and psychological well-being is too high.

It has not been my intention to provide a comprehensive discussion of various drugs, both legal and illegal, in terms of their effects and risks from a physical and psychological perspective. Instead, my purpose has been to encourage you to make an honest self-assessment of the degree to which relying on drugs and alcohol may actually be restricting your choices instead of leading to genuine control of the direction you want to take. If you are interested in doing further reading in this area, I recommended selected chapters in Glasser (1984), Burns (1981), and Emery (1981). For those of you who are interested in the effects of antidepressant drugs and their negative effects on the brain, I recommend Breggin's (1983) *Psychiatric Drugs: Hazards to the Brain.* Another well-documented introduction to the topic of drug use is the book *Drugs: A Factual Account,* by Dusek and Girdano (1980). In their readable book they discuss the social context of drugs, the reasons people use them, and their effects.

TIME OUT FOR PERSONAL REFLECTION

Are you greatly increasing your chances of a heart attack by choosing coronary-prone behavior? The following survey is an adaptation of the characteristics of the Type A personality as described by Friedman and Rosenman (1974). Take this self-inventory to determine to what degree each of these behavioral traits is typical of you. Use this code: A = this is very much *true of me; B = this is* sometimes *true of me; C = this is* rarely *true of me; and D = this is* almost never *true of me.*

1. *I tend to speak rapidly.*
2. *My speech has an explosive quality to it, and I often accentuate many of my words.*
3. *My voice often sounds irritated.*
4. *Most of the time I walk and move with haste.*
5. *I am a fast eater.*
6. *When I eat, I generally read or watch television.*
7. *I typically find myself trying to do more and more in less and less time.*
8. *I persistently feel that I have unfinished projects, even though I work long and hard hours.*
9. *If I have to wait in line or get caught in traffic, I tend to become upset and irritated.*
10. *When others are speaking, I often get impatient in wanting them to make their point.*
11. *I often find myself trying to do too many things at once.*
12. *Many times I attempt to maneuver the conversation around to a topic that interests me.*
13. *When others are speaking, I am generally thinking about what I will say next.*
14. *I feel guilty when I relax or do nothing for several hours or several days.*
15. *I am highly competitive.*
16. *At times I'm afraid to stop, for fear that I won't get enough done.*
17. *I measure my worth as a person by the number of my accomplishments.*

_____   18. *Very often I set impossible tasks and deadlines for myself, and then I try to beat these deadlines.*

_____   19. *There is an urge within me to continually get ahead, for I am never satisfied with where I am.*

_____   20. *Time controls me; I do not control time.*

Two suggestions for using this inventory:

- *Look over the items that you rated as being true of you much of the time. Which of these traits would you most like to change? How can you begin to make these changes?*
- *Have someone who knows you fairly well complete this inventory for you on the basis of how he or she perceives you. Then compare results, and talk about any differences that interest either of you.*

Constructive Reactions to Stress

In order to cope with stress effectively we must first face up to the causes of our problems, and then we must recognize our own part in creating them. Instead of adopting destructive reactions to stress, we can use task-oriented, or constructive, approaches aimed at realistically coping with stressful events. Weiten (1983) describes *constructive coping* as behavioral reactions to stress that tend to be relatively healthy or adaptive. He lists the following characteristics of constructive coping: it involves a direct confrontation with a problem situation; it entails staying in tune with reality; it is based on an accurate and realistic appraisal of a stressful situation, rather than on distorting reality; it involves learning to recognize and inhibit harmful emotional reactions to stress; it entails a conscious and rational effort to evaluate alternative courses of action; and it is not dominated by wishful or irrational thinking. This section focuses on such positive ways to deal with stress.

Developing a Type B Personality.   We have seen how Type A behaviors can endanger our health. Making a conscious decision to acquire a Type B life-style is one important avenue to dealing with stress constructively. Developing a Type B orientation means making clear choices in organizing our life so that we keep stress to a minimum. Transforming oneself from a Type A person entails learning a balance in life, especially between work and play. It involves changing basic attitudes and thoughts so that we do not react so intensely to situations and thus cause stress. Most of all, it demands that we accept full responsibility for how we are living—recognizing that our continual choices influence who we are and that we are not passively programmed and rigidly molded once and for all.

From a personal perspective I know how difficult it is to make the transformation from Type A to Type B. I can't expect to cram my life with activities all semester, fragmenting myself with many stressful situations, and then expect a "day off" to rejuvenate my system. Instead, I am slowly learning that I need to acquire ways of cutting down on those situations that cause stress and to deal differently with the stresses that are inevitable. Taking a few moments out for quiet reflection, learning relaxation exercises, practicing some form of meditation, getting adequate sleep, having a sound diet, keeping physically fit, participating in a regular exercise program, and making other conscious choices that lead to a low-stress life-style are some avenues of maintaining a healthy body and mind.

I must add that making a *basic* change in life-style takes a tremendous degree of determination. As one person who has not yet succeeded at making the change from Type A to Type B, all I can say is "It ain't easy, but if this is a change I sincerely want, then I can do it."

Relaxation.   Another positive approach for dealing with stress is learning to genuinely relax. Before you continue reading, take a few moments to "relax" and to think about how you relax. Do you engage in certain forms of relaxation on a regular basis? What do you consider relaxing? Look over the following list and decide which forms of relaxation are for you. Think about the quality of each form of relaxation and how often you use it.

- sitting in a quiet place for as few as ten minutes a day and just letting your mind wander
- listening to music and fully hearing and feeling it (without making it the background of another activity)
- sleeping deeply and restfully
- being involved in a hobby that gives you pleasure
- engaging in sports that have the effect of calming you
- asking for and receiving a massage
- taking longer than usual in lovemaking
- walking in the woods or on the beach
- closing your eyes and listening to the sounds in nature
- listening to the sounds of your breathing
- practicing some form of meditation each day
- relaxing in a hot tub
- allowing yourself to let go fully with friends
- regularly practicing muscle-relaxation exercises
- practicing some form of self-hypnosis to cut down stress and outside distractions

Consider what gets in your way of achieving the level of relaxation you'd like as often as you'd like. Some of us experience a great deal of difficulty in fully relaxing. For example, I approach relaxation with purpose and intensity. I often make the mistake of trying too hard to relax, which has the effect of making what I am doing one more burden. I can

recall setting out for a vacation with my family saying "We *will* have a good time this week, and we *will* enjoy each other's company!" While I do a lot of walking in the woods, my mind is not often quiet. Frequently I return from such a solitary hike with many ideas for other projects. A constant struggle is to quiet myself enough to become aware of barriers that get in the way of unwinding.

In our complex society many of us encounter obstacles in allowing ourselves to fully relax. Even if we take a few moments in a busy schedule to unwind, our mind may be reeling with thoughts of past or future events. Another problem is simply finding a quiet and private place where we can relax and a time when we will be free from interruptions. Perhaps an important lesson to learn is how to let go for even a few minutes, to learn to unwind while waiting in a line or riding on a bus. Refer to Resource 5 for a relaxation exercise that you can apply as a constructive way of coping with stress.

Meditation. Meditation is another constructive reaction to stress. This method of getting personally focused is enjoying an increased popularity among people of all ages. For some people it still has an aura of mysticism, and they may shy away from it because it seems intricately bound up with elaborate rituals, strange language, strange clothing, and abstract philosophical and spiritual notions. But you don't have to wear exotic garb and sit in a lotus position in order to meditate. Simply sitting quietly and letting your mind wander or looking within can be a simple form of meditation.

As Davis, Eshelman, and McKay (1980) note, meditation can be practiced independently of any religious or philosophical orientation, purely as a means of reducing inner discord and increasing self-knowledge. They describe a variety of methods of meditation and urge readers to select one or more that suit them.

Meditation is effective in creating a deep state of relaxation in a fairly short time. It can be used to prevent or treat high blood pressure and heart disease. It can reduce anxiety and the effects of stress. However, most writers on meditation agree that exercises must be practiced for at least a month for meditation's more profound effects to be experienced.[2] Davis, Eshelman, and McKay (1980) outline four major components of meditation:

- a quiet place with a minimum of external distractions
- a comfortable position that can be held for about 20 minutes without causing stress
- dwelling on an object or a repetitive sound or word while letting thoughts simply pass by
- adopting a passive attitude, which includes letting go of thoughts and distractions and simply returning to the object you are dwelling on

[2]I recommend three books if you would like to do further reading or find a method of meditation that fits you: *The Relaxation and Stress Reduction Workbook*, by Davis, Eshelman, and McKay (1980); *Precision Nirvana*, by Shapiro (1978); and *Journey of Awakening: A Meditator's Guidebook*, by Ram Dass (1978).

WELLNESS AND LIFE-STYLE CHOICES

Dealing constructively with stress can be part of a person's overall striving for "wellness." The concept of wellness fits into a holistic view of health. Traditional medicine focuses on identifying symptoms of illness and curing disease. By contrast, *holistic health* focuses on every facet of human functioning. It emphasizes the intimate relationship between our body and all the other aspects of ourselves—psychological, social, and spiritual. And it stresses positive wellness rather than merely the absence of disabling symptoms. Just as there are many degrees of being ill, there are degrees of wellness.

Wellness as an Active Choice

Wellness entails a lifelong process of taking care of our needs on all levels of human functioning. It implies that we see ourselves as constantly growing and developing. Well people are committed to creating a life-style that contributes to taking care of their physical self, challenging themselves intellectually, expressing the full range of their emotions, finding meaningful interpersonal relationships, and searching for a meaning that will give direction to their life.

A combination of factors contributes to our sense of well-being. Thus, a holistic approach to health must pay attention to our life-style, including a range of specific factors: how we work and play, how we relax, how and what we eat, how we keep physically fit, our relationships with others, and our spiritual needs.

It is beyond the scope of this book to become prescriptive in the areas of creating a life-style that will lead to wellness. My purpose here is to introduce you to the issues involved in wellness and life-style choices, to encourage you to think about the priority you are placing on a general sense of physical and psychological well-being, and to invite you to consider if there are any changes you want to make in your present life-style. There are scores of self-help books on subjects of stress management, exercise, meditation, diet, nutrition, weight control, control of smoking and drinking, and wellness medicine.

One Man's Wellness Program

To make this discussion of wellness and life-style choices more concrete, I'll provide a case illustration of a client who was in one of my therapeutic groups, whom I'll call Kevin. When I first met him in the group, he struck me as being closed-off emotionally, rigid, stoical, and defensive. For many years he had thrown himself completely into his work as an attorney. Although his family life was marked by tension and bickering with his wife, he attempted to block out the stress he was experiencing at home by burying himself in his law cases and by excelling in his career.

When Kevin reached middle age, he began to question how he wanted to continue living. One of the catalysts for his self-searching was a series of heart attacks that his father suffered. He watched his father decline physically, and this jolted him into the realization that both his father's time and his own time were limited. Later Kevin went for a long-overdue physical examination and discovered that he had high blood pressure, that his cholesterol level was abnormally high, and that he was at relatively high risk of having a heart attack himself. He also learned that several of his relatives had died of heart attacks, and he decided that he wanted to reverse what he saw as a self-destructive path. After consultations and discussions with his physician, Kevin decided to change his lifestyle in several ways. He was overeating, his diet was not balanced, he was consuming a great deal of alcohol to relax, and he was "too busy" to do any physical exercise. His new decision involved making contacts with friends. He learned to enjoy playing tennis and raquetball on a regular basis. He took up jogging and reported that, if he had not run in the morning, he felt somewhat sluggish during the day. He radically changed his diet in line with the suggestions from his physician. As a result, he lowered both his cholesterol level and his blood pressure without the use of medication; he also lost 20 pounds and worked himself into excellent physical shape.

Kevin's wellness program did not stop with enhancing his physical being. He developed less tolerance for mediocre family relationships. He and his wife got involved in marital counseling to learn how to bring out the conflicts that were dividing them and to learn how to express their reactions to each other. Previously he had kept most of his feelings to himself and had merely grown silent when he felt unappreciated by his wife. His counseling sessions gave him some tools for expressing his frustrations openly. Eventually, his three sons, his wife, and Kevin had a series of family-therapy sessions. Kevin acknowledged that the home atmosphere was characterized by tension and that he wanted simply to escape from this stress-producing environment. Now he hoped to face the problems that were keeping the family members strangers to one another. For the first time in his life he allowed himself to *express* his caring to his sons and his wife; he let them know how powerless he felt at times to change the home situation, and he felt his sadness and wept. Kevin no longer wanted to be the strong person who could prove that he was unaffected by whatever went on at home. He continued to reach out to his sons, and he made more time to play as well as work. As Kevin learned how to be more emotionally expressive, he reported that he felt more alive physically. He was less tight both physically and emotionally, and he could actually laugh much more.

Let's underscore a few key points in Kevin's case. First of all, he took the time to seriously reflect on the direction he was going in life. He did not engage in self-deception; rather, he admitted that his life-style was not a healthy one. On finding out that heart disease was a part of his family history, he did not shrug his shoulders and assume an indifferent attitude. Instead, he made a decision to take an active part in changing his life on many levels. He cut down on drinking and relied less on alcohol as an escape. He changed his patterns of eating and exercise, which resulted in his feeling better physically and psychologically. Although he was still committed to his law practice, he pursued it less compulsively. He realized that he had missed play in his life, and he sought a better balance between work and play.

With the help of counseling, Kevin realized the high price he was paying for bottling up emotions of hurt, sadness, anger, guilt, and joy. Although he did not give up his logical and analytical dimensions, he allowed himself to be a person who could express what he was feeling. He began questioning the value of living exclusively by logic and calculation, both in his professional and his personal life. As a consequence, he cultivated friendships and let others who were significant to him know that he wanted to be closer to them. Kevin could have asked his physician for a prescription and could have assumed a passive stance toward curing his illness. Instead, he was challenged to review his life to determine what steps he could take to get more from the time he had to live. A person who knew Kevin only casually commented one day that he seemed so much different than he had a year before. She remembered him as being uptight, unfriendly, uncommunicative, angry-looking, and detached. She was surprised at his changes, and she used adjectives such as *warm, open, relaxed, talkative,* and *outgoing* to describe him.

Behavior Modification as a Means to Wellness

At this point you may be seriously concerned about the condition of your body, your use of alcohol and drugs, your smoking, your eating habits, or the amount of exercise you get. We know what is healthy and unhealthy for us, yet we often have difficulties in committing ourselves to a plan for change. Even if you are determined to change certain life-style patterns, taking the first step is often difficult. For most of the above behavioral patterns, you can find support groups and clinics to help you develop a course of action. If you are interested in making these changes on your own, behavior modification can be a most useful tool for improving self-control. In general, a self-directed behavior-modification program involves the application of the principles of learning to changing specific behavior. The assumption is that any behavior that is learned, as our life-style patterns are, can also be unlearned. Those behaviors in our life-style that are not working effectively for us can be reduced or eliminated and then replaced by a set of attitudes and behaviors that will work.

Behavior modification is particularly appropriate if you are working at weight control or smoking control. Below is a summary of the essence of a behavior-modification program.

1. The first step is to specify the target behavior. Vague statements about problematic behavior must be changed into clear statements about specific behaviors that you are willing to change.
2. Next comes the process of simply monitoring your present behavior so that you can become aware of what you are doing. If you want to control smoking, for example, you can begin by simply paying attention to the situations and times when you most crave tobacco.
3. The third step consists of designing a program, or a plan for change. It is essential that your plan be systematic and clear and that you reward yourself for carrying it out. A written contract can be of value here.
4. As you carry out your plan, you will need to revise and fine-tune your program. This will entail finding strategies for dealing with setbacks and the discouragement that comes with meeting barriers to change.
5. The final step consists of bringing your program to an end and evaluating how effective it has been.

Resource 7 provides a discussion of specific steps of a self-change program that you can apply in creating a plan for changing certain behaviors. I recommend Watson's and Tharp's (1985) excellent book *Self-Directed Behavior: Self Modification for Personal Adjustment* if you want a more detailed treatment of how to achieve self-control by using behavioral methods.

Accepting Responsibility for Your Body

It is not unusual these days for people to take the responsibility of living a healthy life. As you are aware, television and popular magazines have special features devoted to informing the public about exercise programs, dietary habits, and ways to manage stress. More health insurance companies are providing payment for preventive medicine; one does not need to look far to find a preventive health clinic. Many communities provide a wide variety of programs aimed at helping people to improve the quality of their life by finding a form of exercise that suits them. Even industry provides time for employees to get involved in exercise programs. Many corporations have come to realize the value of exercising as a way of managing stress and preventing burn-out on the job; they have apparently found that exercising pays off in terms of productivity.

Not all physicians prescribe pills to alleviate the symptoms of what they see as a problematic life-style. Psychologically oriented physicians emphasize the role of *choice* and *responsibility* as critical determinants of our physical and psychological well-being. In their practice they challenge their patients to look at what they are doing to their body through their lack of exercise, the substances they take in, and other damaging behavior. While they may prescribe medication to lower a person's extremely high blood pressure, they inform the patient that medications can do only so much and that what is needed is a radical change in life-style.

Doctors often find, however, that most of the people they see are more interested in getting pills and in removing their symptoms than in changing a stressful life-style. These patients would much rather see themselves as the victim of a heart attack than as responsible for their heart trouble.

A growing number of doctors are thinking in terms of holistic health. Perhaps the key principle underlying this integrated approach is *responsibility*. In commenting on the responsibility we bear for our physical health, Albrecht (1979) makes several points that sum up the issue of who controls our body:

> [Responsibility] is the notion that one's health is almost entirely a function of what one does with one's body and one's thoughts. Poor health behaviors lead to poor health. Immature thinking and reacting lead to negative emotions and unnecessary stress. Overeating, over-smoking, overuse of tobacco, abuse of recreational drugs or patent medicines, and sedentary living are *choices* that one can make or un-make. By taking complete responsibility for your health, you become obligated to yourself to act and live in ways that will guarantee your own total wellness [p. 31].

As you can readily see, it makes a world of difference whether you see yourself as a passive victim or an active agent in the maintenance of your body. If you believe that you simply catch colds or are ill-fated enough to get sick, and if you don't see what you can do to prevent bodily illnesses, then your body is controlling you. But if you recognize that the way you are choosing to lead your life (including accepting responsibility for what you consume, how you exercise, and the stresses you put yourself under) has a direct bearing on your physical and psychological well-being, then you can be in control of your body. At this time in your life, how would you answer these central questions: Do you control your body? Or does your body control you?

TIME OUT FOR PERSONAL REFLECTION

1. *The following are some common rationalizations that people use for not changing patterns of behavior that affect their bodies. Look over these statements and decide what ones, if any, you use. What others do you sometimes use that are not on this list?*

_____ *I don't have the time to exercise every day.*
_____ *No matter how I try to lose weight, nothing seems to work.*
_____ *I sabotage myself, and others sabotage me, in my attempts to lose weight.*
_____ *I'll stop smoking as soon as my life becomes less stressful.*
_____ *When I have a vacation, I'll relax.*
_____ *Even though I drink a lot (or use other drugs), it calms me down and has never interfered with my life.*

_____   *I need a drink (or a marijuana cigarette) to relax.*
_____   *Food isn't important to me; I eat anything I can grab fast.*
_____   *I simply don't have the time to eat three balanced meals a day.*
_____   *Food has gotten so expensive, I just can't afford to eat decent meals
              any more.*
_____   *If I stop smoking, I'll surely gain weight.*
_____   *I simply cannot function without several cups of coffee.*
_____   *If I don't stop smoking, then I might get lung cancer or die a little
              sooner, but we all have to go sometime.*

What other statements could you add to this list?

_____

_____

_____

_____

2. *Complete the following sentences with the first word or phrase that
   comes to mind:*

   a. *One way I abuse my body is* _____

   b. *One way I neglect my body is* _____

   c. *When people notice my physical appearance, I think that* _____

   _____

   d. *When I look at my body in the mirror, I* _____

   e. *I could be healthier if only* _____

   f. *One way I could cut down the stress in my life is* _____

   _____

   g. *If I could change one aspect of my body it would be my* _____

   h. *One way that I relax is* _____

   i. *I'd describe my diet as* _____

   j. *For me, exercising is* _____

CHAPTER SUMMARY

The purpose of this chapter has been to stimulate you to think about how
you are treating your body and how you might take control of your physical and psychological well-being. One enemy of well-being is excessive

stress. A constructive way of dealing with stress is within the framework of wellness and your choice of life-style. We cannot realistically expect to eliminate stress from our life, but we can modify our way of thinking and our life-style to reduce stressful situations and manage stress more effectively.

Conquering stress highlights the importance of a willingness to accept responsibility for what you are doing to your body. A central message is to listen to your body and respect what you hear. By taking time we can experience the world around us through our senses of seeing, hearing, smelling, tasting, and touching. We can also become less of a stranger to our body through relaxation, dance, and movement. Touch is particularly important. For healthy development, both physical and emotional, we need contact, and we need to be touched. Our body image is not something we are born with. We acquire our attitudes about our body. We can challenge some of the attitudes we have picked up, especially if they are self-critical.

I hope you will apply the specific examples emphasized in this chapter. Even if you are not presently concerned with the problems of stress, drug abuse, or weight control, you may have discovered certain attitudes about your body that are self-defeating. A theme of this chapter has been to examine what might be keeping you from really caring about your body or acting on the caring that you say you have. The basic choice is more than a matter of smoking or not smoking, of exercising or not exercising; the basic choice concerns how you feel about yourself and about your life. By accepting responsibility for the feelings and attitudes you have developed about your body, you begin to free yourself from feeling victimized by your body.

In the next few chapters we consider the topics of sex roles, sexuality, love, and intimate relationships. I encourage you to consider how your perceptions of your body affect these areas of your life. Do you shy away from the opposite sex because of your fears about how others will react to your physical being? Is it possible that you keep yourself in a self-imposed prison, unwilling to initiate positive contact with other people, simply because you assume they won't like the way you look? Does your body express your feelings of tenderness, anger, enthusiasm, and so on, or does it tend to be rigid and under control? By examining these and similar questions, you can widen the brackets of freedom in these other areas of your life.

I end this chapter with an invitation to make an honest assessment of how you see your body and how you feel about it, as well as the many ways in which your views influence your behavior. Your subjective evaluation of your body is at least as powerful as your objective physical traits—and it is open to change.

ACTIVITIES AND EXERCISES

1. You may have become motivated enough to want to actively work at changing a pattern of behavior that is related to the health of your body. Some examples of self-directed programs you might want to set up for yourself include eliminating smoking (or some drug); reducing or eliminating alcoholic beverages; designing an effective exercise program; developing a systematic approach to losing weight and maintaining an appropriate weight; and making specific changes in your lifestyle in the direction of reducing stress. Begin by consulting a book such as Williams and Long (1983) or Watson and Tharp (1985) for the details of setting up a program for self-directed behavior change. Then, you might want to read other books in the Suggested Readings to help you with the specific program you'd like to develop.

2. In your journal, keep an account of the stressful situations that you encounter for about a week or so. After each entry you might note items such as: To what degree was the situation a stressful one because of your thoughts, beliefs, and assumptions pertaining to the events? How were you affected? Do you see any ways of dealing with these stresses more effectively?

3. Consider making a written contract, with yourself and some other person, about changing a specific behavior. You could pledge to eliminate snacking, agree to keep a stress journal for a month, or make a contract to begin an exercise program. Check with the person you've signed the contract with frequently to appraise your progress.

4. In your journal, record for one week all the activities that are healthy for your body as well as those that are unhealthy. It could be valuable to record things such as what you eat, stress patterns, smoking and drinking, sleeping habits, exercise, relaxation, and so forth. After you've done this for a week, look over your list and determine whether there are areas that you'd be willing to work on during this semester.

5. Consider some of the following questions as a basis for discovering how your body image affects other aspects of your life. You may tell a close friend how you have answered some of the following questions and ask for honest feedback as one way of checking out your own perceptions of your body. Or you might form a small group in your class in which members can share some of their reactions to their own bodies and the ways in which their feelings have influenced their behavior.

   a. Look at your face in a mirror, and carefully study your facial characteristics. What does your face tell you and others about your personal history? Does your face seem alive and inviting? Or does it reflect fear and tend to keep others away from you?

b. What messages do you express to others through your body?

c. When you look at your body, what does it tell you about the degree of caring you have for yourself? If you say that you care about yourself, yet your body belies this statement, what do you suppose is keeping you from acting on the caring you say you have?

d. When you were a child or adolescent, did your body image keep you from doing certain things that you wanted to do? Do traces of earlier feelings about your body get in the way of doing what you'd like to do now? If so, what are some initial steps you can take to change?

6. Review the section on behavior modification and Resource 7, in which I describe a model for self-directed changes. Think of a specific behavior you would like to change and apply these steps to yourself. Be sure to keep observational records in your journal. After looking over a week's records, decide on a plan for action, and then keep track of your progress.

SUGGESTED READINGS

Albrecht, K. (1979). *Stress and the Manager*. Englewood Cliffs, N.J.: Prentice-Hall. If you were to select just one book on stress management, this would be my top recommendation. The author has many sound ideas and practical suggestions for changing to a low-stress life-style.

Burns, D. D. (1981). *Feeling Good: The New Mood Therapy*. New York: New American Library (Signet). A highly readable and practical self-help book based on the principles of cognitive therapy. The focus is on learning how to control our feelings and actions by becoming aware of and changing our self-defeating thinking. The author stresses a drug-free approach to dealing with depression. He writes about coping with the stresses of daily life and offers a consumer's guide to antidepressant drug therapy.

Dass, R. (1978). *Journey of Awakening: A Meditator's Guidebook*. New York: Bantam. Readers who want to know more about ways of meditating, along with a directory of further resources, will find this book a helpful place to begin.

Davis, M., Eshelman, E. R., & McKay, M. (1980). *The Relaxation and Stress Reduction Workbook*. Richmond, Calif.: New Harbinger Publications. This is an excellent manual for those who want to learn how to relax. Contains practical exercises in body awareness, progressive relaxation, meditation, self-hypnosis, ways of disputing irrational ideas, assertiveness training, time management, and biofeedback.

Emery, G. (1981). *A New Beginning: How You Can Change Your Life through Cognitive Therapy*. New York: Simon & Schuster. An excellent self-help book that describes constructive ways of coping with depression. Of particular value are the author's chapters on controlling the psychological and physical symptoms of depression, dealing with weight gain, overcoming alcohol and drug dependency, handling the stress of motherhood, and coping with the stresses of growing older.

Friedman, M., & Rosenman, R. H. (1974). *Type A Behavior and Your Heart*. Greenwich, Conn.: Fawcett. This pioneering medical team conducted research into the relationship between high-stress life-styles and heart attacks. They've translated their findings in a simple and interesting style. *Must* reading for those who are thinking of changing to a less stressful way of living.

Glasser, W. (1984). *Take Effective Control of Your Life*. New York: Harper & Row. The main message of this book is that we can best control our life by working on changing what we are *doing* and how we are *thinking*. By changing our behavior and our thinking, we are likely to begin to feel different. Of special interest are Glasser's chapters on psychosomatic illness as a creative process, attempting to control our life with addicting drugs, and taking control of our health.

Schwartz, J. (1982). *Letting Go of Stress*. New York: Pinnacle Books. In a very readable manner the author shows ways of learning how to let go of stress without relying on alcohol or drugs. She clearly presents step-by-step exercises covering a 15-day period in the areas of increasing awareness, nutrition, exercise, communication, relaxation, and life-style. There are a number of useful self-evaluation tests on stress, relaxation, rating your risk of heart attack, and physical exercise.

Watson, D. L., & Tharp, R. G. (1985). *Self-Directed Behavior: Self-Modification for Personal Adjustment* (4th ed.). Monterey, Calif.: Brooks/Cole. For those who want to set up a self-directed program to control smoking, eating, or drinking or to promote regular exercise, this book offers useful guidelines for systematically making behavioral changes.

Williams, R. L., & Long, J. D. (1983). *Toward a Self-Managed Life Style* (3rd ed.). Boston: Houghton Mifflin. This is an excellent source for those who want to set up a behavioral program for themselves to deal with areas such as weight control, smoking and drinking, or exercise.

5

SEX ROLES

PRECHAPTER SELF-INVENTORY

Use the following scale to respond: 4 = this statement is true of me *most* of the time; 3 = this statement is true of me *much* of the time; 2 = this statement is true of me *some* of the time; 1 = this statement is true of me *almost none* of the time.

1. It is important to me to be perceived as feminine (masculine).
2. I feel comfortable with my identity as a woman (man).
3. It is relatively easy for me to be both logical and emotional, tough and tender, objective and subjective.
4. I have trouble accepting both women who show "manly" qualities and men who show "womanly" qualities.
5. It is difficult for me to accept in myself traits that are often associated with the opposite sex.
6. I'm uncomfortable with thinking, feeling, or acting in ways that do not conform to society's view of what is appropriate for a man or a woman.
7. I think I'm becoming the kind of man or woman I want to become, regardless of anyone else's ideas about what is expected of my gender.
8. I am glad that I am the sex that I am.
9. I feel discriminated against because of my gender.
10. My parents provided good models of what it means to be a woman and a man.

INTRODUCTION

In the previous chapter you met Kevin, a man who gradually became aware of the costs of living by traditional sex roles and who began to widen his behavioral repertoire. To a great extent he was a product of his social and cultural conditioning. His view of himself as a man was a result of years of traditional child-rearing practices, which were continued in school and reinforced by his culture. For a long time he did not even realize that he was being psychologically restricted by the expectations tied to his gender. This dawning awareness came to him mainly because of a crisis that faced him in mid-life. He was shocked by his father's illness, and he realized the toll that living by traditional roles had taken on his father.

   This crisis was the impetus that helped Kevin review the way he was living and make some choices about changing his future. He began to look at the impact that his definition of maleness was having on all aspects of his life. He realized that he had never questioned his attitudes about sex-role behavior, that he was behaving automatically rather than by choice, and that he was paying a steep price for conforming to a traditional role. It was even more difficult for him to make actual behavioral changes once he decided to be a more expressive man. He struggled against years of conditioning. Although he increased his level of consciousness intellectually through reading and through personal counseling, he had trouble catching up emotionally and behaviorally with what he knew. In other words, his intellectual enlightenment did not easily translate into his feeling differently and acting differently.

All of us are partially the product of our cultural conditioning. This chapter is aimed at challenging you to examine those factors that have directly and indirectly shaped your sex-role identity. With an increased awareness you will be in a better position to assess both the positive and negative effects that your sex-role socialization continues to have on all aspects of your life. This context provides a basis for deciding what changes, if any, you want to make.

In summary, the focus of this chapter is to invite you to think critically about sex-role stereotypes and to form your own standards of what it means to be a woman or a man. You will need to acquire a sense of patience and appreciate the difficulties involved in overcoming certain ingrained attitudes. The real challenge is to transform new attitudes into new ways of behaving.

MALE ROLES

As mentioned earlier, many men in our society live a restricted and deadening life because they have "bought" some cultural myths about what it means to be a male. Unfortunately, too many men are caught in rigid roles and expect sanctions when they deviate from what is supposedly "manly." In this way they become so involved in the many roles they are playing that they eventually become a stranger to themselves. They no longer know what they are like inside, because they put so much energy into maintaining an acceptable male image.

The All-American Male

What is the stereotype of the all-American male, and what aspects of themselves do many males feel they must hide in order to conform to it? In general, the stereotypic male is cool, detached, objective, rational, and strong. A man who attempts to fit himself to the stereotype will suppress most of his feelings, for he sees the subjective world of feelings as being essentially feminine. A number of writers have discussed these issues and identified characteristics of a man living by the stereotype and also those he may attempt to suppress or deny (Basow, 1980; Deaux, 1976; Goldberg, 1976, 1979; Jourard, 1971; Mornell, 1979; Pleck & Sawyer, 1974). The following list of characteristics outlines the limited view of a male's role that many men have accepted to a greater or lesser degree.

- *Independence.* Rather than admitting that he needs anything from anyone, he may live a life of exaggerated independence. He feels he should be able to do by himself whatever needs to be done, and he finds it hard to reach out to others.
- *Aggressiveness.* He feels he must be continually active, aggressive, assertive, and striving. He views the opposites of these traits as signs of weakness, and he fears being seen as weak.
- *Denial of fears.* He won't express his fears, and he probably won't even allow *himself* to experience them. He has the distorted notion that to be afraid means that he lacks courage, so he hides his fears from himself and from others.
- *Protection of his inner self.* He doesn't disclose himself to women, because he is afraid that they will think of him as unmanly if they see his inner core. He keeps himself hidden from other men because they are competitors and, in this sense, potential enemies.
- *Invulnerability.* He cannot make himself vulnerable, as is evidenced by his general unwillingness to disclose much of his inner experiences. He won't let himself feel and express sadness; nor will he cry. To protect himself, he becomes emotionally insulated and puts on a mask of toughness, competence, and decisiveness.
- *Lack of bodily self-awareness.* He doesn't recognize bodily cues that may signal danger. He drives himself unmercifully and views his body as some kind of machine that won't break down or wear out. He may not pay attention to his exhaustion until he collapses from it.
- *Remoteness with other men.* Although he may have plenty of acquaintances, he doesn't have very many male friends he can confide in.
- *Successfulness.* He hides from failure, and he must at all times put on the facade of the successful man. He feels he's expected to succeed and produce, to be "the best," and to get ahead and stay ahead. He has to win, which means that someone else has to lose.
- *Denial of "feminine" qualities.* Because he plays a rigid male role, he doesn't see how he can still be a man and at the same time possess (or reveal) traits that are usually attributed to women. Therefore, he is very controlled, shutting out much of what he could experience and leading an impoverished life as a result. He finds it difficult to express warmth and tenderness.
- *Avoidance of physical contact.* He has a difficult time touching freely. He thinks that he should touch a woman only if it will lead to sex, and he

fears touching other men because he doesn't want to be perceived as a homosexual.

- *Rigid perceptions*. Such men see men and women in rigid categories. Women should be weak, emotional, and submissive; men are expected to be tough, logical, and aggressive.
- *Drive to perform*. The masculine imperative is to live up to the ideal of what a man should be, and there is a pressure to always give a better performance.
- *Devotion to work*. Many men put much of their energy into external signs of success. Thus, little is left over for their wife and children. They often grew up in an environment where women were not given a high value and where relationships were not important. Instead, success, achievement, and productivity were valued.

The Price of Remaining in Traditional Roles

What price must a man pay for denying most of his inner self and putting on a false front? First, he loses a sense of himself because of his concern with being the way he thinks he should be as a male. Writing on the "lethal aspects of the male role," Sidney Jourard (1971) contends that men typically find it difficult to love and be loved. They won't reveal themselves enough to be loved. They hide their loneliness, anxiety, and hunger for affection, thus making it difficult for anyone to love them as they really are.

Another price the guarded male must pay for his seclusion is that he must always be vigilant for fear that someone might discover what is beneath his armor. Jourard puts this point well:

> He may, in an unguarded moment, reveal his true self in its nakedness, thereby exposing his areas of weakness and vulnerability. Naturally, when a person is in hostile territory, he must be continually alert, tense, opaque, and restless. All this implies that trying to seem manly is a kind of work, and work imposes stress and consumes energy. Manliness, then, seems to carry with it a chronic burden of stress and energy expenditure which could be a factor related to man's relatively shorter life span [pp. 35–36].

In his excellent book *The Hazards of Being Male*, Goldberg (1976) cites evidence showing that men tend to die at an earlier age than women do, that they suffer from cardiovascular problems more than women do, that boys do more poorly than girls in school, that men are involved in more crime than women are, and that the suicide rate is higher for males than for females. Goldberg makes the point that all the statistics that point to the hazards of being male actually constitute a description of the crises faced by males in our society. He contends that "the male has become an

artist in the creation of many hidden ways of killing himself" (p. 189) and calls for a "revolution" in male consciousness.[1]

In a later book, *The New Male*, Goldberg (1979) develops the idea that, if men continue to cling to the traditional masculine blueprint, they will end their life as a pathetic throwaway who is abandoned and asleep. He describes such men as alive at 20, machines at 30, and burned out by 40. During their twenties most of their energies are directed toward "making it" while denying important needs and feelings. At 20 these men are typically urgently sexual, restless and passionate about converting their ideas into reality, eager to push themselves to their limits (if they recognize any), curious and adventurous, and optimistic about the possibilities for living. In his early twenties the traditional male is driven by societal pressures to prove his manliness, long before he is aware of who he is and what it is that he really wants for himself. Therefore, he locks himself into a cage and becomes trapped in his life situation, with few apparent choices. At 30 he has convinced himself that he is not a person but a machine that has to function so the job can get done. By his forties he may experience a "male menopause" as his functioning begins to break down. Goldberg sees this decline as the result of years of repression and emotional denial, which

[1]From *The Hazards of Being Male*, by H. Goldberg. Copyright 1976 by Nash Publishing Company. Reprinted by permission.

makes him a danger to both himself and to others. Because his anxiety would be too much to deal with if he were to accept that he had been a self-destructive conformist, he may urge other young men to pay the same dues as he did for entry into the "macho" club.

Challenging Traditional Male Roles

Although this appears to be a gloomy picture of the typical male, we must acknowledge that today more and more men are challenging the conditioning that directs them to fall passively into the traditional male role. I am thinking of several men who *did* recognize that they had allowed themselves to become machines and who realized that they were slaves to a hollow image of themselves. Kevin is an example of such a person. So is Leroy, who told me the following:

> I was a driving and driven man who was too busy to smell the flowers. My single goal in life was to prove myself and become a financial and business success. I was on my way to becoming the president of a corporation, and I was thinking that I had it made. When I got my W-2 form, I became aware that I had made more money than was in my plan for success, yet I had had a miserable year. I decided that I wanted to experience life, to smell more flowers, and to not kill myself with a program that I had never consciously chosen for myself.

Leroy's decision did not come easy. It was, and continues to be, a real struggle for him to admit that he is only human. It is not easy for him to allow himself to experience and express feelings, yet he is making fine strides at becoming a very sensitive, caring, and expressive man. He is actively "talking back" to "inner voices within him" that tell him he *must* keep driving himself, that he *must* constantly set and conquer new goals, and that he does not have the time to enjoy and savor life. For him a turning point was landing in the hospital and almost dying. This jarred him into accepting that he was not an indestructible machine. Commenting on the impact of this experience, Leroy said:

> To me, life was a constant struggle, and I could never let down. Life was a series of performances that involved me pleasing others and then waiting for the applause to come. The applause was never enough, because I prostituted myself. I was always disappointed by the applause, because I felt empty when the applause would die down. So I continued to push myself to give more performances. But out of my illness I began to look at my life and slow down, and I realized there is a world out there that does not solely involve my work. I decided to work no more than 50 hours a week; before getting sick I was working 70 to 90 hours a week. With that extra time, I decided to smell life—there are a lot of roses in life, and the scent is enticing and exciting to me. I'll thrive on it as long as I can breathe it.

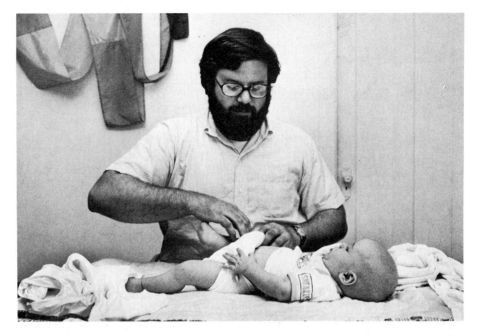

At 37 years of age, Leroy showed the courage to reverse some of the self-destructive patterns that were killing him. He began deciding for himself what kind of man he wanted to be, rather than living by an image of the man that others thought he should be.

Leroy says that he likes roses because of the scent, even though they do have thorns that hurt. He is now convinced that the scent makes up for the thorns. While he experiences more emotional pain than he ever allowed himself to feel before, he also experiences joy and sharing that he never knew before. He and his wife, Angie, lived separately for nearly two years, which apparently helped each of them clarify what they wanted. Although both of them experienced some loneliness, they found inner strength and discovered that they could exist without one another. This time alone helped Leroy take a look at his priorities and clarify some options. Eventually he initiated steps that resulted in the two of them living together again. This time both were stronger as individuals and also had more to give to each other. At the time they decided to live as a couple again, they also got involved in marital counseling as a way of helping them to define a new relationship. They have been reunited for over two years, and they enjoy each other more than they ever had before; they are also able to face each other more directly and fight constructively when this is called for. They have their differences, yet they can talk about them, and neither insists that the other fit the picture of the "ideal person."

Leroy continues to be aware of choosing a less stressful life-style than the one he had before his illness. By resisting the pressures of becoming a "corporation man," he paid the price of losing his job—and later another one. At this time he is unemployed, yet he reports that he feels far less stress now than he did when he worked for the corporation. He is considering two job offers. One involves a considerable amount of travel and professional challenge. The other, while secure, is less challenging and involves no extended travel. Leroy likes having more time with his wife, and they are considering starting a family. He is therefore carefully contemplating which job would most suit his present life-style.

TIME OUT FOR PERSONAL REFLECTION

1. *There are common myths and misconceptions associated with being a woman and being a man. Take the following inventory by writing an "A" in the blank on the left if you agree more than you disagree with the statement or a "D" in the blank if you disagree more than agree. Then, in the next space, answer the statement in the way you think most of your friends and associates of the* same sex *as you would be likely to respond.*

Statements about men:

_____ _____   a. *Men are defined by what they achieve.*
_____ _____   b. *Men are basically aggressive by nature.*
_____ _____   c. *Men have a need to feel superior.*
_____ _____   d. *Men should have more social freedom than women.*
_____ _____   e. *Men should always display courage and be strong.*
_____ _____   f. *Men should protect women.*
_____ _____   g. *Men are primarily concerned about the world of work.*
_____ _____   h. *Men ought to make women feel important.*
_____ _____   i. *Men ought to respond rationally rather than emotionally.*
_____ _____   j. *Men have a basic need to be competitive.*

Statements about women:

_____ _____   a. *Women by nature have a need to have and take care of children.*
_____ _____   b. *Women should be less active than men.*
_____ _____   c. *Women define themselves by giving to others.*
_____ _____   d. *Women should make a primary commitment to the home.*
_____ _____   e. *Women should make the men in their life feel important.*
_____ _____   f. *Women should not have a career if it jeopardizes their family life.*
_____ _____   g. *Women should be faithful to the men in their life.*
_____ _____   h. *Women are typically hurt very easily.*
_____ _____   i. *Women, by nature, are more emotional than logical.*
_____ _____   j. *Women should not be too assertive and surely not aggressive.*

Now, compare your responses with those of others in your class, both men and women. Are there many differences? Also, you could discuss the degree to which your attitudes concerning sex roles might have been influenced by your environment. A lively discussion could be

*geared around determining which of the above statements are per-
ceived as myths and misconceptions and which are seen as "facts of
life."*

2. *Are there genuine sex differences between women and men? Below are
some popular stereotypes. As you did in the above inventory, decide
whether you are more in agreement (A) or disagreement (D) with each
statement.*

   a. *Women are more susceptible to persuasion than are men.*

   b. *Women react with more emotion to stressful events than do men.*

   c. *Women are more passive than men.*

   d. *Women are more interested in people, whereas men are more interested in things.*

   e. *Women are more dependent on love relationships than men.*

   f. *Women are more sensitive to the feelings of others than are men.*

   g. *Women are more accurate than men in understanding nonverbal
signals.*

   h. *Women are less interested in sex than are men.*

SIMILARITIES BETWEEN WOMEN & MEN GREATLY OUTWEIGH THE DIFFERENCES.

_____   _____   *i. Women are more nurturant than men.*
_____   _____   *j. Women tend to be less aggressive than men.*

In reviewing research evidence on the above popular stereotypes, Weiten (1983) found that there was some research evidence to support statements "c," "f," "g," and "j"; research evidence did not support statements "a," "b," "d," "e," "h," and "i." In general, according to Weiten, the stereotypes had little relation to reality. He concluded that the similarities between women and men greatly outweighed the differences. Sex-role stereotypes lead to errors in social perception, and this inaccurate perception is often harmful to one's psychological health and interferes with social relationships.

FEMALE ROLES

Like men, women in our society have suffered from a sexual stereotype. Typically, women have been perceived as weak, fragile, unambitious, helpless, unintelligent, designed by nature for the role of homemaker and mother, unassertive, noncompetitive, and unadventurous. This rigid viewpoint is in the process of changing as many women actively fight the stereotype of the passive, dependent female.

Traditional Roles for Women

How are these sexual stereotypes formed? Deaux (1976) cites evidence that boys and girls are conditioned early in life to accept predetermined sex roles. She indicates, for example, that boys are often seen as curious, active, and independent, while girls are seen as lacking in curiosity, having little initiative, and needing help from boys. Not long ago, reading primers showed men as the ones who solved problems and went to work, while the women were typically shown in the kitchen. Deaux also cites a study showing how television and magazines influence children to accept sex-role stereotypes. Men usually appear in advertisements and commercials when figures who suggest authority are needed; by contrast, women are usually the principal figures when commercials deal with the use of household products. In summary, Deaux makes the point that "parents and other socializing agents convey certain expectations to their children as to what grown-up men and women are like. These impressions may form the basis of stereotypes that are found much later in life" (1976, p. 20).

Are these stereotypes changing? According to Deaux, if children have good models in the home and if they see changes in male and female images in the media, the stereotypes may well change in the future, but

for now "we must conclude that stereotypes are still alive and doing reasonably well in our culture" (p. 21).

In summarizing studies done on sex-role stereotypes, Basow (1980) cites considerable research evidence supporting their existence. Women, more so than men, are seen as exhibiting these qualities: gentleness, sensitivity, ability to express feelings, tactfulness, religiosity, and interest in relationships. Brooks-Gunn and Matthews (1979), in their book *He and She: How Children Develop Their Sex-Role Identity*, write that stereotypes still persist and continue to affect the way we are perceived by others. Sex-role stereotypes influence societal practices, discrimination, individual beliefs, and sex-related behavior itself. The authors contend that sensitizing ourselves to the process of sex-role development can help us to make choices about modifying the results of our socialization.

Challenging Traditional Female Roles

Despite the staying power of sexual stereotypes, increasing numbers of women are rejecting limited views of what a woman is expected to be. They are discovering that they can indeed have many of the traits traditionally attributed to them yet at the same time take a new view of themselves. Today's women are pursuing careers that in earlier times were closed to them. They are demanding equal pay for equal work. Many women are making the choice to postpone marriage and child rearing until they have established themselves in a career, and some are deciding not to have children. Choosing a single life is now an acceptable option. In dual-career marriages there is considerable sharing of responsibilities that previously were allocated to one or the other sex. Women are assuming positions of leadership in government and business. One such significant turning point is the fact that in 1984 a woman ran for vice-president of the United States. There are signs that women are questioning many of the attitudes they have incorporated and that they are resisting the pressures of conforming to traditional sex-role behaviors.

In particular, many women are challenging the pressures put on them to find their satisfactions exclusively or primarily in marriage and the raising of a family. Contending that the "earth mother is dead," Goldberg (1976) writes that contemporary women are showing their true identities. They are no longer willing to conspire with men in fostering the image of themselves as weak, helpless, and designed primarily to take care of men's needs and the needs of their children.

Goldberg views this assertiveness on the part of women as liberating not only for themselves but for men as well, because it frees men from the need to live up to the macho image. When both men and women are free of restrictive roles and thus free to be the persons they *could* be, they can develop authentic relationships with one another based on their individual strengths instead of on a game in which one must be weak so that the other can be strong. In Goldberg's words, "When she is she in her genuine, total, strong femaleness and personhood and he is he in his maleness and personhood, they can begin to revel in the realities and joys of an authentic, interdependent, and genuinely fulfilling interaction" (1976, p. 32).

Difficulties and Fears.   As women begin to challenge their sex-role identity, they often underestimate the difficulties they will encounter. In her popular book *The Cinderella Complex*, Dowling (1981) clearly describes women's struggle in achieving independence. Women's strivings to be independent and successful are accompanied by many fears. As have men, women have been subject to conditioning for many years, and they experience anxiety when they step out of well-defined roles governing their behavior. For example, many women are still not able to enjoy their achievements because of their fear of being perceived as "unfeminine." One of the themes in Dowling's book is that women have not kept pace on an emotional level with what they know intellectually about living more freely. While they may *think* independently, they often *feel* emotionally dependent.

As can be seen, women of today have more options than their counterparts in the past, but this increase brings with it an increase in anxiety.

Well-defined roles can be restrictive, but they can also be secure, and many contemporary women experience difficulty when they look inward and attempt to decide what they want. Moreover, many of these women actually feel uncomfortable with choices that will lead to success. They have been conditioned for so long *not* to experience success in the outside world that they have a real fear of succeeding. Deaux (1976) describes research suggesting that, even though women may have a need to achieve, they may also have a motive to *avoid* achieving too much. They have learned to expect negative social consequences if they do succeed. Deaux indicates that the percentage of women who fear success does not appear to be decreasing greatly.

Certainly, to maximize her options a woman needs to be alert to the danger of keeping herself locked into old roles and denying her talents. She must avoid the pitfall of blaming the dissatisfaction she feels on circumstances outside herself. At the same time, she can recognize that stepping out of old roles can be frightening, and she can try to become aware of what her fears and anxieties are. Just as she can question the traditional female stereotype, she can also question the myth that a successful and independent woman doesn't need anyone and can make it entirely on her own. This trap is very much like the trap that many males fall into and may even represent an assimilation of traditionally male values. Hopefully, a woman can learn that she can achieve independence, exhibit strength, and succeed while at times being dependent and in need of nurturing. Real strength allows either a woman or a man to be needy and to ask for nurturing without feeling personally inadequate.

Some women experience a lack of support and an actual resistance from the men in their life when they do step outside of traditional roles and exercise some of their options. Basow (1980) notes that, since men typically have been the dominant sex, with most of the power, it is difficult for them to share this power with women.

In her counseling practice Marianne finds that many women struggle with attempting to balance a career outside of the home with their career at home. Their husbands, who sometimes see themselves as liberated, are put to the test when they are expected to assume an increasing share in the responsibilities at home. They may say that they want their wives to "emerge and become fulfilled persons," yet they may also send messages such as: "Don't go *too* far!" "Don't abandon the ship by throwing aside the traditional expectations." "Have a life outside of the home, but don't give up any of what you are doing at home." In addition, some of the problems that women experience in going beyond their traditionally expected roles are simply the result of having added an unrealistic load of responsibilities on themselves. While a woman may have to fight her husband's resistance to her change, the major fight is frequently with herself. Her internal war may be far more intense than her confrontations with others. She may say to herself one of the following sentences, some of which are rational and others irrational:

- "I must be a good mother, a good wife, and a good housekeeper."
- "If I don't take care of the kids, who will?"
- "If I'm not around to see that the house is kept up, the place will become unlivable."
- "If I were competent, I could manage both careers, without anything or anyone in my life suffering."

Both husband and wife may need to look at how realistic it is to expect that she can have a career while at the same time retaining all of her responsibilities for cleaning the house, cooking the meals, and being primarily responsible for the children. No easy answers are available, but a continuing redefinition and renegotiation of what either partner is and is not willing to do are essential.

One Woman's Struggle

Susan is one of the many women who are struggling to break out of rigid, traditional roles that are thwarting their move toward greater independence. She married at an early age. In high school she was an exceptional student and had aspirations to go to college but was discouraged from doing so by her family. They encouraged her to marry the "nice guy" whom she had been dating through high school, letting her know that she would risk losing him if she went off to college. Her parents maintained that he could provide a good future for her and that it was not necessary for her to pursue college or a career. Without much questioning of what she was told, she got married and had two children. To an outside observer, it appeared that she had a good life, that she was well provided for, and that she and her husband were getting along well.

In reflecting over the history of her marriage, Susan remembers first feeling restless and dissatisfied with her life when her children went to school. Her husband, David, was advancing in his career and was getting most of his satisfaction from his work. Around him she felt rather dull and had a vague feeling that something was missing from her life. She had never forgotten her aspiration to attend college, and eventually she enrolled. Although David was not supportive initially, he later encouraged her to complete her education. But he made it clear that he expected her not to neglect her primary responsibilities to the family.

As Susan pursued her college education, she was often torn between performing her multiple and sometimes conflicting roles. She was an excellent student, she loved her association with her peers, and she sometimes felt guilty about how much she was enjoying being away from her family. For the first time in her life she was being known as herself and not as someone's daughter or wife. Even though she enjoyed her academic success, it frightened her. It was easy for David to trigger her guilt over not being an adequate mother and wife. Although at times he felt threatened by her increasing independence from him, he did like and respect the person she was becoming. And she herself liked her ever-growing ability to stand on her own two feet. Neither of them talked about divorce, but she felt reassured that she was staying with him out of choice and that she wanted him more than she needed him.

Susan's situation demonstrates that women who for many years have followed traditional roles can successfully leave them and define new roles for themselves. Some of the themes that Susan, and many women like her, struggle with are dependence versus independence, fear of success, looking outside of one's self for support and direction, expecting to be taken care of by others, and questioning the expectations of others.

You might take a few minutes to think about couples you know to see if any of them have much in common with Susan and David. Do you think that deviating from traditional sex roles will have a positive or negative impact on a couple's relationship? Can you think of ways that each individual can continue to grow as a person without putting undue stress on a relationship? Do you have any concerns about becoming the person you want to become yet at the same time not jeopardizing a relationship with another person?

TIME OUT FOR PERSONAL REFLECTION

Collette Dowling's national best-seller The Cinderella Complex *describes women's hidden fear of independence and the roots of their inner conflicts as they struggle toward liberation. What follows are some of the points Dowling makes in her book. After reading each statement, place an "A" in the blank if you agree more than you disagree with it, and place a "D" in the blank if you disagree more than you agree with it.*

1. *Freedom and independence can't be wrested from others, from society, or from men; it can only be achieved, painstakingly, from within.*
2. *Liberated women are able to move toward the things that are satisfying to them and away from those that are not.*
3. *Women in our society have been conditioned to fear success.*
4. *Most women actually have a fear of independence.*
5. *Women have typically been brought up thinking that asserting themselves is unfeminine.*
6. *Women's anxiety over failure relates to their feeling inadequate and defenseless in the world.*
7. *Although there is a tendency of women to try to solve their problems by changing things externally (getting married, changing jobs, fighting*

for women's rights), such external changes will not help them to change self-destructive attitudes.

_____ 8. *Women who want to achieve a better self-image must begin by recognizing what's going on inside of them.*

_____ 9. *Women will not experience real change and genuine emancipation until they combat the anxieties that prevent them from feeling competent and whole as persons.*

_____ 10. *Ultimately, women will not achieve genuine liberation from anyone other than themselves.*

The central message of Dowling's book is that psychological dependency, or the wish to be taken care of by others, is the major force holding women down. The author's thesis is that, like Cinderella, women today are still waiting for something or someone external to transform their life. What are your reactions to Dowling's thesis? What path do you think women need to take to free them from the restrictions of their sex-role socialization and to achieve psychological independence?

_____

_____

_____

_____

_____

LIBERATION FOR BOTH WOMEN AND MEN

The increasing liberation of women has also stimulated to some degree the liberation of men. Warren Farrell (1975) contends that, if a man were relieved of the responsibility of being the primary breadwinner, he would probably have far fewer fears about losing his job and feel freer to pursue a line of work that interested and excited him. He might feel less pressured to be the sole source of his spouse's happiness, less hassled by staying afloat in competition, and more open to deriving satisfaction from something other than his work. He might be more interested in spending time with his children, in pursuing hobbies, and in developing relationships based on feelings rather than on security. Finally, he would probably experience less anxiety about his sex role and might develop a set of values that gave a new richness to living.

I want to emphasize that both sexes need to remain open to the other and to change their attitudes if they are interested in releasing themselves from stereotyped roles. People of both sexes seem to be in a transitional period in which they are redefining themselves and ridding themselves of

old stereotypes; yet too often they are needlessly fighting with each other when they could be helping each other to recognize that they have *both* been conditioned for many years and that they need to be patient as each learns new patterns of thought and behavior.

Many women and men want the same thing—to loosen the rigid sex-role expectations that have trapped them. Many men recognize a need to broaden their view of themselves to include capacities that have been traditionally stereotyped as feminine and that they have consequently denied in themselves. Many women are seeking to give expression to a side of themselves that has been associated with males. As men and women alike pay closer attention to attitudes that are deeply ingrained in themselves, they may find that they haven't caught up emotionally with their intellectual level of awareness. Although we might well be "liberated" intellectually and *know* what we want, many of us have difficulty in *feeling* OK about what we want. The challenge is getting the two together!

Alternatives to Rigid Sex Roles

The fact that certain male and female stereotypes have been prevalent in our culture doesn't mean that all men and women live within these narrow confines. Nevertheless, many people uncritically accept rigid definitions of their roles, while others just as uncritically reject them; and probably even liberated people are affected by some vestiges of sexual stereotypes. Fortunately, there is much challenging of traditional perspectives among the college students I come in contact with. For instance, more and more men are apparently realizing that they can combine self-confidence, assertiveness, and power with tenderness, warmth, and self-expressiveness. The macho male doesn't seem to be admired or respected by either the men or the women I encounter on the university campus.

The alternative to living according to a stereotype is to realize that we can actively define our own standards of what we want to be like as women or as men. We don't have to blindly accept roles and expectations that have been imposed on us or remain victims of our early conditioning. We can begin to achieve autonomy in our sexual identity by looking at how we have formed our ideals and standards and who our models have been; then we can decide whether these are the standards we want to use in defining ourselves now.

One appealing alternative to rigid sex-role stereotypes is the concept of *androgyny,* or the coexistence of male and female characteristics in the same person. We all secrete some male and female hormones, and many psychologists postulate that we also have both feminine and masculine psychological characteristics. For example, Carl Jung developed the notions of the *animus* and the *anima,* which refer to the (usually hidden) masculine and feminine aspects within us. Taken together, the *animus* and the *anima* reflect Jung's conception of humans as bisexual in nature. Since women share in some of the psychological characteristics of men (through their *animus*), and since men possess some feminine aspects (through their *anima*), both are better enabled to understand the opposite sex. Jung was very insistent that women and men must express both dimensions of their personality. Failure to do so results in one-sided development. Thus, becoming fully human entails the expression of the full range of these personality characteristics.[2]

Deaux (1976) cites research indicating that an androgynous person has a wider range of capacities than a person who lives by sex-typed expectations. For example, an androgynous person can show "masculine" assertiveness or "feminine" warmth, depending on what a situation calls for. For Deaux, androgyny is a promising concept that deserves further attention. One of the central themes of her book *The Behavior of Women and Men* is that there are relatively few characteristics in which women and men consistently differ:

> Men and women both seem to be capable of being aggressive, helpful, and alternately cooperative and competitive. In other words, there is little evidence that the nature of women and men is so inherently

[2]For those who wish to pursue Jung's ideas further, a good basic book is *A Primer of Jungian Psychology* (Hall & Nordby, 1973).

different that we are justified in making stereotyped generalizations [Deaux, 1976, p. 144].

Basow (1980), in her book *Sex-Role Stereotypes: Traditions and Alternatives,* writes that androgyny does not imply being neuter or, indeed, anything else about one's sexual orientation. Rather, it refers to a person's flexibility in sex-role behaviors. Thus, androgynous people may perceive themselves as being understanding, affectionate, and considerate *and* self-reliant, independent, and firm.

According to Basow, the ultimate goal is to move toward androgyny *and beyond* by transcending traditional sex-role polarities to reach a new level of synthesis. Thus, a person is able to move freely in a variety of situations. The same person could be compassionate with a friend, assertive with a fellow worker, and tender with a child. In this view, the world is not divided into polarities of masculinity and femininity; rather, people have a range of potentials that can be adapted to a range of situations.

In his stimulating book *Passive Men, Wild Women,* Mornell (1979) calls for us to learn to accept all sides of our complex personality. He discourages looking for easy answers that speak about dependence *or* independence, tenderness *or* tough-mindedness, dominance *or* submissiveness, and being a work person *or* a home person. For Mornell,

> the ultimate answer . . . *begins* with our refusing to accept the man as passive and the woman as wild, and in our seeing the problem for what it is. Let us accept and even enjoy our basic differences. Let us learn with and from each other what we may have never learned from our own fathers, mothers, or our society: how to accept our human differences and still be strong individuals, active partners, and involved lovers [1979, p. 94].

The real challenge is for us to choose the kind of woman or man we want to be and not be determined by passive acceptance of a cultural stereotype or blind identification with some form of rebellion.

At this point take a few minutes to refer to the Sex-Role Inventory (Resource 8). Doing so is a way for you to assess to what degree you are androgynous.

TIME OUT FOR PERSONAL REFLECTION

1. The following statements may help you assess how you see yourself in relation to sex roles. Place a "T" before each statement that generally applies to you and an "F" before each one that generally doesn't apply to you. Be sure to respond as you are now, *rather than as you'd like to be.*

_____   *I'd rather be rational than emotional.*
_____   *I'm more an active person than a passive person.*
_____   *I'm more cooperative than I am competitive.*
_____   *I tend to express my feelings rather than keeping them hidden.*
_____   *I tend to live by what is expected of my sex.*
_____   *I see myself as possessing both masculine and feminine characteristics.*
_____   *I'm afraid of deviating very much from the customary sex-role norms.*
_____   *I'm adventurous in most situations.*
_____   *I feel OK about expressing both negative and positive feelings.*
_____   *I'm continually striving for success.*
_____   *I fear success as much as I fear failure.*

Now look over your responses. Which characteristics, if any, would you like to change in yourself?

_____

_____

_____

2. *What are some of your reactions to the changes in women's view of their sex role? What impact do you think the feminist movement has had on women? on men?*

_____

_____

_____

_____

_____

3. *What do you think of the concept of androgyny? Would you like to possess more of the qualities you associate with the opposite sex? If so, what are they? Are there any ways in which you feel limited or restricted by rigid sex-role definitions and expectations?*

_____

_____

_____

_____

_____

CHAPTER SUMMARY

Many men have become prisoners of a stereotypic role that they feel they must live by. Writers who address the problems of traditional male roles have focused on characteristics such as independence, aggressiveness, denial of fears, self-protection, lack of bodily awareness, denial of "feminine" qualities, rigidity, being driven by work, and fears of intimacy. Fortunately, an increasing number of men are challenging the restrictions of these traditional roles, for they are realizing the price that they must pay by living by certain cultural injunctions.

Women, too, have been restricted by their cultural conditioning and by accepting sex-role stereotypes that have kept them in an inferior position in the past. Despite the staying power of these traditional female role expectations, more and more women are rejecting the limited vision of what a woman is "expected" to be. Like men, women are gaining increased intellectual awareness of alternative roles they can adopt, yet they often struggle emotionally in *feeling* and *acting* in ways that are different from their upbringing. The challenge for both sexes is to keep pace on an emotional level with what they know intellectually about living more freely.

In this chapter I've encouraged you to think about your attitudes and values concerning sex roles and to take a close look at how you developed them. Granted that there are definite cultural pressures to adopt given sex roles, we are not hopelessly cemented into a rigid way of being. We can challenge those sex-role expectations that seem restricting to us, and we can then determine if the costs of having adopted certain roles are worth the potential gains. In asking you to examine the basis of your sex-role expectations and your concept of what constitutes a woman or a man, I've stressed the idea that ultimately you can decide for yourself what kind of woman or man you want to be, instead of following the expectations of others.

ACTIVITIES AND EXERCISES

1. Write down the characteristics you associate with being a woman (or feminine) and being a man (or masculine). Then think about how you acquired these views and to what degree you're satisfied with them. Refer to the Time Out for Personal Reflection on page 140 for a review of popular stereotypes associated with men and women.
2. The chapter has developed the idea that many men and women are

challenging traditional roles. Based on your own observations, to what extent do you find this to be true? Do your friends typically accept traditional roles, or do they tend to challenge society's expectations?

3. Interview people from a cultural group different from your own. Describe some of the common gender stereotypes mentioned in this chapter and determine if such stereotypes are true of the other cultural group.

4. Make a list of sex-role stereotypes that apply to men and a list of those that apply to women. Then select people of various ages, and ask them to say how much they agree or disagree with each of these stereotypes. If several people bring their results to class, you might have the basis of an interesting panel discussion.

5. For a week or two, pay close attention to the messages that you see transmitted on television, both in programs and in commercials, regarding sex roles and expectations of women and men. Record your impressions in your journal.

SUGGESTED READINGS

Basow, S. A. (1980). *Sex-Role Stereotypes: Traditions and Alternatives*. Monterey, Calif.: Brooks/Cole. This book is aimed at exploring these questions: How did sex-role stereotypes originate? How are they maintained and transmitted? How can one break free from them and change? Breaking free of stereotypes is aided by the concept of androgyny, which aims at a flexible integration of masculine and feminine attributes in one person.

Brooks-Gunn, J., & Matthews, W. S. (1979). *He and She: How Children Develop Their Sex-Role Identity*. Englewood Cliffs, N.J.: Prentice-Hall (Spectrum). A thought-provoking and personal book that challenges readers to examine patterns of socialization and the bases upon which they learned to become "feminine" or "masculine." The development of sex-role identity is traced from infancy through adolescence. The book contains a comprehensive bibliography for those who wish to pursue their study further.

Deaux, K. (1976). *The Behavior of Women and Men*. Monterey, Calif.: Brooks/Cole. A very informative work that deals with both stereotypes and self-evaluations of women and men. The book also includes an excellent treatment of the concept of androgyny.

Goldberg, H. (1976). *The Hazards of Being Male*. New York: Nash. An excellent treatment of the stereotypes of masculinity. The author describes the traps males have fallen into and ways of getting out of them.

Goldberg, H. (1979). *The New Male*. New York: New American Library (Signet). The author writes about how changes in each sex affect the other. He describes the crisis of the contemporary male and makes some suggestions for how to stop being a machine and become a person.

Kiley, D. (1983). *The Peter Pan Syndrome.* New York: Avon. This best-seller describes men who have never grown up. The main characteristics of the syndrome are irresponsibility, anxiety, loneliness, sex-role conflict, narcissism, chauvinism, social impotence, and despondency.

Mornell, P. (1979). *Passive Men, Wild Women.* New York: Ballantine. The author makes the point that men and women often react to and bring out each other's worst side. In a clear style, he describes men who are alive at work and dead at home and talks about the problems of passionate women who live with passive men.

6

SEXUALITY

PRECHAPTER SELF-INVENTORY

Use the following scale to respond: 4 = this statement is true of me *most* of the time; 3 = this statement is true of me *much* of the time; 2 = this statement is true of me *some* of the time; 1 = this statement is true of me *almost none* of the time.

————————   1. I think that the quality of a sexual relationship usually depends on the general quality of the relationship.

————————   2. I believe that exercising sexual freedom creates corresponding responsibilities.

————————   3. I find it easy to talk openly and honestly about sexuality with at least one other person.

————————   4. For me, sex without love is unsatisfying.

————————   5. I experience guilt or shame over sexuality.

————————   6. I have found that sex-role definitions and stereotypes get in the way of mutually satisfying sexual relations.

————————   7. Sensual experiences do not necessarily have to be sexual.

————————   8. Performance standards and expectations get in the way of my enjoying sensual and sexual experiences.

————————   9. I have struggled to find my own values pertaining to sexual behavior.

————————   10. I believe that I acquired healthy attitudes about sexuality from my parents.

INTRODUCTION

People of all ages experience difficulty at times in talking openly about sexual matters. This lack of communication contributes to the perpetuation of myths and misinformation about sexuality. It is true that the media are giving increased attention to all aspects of sexual behavior, to the point of bombarding us with new information and trends. Almost nothing is unmentionable in the popular media. Yet this increased knowledge regarding sexuality does not appear to have resulted in encouraging all people to talk more freely about their own sexual concerns, nor has it always reduced their anxiety about sexuality. For many people sex remains a delicate topic, to the extent that they find it difficult to communicate their sexual wants, especially to a person close to them.

A goal of this chapter is to introduce the idea of learning how to recognize and openly express our sexual concerns. Too many people suffer from needless guilt, shame, worries, and inhibition merely because they keep their concerns about sexuality secret, largely out of embarrassment. Moreover, keeping their concerns to themselves can hinder their efforts to determine their own values regarding sex. In this chapter I ask you to examine your values and attitudes toward sexuality and to determine what choices *you* want to make in this area of your life.

Myths and Misconceptions about Sexuality

What follows are some illustrations of statements that I consider to be misconceptions about sex. As you read over this list, ask yourself what your attitudes are and where you developed these beliefs. Are they working for you? Could any of the following statements apply to you? How might some of these statements affect your ability to make free choices concerning sexuality?

- If I allow myself to become sexual, I'll get into trouble.
- Women should be less active than men in sex.
- Women are not as sexy when they initiate.
- As you get older, you're bound to lose interest in sex.
- If my partner really loved me, I would not have to tell him or her what I liked or wanted; knowing what I need intuitively without my asking is a sign of love.
- If I had negative conditioning regarding sex as I was growing up, I can't hope to overcome this limitation and am doomed never to fully enjoy sexual experiences.
- Acting without any guilt or restrictions is what is meant by being sexually free.
- The more a person knows about the mechanics of sex, the more he or she will be satisfied with sexual relationships.
- I am not responsible for the level of my sexual satisfaction.
- My partner would be offended and hurt if I told him or her what I liked and wanted.
- Some people find that the only place they get along well together is in bed.
- Being sexually attracted to a person other than my partner implies that I don't really find my partner sexually exciting.
- There is only one right person for me.
- Multiple sexual relationships enhance a primary relationship.
- An exclusive relationship ensures a greater degree of emotional and sexual intensity than is true of an open relationship.
- The inability or unwillingness to engage in multiple sexual relationships indicates a lack of trust in oneself or at least a basic insecurity.
- The more physically attractive a person is, the more sexually exciting he or she is.
- With the passage of time, any sexual relationship is bound to become less exciting or grow stale.

What are a few sexual myths or misconceptions you think ought to be added to this list?

_____

_____

_____

_____

LEARNING TO TALK OPENLY ABOUT SEXUAL ISSUES

As in other areas of life, we sometimes saddle ourselves with beliefs about sex that we have not given much thought to. Open discussion with those you are intimate with, as well as an honest exchange of views in your class, can do a lot to help you challenge some of the unexamined attitudes you have about this significant area of your life. At this time I suggest that you refer to Resource 9, How Much Do You Know about Sexuality? Take this brief test to assess your knowledge about sexuality *before* continuing with this chapter.

Sharing Sexual Concerns

One might expect that young people today would be able to discuss openly and frankly the concerns they have about sex. Students will discuss attitudes about sexual behavior in a general way, but they show considerable resistance to speaking of their own sexual concerns, fears, and conflicts. I've come to believe that it can be a great service simply to provide a climate in which people can feel free to examine their personal concerns. A particularly valuable technique is to give women and men an opportunity to discuss sexual issues in separate groups and then come together to share the concerns they've discovered. Typically, both men and women appreciate the chance to explore their sexual fears, expectations, secrets, and wishes, as well as their concerns about the normality of their bodies and feelings. Then, when the male and female groups come together, the participants usually find that there is much common ground, and the experience of making this discovery can be very therapeutic. For instance, men may fear becoming impotent, not performing up to some expected standard, being lousy lovers, or not being "man enough." When the men and women meet as one group, the men may be surprised to discover that women worry about having to achieve orgasm (or several of them) every time they have sex and that they, too, have fears about their

sexual desirability. When people talk about these concerns in a direct way, much game playing and putting on of false fronts can be dispensed with.

My work with therapeutic groups continues to teach me how much we need to learn how to talk with each other about sexual concerns. Many people suffer from unrealistic fears that they are alone in their feelings and concerns about their sexuality. If we could learn how to initiate open discussion of these issues, we might find that genuine sexual freedom is possible. We could shed many of the fears that needlessly hamper our joy in freely experiencing sex.

In the past there was clearly a taboo against openly discussing sexual topics. Today, bookstores are flooded with paperbacks devoted to improving one's sex life. Although people may come to a counselor with greater awareness of sexuality, it is clear that many of them have not been able to translate their knowledge into a more satisfying sex life. In fact, their increased awareness of what is normal for women and men has sometimes had the effect of compounding their problems. They may burden themselves with expectations of what their sex life *should* be like, according to the latest studies. Counselors discover that couples are often very uncomfortable in communicating their sexual likes and dislikes, their personal fears, and the shame and guilt they sometimes have about sex. They still operate on the old myth that, if their mate really loves them, then he or she should know intuitively what gives them pleasure. To ask for what one wants sexually is often seen as diminishing the value of what is received.

Nevertheless, the outlook in this area is not totally negative. Whereas in the past a couple with sexual problems might have kept such problems locked behind their bedroom door, the trend now is toward a willingness to acknowledge these problems and to seek help. Indeed, many people are able to apply their knowledge about sexuality to enhancing their sex life. Many more are challenging the myths pertaining to sex.

At this point let me describe some of the typical concerns that are openly aired by both men and women in discussion groups I've participated in. These concerns might be expressed as follows:

- "I often wonder what excites my partner and what that person would like, yet I seldom ask. I suppose it's important for me to learn how to initiate by asking and also how to tell the other person what *I* enjoy."
- "So often I doubt my capacity as a lover. I'd like to know what my partner thinks. Perhaps one thing that I can learn to do is to share this concern with him (her)."
- "I worry about my body. Am I normal? How do I compare with others? Am I too big? too small? Am I proportioned properly? Do others find me attractive? Do I find myself attractive? What can I do to increase my own appeal to myself and to others?"
- "Am I responsible if my partner's dissatisfied?"
- "Sex can be fun, I suppose, but often I'm much too serious. It's really difficult for me to be playful and to let go without feeling foolish—and not just in regard to sex. It isn't easy for me to be spontaneous."
- "There are many times when I feel that my spouse is bored with sex, and that makes me wonder whether I'm sexually attractive to her (him)."
- "There are times when I desire sex and initiate it, and my husband (wife) lets me know in subtle or even direct ways that he (she) isn't interested. Then I feel almost like a beggar. This kind of experience makes me not want to initiate any more."
- "As a woman, I'd really like to know how other women feel after a sexual experience. Do they normally feel fulfilled? What prevents them from enjoying sex? How do they decide who's at fault when they don't have a positive experience?"
- "As a man, I frequently worry about performance standards, and that gets in the way of my making love freely and spontaneously. It's a burden to me to worry about doing the right things and being sexually powerful, and I often wonder what other men experience in this area."
- "There seem to be two extremes in sex: we can be overly concerned with pleasing our partner and therefore take too much responsibility for their sexual gratification, or we can become so involved with our own pleasure that we don't concern ourselves with our partner's feelings or needs. I ask myself how I can discover a balance—how I can be selfish enough to seek my own pleasure yet sensitive enough to take care of my partner's needs."

- "Sometimes I get scared of women (men), and I struggle with myself over whether I should let the other person know that I feel threatened. Will I be perceived as weak? Is it so terrible to be weak at times? Can I be weak and still be strong?"
- "I frequently feel guilty over my sexual feelings, but there are times when I wonder whether I really want to free myself of guilt feelings. What would happen if I were free of guilt? Would I give up all control?"
- "I worry a lot about being feminine (masculine) and all that it entails. I'm trying to separate out what I've been conditioned to believe about the way a woman (man) is supposed to be, yet I still have a hard time deciding for myself the kind of woman (man) I want to be. I want to find my own standards and not be haunted by external standards of what I should be and feel."
- "Can sex be an attempt to overcome my feelings of isolation and separation? There are times when I think I'm running into a sexual relationship because I feel lonely."
- "I've wondered whether we are by nature monogamous. I know I'd like to experience others sexually, but I surely don't want my mate to have these same experiences."
- "There are times lately when I don't seem to be enjoying sex much. In the past year, I haven't been able to experience orgasm, and the man that I'm living with thinks it's his fault. What's happening? Why am I not as sexually responsive as I used to be with him?"
- "I feel very open and trusting in talking about my sexuality in this group, and I'd very much like to experience this with my partner. I want to be able to be direct and avoid getting involved in sexual games. I need to learn how to initiate this kind of open dialogue."
- "There are times when I really don't crave intercourse but would still like to be held and touched and caressed. I wish my partner could understand this about me and not take it as a personal rejection when for some reason I simply don't want intercourse."
- "I really felt humiliated when I became impotent—I was sure she saw me as unmanly. I'm glad to learn that this is a common experience with other men and that I'm not abnormal."

SEX AND GUILT

Guilt over Sexual Feelings

Most of us have learned certain taboos about sex. We often feel guilty about our *feelings,* even if we don't act on them. Guilt is commonly experienced in connection with homosexual fantasies and impulses, feelings of sexual attraction toward members of one's family, sexual feelings toward people other than one's spouse, enjoyment of sexuality, and too much (or too little) desire for sex. Even though we intensely fear such feelings, we can and should learn to accept them as legitimate. Moreover, simply having feelings doesn't mean that we're impelled to act on them.

As is the case of shame over our bodies, we need to become aware of our guilt and then to reexamine it to determine whether we're needlessly burdening ourselves. Not all guilt is unhealthy and irrational, of course, but there is a real value in learning to challenge guilt feelings and to rid ourselves of those that are *unrealistic*.

For many of my earlier years I experienced a great deal of guilt over my sexual feelings and fantasies. I believe that my guilt was largely due to the influence of a strict religious education that took a strong stand on sexual morality. Even though I've consciously struggled to overcome some of this influence, I still experience traces of old guilt. As in so many other areas, I find that early lessons in regard to sex are difficult to unlearn. Consequently, it has been important for me to continue to challenge old guilt patterns that interfere with my sexual enjoyment, while at the same time developing a personal ethical code that I can live by with integrity and self-respect.

Many people express some very real fears as they begin to recognize and accept their sexuality. A common fear is that, if we recognize or accept our sexual feelings, our impulses will sweep us away, leaving us out of control. It's important to learn that we can accept the full range of our sexual feelings yet decide for ourselves what we will *do* about them. For instance, I remember a man who said that he felt satisfied with his marriage and found his wife exciting but was troubled because he found other women appealing and sometimes desired them. Even though he had made a decision not to have extramarital affairs, he still experienced a high level of anxiety over simply having sexual feelings toward other women. At some level he believed that he might be more likely to *act* on his feelings if he fully accepted that he had them. In my opinion, he was torturing himself needlessly. I saw it as important that he learn to discriminate between having sexual feelings and deciding to take certain actions and that he learn to trust his own decisions.

In making responsible, inner-directed choices of whether to act on sexual feelings, many people find questions such as the following to be helpful guidelines: Will my actions hurt another person or myself? Will my actions limit another person's freedom? Will my actions exploit another's rights? Are my actions consistent with my commitments? Of course, each of us must decide on our own moral guidelines, but it seems unrealistic to expect that we can or should control our feelings in the same way that we can control our actions. By controlling our actions, we define who we are; by trying to deny or banish our feelings, we only become alienated from ourselves.

Guilt over Sexual Experiences

While some people are convinced that in these "modern times" college students do not suffer guilt feelings related to sexual behaviors, my observations show me that this is not the case. College students, whether single or married, young or middle-aged, often report a variety of experiences over which they feel guilty. Guilt may be related to masturbation, extramarital (or "extrapartner") affairs, homosexual behavior, sexual practices that are sometimes considered deviant, and the practice of having sex with many partners.

Sources of Guilt.   Sex therapists emphasize early sexual learning as a crucial factor in one's later sexual adjustment. They assume that current guilt feelings often stem from both unconscious and conscious decisions that were made in response to verbal and nonverbal messages about sexuality.

In their comprehensive volume *Sexual Choices*, Nass, Libby, and Fisher (1984) discuss the acquiring of sexual information and its relationship to developing guilt feelings. They write that our early recollections of where we learned about sex are typically fuzzy. Although we may remember selected incidents, where and when we developed certain attitudes and feelings about sex are often not a part of our consciousness. According to these authors, some of the major sources of basic information on sexual matters are parents, peers, the media, and sex-education programs.

Nass, Libby, and Fisher see parents as the earliest shapers of sexual attitudes. For example, erotic activities such as masturbation and sex play may result in punishment, or they may not be given any labels that children can understand. This process of "nonlabeling" of erotic activities and body parts can lead children to deny their own sexuality. If children are not given words for their sexual experiences, they can easily develop inaccurate beliefs and guilt feelings pertaining to natural feelings and behavior. If parents restrict their vocabulary by referring to the genitals as simply organs of excretion, then children are likely to assume that sexual pleasure is "dirty" or unnatural. Such distortions or omissions of information create a hidden attitude toward sexuality through which later sex information is bound to be filtered.

Peers often fill the void left by parents. However, reliance on the same-sex peer group usually results in learning inaccurate sexual information, which can later lead to fears and guilt over sexual feelings and activities. Most sex information from the peer group is imparted during the early teen years. Many distorted notions are incorporated, such as: "If you masturbate, your penis will fall off." "Kissing may lead to getting pregnant."

Movies, television, magazines, and newspapers provide information that is often a source of negative learning about sexuality. Material dealing with rape, violent sex, and venereal disease is blatantly presented to children. This slanted information often produces unrealistic and unbalanced attitudes about sexuality and ultimately fosters fears and guilt that can have a powerful impact on the ability to enjoy sex as an adult.

The main point is that we acquire a sense of guilt over sexual feelings and experiences as a result of a wide diversity of sources of information and *mis*information. As was mentioned, becoming aware of early verbal and nonverbal messages about sexuality is essential if we hope to free ourselves of guilt.

An Example: Incest Guilt.   In our therapeutic groups Marianne and I find that the participants have a difficult time in working through the guilt they feel over certain sexual experiences. As a common illustration, I'll use the example of incest.

In groups designed for personal growth and for relatively well-functioning people, we find a startling number of women who report incidents of incest and sexual experimentation with fathers, uncles, stepfathers, grandfathers, and brothers. Many women will bring up the matter because they feel burdened with guilt, rage, hurt, and confusion over having been taken advantage of sexually. Some are both confused and guilty, because even though they may feel like a victim (and in most cases they were), at the same time they may see themselves as a conspirator. They may believe that they were at least partly to blame in that they led the man on or enjoyed the act (as well as fearing it at the same time). Typically, these experiences happen in childhood or early adolescence; the women remember feeling helpless at the time, not knowing how to stop the man and also being afraid to tell anyone. Once they bring out these past experiences, intense, pent-up emotions surface, such as hatred and rage for having been treated in such a way and feelings of having been raped and used.

The effects of these early childhood experiences can be far reaching and contemporary, in that a woman's ability to form sexually satisfying relationships may be impaired by events that she has kept inside of herself for many years. She may resent all men, associating them with the father or other man who initially took advantage of her. If she couldn't trust her own father, then what man can she trust? She may have a hard time trusting men's feelings of affection for her, thinking that they are merely trying to get her to have sex with them. She may keep control of relationships by not letting herself be open with men or be sexually playful and free with them. Her fear is that, if she gives up her control, she will be hurt again. She may rarely or never allow herself to fully give in to sexual pleasure during intercourse. Her guilt over sexual feelings and her negative conditioning prevents her from being open to enjoying a satisfying sexual relationship. She may still blame men for her feelings of guilt and her sexual nonresponsiveness.

We've found that it is therapeutic for most of these women to simply share this burden that they've been carrying alone for so many years. In a climate of support, trust, care, and respect, these women can *begin* a healing process that will eventually allow them to shed needless guilt. Before this healing can occur, they generally need to fully express bottled-up feelings, usually of anger and hatred. We stress that what is important is that this catharsis occur in the group in *symbolic* ways; it is not necessarily recommended that they confront the men who initiated sexual activities with them. Sometimes the man in question will no longer be alive, or the woman might decide that she does not want to go to her uncle and discuss the times he took advantage of her when she was 11 years old. Through role playing, release of feelings, and sharing of her conflicts with others in the group, she often finds that she is not alone in her plight, and she begins to put these experiences into a new perspective. While she will never forget these experiences, she can begin the process of letting go of feelings of self-blame. In doing so, she is also freeing herself of the control these sexual experiences (and the feelings associated with them) have had over her ability to form intimate relationships with men.

If you are interested in doing further reading on the psychological aspects of incest, including its causes, effects, and treatment approaches, I recommend Karin Meiselman's (1978) book *Incest*.

TIME OUT FOR PERSONAL REFLECTION

1. *Complete the following statements pertaining to sexuality:*

   a. *I first learned about sex through* _____

   _____

   b. *My earliest memory about sex is* _____

   _____

   c. *The way this memory affects me now is* _____

   _____

   d. *One verbal sexual message I received from my parents was* _____

   _____

   e. *One nonverbal sexual message I received from my parents was* ____

   _____

f. An expectation I have about sex is _____

_____

g. When the topic of sexuality comes up I usually _____

_____

h. While I was growing up, a sexual taboo I had was _____

_____

2. What are your reactions to the fact that the topic of sexuality is being discussed in this book and in your class?

_____

_____

_____

_____

3. List a couple of the myths and misconceptions that have most affected you personally.

_____

_____

_____

_____

4. List some ways in which you might deny your sexuality.

_____

_____

_____

_____

5. Are there any steps you'd like to take toward learning to accept your body and your sexuality more than you do now? If so, what are they?

_____

_____

_____

_____

6. *Do you experience guilt over sexual feelings? If so, what specific feelings give rise to guilt for you?*

_____

_____

_____

_____

7. *How openly are you able to discuss sexuality in a personal way? Would you like to be more open in discussing your sexuality or sexual issues? If so, what is preventing this openness?*

_____

_____

_____

_____

8. *What are some personal issues relating to sex that you're willing to discuss in your class group? What are some areas that you would not be willing to share or explore?*

_____

_____

_____

_____

LEARNING TO ENJOY SENSUALITY AND SEXUALITY

Sensual experiences involve the enjoyment of all of our senses and can be enjoyed separately from sexual experiences. People often confuse sensuality with sexuality, especially by concluding that sensuality necessarily leads to sexual experiences. As we've seen, performance standards and expectations often get in the way of people's sensual and sexual pleasure, particularly in the case of men. Many men report that they feel a need to perform "up to standard," and they burden themselves with the stress of worrying about what is expected of them. Some men are not content to be themselves but think they must be *supermen*, particularly in the area of

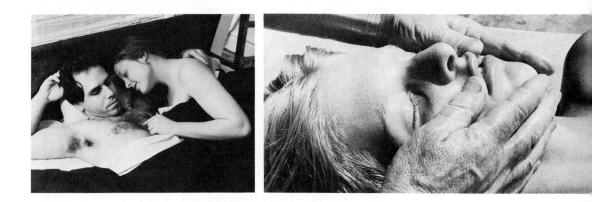

sexual attractiveness and performance. They measure themselves by unrealistic standards and may greatly fear losing their sexual power. Instead of enjoying sexual and sensual experiences, they become orgasm oriented. They often place heavy expectations on women to climax as well, in order to reaffirm their view that they are more than sexually adequate. With this type of orientation toward sex, it is no wonder that these men fear two problems in particular: impotence and premature ejaculation.

Listening to Our Body

I like the way Goldberg (1976) deals with the meaning these sexual problems often have. In a chapter entitled "The Wisdom of the Penis," Goldberg says that impotence can really be a message that a man doesn't want to have sex with this particular woman at this particular time; it doesn't necessarily mean that he has lost his potency in general. Goldberg makes a strong case that men should have sex only when they are genuinely aroused and excited; otherwise, they are inviting impotence. "The penis," he writes, "is not a piece of plumbing that functions capriciously. It is an expression of the total self. In these days of overintellectualization it is perhaps the only remaining sensitive and revealing barometer of the male's true sexual feelings" (p. 39). In similar fashion, Goldberg interprets premature ejaculation as the body's way of saying "I really don't want to do this, but, if I must, let's get it over with as fast as possible." In short, if we can learn to pay attention to what our bodies are telling us, they can teach us ways of enjoying a sensual and sexual life. Much the same point is made by Jourard (1971) in writing on the delight and ecstasy that a sexual experience can bring. The body, says Jourard, doesn't lie: "If she wants me and I don't want her, I cannot lie. My body speaks the truth. And I cannot take her unless she gives herself. Her body cannot lie" (p. 53).

It should be added that sexual dysfunction can occur for any one of a number of reasons, including, in some cases, physical ones. In the majority of cases, however, a problem such as impotence is due to psychological factors. For example, in addition to the lack of desire to have sex with a certain person at a certain time, impotence may result from feelings of guilt, prolonged depression, anxiety about personal adequacy, or a generally low level of self-esteem. Most men for whom impotence becomes a problem might be well advised to ask "What is my body telling me?"

Asking for What We Want

Paying attention to the messages of our body is only a first step. We still need to learn how to express to our partner *specifically* what we like and don't like sexually. I've found that both men and women tend to keep their sexual preferences and dislikes to themselves instead of sharing them with their partner. They've accepted the misconception that their partner should know intuitively what they like and don't like, and they resist telling their partner what feels good to them out of fear that their lovemaking will become mechanical or that their partner will only be trying to please them. I'm thinking of the man who said that he felt "very uptight" because he considered oral sex morally wrong and thought of it as a type of perversion. He engaged in it anyway, without much enthusiasm, because he felt his wife expected it and because he thought that, if he didn't, she would be disappointed in him as a man. It would have been very important for him to openly express his reluctance to her, instead of keeping it a secret.

Often a woman will complain that she doesn't derive as much enjoyment from sexual intercourse as she might because the man either is too concerned with his own pleasure or is orgasm oriented and sees touching, holding, and caressing only as necessary duties he must perform to obtain "the real thing." Thus, she may say that he rolls over in bed as soon as he is satisfied, even if she's left frustrated. Although she may require touching and considerable foreplay and afterplay, he may not recognize her needs. For this reason, she needs to express to him what it feels like to be left unsatisfied. She must do this without attacking him, which would only raise his defenses.

It is not uncommon for a woman to ask a question such as: "Does touching always have to lead to sex?" She is probably implying that there is a significant dimension missing for her in lovemaking—namely, the sensual aspect. Being sensual is an important part of a sexual experience. Sensuality pertains to fully experiencing all of our senses, not just sensations in our genitals. There are many parts of the body that are sensual and that can contribute to our enjoyment of sex. Far too often people who meet for a sexual encounter are too oriented toward orgasm. Although there is great enjoyment in the orgasmic experience, people are missing out on another source of enjoyment by not giving pleasure to themselves and their partner with other stimulation.

People sometimes engage in sexual intercourse when what they actually want is to be touched and embraced and to feel sensual in all parts of their body. They may feel deeply frustrated when their need for a sensual experience quickly culminates with an orgasm. If this becomes a pattern, people may find that there is a feeling of emptiness attached to their sex life. Sex then becomes either a duty or a routine event. One or both of the partners are likely to feel used or cheated and eventually may not look forward to having sex.

The Sensate-Focus Exercise.   One way for couples to become more aware of and to appreciate their sensuality is the sensate-focus exercise. This exercise was originally developed by Masters and Johnson (1980) as a technique in a treatment plan for sexual dysfunctions. The sensate-focus experience involves people's taking time to make contact with each other, paying attention to the sensations of their entire body, learning how to ask for what they want, and receiving pleasure without feeling pressured or guilty. It consists of having the couple forgo sexual intercourse and orgasm for a period of time. This is done so that there is no demand to perform sexually and so that the goal of orgasm is not made the primary one. Instead, the partners limit their erotic activity to gently touching and caressing each other's body. Freed from such pressures, both the woman and the man are often able to experience full erotic and sensuous sensations for the first time. The general instructions given to a couple are:

"One of you will be the giver, and the other the receiver. As the receiver, your only responsibility is to take and enjoy, and to communicate verbally or nonverbally what is pleasurable. It is important that you do not worry about whether the giver is getting tired or anything else. You are to be selfish and to concentrate on your sensations over your entire body. The giver focuses on the feelings and sensations of giving the partner pleasure. Each of you takes a turn in being in the role of giver and receiver. To prolong the experience of sensuality, avoid touching genitals."

Although this kind of approach might sound simple, it's surprising how many couples have never tried it. These people have restricted the pleasure they could give to their partner and receive for themselves, merely because they didn't think it was right to ask directly for what they wanted.

SEX AND INTIMACY

Intimacy can be conceived of as a close emotional relationship characterized by a deep level of caring for another person. It is a basic component of all loving relationships, as we will see in the next two chapters, which deal with love and intimacy. Although intimacy is a part of every loving relationship, it is a mistake to assume that sexuality is a part of all loving and intimate relationships. Chapter 8 explores many forms of intimate relationships that do not involve sex.

Increasing our sexual awareness can include becoming more sensitive to the ways in which we sometimes engage in sex as a means to some end. For instance, sexual activity can be used as a way of actually preventing the development of intimacy. It can also be a way of avoiding experiencing our aloneness, our isolation, and our feelings of distance from others. Sex can be an escape into activity, a way of avoiding inner emptiness. When it is being used in any of these ways, it can take on a driving or compulsive quality that detracts from its spontaneity and leaves us unfulfilled. Sex used as a way of filling inner emptiness becomes a mechanical act, divorced of any passion, feeling, or caring. Then it only deepens our feelings of isolation and detachment.

In spite of the fact that we live in an age of sexual liberation, many people do not experience genuine satisfaction in their sexual relationships. Rollo May (1981) develops the thesis that sex without intimacy as a lifestyle leads to enslavement and the emotional deadening of a person. In his clinical experience as a psychotherapist, May has observed that people who engage in sex without intimacy have little capacity for feeling and become sex machines who function mechanically instead of lovingly. As May puts it, "The danger is that these detached persons who are afraid of intimacy will move toward a robotlike existence, heralded by the drying up of their emotions not only on sexual levels, but on all levels, supported by the motto 'Sex does not involve intimacy anyway' " (1981, p. 153). In short, May contends that the trend toward sex without intimacy in our culture is closely associated with the loss of the capacity to feel any emotions.

In my professional work with clients and college students I have observed a trend away from casual sexual encounters without any emotional attachment. Those who have left sexually exclusive relationships may look forward to sex with a variety of partners. For a time, some of them may be drawn to "sport sex" as they experience their newly found "freedom." Many report, however, that they eventually tire of such relationships and find themselves searching for intimacy as a vital part of their sexual involvements. Ultimately, they are seeking to be loved by a special person, and they want to trust giving their love in return. What they appear to want is much like May's view of intimacy and love. His perspective is that love is a state of being characterized by both a physical and emotional sharing. To him, "Intimacy is the sharing between two people not only of their bodies, but also of their hopes, fears, anxieties and aspirations" (1981, p. 149).

It might be well to reflect on how sex can be used to either enhance or diminish ourselves and our partner as persons. We can ask ourselves such questions as: Are my intimate relationships based on a need to conquer or exert power over someone else? Or are they based on a genuine desire to become intimate, to share, to experience joy and pleasure, to both give and receive? Asking ourselves what we want in our relationships and what uses sex serves for us may also help us avoid the overemphasis on technique and performance that frequently detracts from sexual experiences. Although technique and knowledge are important, they are not ends in themselves, and overemphasizing them can cause us to become oblivious to the *persons* we have sex with. An abundance of anxiety over performance and technique can only impede sexual enjoyment and rob the experience of genuine intimacy and caring.

TIME OUT FOR PERSONAL REFLECTION

1. *Complete the following sentences:*

    a. *To me, being sensual means* _____

    _____

    b. *To me, being sexual means* _____

    _____

    c. *Sex without intimacy is* _____

    _____

    d. *Sex can be an empty experience when* _____

    _____

    e. *Sex can be most fulfilling when* _____

    _____

2. *Look over the following list, quickly checking the words that you associate with sex.*

___ fun	___ dirty	___ routine
___ ecstasy	___ shameful	___ closeness
___ procreation	___ joy	___ release
___ beautiful	___ pressure	___ sinful
___ duty	___ performance	___ guilty
___ trust	___ experimentation	___ vulnerability

Now look over the words you've checked and see whether there are any significant patterns in your responses. What can you say by way of summary about your attitudes toward sex?

_____

_____

_____

_____

DEVELOPING OUR OWN SEXUAL VALUES

During the past couple of decades a change has occurred in our society that many people term a sexual revolution. Certainly, there has been an open questioning of society's sexual standards and practices, accompanied by the growing belief that individuals can and should decide for themselves what acceptable sexual practices are. Previously, many people did not have to struggle to decide what was moral or immoral, since they took the standards of sexual behavior from external sources. This is not to say that they were necessarily moral, even by their own standards, for they may have been more secretive about their sexual activities and may also have suffered more guilt than do many people today.

Although I believe that it's desirable for people to bring sexual issues into the open and talk freely without the guilt and shame their parents may have experienced, I also believe that we need to form consistent value systems on which to base our behavior, including our sexual behavior. The change in sexual attitudes can give us the freedom to be sexually responsible—to determine our own values and govern our own behavior.

For much of the earlier part of my life I looked outside myself for the answers to sexual issues. Instead of struggling to find values that would be my own, I accepted the guidelines that came ready-made from my church. Although it was comfortable for me at the time, I now see this acceptance of external standards as an avoidance of my responsibility to define my own sexual ethics, as well as an avoidance of the anxiety I would have experienced in attempting to do so. Since then I've come to recognize the importance of dealing with sexual issues in a way that has meaning for me and that I can live with.

I frequently get the impression that it isn't in vogue to talk about sexual values and ethics; many people seem to prefer to follow their spontaneous impulses without weighing the place of values in their decisions. Of course, designing a personal and meaningful set of sexual ethics is not an easy task. It can be accomplished only through a process of honest ques-

tioning. Our questioning can start with the values we presently have: What is their source? Do they fit in with our views of ourselves in other areas of our life? Which of them should we keep in order to live responsibly and with enjoyment? Which should we reject? Achieving freedom doesn't have to mean shedding all our past beliefs or values. Whether we keep or reject them in whole or in part, we can refuse to allow someone besides ourselves to make our decisions for us. It can be tempting to allow others (whether past authorities or present acquaintances) to tell us what is right and wrong and design our life for us, for then we don't have to wrestle with tough decisions ourselves. If we fail to create our own values and choose for ourselves, however, we surrender our autonomy and run the risk of becoming alienated from ourselves.

Although sex is a natural urge, the place that sex occupies in our life and the attitudes we have toward it are very much a matter of free choice. We are free to answer for ourselves such basic questions as: Does sex necessarily have to include love? Can we have love without sex? Are love and sex the foundations for marriage? What is the purpose of sex? Should love precede sex?

In their book *Sexual Awareness: Enhancing Sexual Pleasure*, McCarthy and McCarthy (1984) make the observation that we have gone from a sexually repressed, ignorant, and inhibited culture to a performance-oriented and confused sexual culture. They assert that, the more knowledge people have about sexuality, the better they can choose to integrate sexual expression into their life. Contending that sexuality cannot be value-free, they develop the following guidelines for sexual awareness, sexual functioning, and making choices pertaining to sexual expression:

- Sexuality is a basic part of our existence and is not to be considered inherently evil.
- Our sexuality is a positive and integral part of our personality.
- It is our responsibility to choose how we will express our sexuality. Since sexuality can enhance our life, it should not contribute to anxiety and guilt.
- At its best a sexual relationship involves trust, respect, and concern for our partner.
- An intimate relationship is the most satisfying way to express our sexuality.

Developing our own values means assuming responsibility for ourselves, which for me includes taking into consideration how others may be affected by our choices while allowing them to take responsibility for theirs. I make the assumption that, in an adult relationship, the parties involved are capable of taking personal responsibility for their own actions. Consequently, I think it's difficult to be used or manipulated unless we allow others to use or manipulate us. Generally, we cannot be exploited unless we collaborate in this activity. For example, in the case of premarital or extramarital sex, each person must weigh such questions as: Do I really want to pursue a sexual relationship with this person at this time? Is the price worth it? What are my commitments? Who else is involved, and who could be hurt? Might this be a positive or a negative experience? How does my decision fit in with my values generally?

In summary, it's no easier to achieve sexual autonomy than it is to achieve autonomy in the other areas of our life. While challenging our values, we need to take a careful look at ways in which we could easily engage in self-deception by adjusting our behavior to whatever we might desire at the moment. We also need to pay attention to how we feel about ourselves in regard to our past sexual experience. Perhaps, in doing so, we can use our level of self-respect as one important guide to our future behavior. That is, we can each ask "Do I feel enhanced or diminished by my past experience?"

HOMOSEXUALITY AS AN ALTERNATIVE LIFE-STYLE

Homosexual relationships are becoming the avowed preference of an increasing number of people in our society. The challenge is how to help both heterosexuals and homosexuals recognize that homosexuality is a viable alternative life-style for many people. The gay movement has made significant strides toward gaining such recognition and acceptance. In many states acknowledged homosexuals are holding public office.

There is a controversy over the origin of homosexuality. Some experts argue that one's sexual preference is at least partly a function of genetic or physiological factors, and others contend that homosexuality is entirely learned behavior. Some maintain that there is both an internal predisposition and an environmental dimension to the shaping of one's sexual preference. And there are those who assert that sexual identity is strictly a matter of choice at some point in one's life. The resolution of this controversy is beyond the scope of this book. The focus of this section is to consider how the themes of this chapter can apply equally to homosexual and heterosexual relationships.

Nass, Libby, and Fisher (1984) report that sociologists now view homosexuality not as a perversion or deviance but as an orientation that is neither good nor bad in itself. Homosexuality can be regarded as another style of expressing sexuality; this style can be healthy or unhealthy, depending on the person and the social and psychological dynamics. Sociologists hold that the fact that homosexuality is minority behavior is not a sufficient reason for denying it acceptance.

In the past, many people felt ashamed and abnormal because of homosexual preferences. Heterosexuals frequently categorized them as deviates and as sick or immoral. For these and other reasons many homosexuals were forced to conceal their preferences, perhaps even to themselves. Today, the gay movement is actively challenging the stigma attached to this alternative life-style, and those who choose it are increasingly asserting their right to live as they choose, without discrimination. Nevertheless, much of the public continues to cling to stereotypes, prejudices, and misconceptions regarding homosexual behavior.

In their book *Counseling with Gay Men and Women*, Woodman and Lenna (1980) define the gay movement as a demand for equal rights and equal protection under the law. These rights include the right to choose how to live creatively and socially. As a part of the liberation effort there are two aims: (1) the recognition of homosexuality as not abnormal or aberrant, and (2) the dismantling or restructuring of discriminatory social institutions. This movement has implications on both the individual and collective levels. As individuals, many gay people are no longer willing to remain passive when others define reality in ways that are contrary to

their feelings and experiences. Collectively, gay people are banding together by forming organizations to fight institutionalized oppression. Woodman and Lenna provide the following picture of an alternative lifestyle:

> The contemporary gay perspectives are that homosexual life-styles are not only alternative but also totally positive and legitimate. Being gay is not seen as merely engaging in homosexual behavior but as a gestalt of personal feelings and a network of social relationships in which sexual and affectional preferences play a role [1980, p. 9].

In basic agreement with the perspective described by Woodman and Lenna is the concept of "homosexuality as beyond deviance" as advocated by Nass, Libby, and Fisher (1984). They write that homosexuals have organized to free themselves from the fears and stigmas of the past, mainly by trying to reeducate the public. According to them, these organized efforts have promoted greater acceptance of homosexual choices by some people, and many gays have been helped to develop a more positive self-image.

A further problem consists in the labeling done by both heterosexuals and homosexuals. Nass, Libby, and Fisher contend that applying labels to people can restrict their possibilities in developing an identity. They suggest the phrasing "He is now involved in a homosexual relationship" as preferable to "He *is* a homosexual." The former statement allows for the possibility that one's gender preference is a choice subject to change, rather than a permanent condition. Also, a person has many other dimensions besides sexual orientation, and the label of "gay" or "homosexual" can easily reduce a person's identity to a merely sexual one.

Moses and Hawkins (1982) take the position that labeling people as "lesbian" or "homosexual" often leads others to react negatively to them on the basis of the label. They argue for a move away from slapping labels on people—labels that often become a part of their self-concepts.

In categorizing relationships as heterosexual or homosexual, we sometimes forget that sex is not the only aspect of a relationship. Here I would only urge the same points I've made earlier in this chapter—namely, that whatever choice we make, we need to examine the bases for it, whether it is the best choice for us, and whether it is compatible with our own values. Just as I'm concerned that people might choose or reject certain sex roles because of others' expectations, so too I am concerned that people may reject a gay life-style merely because others condemn it or adopt it merely because they are unquestioningly following a liberation movement. For me, what is most important is that we define ourselves, that we assume the responsibility for our own choices, and that we feel that we can live out our choices with inner integrity.

TIME OUT FOR PERSONAL REFLECTION

1. *What influences have shaped your attitudes and values concerning sexuality? In the following list, indicate the importance of each factor by placing a 1 in the blank if it was* very important, *a 2 if it was* somewhat important, *and a 3 if it was* unimportant. *For each item that you mark with a 1 or a 2, indicate briefly the nature of that influence.*

_____   *parents* _____

_____   *church* _____

_____   *friends* _____

_____   *siblings* _____

_____   *movies* _____

_____   *school* _____

_____   *books* _____

_____   *television* _____

_____   *spouse* _____

_____   *grandparents* _____

_____   *your own experiences* _____

_____   *other influential factors:* _____

_____

2. *Try making a list of specific values you hold regarding sexual issues. As a beginning, you might respond to the following questions:*

    a. *How do you feel about promiscuity?*

        _____

        _____

        _____

        _____

    b. *What is your view of sex outside of marriage?*

        _____

        _____

        _____

        _____

    c. *Do you think it's legitimate to separate love and sex?*

        _____

        _____

        _____

        _____

    d. *How do you feel about having sex with a person you don't like or respect?*

        _____

        _____

        _____

        _____

    e. *List other specific values or convictions you have concerning sexual behavior.*

        _____

        _____

        _____

        _____

3. *What are your reactions to those people who choose homosexuality as an alternative life-style?*

_____

_____

_____

_____

4. *How do you feel about homosexual experiences for yourself?*

_____

_____

_____

_____

5. *What are your views concerning the gay movement? Do you believe that the rights of homosexuals have been denied? Do you think that people who openly profess a gay life-style have rights equal to those of heterosexuals and should not be denied a specific job because of their sexual preference alone?*

_____

_____

_____

_____

_____

CHAPTER SUMMARY

Sexuality is a part of your personhood and should not be thought of as merely an activity divorced from your feelings, values, and relationships. Although our childhood and adolescent experiences do have an impact on the shaping of our present attitudes and behavior toward sex, we are in a position to modify this area of our life if we are not satisfied with ourselves as sexual beings.

One significant step toward evaluating our sexual attitudes is to become aware of the myths and misconceptions that we may harbor. It helps to review where and how we acquired our views about sexuality. Have the sources of your sexual knowledge and values been healthy models? Have you questioned the ways in which your attitudes affect the way you feel about yourself sexually? Is your sexuality an expression of yourself as a complete person?

Another step toward developing our own sexual views is to learn to be open in talking about our sexual concerns, including fears and desires, with at least one other person whom we trust. Guilt feelings may be based on irrational premises, and we may be burdening ourselves needlessly with feeling guilty about normal feelings and behavior. We may feel very alone when it comes to our sexual feelings, fantasies, fears, feelings, and actions. By sharing some of these concerns with others, we are likely to find out that we are not the only ones with such concerns.

If we are successful in dealing with barriers that prevent us from acknowledging, experiencing, and expressing our sexuality, then we increase our chances of learning how to enjoy both sensuality and sexuality. Sensuality can be a significant path toward creating satisfying sexual relationships, and we can learn to become sensual beings even if we decide not to have sexual relationships with others. Sensuality implies a full awareness and a sensitivity to the pleasures of sight, sound, smell, taste, and touch. We can enjoy sensuality without being sexual, and it is a mistake to conclude that sensuality necessarily leads to sexual behavior. Nevertheless, sensuality is very important in enhancing sexual relationships. Intimacy, or the emotional sharing with a person we care for, is another ingredient of joyful sex. As a habitual style, sex without intimacy tends to lead to a basic sense of frustration, emptiness, and emotional deadness.

The place that sex occupies in our life and the attitudes we have toward it are very much a matter of free choice. It is no easier to achieve sexual autonomy than it is to achieve autonomy in other areas of life.

The themes explored in this chapter can be applied equally to both heterosexual and homosexual life-styles. Although there is a controversy over the origin of homosexuality, it is clear that this is the preferred lifestyle of many. Rather than labeling homosexuals, it is helpful to focus on understanding their concerns and struggles as persons.

The following two chapters—on love and intimate relationships—are really impossible to separate from the themes of this chapter. I encourage you to think about love, sex, and intimacy as an integrated dimension of a rich life.

ACTIVITIES AND EXERCISES

1. Write down some of your major questions or concerns regarding sexuality. You might consider discussing these issues with a friend, your partner (if you're involved in an intimate relationship), or your class group.

2. In your journal, trace the evolution of your sexual history. What were some important experiences for you, and what did you learn from these experiences?

3. Discuss with some friends various aspects of homosexuality as a lifestyle. What trends do you see regarding acceptance or rejection of those who choose homosexual relationships?

4. List as many common slang words as you are able to think of pertaining to (a) the male genitals, (b) the female genitals, and (c) sexual intercourse. As you review this list, what sexual attitudes seem to be expressed? What do you think this list implies about your culture's attitude toward sexuality? Explore the hypothesis that the more rigid, uncomfortable, and embarrassed a particular culture is about sex, the more negative are the words used to describe sexual functioning.

5. Incest is a universal taboo. Explore some of the reasons for this taboo. You might investigate cross-cultural attitudes pertaining to incest. Do you view sexual experimentation between siblings during childhood as incest? Discuss.

6. The media are giving increasing attention to the topics of incest and sexual abuse of children. What do you think this current interest in these subjects implies?

7. What sexual modeling did you see in your parents? What attitudes and values about sex did they convey to you, both implicitly and explicitly? What would you most want to communicate to your children about sex?

SUGGESTED READINGS

Koestenbaum, P. (1974). *Existential Sexuality: Choosing to Love*. Englewood Cliffs, N.J.: Prentice-Hall (Spectrum). A thoughtfully written book that stresses the freedom and responsibility you have to choose your kind of sex and to give meaning to sex.

Masters, W. H., & Johnson, V. E. (1974). *The Pleasure Bond*. New York: Bantam. Focuses on marital themes and a range of topics such as sexual fidelity, extramarital sex, touching, commitment, and second marriages.

McCarthy, B., & McCarthy, E. (1984). *Sexual Awareness: Enhancing Sexual Pleasure*. New York: Carroll & Graf. A readable guide to sensual experiencing and sexuality. Some topics include the pleasures of nonsexual touching, the key to maintaining sexual intimacy, becoming a sexual person, and overcoming sexual problems.

Moses, A. E., & Hawkins, R. O. (1982). *Counseling Lesbian Women and Gay Men: A Life-Issues Approach*. St. Louis: C. V. Mosby. A comprehensive and well-written book that describes the gay experience and deals with special issues in counseling gay clients. The authors offer some specific suggestions for positive intervention with gay people. Contains a very comprehensive bibliography for those who wish to pursue further study of the subject of homosexuality.

Nass, G. D., Libby, R. W., & Fisher, M. P. (1984). *Sexual Choices: An Introduction to Human Sexuality* (2nd ed.). Monterey, Calif.: Wadsworth Health Sciences. A fairly complete and comprehensive textbook on human sexuality. Some of the topics discussed are developing a sexual identity and sexual relationships, early sexual learning, homosexual and bisexual preferences, marriage and alternative life-styles, intimacy and the elderly, women's liberation and sexual choices, sexual assault, enhancing sexual health, wanted and unwanted conception, and birth control.

LOVE

PRECHAPTER SELF-INVENTORY

Use the following scale to respond: 4 = this statement is true of me *most* of the time; 3 = this statement is true of me *much* of the time; 2 = this statement is true of me *some* of the time; 1 = this statement is true of me *almost none* of the time.

_____   1. Loving more than one person of the opposite sex diminishes my capacity to be deeply involved with another person.
_____   2. I have a fear of losing others' love.
_____   3. When I experience hurt or frustration in love, I find it more difficult to continue to risk loving.
_____   4. I make myself known and transparent to those I love.
_____   5. I find it difficult to express loving feelings toward members of the same sex.
_____   6. I am as afraid of being accepted as I am of being rejected by those I love.
_____   7. I have to take some risks if I'm to open myself to loving.
_____   8. In my loving relationships there is complete trust and an absence of fear.
_____   9. I accept those whom I love as they are, without challenging them to be different.
_____   10. I expect constant closeness and intimacy with those I love.

INTRODUCTION

In this chapter I invite you to look carefully at your style of loving by examining your choices and decisions concerning your ability to give and receive love. People often say either that they have love in their life or that they don't. I make the assumption that the issue is not as clear-cut as this and that we all have the capacity to become better at loving. We can look at the situations that we put ourselves in and that we create for ourselves and then consider how conducive these are to the sharing of love. We can also look at our attitudes toward love. Some of the questions we can examine are: Is love active or passive? Do we fall in and out of love? How much are we responsible for creating a climate in which we can love others and receive love from them? Do we have romantic and unrealistic ideals of what love should be? If so, how can we challenge them? In what ways does love change as we change?

As you read this chapter, I hope that you'll try to apply the issues I discuss to your own experience of love and that you'll consider the degree

to which you're now able to appreciate and love yourself. I also hope that you'll review your own need for love as well as your fears of loving and that you may come to recognize whether there are barriers within yourself that prevent you from experiencing the level of love you're capable of.

OUR NEED TO LOVE AND TO BE LOVED

I believe that, in order to fully develop as people and enjoy a rich existence, we need to care about others and have them return this care to us. To me, a loveless life is characterized by a joyless isolation and alienation. Our need for love includes the need to know that, at least in one person's world, our existence makes a difference. If we exclude ourselves from physical and emotional closeness with others, we pay the price of experiencing emotional and physical deprivation.

People express their need to love and to be loved in many ways, a few of which are revealed in the following statements:

- "I need to have someone in my life I can actively care for. I need to let that person know he (she) makes a difference in my life, and I need to know I make a difference in his (her) life."
- "I want to feel loved and accepted for who I am now, not for what the other person thinks I should be in order to be worthy of acceptance."
- "Although I enjoy my own company, I also have a need for people in my life. I want to reach out to certain people, and I hope they'll want something from me."
- "It's true that loving and being loved is frightening, but I'd rather open myself up and risk what loving entails than close myself off from this experience."
- "I'm finding out that I'm a person who does need others and that I have more of a capacity to give something to others than I thought I had."

- "I'm beginning to realize that I need to learn how to love myself more fully, for up until now I've limited myself by discounting my worth. I want to learn how to appreciate myself and accept myself in spite of my imperfections. Then maybe I'll be able to really believe that others can love me."
- "There are times when I want to share my joys, my dreams, my anxieties, and my uncertainties with another person, and at these times I want to feel heard and understood."

Of course, there are many ways to harden ourselves so that we won't experience a need for love. We can close ourselves off from needing anything from anybody; we can isolate ourselves by never reaching out to another; we can refuse to trust others and to make ourselves vulnerable; we can cling to an early decision that we are basically unlovable. It's important to recognize, however, that *we* make these decisions about love—and *we* pay the price. In whatever way we deaden ourselves to our own need for love, the question is: Is the safety we achieve worth the price we pay for it?

BARRIERS TO LOVING AND BEING LOVED

Self-Doubt and Lack of Self-Love

Despite our need for love, then, we often put barriers in the way of our attempts to give and to receive love. One common obstacle consists of the messages we sometimes send to others concerning ourselves. If we enter relationships convinced that nobody could possibly love us, we will give this message to others in many subtle ways. We thus create a self-fulfilling prophecy, whereby we make the very thing we fear come true by telling both ourselves and others that life can be no other way.

If you are convinced that you're unlovable, your conviction is probably related to decisions you made about yourself during your childhood or adolescent years. At one time, perhaps, you decided that you wouldn't be loved *unless* you did certain expected things or lived up to another's design for your life. For example, one such decision is: "Unless I produce, I won't be loved. To be loved, I must produce good grades, become successful, and make the most of my life." Such a decision can make it difficult to convince yourself later on in life that you can be loved even if you're not productive.

People sometimes have a difficult time believing that they are lovable for *who* they are, and they may discount the love others give them as

"NO ONE COULD POSSIBLY LOVE ME..."

being contingent on a single characteristic of their personality. For example, think for a moment of how many times you have completed this sentence in any of the following ways: People love me only because I am . . . pretty, bright and witty, good in sports, a good student, a fine provider, attractive, accomplished, cooperative and considerate, a good father (mother), a good husband (wife), and so forth.

If you limit your ability to receive love from others by telling yourself (and by convincing others) that you are loved primarily for a single trait, it would be well to challenge this assumption. For example, if you say "You only love me because of my body," you might try to realize that your body is *one* of your assets. You can learn to appreciate this asset without assuming that it is all there is to the person you are. If you have trouble seeing any desirable characteristics besides your physical attractiveness, you are likely to give others messages that your primary value is bound up in appearances. Ideally, you will come to accept that being a physically attractive person makes it easier for others to notice you and want to initiate a contact with you. However, you don't need to limit yourself by depending exclusively on how you look, for you can work at developing other traits. The danger here consists of relying on physical attractiveness as a basis for building and maintaining a relationship. Regardless of the characteristic, if you rely exclusively on it as a source of gaining love from others (or from yourself), your ability to be loved is in a tenuous state.

In my own life I have had to struggle for a long time in recognizing and accepting my lovability. It would be easy for me to say "People love me only because I'm productive—because I write books, am an energetic teacher, am a good organizer, and work hard." The truth is, my productivity may attract certain people to me, and it may have something to do with the reasons others love me. However, it would be a faulty assumption to equate my total worth as a person with my productivity. It has taken me a long time to begin to believe that others love me for something other than my accomplishments; in fact, they may love me *despite* my driven-ness and my own need to produce. I continue to learn that my compulsive energy and drive often put distance between those people who love me (and those I love) and myself. Thus, a lesson that I'm continuing to learn is that the very thing I sometimes believe I *must* do or be in order to be loved actually gets in the way of others' loving me.

My point here is not just that we sometimes imagine that *other people* have expectations we must meet in order to be loved; we often obstruct our ability to love and receive love by *our own* unwillingness to accept what we actually are, as opposed to what we think we should be. For instance, I think it's essential for me to remember that I have difficulty in feeling worthy apart from my productivity. It's not always easy for me to acknowledge this difficulty to myself, and I have a tendency to distort or overlook it. I can easily convince myself that I *should* have worked this issue out by now, that I really should be beyond this limitation and should feel different. However, my only hope for changing this early decision about my self-worth is to recognize how I actually feel, think, and behave. Once I accept some of my self-limiting attitudes as part of me, I can actively be alert for manifestations of them, and I can challenge their validity.

Thus, a real limitation of our ability to love others is the degree to which we are unable to love and appreciate ourselves. I find over and over that, as we begin to learn to appreciate ourselves, we have some basis for actively loving others and accepting their love. A major stumbling block for many people is that they refuse to look at themselves, focusing instead on what they can do to "give" to others. I believe that we can give the most when we recognize our own worth and our own limitations. However, I also want to stress that early decisions about ourselves aren't easy to erase. In many subtle ways, they continue to manifest themselves. Consequently, we must continually challenge the validity of our assumptions and be alert for the obstacles we put in the way of our loving and being loved.

Learning to Love and Appreciate Ourselves.   Some people are reluctant to speak of their self-love, because they have been brought up to think that self-love is purely egocentric. Yet unless we learn how to love ourselves, we'll encounter difficulties in loving others and in allowing them to express their love for us. We can't very well give to others what we don't possess ourselves. And if we can't appreciate our own worth, how can we believe others when they say that they see value in us?

Having love for ourselves doesn't imply having an exaggerated picture of our own importance or placing ourselves above others or at the center of the universe. Rather, it implies having respect for ourselves, even though we're imperfect. It entails caring about our life and striving to become the person we are capable of becoming.

Many writers have stressed the necessity of self-love as a condition of love for others. In *The Art of Loving*, Erich Fromm (1956) describes self-love as a respect for our own integrity and uniqueness, and he maintains that it cannot be separated from love and understanding of others. In his beautiful book *Love*, Buscaglia (1972) also writes that to love others we must first love ourselves, for we cannot give what we haven't ourselves learned and experienced. Buscaglia describes the loving of oneself as "the discovery of the true wonder of you; not only the present you, but the many possibilities of you" (p. 99).

As we grow to treat ourselves with increasing respect and regard, we increase our ability to fully accept the love that others might want to give us; at the same time, we have the foundation for genuinely loving others. I agree with Hodge (1967) when he says: "Love of one's self is not antagonistic to having satisfying relationships. On the contrary, we are free to love others only as we become free to love ourselves" (p. 221).[1] Mayeroff (1971) agrees, saying in *On Caring*, "If I am unable to care for myself, I am unable to care for another person" (p. 49).[2] To care for ourselves, Mayeroff adds, we need to be responsive to our own needs for growth; we also need to feel at one with ourselves rather than estranged from ourselves. Furthermore, caring for ourselves and caring for others are mutually dependent: "I can only fulfill myself by serving someone or something apart from myself, and if I am unable to care for anyone or anything separate from me, I am unable to care for myself" (p. 48).

In counseling situations I often ask clients who only give to others and who have a difficult time taking for themselves: "Do *you* deserve what you so freely give to others?" "Could you begin to consider being as kind to yourself as you are to others?" "If your own well runs dry, will you be able to give to others?"

Our Fear of Love

There are other barriers to love besides a lack of self-love. Despite our need for love, we often fear loving and being loved. Our fear can lead us to seal off our need to experience love, and it can dull our capacity to care about others. Love doesn't come with guarantees; we can't be sure that another person will always love us, and we do lose loved ones. As Hodge (1967) insists, we can't eliminate the possibility that we will be hurt if we choose to love. Our loved ones may die or be injured or become painfully

---

[1]This and all other quotations from this source from *Your Fear of Love*, by M. Hodge. Copyright 1967 by Doubleday & Company, Inc. Reprinted by permission.

[2]This and all other quotations from this source from *On Caring*, by M. Mayeroff. Copyright © 1971 by Harper & Row, Publishers, Inc. Reprinted by permission of the publishers, Perennial Library.

ill; they may simply be mistrustful of our caring. In Hodge's words, "These are painful experiences, and we cannot avoid them if we choose to love. It is part of the human dilemma that love always includes the element of hurt" (p. 266).

There are some common fears of risking in love. Most of them are related to rejection, loss, the failure of love to be reciprocated, and uneasiness with intensity. Some of them might be expressed as follows:

- "Since I once got badly hurt in a love relationship, I'm not willing to take the chance of trusting again."
- "I fear allowing myself to love others because of the possibility that they will be seriously injured, contract a terrible illness, or die. I don't want to let them matter that much; that way, if I lose them, it won't hurt as much as if they really mattered."
- "My fear is that love will never be as good as I imagine it to be—that my ideal notions will never be matched in reality."
- "I'm afraid of loving others because they might want more from me than I'm willing to give, and I might feel suffocated."
- "I'm afraid that I'm basically unlovable and that, when you really get to know me, you'll want little to do with me."
- "My fear is that I'm loved not for who I am but for the functions that I perform and the roles that I serve. If I ceased doing these things, I would no longer be loved. It's hard for me to imagine that I'm loved simply for myself."
- "Emotional closeness is scary for me, because if I care deeply for a person and permit her to care about me, then I'm vulnerable."
- "One great fear is that people in my world will be indifferent to me— that they simply won't give a damn about my existence."
- "In many ways it's easier for me to take rejection than acceptance. It's hard for me to accept compliments or to be close and intimate. If people tell me that they want to care for me, I feel I've taken on a burden, and I'm afraid of letting them down."
- "I've never really allowed myself to look at whether I'm lovable. My fear is that I will search deep within myself and find little for another to love. What will I do if I discover that I'm grotesque, or hollow and empty, or incapable of giving or receiving?"

Loving demands courage, for there are always risks involved. I like the way Hodge (1967) expresses it:

> If we postponed the experience and expression of love until we no longer feared it, we would postpone it forever. Some people do appear to use their fear of love as a perpetual excuse for stalemated living— loving and trembling seem to go together. If we desire love we must learn to love in spite of our fears [pp. 267–268].

TIME OUT FOR PERSONAL REFLECTION

1. Who are some of the people that have made the most difference in your life, and in what ways were they important?

   a. _____

   b. _____

   c. _____

   d. _____

   e. _____

2. How do you express your love to others? Check the responses that apply to you, and add any other ways in which you show love, affection, and caring.

   _____ a. by telling the other person that I love him or her
   _____ b. through touching and other nonverbal means
   _____ c. by doing special things for the person
   _____ d. by making myself known to the person
   _____ e. by becoming vulnerable and trusting
   _____ f. by buying the person gifts

   g. _____

   _____

3. How do you express to another person your own need to receive love, affection, and caring?

   _____ a. by telling him or her that I need to be loved
   _____ b. by being open and trusting

   c. _____

   _____

4. List some specific fears that you have concerning loving others.

   _____

   _____

   _____

   _____

5. *Mention some barriers within yourself that prevent you from fully loving others. (Examples: extreme selfishness, lack of caring, fear of vulnerability, fear of being responsible for another.)*

_____

_____

_____

_____

6. *Mention some barriers within yourself that prevent others from loving you or that prevent you from fully receiving their love. (Examples: being overly suspicious, refusing to accept others' love, feeling a lack of self-worth, needing to return their love.)*

_____

_____

_____

_____

7. *List some qualities you have that you deem lovable. (Examples: my ability to care for others, my sense of humor.)*

_____

_____

_____

_____

8. *List some specific ways in which you might become a more lovable person. (Examples: increasing my feelings of self-worth, trusting others more, taking better care of my physical appearance.)*

_____

_____

_____

_____

9. *What did you learn about yourself from these exercises? Would you want to be your own best friend?*

_____

_____

_____

_____

Myths and Misconceptions about Love

There are many myths and misconceptions about love that inhibit our ability to love fully and to receive love from others. Some of the more common beliefs that need to be challenged are discussed below.

The Myth of Eternal Love.   I believe that the notion that love will endure forever is nonsense. This idea can deceive us into feeling a sense of security that simply has no basis in reality. There are no guarantees that our love (or another's love for us) will last a lifetime. That would be true only if we never changed. On the contrary, I think that the intensity and the degree of our love changes as we change. We may experience stages of love with one person, deepening our love and finding new levels of richness; there is also the chance that each of us will grow in different directions or outgrow the love we once shared.

The Myth that Love Is Fleeting.   On the opposite end of the spectrum is the notion that love is strictly temporary. I am thinking of one person who

DO YOU GUARANTEE THAT ?

found himself to be in love with different women as often as his moods changed. One day he would claim that he loved Sara and wanted to be committed to her in an exclusive relationship, but in a short while he would grow tired of Sara and find himself in love with Peggy and would maintain that he wanted an intense and exclusive relationship with her. For him, love was strictly a here-and-now feeling. I don't believe that such changeable feelings constitute real love. In most intense, long-term relationships, there are times when the alliance is characterized by deadness, frustration, strife, or conflict. There inevitably are times when we feel "stuck" with a person, and at such times we may consider dissolving the relationship. If our attitude is "I'll stay while things are rosy, but as soon as things get stormy or dull, I'll split and look elsewhere for something more interesting," then it's worth asking what kind of love it is that crumbles with the first crisis. For me, authentic love means recognizing when we're stuck in an unsatisfying place but being willing to challenge the reasons for the deadness and caring enough about the other person to stay and work on breaking through the impasse.

The Myth that Love Implies Constant Closeness.   I feel strongly that most of us can tolerate only so much closeness and that the other side of this need is our desire for distance. I am fond of Kahlil Gibran's words in *The Prophet:* "And stand together yet not too near together: For the pillars of the temple stand apart, and the oak tree and the cypress grow not in each other's shadow."[3]

There are times when a separation from our loved one can be very healthy. At these times we can renew our need for the other person and also allow ourselves to become centered again. If we fail to separate when we feel the need to do so, we'll surely strain the relationship. I'm thinking now of a man who refused to spend a weekend without his wife and children, even though he said he wanted some time for himself. The myth of constant closeness and constant togetherness in love prevented him from taking private time just for himself. It might also have been that the myth covered up certain fears. What if he discovered that his wife and children managed very well without him? What if he found that he couldn't stand his own company for a few days and that the reason for "togetherness" was to keep him from boring himself?

The Myth that We Fall in and out of Love.   A common notion is that we "fall" in love—that we passively wait for the right person to come along and sweep us off our feet. According to this view, love is something that

---

[3]This and all other quotations from this source reprinted from *The Prophet*, by Kahlil Gibran, with permission of the publisher, Alfred A. Knopf, Inc. Copyright 1923 by Kahlil Gibran; renewal copyright 1951 by Administrators C.T.A. of Kahlil Gibran Estate, and Mary G. Gibran.

happens *to* us. In contrast, I see love as being *active*, something we ourselves create. *We* make love happen.

Numerous writers have discussed this concept of love as an activity. Mayeroff (1971) asserts that patience is an important part of loving, for it enables others to grow in their own way and at their own pace. He adds "Patience is not waiting passively for something to happen, but is a kind of participation with the other in which we give fully of ourselves" (p. 17). In *Let Me Live!* Lyon (1975) writes that love is a *verb* that implies *acts* of loving. Active lovers, he says, are *greedy* in the sense that they want much from life and from love. "To achieve this goal they are willing to gamble. As gamblers, they are ready to play for high stakes by committing themselves first and fully" (p. 80). To Lyon, the "one basic fact of life" is that, in the long run, we get from life and love what we deserve:

> If you choose to fall in love, you will fall—or be pushed—out of love. If you live as an alien, yours will be a life of alienation. If you passively wait for love to happen to you, you will wait an eternity. But should you reach, grab, seek, act, risk—then you will find that there *is* life after birth [p. 81].

Buscaglia (1972) also criticizes the phrase "to fall in love." He contends that it's more accurate to say we *grow* in love, which implies an activity of choosing: "Love is active, not passive. It is continually engaged in the process of opening new doors and windows so that fresh ideas and questions can be admitted" (p. 69). For Buscaglia, love is like a "continual feast to be nourished upon. It sets an appetizing, attractive, gourmet table, but it cannot force anyone to eat. It allows each the freedom to select and reject according to his taste" (p. 69). In *The Art of Loving*, Fromm (1956) also describes love as an active agent: "Love is an activity, not a passive affect; it is a 'standing in,' not a 'falling for.' In the most general way, the active character of love can be described by stating that love is primarily *giving*, not receiving" (p. 22).[4]

People often say "I love you" and at the same time are hard pressed to describe the active way in which they show this love. Declaring "I love you just because . . ." may not be enough. Words can be easily overused and become hollow. The loved one may be more convinced by actions than by words.

In summary, active love is something that we can choose to share with others. We don't lose love by sharing it but rather increase it. This thought leads me to the next myth.

The Myth of the Exclusiveness of Love.   We sometimes think of love as a limited quantity that we must carefully dole out and conserve. We may

---

[4]This and all other quotations from this source from *The Art of Loving*, by E. Fromm. Copyright © 1956 by Harper & Row, Publishers, Inc. Reprinted by permission of the publishers.

believe that we are capable of loving only one other person—that there is one right person for each of us and that our fate is to find this singular soul. I believe, however, that one of the signs of genuine love is that it is expansive rather than exclusive. By opening myself to loving others, I open myself to loving one person more deeply. The need to restrict love to just one person seems irrationally based on our need to feel that we are irreplaceable.

In some senses, though, we may choose to make our love exclusive or special. For example, two people may choose not to have sexual relationships with others, because they realize that doing so might interfere with their capacity to freely open up and trust each other. Nevertheless, their sexual exclusivity does not have to mean that they cannot genuinely love others as well.

Jealousy is an issue that can be mentioned here. For example, Joe may feel insulted if he discovers that his wife, Carol, finds certain other men sexually attractive. Even if Carol and Joe have an agreement not to have sexual relationships with others, Joe might be threatened and angry over the mere fact that Carol has sexual *feelings* for other men. He may wrongly assume: "What is the matter with me that Carol has to look at other men? If I were enough of a man for her, then I should be able to satisfy all of her needs, and she would not find other men sexually attractive. Her interest in other men is a sign that something is wrong with me!" Jealousy can easily get out of proportion when it controls the person, instead of the person controlling it. On the other hand, I think it is a mistaken assumption to equate an absence of jealousy with an absence of love. Carol might be upset if Joe did not display any jealousy toward her, insisting that this meant that he was indifferent to her or that he had come to take her for granted.

The Myth that True Love Is Selfless.   We may have been conditioned to believe that genuine love implies that we forget ourselves. It is a myth that true love means giving selflessly. For one thing, love also means *taking*. If you cannot allow others to give to you and cannot take their expressions of love, you are likely eventually to become drained or to become resentful of your continual giving. For another thing, in giving to others we do meet many of our own needs, and I see nothing wrong in this, as long as we can admit it. For example, a mother who never says no to any demands made by her children may not be aware of the ways that she has conditioned them to depend on her. They may be unaware that she has any needs of her own, for she hides them so well. In fact, she may set them up to take advantage of her out of her need to feel significant. In other words, her "giving" is actually an outgrowth of her need to feel like a good mother, rather than an honest expression of love for her children.

I am not implying that giving to others or the desire to express our love to others is necessarily a problem. Rather, I hope to stress that we should recognize our own needs and should allow others to take care of us and return the love we show to them.

AUTHENTIC AND INAUTHENTIC LOVE

"Love" That Stifles

It isn't always easy to distinguish between authentic love, which enhances us and those we love, and the kind of "love" that diminishes ourselves and those to whom we attempt to give it. Certainly, there are forms of pseudo-love that parade as real love but that have the effect of crippling not only ourselves but also those we say we love. Later in this section I describe my view of genuine love; here, I want to list some signs of what I consider inauthentic love. This list isn't rigid or definitive, but it may give you some ideas you can use in thinking about the quality of your love.

I believe my love is inauthentic when:

- I have an inordinate need to control the other person.
- I cannot allow my loved ones the freedom to decide for themselves but in many ways dictate how they should be in order to be loved by me.
- There are threats attached to my loving.
- I really don't trust the other person or let the other person trust me.
- I refuse to allow the other person to grow and change, because I fear that I won't know how to respond to his or her new self.
- I treat the loved one like a possession.
- I expect or demand that the other person do for me things I'm unwilling to do for myself.
- My expectations are unrealistic.
- I expect the other person to fill my emptiness, while I avoid doing much about filling myself.
- I refuse to make any type of commitment, keeping myself free but at the same time keeping the other person uncertain about my intentions.
- I won't share my thoughts, my feelings, and my soul with the other person.
- I expect the other person to be an open book to me, while I remain closed.

I'm quite sure that all of us can find some of these manifestations of inauthentic love occurring in our relationships, and I don't think that means our love is necessarily phony. For instance, at times we might be reluctant to let another person into our private life, might have excessive expectations, or might attempt to impose our agenda on others "for their own good." What is essential is to be honest with ourselves and to recognize when we are doing things that are not expressions of genuine love, for then we can change these patterns.

Some Meanings of Authentic Love

So far, I've discussed mostly what I think love is *not*. Now I'd like to share some of the positive meanings love has for me.

Love means that I *know* the person I love. I'm aware of the many facets of the other person—not just the beautiful side but also the limitations, inconsistencies, and flaws. I have an awareness of the other's feelings and thoughts, and I experience something of the core of that person. I can penetrate social masks and roles and see the other person on a deeper level.

Love means that I *care* about the welfare of the person I love. To the extent that it is genuine, my caring is not a smothering of the person or a possessive clinging. On the contrary, my caring liberates both of us. If I care about you, I'm concerned about your growth, and I hope you will become all that you can become. Consequently, I don't put up roadblocks to your personal growth, even though it may result in my discomfort at times.

Love means having *respect* for the *dignity* of the person I love. If I love you, I can see you as a separate person, with your own values and thoughts and feelings, and I do not insist that you surrender your identity and conform to an image of what I expect you to be for me. I can allow and encourage you to stand alone and to be who you are, and I avoid treating you as an object or using you primarily to gratify my own needs.

Love means having a *responsibility* toward the person I love. If I love you, I'm responsive to most of your major needs as a person. This responsibility does not entail my doing for you what you are capable of doing for yourself; nor does it mean that I run your life for you. It *does* imply acknowledging that what I am and what I do affects you, so that I am directly involved in your happiness and your misery. A lover does have the capacity to hurt or neglect the loved one, and in this sense I see that love entails an acceptance of some responsibility for the impact on you of my way of being.

Love means *growth* for both myself and the person I love. If I love you, I am growing as a result of my love. You are a stimulant for me to become more fully what I might become, and my loving enhances your being as well. We each grow as a result of caring and being cared for; we each share in an enriching experience that does not detract from our being.

Love means making a *commitment* to the person I love. This commitment does not entail surrendering our total selves to each other; nor does it imply that the relationship is necessarily permanent. It does entail a willingness to stay with each other in times of pain, uncertainty, struggle, and despair, as well as in times of calm and enjoyment.

Love means a *sharing with* and an *experiencing with* the person I love. My love for you implies that I want to spend time with you, share meaningful aspects of your life with you, and experience with you what is meaningful in your life.

Love means *trusting* the person I love. If I love you, I trust that you will accept my caring and my love and that you won't deliberately hurt me. I trust that you will find me lovable and that you won't abandon me; I trust the reciprocal nature of our love. If we trust each other, we are willing to be open to each other and can shed masks and pretenses and reveal our true selves.

Love means that I am *vulnerable*. If I open myself up to you in trust, then I am also vulnerable to experiencing hurt and rejection and loss. Since you aren't perfect, you have the capacity to hurt me; and, since there are no guarantees in love, there is no real security that your love will last forever.

Love is *freeing*. Love is freely given, not doled out on demand. At the same time, my love for you is not contingent on whether you fulfill my expectations of you. Authentic love does not imply "I'll love you when you become perfect or when you become what I expect you to become." Nevertheless, love is not *unconditional*. Although genuine love is not based on whether we live up to each other's expectations, this does not imply that I will be loved and accepted regardless of what I do or who I become. I can destroy or lessen your love for me, just as I can work to enhance it.

Love is *expansive*. If I love you, I encourage you to reach out and develop other relationships. Although our love for each other and our commitment to each other might preclude certain actions on our parts, we are not totally and exclusively wedded to each other. It is a pseudo-love that cements one person to another in such a way that he or she is not given room to grow.

Love means having a *want* for the person I love without having a *need* for that person in order to be a separate identity. If I am nothing without you, then I'm not really free to love you. If I love you and you leave, I'll experience a loss and be sad and lonely, but I'll still be able to survive. If I am overly dependent on you for my meaning and my survival, then I am not free to challenge our relationship; nor am I free to challenge and confront you. Because of my fear of losing you, I'll settle for less than I want, and this settling will surely lead to feelings of resentment.

Love means *identifying* with the person I love. If I love you, I can empathize with you and see the world through your eyes. I can identify with you because I'm able to see myself in you and you in me. This closeness does not imply a continual "togetherness," for distance and separation are sometimes essential in a loving relationship. Distance can intensify a loving bond, and it can help us rediscover ourselves, so that we are able to meet each other in a new way.

Love is *selfish*. I can only love you if I genuinely love, value, appreciate, and respect myself. If I am empty, then all I can give you is my emptiness. If I feel that I'm complete and worthwhile in myself, then I'm able to give to you out of my fullness. One of the best ways for me to give you love is by fully enjoying myself with you.

Love can tolerate *imperfection*. In a love relationship there are times of boredom, times when I may feel like giving up, times of real strain, and times I experience an impasse. Authentic love does not imply perpetual happiness. I can stay during rough times, however, because I can remember what we had together in the past, and I can envision what we will have together in our future if we care enough to face our problems and work them through.

I would like to conclude this discussion of the meanings authentic love has for me by sharing a few thoughts from Fromm's *The Art of Loving* (1956). I'm fond of Fromm's description of mature love, which for me sums up the essential characteristics of authentic love:

> Mature love is union under the condition of preserving one's integrity, one's individuality. Love is an active power in man; a power which breaks through the walls which separate man from his fellow men, which unites him with others; love makes him overcome the sense of isolation and separateness, yet it permits him to be himself, to retain his integrity. In love this paradox occurs that two beings become one and yet remain two [pp. 20–21].

IS IT WORTH IT TO LOVE?

Often I hear people say something like "Sure, I need to love and to be loved, but is it *really* worth it?" Underlying this question is a series of other questions: Can I survive without love? Is the risk of rejection and loss worth taking? Are the rewards of opening myself up as great as the risks?

It would be comforting to know an absolute answer to these questions, but I fear that each of us must struggle to decide for ourselves whether it's worth it to love. It seems to me that our first task is to decide whether we prefer isolation to intimacy. Of course, our choice is not between extreme isolation and constant intimacy; surely there are degrees of both. But we do need to decide whether to experiment with extending our narrow world to include significant others. We can increasingly open ourselves to another and discover for ourselves what that is like for us; alternatively, we can decide that people are basically unreliable or not worth the risk and that it's better to be safe and go hungry emotionally. We can also decide how far we choose to trust and how important loving and being loved will be in our life.

Suppose now that you feel unable to love or to give love and thus feel isolated, but that you'd like to learn how to become more intimate. You might begin by acknowledging this reality to yourself, as well as to those in your life with whom you'd like to become more intimate. In this way you can take some significant beginning steps.

In answering the question of whether it's worth it to you to love, you can also challenge some of your attitudes and beliefs concerning acceptance and rejection. I've encountered many people who believe that it isn't worth it to love because of the possibility of experiencing rejection. If you feel this way, you can decide whether to stop at this barrier. You can ask yourself: "What's so catastrophic about being rejected? Will I die if someone I love leaves me? Can I survive the emotional hurt that comes with disappointment in love?"

Hodge (1967) writes that, as adults, we're no longer helpless and that we can do something about rejection and hurt. We can choose to leave relationships that aren't satisfying; we can learn to survive hurt, even though it may be painful; and we can realize that being rejected by a person doesn't mean that we are fundamentally unlovable. I very much like the last line in Hodge's *Your Fear of Love*, and I ask you to consider how it may apply to you: "We can discover for ourselves that it is worth the risk to love, even though we tremble and even though we know we will sometimes experience the hurt we fear" (p. 270).

TIME OUT FOR PERSONAL REFLECTION

1. *The following are some possible reasons for thinking that it is or isn't worth it to love. Check the ones that fit your own thoughts and feelings.*

   It's worth it to love, because

   _____ *of the joy involved when two people love each other.*
   _____ *the rewards are greater than the risks.*
   _____ *a life without love is empty.*

   List other reasons:

   _____

   _____

   It isn't worth it to love, because

   _____ *of the pain involved when love is not returned.*
   _____ *the risks are not worth the possible rewards.*

———————   *it's better to be alone than with someone you might no longer love (or who might no longer love you).*

List other reasons:

_____

_____

2. *What is your answer to the question of whether it's worth it to love?*

_____

_____

_____

_____

3. *Review my list of the meanings love has for me, and then list some of the meanings love has for you.*

_____

_____

_____

_____

4. *Think of someone you love. What specifically do you love about that person? (Example: I love his sensitivity.) Then, list specific ways that you show your love to this person. (Example: I spend time with her. I enjoy doing things that make her happy.)*

_____

_____

_____

_____

5. *What are some questions you have regarding the ideas discussed so far in this chapter? Which ones would you most like to hear the others in your class respond to?*

_____

_____

_____

_____

LOVE AND SEXUALITY

Although I treat the issues of love, sex, and intimacy in different chapters, these topics cannot really be completely separated. So I hope you'll try to make some connections by integrating the ideas of the three chapters and by applying them to yourself. The following exercises should help get you started.

A Personal Inventory on Love and Sexuality

After you've worked through the following questions and indicated the responses that actually apply to you now, you might want to take the inventory again and give the responses that indicate how you'd like to be. Feel free to circle more than one response for a given item or to write your own response on the blank line. You may want to take the inventory again at the end of the course to see whether, or to what degree, any of your beliefs, attitudes, and values concerning love and sexuality have changed.

1. As far as my need for love is concerned,
    a. I can give love, but it's difficult for me to receive love.
    b. I can accept love, but it's difficult for me to give love.
    c. Neither giving nor accepting love is especially difficult for me.
    d. Both giving and accepting love are difficult for me.

    e. _____

2. I feel that I have been loved by another person
    a. only once in my life.
    b. never in my life.
    c. many times in my life.
    d. as often as I've chosen to open up to another.

    e. _____

3. When it comes to self-love and appreciation of myself,
    a. I have a healthy regard and respect for myself.
    b. I find the idea of self-love objectionable.
    c. I encounter great difficulty in appreciating myself.
    d. I'm generally able to love myself, but there are parts of myself that I dislike.

    e. _____

4. I love others because
    a. I want their love and acceptance in return.
    b. I fear being alone if I don't.

c. I like the feeling of loving another.
d. I derive joy from giving to another person.

e. _____

5. To me, love is best described as
   a. giving to another out of my fullness as a person.
   b. thinking more of the other person than I do of myself.
   c. relating to another in the hope that I'll not feel so empty.
   d. caring for another to the same degree that I care about myself.

   e. _____

6. My greatest fear of loving and being loved is
   a. that I will have nothing to give another person.
   b. that I will be vulnerable and may be rejected.
   c. that I might be accepted and then not know what to do with this acceptance.
   d. that I will feel tied down and that my freedom will be restricted.

   e. _____

7. In regard to commitment in a loving relationship, I believe that
   a. without commitment there is no real love.
   b. commitment means I love that person exclusively.
   c. commitment means that I stay with the person in times of crisis and attempt to change things.
   d. commitment is not necessary for love.

   e. _____

8. For me, the relationship between love and sex is that
   a. love often develops *after* a sexual relationship.
   b. sex without love is unsatisfying.
   c. the two must always be present in an intimate relationship with another person of the opposite sex.
   d. sex can be very exciting and gratifying without a love relationship.

   e. _____

9. I could become more lovable by
   a. becoming more sensitive to the other person.
   b. learning to love and care for myself more than I do now.
   c. doing what I think others expect of me.
   d. being more genuinely myself, without roles and pretenses.

   e. _____

10. If I loved a person who did not love me in return, I would
    a. never trust another love relationship.

b. feel devastated.

c. convince myself that I really didn't care.

d. feel hurt but eventually open myself to others.

e. _____

11. In love relationships, generally I
   a. settle for what I have with the other person as long as things are comfortable.
   b. constantly seek to improve the relationship.
   c. am willing to talk openly about things I don't like in myself and in the other person.
   d. am able to express positive feelings but unable to express negative feelings.

   e. _____

12. When it comes to talking about sexuality,
   a. I encounter difficulty, especially with my partner.
   b. I feel free in discussing sexual issues openly.
   c. I usually become defensive.
   d. I'm willing to reveal my feelings if I trust the other person.

   e. _____

13. My attitudes and values toward sexuality have been influenced principally by
   a. my parents.
   b. my friends and peers.
   c. my church.
   d. my school experiences.

   e. _____

14. I think that social norms and expectations
   a. encourage the dichotomy between male and female roles.
   b. impose heavy performance standards on men.
   c. make it very difficult to develop one's own ideas about what constitutes normal sexuality.
   d. clash with my own upbringing.

   e. _____

15. I think that sexual attitudes could be improved by
   a. giving children more information while they are growing up.
   b. teaching principles of religion.
   c. increasing people's knowledge about the physical and emotional aspects of sexuality.

     d. allowing people to freely discuss their sexual values and conflicts in small groups.

     e. _____

Here are a few suggestions of things you can do after you've finished this inventory:

1. You can use any of the items that strike you as points of departure for your journal writing.
2. If you're involved in an intimate relationship, you can ask the other person to take the inventory and then share and compare your responses. Your responses can be used as a basis for dialogue on these important issues.
3. You can write down other questions that occurred to you as you took this inventory, and you can bring these questions to class.
4. Your class can form small groups in which to discuss the items that had the most meaning for each person.

A Sentence-Completion Exercise on Love and Sex

Complete the following sentences by quickly writing down your immediate response.

1. My greatest fear of love is _____

2. To me, love without sex is _____

3. To me, love with sex is _____

4. To me, sex without love is _____

5. I need love because _____

6. I feel most loved when _____

7. One lovable quality about me is _____

8. I could increase my ability to love others by _____

_____

9. I express my love for others primarily by _____

_____

10. To me, love means primarily _____

11. If nobody loved me, _____

12. For me, the greatest risk in loving others is _____

_____

13. For me, the greatest risk in letting others love me is _____

_____

14. When I'm with those I love, I _____

_____

15. When I'm separated from my loved ones, I _____

_____

CHAPTER SUMMARY

Although we have a need to love and to be loved, most of us encounter barriers to meeting these needs. Our self-doubt and assumptions that we are not worthy of being loved are perhaps the major roadblocks to loving others and to remaining open to receiving love from others. Although many of us have been brought up believing that self-love is egotistical, in reality we are not able to love others unless we love and appreciate ourselves. How can we give to others that which we first do not possess ourselves? Our fear of love is another major impediment to loving. Many people would like there to be guarantees that our love for special people will last as long as we live, but the stark reality is that there are no guarantees. It helps to realize that loving and trembling go together and to accept that we must learn to love in spite of our fears.

There are a number of myths and misconceptions about love that make it difficult to be open to giving and receiving love, a few of which are the myth of eternal love, the myth that love implies constant closeness, the myth of the exclusiveness of love, the myth that true love means we are selfless, and the myth of falling in love. Although love that is genuine results in the growth of both persons, some "love" has a stifling impact. Not all that poses as real love is authentic, and one of the major challenges is to decide for ourselves the meanings of authentic love. By recognizing our attitudes about loving, we can increase our ability to choose the ways in which we behave in our love relationships.

Now list some of the ideas that seemed most significant to you or that you'd most like to remember.

_____

_____

_____

_____

_____

ACTIVITIES AND EXERCISES

1. Mention some early decisions that you made regarding your own ability to love or to be loved, such as:

   - "I'm not lovable unless I produce."
   - "I'm not lovable unless I meet others' expectations."
   - "I won't love another because of my fears of rejection."
   - "I'm not worthy of being loved."

   Write down some of the messages that you've received and perhaps accepted uncritically. How has your ability to feel loved or to give love been restricted by these messages and decisions?
2. Ask several people to give their responses to the question "Is it worth it to love?" Bring these responses to class, and share them with others.
3. For a period of at least a week, pay close attention to the messages conveyed by the media concerning love. What picture of love do you get from television? What do popular songs portray about love? Make a list of some common myths regarding love that you see promoted by the media. Some of these myths might include:

   - Love means that two people never argue or disagree.
   - Love implies giving up one's identity.
   - Love implies constant closeness and romance.
   - Love means rarely having negative feelings toward those you love.

4. How much do you agree with the proposition that you can't fully love others unless you first love yourself? How does this apply to you? In your journal, you might want to write some notes to yourself concerning the situations in which you don't appreciate yourself. You might also keep a record of the times and events when you do value and respect yourself.
5. How important is love in your life right now? Do you feel that you love others in the ways you'd like to? Do you feel that you're loved by others in the ways you want to be?
6. Are you an active lover or a passive lover? You might try writing down the ways in which you demonstrate your caring for those you love and then ask them to read your list and discuss with you how they see your style of loving.

SUGGESTED READINGS

Buscaglia, L. (1972). *Love*. Thorofare, N.J.: Charles B. Slack. This is a very personal and beautiful book of random thoughts on the meanings of love.

Buscaglia, L. (1982). *Living, Loving, and Learning.* New York: Ballantine. This popular book is a collection of some of Buscaglia's lectures on love. Some topics are viewing love as a behavior modifier, building bridges not barriers, choosing life, and speaking of love.

Fromm, E. (1956; paperback edition, 1974). *The Art of Loving.* New York: Harper & Row (Colophon). Love in all its aspects is the subject. Fromm presents a philosophy of love in a book that can be read several times for new insights.

Gibran, K. (1923). *The Prophet.* New York: Knopf. A rich, poetic treatment of many facets of life, including love, marriage, giving, work, freedom, children, death, friendship, self-knowledge, and so on.

Hodge, M. (1967). *Your Fear of Love.* Garden City, N.Y.: Doubleday. This is a very useful and easy-to-read book that describes how fears originate and how they can prevent us from loving. Hodge gives a personal and down-to-earth treatment of topics such as freedom, anger, sex, manhood, and womanhood. He also explores the concept of living to be ourselves, which includes learning to love ourselves and to live spontaneously.

Jourard, S. (1971). *The Transparent Self: Self-Disclosure and Well-Being* (rev. ed.). New York: Van Nostrand. Jourard contends that we have many ways of concealing our real selves and that we use masks and roles to keep from being open. He makes a case for the value of being transparent in human relationships. The book includes some excellent essays on love, sex, marriage, and the lethal aspects of male roles.

Powell, J. (1969). *Why Am I Afraid to Tell You Who I Am?* Nile, Ill.: Argus. In this sequel to the author's popular *Why Am I Afraid to Love?* the theme of growing through open relationships is explored.

8

INTIMATE RELATIONSHIPS

PRECHAPTER SELF-INVENTORY

Use the following scale to respond: 4 = this statement is true of me *most* of the time; 3 = this statement is true of me *much* of the time; 2 = this statement is true of me *some* of the time; 1 = this statement is true of me *almost none* of the time.

1. I consider the absence of conflict and crisis as a sign of a good relationship.
2. For me, it's difficult to have many close relationships at one time.
3. If I'm involved in a satisfactory relationship, I won't feel attracted to others besides my partner.
4. I believe that the mark of a successful relationship is that I enjoy being both with and without the other person.
5. I would like to find intimacy with one other person.
6. At times, wanting too much from another person causes me difficulties in the relationship.
7. I think that an exclusive relationship is bound to become dull, predictable, and unexciting.
8. I know what I'm looking for in a relationship.
9. I have what I want in terms of intimacy with others.
10. I can be emotionally intimate with another person without being physically intimate with that person.

INTRODUCTION

Much of this chapter focuses on marriage as one typical form of intimate relationship. Although many students either aren't married or are actively involved in some alternative life-style, there seems to be ample reason to dwell on this type of intimate relationship. Marriage is still one of the most widely practiced life-styles in our society, particularly if the term *marriage* is construed broadly to include the many couples who consider themselves committed to an intense relationship even though they are not legally married as well as those who are creating marriages that are different in many respects from the traditional kind. I do want to stress, however, that whether we choose to marry or not we can be involved in many different types of intimate relationship, and much of what is true for marriage is true for these other types as well. Allowing for the differences in relationships, the signs of growth and meaningfulness are much the same, and so are the problems. Consequently, whatever life-style you choose, you can use the ideas in this chapter as a basis for thinking about the role of intimacy in your life.

TYPES OF INTIMACY

As we saw earlier, Erikson maintains that the challenge of forming intimate relationships is the major task of early adulthood. Intimacy implies
that we are able to share significant aspects of ourselves with others. Although marriage is one of the most common ways we can share ourselves
with another physically and psychologically, there are other ways of experiencing and expressing intimacy besides being married. One significant
type of intimate relationship is that between parents and children. Many
of the ideas in this chapter can be applied to bettering your relationships
with your parents or your children. You can take a fresh look at these
relationships, including both their frustrations and their delights, and you
can think about how you might initiate some changes.

I'm thinking now of David, who told me about how little closeness he
had experienced with his father. He saw his father as a "rock," yet he
deeply wished that he could be physically and emotionally close to him.
David made the difficult decision to talk to his father and tell him exactly
how he felt and what he wanted. Instead of the cold rebuff he had expected, he found that his father reached out to him and admitted that he,

too, wanted to be close but that he felt awkward in asking for it—and that he had feared *David's* rejection!

The experience David had with his father could have occurred in any intimate relationship. We can experience feelings of awkwardness, unexpressed desires, and fears of rejection with our friends, lovers, spouses, parents, or children. Thus, many of the suggestions I make in this chapter in regard to couples apply also to other significant relationships. In particular, you can use the ideas about growth and change to improve your relationship with your parents or children, especially if you recognize that either you or they have outgrown the relationship you had previously.

Deep and meaningful friendships with persons of either sex are another type of intimacy. In my own life, I feel very fortunate in having several close friends. With all these women and men I feel the freedom to be fully myself, which includes being vulnerable, trusting them, caring for them, enjoying my time with them, and knowing that each of the relationships is a two-way street. I believe it's important to think about how free we feel with our closest friends, the respect we give them and the respect we receive from them, and the degree to which we feel enriched by each friendship. As you read this chapter, I hope you'll reflect on the quality of your friendships and on what you can do to make them better.

The intimacy we share with another person can be emotional, intellectual, physical, spiritual, or any combination of these. It can be exclusive or nonexclusive, long-term or brief. For example, many of the participants in the personal-growth groups that Marianne and I conduct become very emotionally involved with one another. During the space of a week in which they share their struggles, they develop a closeness that is real and meaningful, even though they may not keep in touch once the week is over. At the same time, I've observed how reluctant many people are to open themselves up emotionally in such short-term situations as a weekend personal-growth group, because they want to avoid the sadness of parting. They might say "What if we do get close and really care for one another here? I hate to see all this intimacy come to an end when the workshop is over!" Bonds of intimacy and friendship can be formed in a short period, however, and subsequent distance in space and time need not diminish the quality of the friendships we form. For example, Marianne and I are very close with a couple who live 500 miles away. Even though we see one another only for several days each year, our contact is meaningful, and we experience a continuity in the relationship when we're together. We don't need to engage in small talk, and we have very personal conversations and intimate moments. To take another example, several years ago Marianne met a foreign-exchange student from Norway. They had a relatively short time together, but they developed a genuine friendship that they keep alive through correspondence and occasional visits to each other's country. Both of them continue to benefit from their exchanges to this day.

Experiences such as the ones I've just described convince me that we only rob ourselves when we avoid intimacy. We may pass up the chance to really get to know neighbors and new acquaintances, because we fear that either we or our new friends will move and that the friendship will come to an end. Similarly, we may not want to open ourselves to intimacy with sick or dying persons, because we fear the pain of losing them. Although such fears may be natural ones, too often we allow them to cheat us of the uniquely rich experience of being truly close to another person. We can enhance our life greatly by daring to care about others and fully savoring the time we can share with them now.

As you read the remainder of this chapter, I hope that you'll spend time thinking about the quality of all the various kinds of intimacy you experience in your life now. Are you involved in the kinds of intimate relationships that you want to be involved in? How can you enhance your relationships? What are *you* willing to do to improve them? What is your view of a growing relationship? I also hope that you'll think of ways to apply the themes I discuss in connection with couples to the many types of relationship in your life.

The one idea I most want to stress is that you can choose the kinds of intimate relationship you want to experience. Often, we fail to make our own choices and instead fall into a certain type of relationship because we think "This is the way it's *supposed* to be." For example, I wonder how many people marry who in reality might prefer to remain single—particularly women, who often feel the pressure to marry and have a family because it's "natural" for them to do so. Instead of blindly accepting that relationships must be a certain way or that only one type of life-style is possible, you have the choice of giving real thought to the question of what types of intimacy have meaning for you.

TIME OUT FOR PERSONAL REFLECTION

1. *What do you look for in a person you'd like to marry or form an intimate relationship with? For each item, put a 1 in the space if the quality is* very important *to you, a 2 if it is* somewhat important, *and a 3 if it is* not very important.

_____   *intelligence*
_____   *character (a strong sense of values)*
_____   *physical appearance and attractiveness*
_____   *money and possessions*
_____   *charm*

_____ *prestige and status*
_____ *a strong sense of identity*
_____ *expressiveness and tendency to be outgoing*
_____ *a sense of humor*
_____ *caring and sensitivity*
_____ *power*
_____ *independence*
_____ *a quiet person*
_____ *someone who will make decisions for me*
_____ *someone I can lean on*
_____ *someone who will lean on me*
_____ *someone I can't live without*
_____ *someone who works hard and is disciplined*
_____ *someone who likes to play and have fun*
_____ *someone who has values similar to mine*
_____ *someone I'd like to grow old with*

Now list the three qualities that you value most in a person when you are considering an intimate relationship.

_____

_____

_____

_____

2. *Why do you think a person might want an intimate relationship with you? Look over the qualities listed above, and then list the qualities you see yourself as having.*

_____

_____

_____

_____

3. *Identify the kinds of intimate relationship you have chosen so far in your life. If you aren't presently involved in any significant intimate relationships, would you like to be?*

_____

_____

_____

_____

4. *What do you get from being involved in a significant relationship? Check the responses that apply to you, and add your own on the lines provided.*

_____ *a feeling of being cared for*
_____ *a sense of importance*
_____ *joy in being able to care for another person*
_____ *excitement*
_____ *the feeling of not being alone in the world*
_____ *sharing and companionship*

Other:

_____

_____

_____

_____

MEANINGFUL RELATIONSHIPS: A PERSONAL VIEW

In this section I share my view of the characteristics of a meaningful relationship. Although it may appear that these guidelines pertain to couples, most of them are also relevant to other interpersonal relationships, such as those between parent and child and between friends of the same or opposite sex. In a broader sense you can apply these guidelines to any significant relationship that you have and want to examine. Take, for example, the guideline "The two persons are willing to work at keeping their relationship alive." Sometimes parents and children take each other for granted and rarely spend time talking about how they are getting along. Either parent or child may expect the other to assume the major responsibility for their relationship. The same principle applies to friends or to spouses. As you look over my list, adapt it to your own relationships, keeping in mind your particular cultural values. What qualities do *you* think are most important in your relationships?

I see intimate relationships as most meaningful when they are dynamic and evolving rather than fixed or final. Thus, there may be periods of joy and excitement followed by times of struggle, pain, and distance. Unless two persons have settled for complacency, there are probably not too many long periods in which they are the same with each other. As long as they are growing and changing, both separately and as a couple, their relationship is bound to change as well. As I look at intimacy from this growth-and-change perspective, the following are some of the qualities of a relationship that seem most important to me.

• *Each person in the relationship has a separate identity.* I like the way Kahlil Gibran (1923) expresses this thought in *The Prophet:* "But let there be spaces in your togetherness, and let the winds of the heavens dance between you" (p. 16).

• *Although each person desires the other, each can survive without the other.* They are not so tightly bound together that, if they are separated, one or the other becomes lost and empty. For example, there are those couples who are rarely apart. They may labor under the myth that a desire for time alone is an indication that something is amiss in their relationship. They may not realize the potential strain on their relationship if they see their identity only as a couple (without separate identities). Some couples split up because they eventually feel suffocated. They did not give each other the distance necessary to develop as individuals.

• *Each is able to talk openly with the other about matters of significance to the relationship.* They are willing to engage in dialogue about the quality of what they have together. They can openly express grievances and let each other know the changes they desire.

• *Each person assumes responsibility for his or her own level of happiness and refrains from blaming the other if he or she is unhappy.* Of course, in a close relationship, the unhappiness of one person is bound to affect the other, but no one should expect another person to *make* him or her happy, fulfilled, or excited.

• *The two persons are willing to work at keeping their relationship alive.* Meaningful relationships are not easy to come by. Nor are they stagnant. If we hope to keep a relationship vital, we must reevaluate and revise our way of being with each other from time to time. Like a book, relationships need to be updated. Some experimentation is needed, and this entails effort.

• *The two persons are able to have fun and to play together; they enjoy doing things with each other.* It is easy to become so serious that we forget to take the time to enjoy those we love. One way of changing drab relationships is to become aware of the infrequency of playful moments and then determine what things are getting in the way of enjoying life.

• *Each person is growing, changing, and opening up to new experiences.* I believe that, if we cannot make it alone, we cannot make it with another person. When we rely on others for our personal fulfillment and confirmation as persons, then we are in trouble. For me, the best way to build solid relationships with others is to work on developing our own centeredness and to be willing to do what is necessary to grow as individuals.

• *If the relationship contains a sexual component, each person makes some attempt to keep the romance alive.* They may not always experience

the intensity and novelty of the early period of their relationship, but they can devise ways of creating a climate in which they can experience romance and closeness. They may go places they haven't been to before or otherwise vary their routine in small ways. They recognize when their sex life is getting dull and look for ways to rejuvenate the boring aspects of their life together. In their lovemaking they are sensitive to each other's needs and desires; at the same time, they are able to ask each other for what they want and need.

• *The two persons are equal in the relationship.* People who feel that they are typically the "givers" and that their partners are usually unavailable when they need them might question the balance in their relationships. Also, each person might ask whether he or she feels OK in the presence of the other. In some relationships, one person may feel compelled to assume a superior position relative to the other—for example, to be very willing to listen and give advice yet unwilling to go to the other person and show any vulnerability or need.

• *Each person actively demonstrates concern for the other.* In a vital relationship the partners do more than just talk about how much they value each other. The actions they perform show their care and concern more eloquently than any words.

• *Each person finds meaning and sources of nourishment outside the relationship.* Their lives did not begin when they met each other; nor would their lives end if they should part.

• *Each avoids manipulating, exploiting, and using the other.* They each respect and care for the other and are willing to see the world through the other's eyes.

• *Each person is moving in a direction in life that is personally meaningful.* They are each excited about the quality of their lives and their projects. Both of them basically like who they are and what they are becoming.

• *If they are married, they stay married out of choice, not simply for the sake of their children, out of duty, or because of convenience.* They choose to stay together even if things get rough or if they sometimes experience emptiness in their marriage. They share a commitment to look at what is wrong in their relationship and to work on changing undesirable situations.

• *Each person recognizes the need for solitude and is willing to create the time in which to be alone.* Moreover, each recognizes the other's need for private times.

• *Each avoids assuming an attitude of ownership toward the other.* Although they may experience jealousy at times, they do not demand that the other person deaden his or her feelings for others.

• *Each shows some flexibility in role behavior.* They are willing to share chores and activities rather than to refuse on the ground that a certain activity isn't "masculine" or "feminine." They may even reverse roles at times.

• *They do not expect the other to do for them what they are capable of doing for themselves.* They don't expect the other person to make them feel alive, take away their boredom, assume their risks, or make them feel valued and important. Each is working toward creating his or her own autonomous identity. Consequently, neither person depends on the other for confirmation of his or her personal worth; nor does one walk in the shadow of the other.

• *Each discloses himself or herself to the other.* They need not indiscriminately share every secret, but they are able to share whatever is germane to the relationship. They are each willing to make themselves known to the other in significant ways, which may include sharing joy, expectations, frustrations, dreams, fears, boredom, excitement, and other feelings.

• *Each allows the other a sense of privacy.* Because they recognize each other's individual integrity, they avoid prying into every thought or manipulating the other to disclose what he or she wants to keep private.

• *Each person has a desire to give to the other.* They have an interest in each other's welfare and a desire to see that the other person is fulfilled. Thus, they go beyond thinking only of what the other person can do for them.

• *They encourage each other to become all that they are capable of becoming.* Unfortunately, people often have an investment in keeping those with whom they are intimately involved from changing. Their expectations and needs may lead them to resist changes in their partner and thus make it difficult for their partner to grow. However, if they recognize their fears, they can challenge their need to block their partner's progress. On the other hand, people sometimes hinder their partner's growth by refusing to give them a chance to change or refusing to believe in their ability to do so. They can encounter this tendency in themselves by expressing their own desires, without nagging and faultfinding, and by caring enough to challenge their partner when it seems appropriate to do so.

• *Each has a commitment to the other.* The more I work with couples, the more I see commitment as a vital part of an intimate relationship. By commitment, I mean that the people involved have an investment in their future together and that they are willing to stay with each other in times of crisis and conflict. Although many people express an aversion to any long-term commitment in a relationship, I wonder how deeply they will allow themselves to be loved if they believe that the relationship can be dissolved on a whim when things look bleak. Perhaps, for some people, a fear of intimacy gets in the way of developing a sense of commitment. Loving and being loved is both exciting and frightening, and we may have to struggle with the issue of how much anxiety we want to tolerate. Commitment to another person involves risk and carries a price, but it is an essential part of an intimate relationship.

One of the reviewers of this book made the comment that the single major interest among college students is creating and maintaining friendships, especially intimate relationships. There is no single or easy prescription for success in this case, but I do think that developing meaningful relationships entails the willingness to struggle.

I am struck with how many college students encounter difficulties in keeping intimate relationships alive. There are some choices you can make that I think will increase your chances of developing lasting friendships. These choices include: being tolerant of differences between your friends and yourself; learning to become aware of conflicts and dealing with them constructively; being willing to let the other person know how you are affected in the relationship; staying in the relationship even though you may experience a fear of rejection; checking out your assumptions with others instead of deciding for them what they are thinking and feeling; being willing to make yourself vulnerable and to take risks; keeping yourself open about how you feel about your relationships with others; and avoiding the temptation to live up to others' expectations instead of being true to yourself.

In summary, creating and maintaining friendships and intimate relationships requires hard work and the willingness to ride out hard times. Further, in order to be a good friend to another, you must first be a good friend to yourself, which implies knowing yourself and caring about yourself. The following Time Out asks you to focus on some of the ways in which you see yourself as an alive and growing person, which is the foundation of building meaningful relationships.

TIME OUT FOR PERSONAL REFLECTION

1. *What are some ways in which you see yourself as growing? In what ways do you see yourself as resisting personal growth by sticking with old and comfortable patterns, even if they don't work? To facilitate your reflection, look over the following statements, and mark each one with a "T" or an "F," depending on whether you think it generally applies to you.*

_____ *I keep myself attractive.*

_____ *If I'm involved in an intimate relationship, I tell the other person what I want.*

_____ *I'm willing to try new things.*

_____ *Rather than settling for comfort in a relationship or in life, I ask for more.*

_____ *If I'm involved in an intimate relationship, I tell the other person what I'm feeling.*

_____ *I'm engaged in projects that are meaningful to me.*

2. *List other ways in which you're growing:*

_____

_____

_____

_____

3. *List some ways in which you resist personal growth:*

_____

_____

_____

_____

4. *In what ways do you see the person with whom you're most intimate growing and/or resisting growth?*

_____

_____

_____

_____

5. *If you're involved in a couple relationship, in what ways do you think you and your partner are growing closer? In what ways are you going in different directions?*

_____

_____

_____

_____

6. *Are you satisfied with the relationship you've just described? If not, what would you most like to change? How might you go about it?*

_____

_____

_____

_____

7. *What did you learn from doing these exercises?*

_____

_____

_____

_____

A suggestion for using this Time Out: If you're involved in a couple relationship, have your partner respond to the questions on a separate sheet of paper. Then compare your answers and discuss areas of agreement and disagreement.

DEALING WITH COMMUNICATION BLOCKS

A number of barriers to effective communication can inhibit the developing and maintaining of intimate relationships. Some of these barriers are failing to really listen to another person; selective listening—that is, hearing only what we want to hear; being overly concerned with getting our point across without considering the other's views; silently rehearsing what we will say next as we are "listening"; becoming defensive, with self-protection our primary concern; and attempting to change others rather than first attempting to understand them. In all of these cases we are focused so much on ourselves that we cannot appreciate what the other person is thinking and feeling.

The renowned psychologist Carl Rogers (1961) has written extensively on ways to improve interpersonal relationships. For him, the main block to effective communication is our tendency to evaluate and judge the statements of others. Rogers believes that what gets in the way of understanding another is the tendency to approve or disapprove, the unwillingness to put ourselves in the other's frame of reference, and the fear of being changed ourselves if we really listen to and understand a person with a viewpoint different from our own. I like his suggestion for testing the quality of our understanding of someone:

> The next time you get into an argument with your wife, or your friend, or with a small group of friends, just stop the discussion for a moment and for an experiment, institute this rule. "Each person can speak up for himself *only* after he has first restated the ideas and feelings of the previous speaker accurately, and to that speaker's satisfaction" [1961, p. 332].

Carrying out this experiment implies that you must strive to genuinely understand another person and achieve his or her perspective. Although being able to respect another person's thoughts and feelings to the extent of being able to summarize them may sound simple, it can be extremely difficult to put into practice. It involves challenging yourself to go beyond merely tuning in to what you find convenient to hear, examining your assumptions and prejudices, not attributing meanings to statements that were not intended, and not coming to quick conclusions based on superficial listening. If you are successful in challenging yourself in these ways, you can enter the subjective world of the significant person in your life; that is, you can acquire empathy, which is the necessary foundation for all intimate relationships. I fully agree with Rogers' (1980) contention that the sensitive companionship offered by an empathic person is healing and that such a deep understanding is a precious gift to another.

Effective Interpersonal Communication

When two people are communicating meaningfully, they are involved in many of the following processes: They are facing each other and making eye contact, and one is listening while the other speaks. They do not rehearse their response while the other is speaking. The listener is able to summarize accurately what the speaker has said. The language is specific and concrete. The speaker makes personal statements instead of bombarding the other with impersonal questions. The listener takes a moment to reflect on what was said and on how he or she is affected before immediately responding. There is a sincere effort to walk in the shoes of the other person. Although each has reactions to what the other is saying, there is an absence of critical judgment. Each of the parties can be honest and direct without insensitively damaging the other's dignity. Each makes "I" statements, rather than second guessing and speaking for the other. There is a willingness to check out assumptions and to avoid stereotyping. There is a respect for each other's differences and an avoidance of pressuring each other to accept a point of view. There is a congruency (or a matching) between the verbal and nonverbal messages. Each person is open to letting the other know how he or she is affected by the other. Neither person is being mysterious by expecting the other to decode his or her message.

The process described above is essential for fostering any kind of meaningful relationship. You might be your own observer while you are communicating and take note of the degree to which you practice the above principles. Decide if the quality of your relationships is satisfying to you. If you determine that you want to improve certain relationships, it will be helpful to begin by working on one of these qualities at a time.

Communicating with Your Parents

One focus of this chapter is on relationships between couples, which is a theme of virtually every personal-growth group I have led. My experience with these groups has taught me how central our relationship with our parents is and how it affects all of our other interpersonal relationships. We learn from our parents how to deal with the rest of the world. We are often unaware of the impact our parents had, and continue to have, on us. My groups are made up of people of various ages, sociocultural backgrounds, life experiences, and vocations. Yet many of the members have ongoing struggles with their parents. It is not uncommon to have a 60-year-old man and a 20-year-old woman express their frustration over not being accepted and affirmed by their parents. They are working very hard at obtaining the parental approval that they are convinced they need.

I think it is important that we recognize the present effect that our parents are having on us and then decide the degree to which we like this effect. At different times in your life you might want to reevaluate your relationship with your parents to see if there are some ways you'd like to be different with them. On the one hand, we sometimes have problems in letting our parents be other than they were when we were children. Although they may continue to treat us as children, it could be that we behave around them as we did as children and provoke their response. On the other hand, parents at times are reluctant to give up old parental roles; this does not mean that we cannot be different with them. We are often angry at them for the very things we are not willing to do, such as initiating closer contact or making time for the relationship. We complain that they are not recognizing us, and at the same time we do not recognize them. I invite you to consider revising certain relationships with your par-

ents. If you really want to be able to talk with them more intimately, you can take the first step. Again, the principles of effective communication can be applied in the enrichment of the time you spend with your parents.

SOURCES OF CONFLICT IN INTIMATE RELATIONSHIPS

A major problem that arises in intimate relationships is boredom or a sense of predictability. Regardless of how exciting and innovative a person or a couple might be, it seems inevitable that a feeling of staleness will set in at times. When this occurs, the couple can try to avoid confronting their boredom by denying its existence, or they can frankly recognize it and share it with each other. In my own experience, I find that accepting my share of responsibility for my boredom, as opposed to making my wife responsible for it, gives me a place to begin dealing with it. In general, if I'm not bored with myself, the chances are that our relationship will not *remain* dull, even though we sometimes experience a feeling of stagnation with each other.

In an address he gave a meeting of the American Association of Marriage and Family Counselors, Sidney Jourard described marriage as a dia-

logue that ends as soon as habitual ways of acting set in. He maintained that people are frequently not very creative when it comes to finding new ways of living with each other and that they tend to fall into the same ruts day after day, year after year. Moreover, many people—whether married or living together—seem to seek only superficial relationships in order to avoid risk. In Jourard's words: "The silent shrieks of pain deafen me. To be married is for many boredom or hell. To be unmarried, legally or unlegally, as many experience it is hell and despair."[1] To this lethal image of marriage and living together, Jourard proposed an alternative, life-giving model. His theme was that "Marriage Is for Life"—not in the sense of having to last a lifetime, but in the sense of giving life to the people involved. As a way of freeing ourselves from deadening ways of living together, Jourard suggested that we might have several different "marriages" with the same person. We could recognize that, at its best, marriage is a relationship that generates change through dialogue. Instead of being threatened by change, we could welcome it as necessary for keeping the relationship alive.

For Jourard, therefore, we can have a series of marriages with the same person by divorcing ourselves from dead patterns and taking our dissatisfaction as a sign that it is time for new growth. In this way, we may be able to establish a new relationship with the same person. Jourard emphasized that divorce often means that one or the other partner has made a deci-

---

[1]From "Marriage Is for Life," by Sidney Jourard. *Journal of Marriage and the Family,* July 1975, pp. 199–208.

sion not to live in the same manner as before. The meaning of a decision to divorce can thus be similar to the meaning of a suicide, in the sense that people who contemplate suicide often are saying, in part, that they are no longer willing to live in the same way as they have been living. Similarly, the changes that occur in an intimate relationship can lead one or both parties to feel that they are at an impasse and that ending the relationship is the only way out.

Personal Reflections on a Marriage

One of the signs of a growing marriage might well be that the two partners have "married and divorced" each other several times, in the sense that they see their marriage as a process of reevaluating old roles and arrangements. They separate themselves from archaic ways of being with each other and are open to a "new marriage" through renegotiation of their relationship. In this way, a marriage can be seen as something that evolves, not as a static entity.

Recently, when Marianne and I were on a vacation, we talked about the evolution and development of our marriage. At the time of our first meeting she was a German foreign-exchange student who would soon return home, and I was her high-school English teacher. We both initially resisted involvement with each other because we feared intimacy and commitment. We were sure that the relationship would eventually end.

However, things did not work out as we had expected. Over a long period of struggle and internal conflict, we made a decision to marry. Part of what made this decision difficult was our differing religious and cultural backgrounds. During our first year of marriage we each defined (or simply fell into) our respective traditional roles, which we did not challenge. Marianne modeled her vision of what a wife should be after her own parents; I was very much influenced by my parents' marriage. I found comfort in the fact that Marianne saw her primary function as taking care of the house and cooking. Control was very much of an issue for each of us, and we had our share of conflicts over our need for control of the other.

We were also in different places emotionally. Marianne was experiencing sadness and loss over leaving her country and her family, and she had not yet found a new identity. At the same time I was excited about completing my doctoral studies and getting involved in my new teaching career. I was impatient with her for not quickly resolving her difficulties and finding her own source of nourishment.

A turning point in our marriage was having a child, and then another one 18 months later. Having children brought up the issue of how we wanted to rear them, as well as our feelings about being parents. Becoming parents was something that we never really examined, for we both simply assumed that one of the reasons for marrying was to have children.

Another turning point involved Marianne's decision to go to college. She did what she had never dreamed of doing—namely, getting an advanced education. She challenged her conditioning, which did not include college in her plan for life. Encouraged by both the American family she had lived with, other close friends, and myself, she eventually got her master's degree in counseling and a license as a marriage and family therapist.

Marianne and I have found a common interest by sharing many professional activities, including writing books together, leading groups and workshops, and having both joint and independent professional practices. Our professional cooperation has enhanced our marriage, as we are able to share work that has a great deal of meaning to both of us.

I do not want to imply that we have worked through all of our sources of conflicts once and for all; we frequently have our differences and difficulties. Associated with the development of our marriage, there have been a number of crises, conflicts, and battles over control. We have had to learn to accept each other's differences, to decide what kind of parents each of us would be, to renegotiate roles and functions, and to evaluate and set priorities. We both recognize that our involvement in home and work differs. Marianne struggled in particular with the issue of balancing her duties as a student and, later, as a professional with those of a mother and a wife. While it seems easier for her now to balance her professional life with her family life, this continues to be a struggle for me.

Although there continue to be some conflicts in our relationship, we are willing to talk about what we want changed and how to do it. We realize how easy it is to get so involved in our separate lives that we fail to see the impact on our marriage and family life; we continue to learn the value of taking time to put our lives in perspective, to evaluate our ways, and to make some new choices. We realize that we need to know ourselves and develop our separate identities if we hope to have a meaningful relationship with each other. And while we value this relationship and continue to grow from it, we do not depend on each other for our survival as individuals.

TIME OUT FOR PERSONAL REFLECTION

The following questions are designed primarily for people who are involved in couple relationships. If you're not involved in such a relationship, you can apply them to whatever relationship is most significant to you right now (for instance, with your parents, children, or closest friend).

1. *What are some sources of conflict in your relationship? Check any of the following items that apply to you, and list any other areas of conflict on the lines provided.*

————————   *spending money*
————————   *use of free time*
————————   *what to do about boredom*
————————   *investment of energy in work*
————————   *interest in others of the opposite sex*
————————   *outside friendships*
————————   *wanting children*
————————   *how to deal with children*
————————   *differences in basic values*
————————   *in-laws*
————————   *sexual needs and satisfaction*
————————   *expression of caring and loving*
————————   *power struggles*
————————   *role conflicts*

Other areas of conflict:

————————————————————————————————————

————————————————————————————————————

————————————————————————————————————

————————————————————————————————————

2. *How do you generally cope with these conflicts in your relationship? Check the items that most apply to you.*

————————   *by open dialogue*
————————   *by avoidance*
————————   *by fighting and arguing*
————————   *by compromising*
————————   *by getting involved with other people or in projects*

List other ways in which you deal with conflicts in your relationship:

————————————————————————————————————

————————————————————————————————————

————————————————————————————————————

————————————————————————————————————

3. *Mention one conflict that you would like to resolve, and write down what you'd be willing to do in order to help resolve it.*

The conflict is ————————————————————————————

To attempt a resolution, I'm willing to _____

_____

4. *List some ways in which you're changed during the period of your relationship. How have your changes affected the relationship?*

_____

_____

_____

_____

5. *To what extent do you have an identity apart from the relationship? How much do you need (and depend) on the other person? Imagine that he or she is no longer in your life, and write down how your life might be different.*

_____

_____

_____

_____

6. *If you were to develop a marriage contract (or a living-together arrangement), what specific points would you most want to include?*

_____

_____

_____

_____

DIVORCE AND SEPARATION

Earlier in this chapter I mentioned Jourard's concept of establishing new marriages with the same person and suggested that a crisis doesn't have to mean that a relationship must or should end. In fact, an impasse can become a turning point that enables two people to create a new way of life together. If they both care enough about their investment in each other, and if they are committed to doing the work that is necessary to change old patterns and establish more productive ones, a crisis can actually save their relationship.

People often decide on divorcing without really giving themselves or their partner a chance to face a particular crisis and work it through. For example, a man begins to see how deadening his marriage is for him and to realize how he has contributed to his own unhappiness in it. As a result of changes in his perceptions and attitudes, he decides that he no longer wants to live with a woman in this deadening fashion. However, rather than deciding to simply end the marriage, he might allow his partner to really see and experience him as the different person he is becoming. Moreover, he might encourage her to change as well, instead of giving up on her too quickly. His progress toward becoming a more integrated person might well inspire her to work actively toward her own internal changes. This kind of work on the part of both persons takes understanding and patience, but they may find that they can meet each other as new and changing persons and form a very different kind of relationship.

Sometimes, of course, ending a relationship is the wisest course. Divorce can then be an act of courage that makes a new beginning possible. My concern is only that too many couples may not be committed enough to each other to stay together in times of crisis and struggle. As a result, they may separate at the very time when they could be making a new start.

How do two people know when a divorce is the best solution? No categorical answer can be given to this question. However, before two people do decide to split up, they might consider at least the following questions:

• Has each of them sought personal therapy or counseling? Perhaps their exploration of themselves would lead to changes that allow them to renew or strengthen their relationship.

• Have they considered marital counseling as a couple? Have they attended a couples' group or workshop to explore alternatives for their future? If they do get involved in marriage counseling of any type, is each doing so willingly, or is one of them merely going along to placate the other?

• Are both parties really interested in preserving their marriage? Perhaps one or both are not interested in keeping the *old* relationship, but it is vital that they both at least want a life together. I routinely ask both members of a couple in difficulties to decide whether they even want to live with the other person. Some of the responses people give include: "I don't really know. I've lost hope for any real change, and at this point I find it difficult to care whether we stay together or not." "I'm sure that I don't want to live with this person any more; I just don't care enough to work on improving things between us. I'm here so that we can separate cleanly and finish the business between us." "Even though we're going through some turmoil right now, I would very much like to care enough to make things better. Frankly, I'm not too hopeful, but I'm willing to give it a try." Whatever their responses, it's imperative that they each know how they feel about the possibility of renewing their relationship.

• Have they each taken the time to be alone, to get themselves in focus, and to decide what kind of life they want for themselves and with others?

• As a couple, have they taken time to be with each other for even a weekend? I'm continually surprised at how few couples arrange for time alone with each other. It's almost as if many couples fear discovering that they really have little to say to each other. This discovery in itself might be very useful, for at least they might be able to do something about the situation if they confronted it; but many couples seem to arrange their lives in such a way that they block any possibilities for intimacy. They eat dinner together with the television set blasting, or they spend all their time together taking care of their children, or they simply refuse to make time to be together.

• What do they each expect from the divorce? Frequently, problems in a marriage are reflections of internal conflicts within the individuals in that marriage. For this reason, I usually recommend that couples involved in marital counseling also engage in their own personal therapy or counseling. In general, unless there are some changes within the individuals, the problems they experienced may not end with the divorce. In fact, many who do divorce with the expectation of finding increased joy and freedom discover instead that they are still miserable, lonely, depressed, and anxious. Lacking insight into themselves, they may soon find a new partner very much like the one they divorced and repeat the same dynamics. Thus, a woman who finally decides to leave a man she thinks of as weak and passive may find a similar man to live with again, unless she comes to understand why she needs or wants to align herself with this sort of person. Or a man who contends that he has "put up with" his wife for over 20 years may find a similar person unless he understands what motivated him to stay with his first wife for so long. It seems essential, therefore, that each come to know as clearly as possible why they are divorcing and that they look at the changes they may need to make in themselves as well as in their circumstances.

Sometimes one or both members of a couple identify strong reasons for separating but say that, for one reason or another, they are not free to do so. This kind of reasoning is always worth examining, however, since an attitude of "I couldn't possibly leave" will not help either partner to make a free and sound choice. Some of the reasons people give for refusing to divorce include the following:

• "I have an investment of 15 years in this marriage, and to leave now would mean that these 15 years have been wasted." A person who feels this way might ask himself or herself: "If I really don't see much potential for change, and if my partner has consistently and over a long period of time rebuffed any moves that might lead to improving our relationship, should I stay another 15 years and have 30 years to regret?"

• "I can't leave because of the kids, but I do plan on leaving as soon as they get into high school." I often think that this kind of thinking burdens children with unnecessary guilt. In a sense, it makes them responsible for the unhappiness of their parents. I would ask: Why place the burden on them if *you* stay in a place where you say you don't want to be? And will you find another reason to cement yourself to your partner once your children grow up?

• "Since the children need both a mother and a father, I cannot consider breaking up our marriage." True, children do need both a father and a mother. But it's worth asking whether they will get much of value from either parent if they see them despising each other. How useful is the model that parents present when they stay together and the children see how little joy they experience? Might they not get more from the two parents separately? Wouldn't the parents set a better and more honest example if they openly admitted that they no longer really choose to remain together?

• "I'm afraid to divorce because I might find that I would be even more lonely than I am now." Certainly, loneliness is a real possibility. There are no guarantees that a new relationship will be established after the divorce. However, we might be more lonely living with someone we didn't like, much less love, than we would be if we were living alone. Living alone might bring far more serenity and inner strength than remaining in a relationship that is no longer right. Moreover, whether a new relationship can be established depends to a great degree on a person's self-perception. The more people become attractive to themselves, the greater the chance that others will see them as attractive.

• "One thing that holds me back from separating is that I might discover that I left too soon and that I didn't give us a fair chance." To avoid this regret, a couple should explore all the possibilities for creating a new relationship *before* making the decision to dissolve their marriage. There does come a point, however, at which a person must finally take a stand and decide, and then I see it as fruitless to brood continually over whether he or she did the right thing.

In summary, we limit our options unnecessarily whenever we tell ourselves that we *can't possibly* take a certain course of action. Before deciding to terminate a relationship, we can ask whether we've really given the other person (and ourselves) a chance to establish something new. By the same token, if we decide that we want to end the relationship but can't, it's worth asking whether we're not simply evading the responsibility for creating our own happiness. Neither keeping a relationship alive and growing nor ending one that no longer is right for us is easy, and it's tempting to find ways of putting the responsibility for our decisions on our children, mates, or circumstances. We take a real step toward genuine freedom when we fully accept that, whatever we decide, the choice is ours to make.

TIME OUT FOR PERSONAL REFLECTION

Complete the following sentences by writing down the first responses that come to mind. Suggestion: Ask your partner or a close friend to do the exercise on a separate sheet of paper; then compare and discuss your responses.

1. *To me, intimacy means* _____

   _____

2. *The most important thing in making an intimate relationship successful is* _____

   _____

3. *The thing I most fear about an intimate relationship is* _____

   _____

4. *When an intimate relationship becomes stale, I usually* _____

   _____

5. *One of the reasons I need another person is* _____

   _____

6. *One conflict that I have concerning intimate relationships is* _____

   _____

7. *In an intimate relationship, it's unrealistic to expect that* _____

   _____

8. *To me, commitment means* _____

   _____

9. *My views about marriage have been most influenced by* _____

   _____

10. *I have encouraged my partner to grow by* _____

    _____

11. *My partner has encouraged me to grow by* _____

    _____

ON CHOOSING THE SINGLE LIFE

While this chapter has so far focused on the intimacy we share with others through relationships, let us not forget the importance of intimacy with ourselves. I fear for the security of those people who depend exclusively on others to be friends while neglecting the value of learning to make friends with themselves.

In this regard, there are some people who choose to remain single (for a time or throughout their life). Some decide that marriage or any other type of committed relationship is not for them. Unfortunately, society has tended to be more accepting of this as a life-style for men than for women. Many single women are told by others that they *should* be getting married, and under this pressure some of them begin to question their own worth. Even though they enjoy their single life-style, they may eventually "choose" marriage because they begin to wonder what is wrong with them.

More women today are resisting this pressure to get married and have a family, and more women are waiting until later in life to get involved in a committed relationship. There are intrinsic values and limitations in both a marriage and a single life. Yet what I think is critical is that we weigh the pros and cons of each and freely make the choice of how we most want to live, rather than passively following someone else's script for us.

Difficulties in Being Single

The following case typifies the problems and challenges many young women face if they choose a single life-style. June likes the advantages of being single, yet she struggles with nagging doubts over whether she is missing more by not getting married, particularly when she has someone in mind whom she is fond of.

June has a successful teaching career at age 27. She earns a good salary, is living in her own house, is free to pursue additional education, and enjoys the freedom of traveling in many countries of the world. She has nobody to answer to in terms of considering changing her career. She says that her many male and female friends provide nourishment to her. She also enjoys many sports and other leisure activities. She feels a sense of accomplishment and independence, something that few people her age do.

At times June struggles with the internal pressure that she will never get married. She also feels external pressure from the man she is now having a close relationship with. But she is also very afraid to give in to his urgings to get married. While she enjoys the intimacy with him, she does not feel ready to commit herself to marriage. Though she does tell herself that she really *should* be ready at her age to take this step, she realizes that the price of getting married would be giving up much of what she values in her single life-style.

June judges herself as being too selfish to make compromises and consider her friend's needs and demands. She tells herself at times that perhaps she should be willing to give up more of what she wants so that she could share a life with him. She wonders about her chances for ever marrying if she fails to take this opportunity. Her family is also applying pressure to her to marry and not spoil a good relationship. At this time June is still searching within herself for her answer. Does she really want to get married? Who is telling her that she should get married? Does she equate being single with a lonely life? And does she want to get married because she is afraid of being seen as a spinster?

Rewards of the Single Life

Today more people are willing to remain single and defy cultural expectations. They are feeling more secure about their choice of the single life. Fewer divorced people rush to find a new mate. They tend to take more time in developing a new relationship, or they remain single. The single parent is common today. There is a cultural trend against viewing being single as a second choice or simply as a fate for those who cannot find a mate. Being single does not mean that one is deficient in social skills.

A recent television series on the single life-style included group interviews with about 20 people from various states. Groups of singles were interviewed about four main topics: being single by choice, finding oneself suddenly single, the sexual revolution, and the marriage of longtime single persons. Most of those interviewed said that there were advantages to being single, such as personal freedom, not being responsible to anyone but themselves, and not having to consider how their actions affected others. It was interesting to note, however, that those who said that they were single by choice also reported missing "that one special person" whom they could confide in about anything. They noted that they did not like casual relationships as a steady diet. Some of the women mentioned the pressure of time if they wanted to have children.

Those who found themselves suddenly single, either through divorce or death, experienced rejection as a key theme in their life. Although they felt pain over their loss and resented the absence of the security they had had in the relationship, this experience proved to be a catalyst for their growth. Some said: "I have been able to do things alone that I never thought possible." "I could meet many of my needs through a support system." "I have been more independent than I ever dreamed."

In terms of sex and the single life, many acknowledged that sex was readily available with many partners. Yet most of them did not find that casual sexual relationships were satisfying to them for very long. They most valued an emotional relationship as an important dimension of a sexual relationship.

Of those who had been single for a long time and had recently married, there was agreement that they had enjoyed their single-life style and also enjoyed being involved in a primary relationship. None of them remarked that they had married because of societal pressures, nor did any of them report having felt odd because of their singlehood. One women said: "I was single, not waiting to be married, yet open to getting married." Some eventually got married because they met a person with whom they wanted a long-term relationship.

CHAPTER SUMMARY

In this chapter I've encouraged you to think about what characterizes a growing, meaningful relationship and to ask yourself such questions as: Do I have what I want in my intimate relationships? Do I desire more (or less) intimacy? What changes would I most like to make in my intimate relationships? In each of my relationships, can both the other person and I maintain our separate identities and at the same time develop a strong bond that enhances us as individuals?

A major barrier in developing and maintaining an intimate relationship is our tendency to evaluate and judge others. By attempting to change others we typically increase their defensiveness. A key characteristic of a meaningful relationship is the ability of the people involved to listen and to respond to each other. They are able to communicate effectively, and they are committed to staying in the relationship even when communication appears to have broken down. They realize that maintaining a relationship entails dedication and hard work. Although there are many sources of conflict in intimate relationships, a major problem is a sense of predictability that comes with knowing another person well. It takes both imagination and effort to think of ways to revise our relationships so that they remain alive.

At times couples decide that their marriage is "dead," and they give serious consideration to divorce. Although this may be a solution for some situations, a marriage that has lost life can also be reinvented so that both persons are growing in the relationship. Again, commitment is essential to stay in the marriage for some time to work through those issues that are dividing them and causing them conflict.

People can still experience intimacy with others even though they choose the single life-style. Today there is a greater acceptance of being single, and this way of living does not have to be thought of as "second best." Although there are difficulties in being single, there are also some distinct advantages and rewards to this life-style.

The ideal picture I've drawn of a growing relationship is not a dogmatic or necessarily complete one; nor will your relationships, however good they are, always approximate it. I've tried to say what I think intimacy is like at its best, and my hope is that these reflections will stimulate your own independent thinking. You can begin by honestly assessing the present state of your intimate relationships and recognizing how they really are (as opposed to how you wish they were). Then you can begin to consider the choices that can lead to positive change in those areas you're dissatisfied with. Throughout this chapter I've emphasized that we must actively work on recognizing problems in ourselves and in our relationships if we are to make intimacy as rewarding as it can be. Finally, I've stressed that you can choose the kinds of intimacy you want in your life.

Now list some key ideas that you want to remember.

ACTIVITIES AND EXERCISES

Some of the following activities are appropriate for you to do on your own; others are designed for two persons in an intimate relationship to do together. Select the ones that have the most meaning for you, and consider sharing the results with the other members of your class.

1. In your journal, write down some reflections on your parents' relationship. Consider such questions as the following:

   - Would you like to have the same kind of relationship your parents have had? What are some of the things you like best about their relationship? What are some features of their relationship that you would not want to have in your own marriage?
   - How have your own views, attitudes, and practices regarding marriage and intimacy been affected by your parents' relationship? Discuss the impact of their relationship on your own marriage, intimate relationship, or views about marriage and intimacy.

2. How much self-disclosure, honesty, and openness do you want in your intimate relationships? In your journal, reflect on how much you would share your feelings concerning each of the following with your partner. Then discuss how you would like your partner to respond to this same question.

   - your sexual fantasies about another person
   - your secrets
   - your need for support from your partner
   - your angry feelings
   - your dreams
   - your desire for an affair with someone else
   - your behavior if you did decide to have an affair
   - your friendships with persons of the opposite sex
   - your ideas on religion and your philosophy of life
   - the times when you feel inadequate as a person
   - the times when you feel extremely close and loving toward your partner
   - the times in your relationship when you feel boredom, staleness, hostility, detachment, and so on

   After you've answered this question for yourself, think about how open you want *your partner* to be with *you*. If your partner were doing this exercise, what answers do you wish he or she would give for each of the preceding items?

3. Over a period of about a week, do some writing about the evolution of your relationship, and ask your partner to do the same. Consider issues such as: Why were we initially attracted to each other? How have we changed since we first met? Do I like these changes? What would I most like to change about our life together? What are the best things we have going for us? What are some problem areas we need to explore? If I could do it over again, would I select the same person? What's the future of our life together? What would I like to see us doing differently? After you've each written about these and any other questions that are significant for you, read each other's work and discuss where you want to go from here. This activity can stimulate you to talk more openly with each other and can also give each of you the chance to see how the other perceives the quality of your relationship.

4. As you look at various television shows, keep a record of the messages you get regarding marriage, family life, and intimacy. What are some common stereotypes? What sex roles are portrayed? What myths do you think are being presented? After you've kept a record for a couple of weeks or so, write down some of the attitudes that you think you

have incorporated from television and other media about marriage, family life, and intimacy.

SUGGESTED READINGS

Bach, G., & Wyden, P. (1969). *The Intimate Enemy: How to Fight Fair in Love and Marriage*. New York: Morrow. This book deals with a wide range of marital games and proposes guidelines for "fighting fair."

Cargan, L., & Malko, M. (1982). *Singles: Myths and Realities*. Beverly Hills, Calif.: Sage. The authors give a comprehensive treatment on the single life-style, including a discussion of the use of leisure time, loneliness, sex in the singles world, and singles and their parents.

Lasswell, M., & Lobsenz, N. (1976). *No-Fault Marriage: The New Technique of Self-Counseling and What It Can Help You Do*. New York: Ballantine Books. This book is designed to help couples look at their own marriage and apply some of the counseling and communication skills that they can learn in marriage counseling. The authors point out why "winning" doesn't work in marital situations.

May, R. (1974). *Love and Will*. New York: Dell. Presenting much insightful material, May discusses paradoxes of love and sex, sex without love, love and death, the relationship of love and will, and the meaning of caring.

Mayeroff, M. (1971). *On Caring*. New York: Harper & Row. This is a sensitive book on the philosophy of caring as a dimension of loving. Mayeroff discusses how caring can give meaning to life and help both oneself and the other person to grow.

Schwartz, R., & Schwartz, L. J. (1980). *Becoming a Couple: Making the Most of Every Stage of Your Relationship*. Englewood Cliffs, N.J.: Prentice-Hall (Spectrum). This book provides some useful ideas that can help couples recognize the various stages of marital development. The focus is on a no-fault structure within which couples avoid the pitfalls of playing blaming games.

9

LONELINESS
AND SOLITUDE

PRECHAPTER SELF-INVENTORY

Use the following scale to respond: 4 = this statement is true of me *most* of the time; 3 = this statement is true of me *much* of the time; 2 = this statement is true of me *some* of the time; 1 = this statement is true of me *almost none* of the time.

_____   1. I stay in unsatisfactory relationships just to avoid being lonely.

_____   2. Knowing that I am ultimately on my own in the world gives me a sense of strength and power.

_____   3. I don't know what to do with my time when I'm alone.

_____   4. I have experienced being lonely in a crowd.

_____   5. I cannot escape loneliness completely.

_____   6. I find little value in experiencing loneliness.

_____   7. My childhood was a lonely period in my life.

_____   8. My adolescent years were lonely ones for me.

_____   9. Loneliness is a problem for me in my life now.

_____   10. I generally arrange for time alone so that I can gain some perspective on what is important and what is unimportant in my life.

INTRODUCTION

In the last chapter our focus was on intimacy and interpersonal relationships. We now turn to the discussion of being alone, the experience of loneliness, and the creative use of solitude. Being with others and being with ourselves are best understood as two sides of the same coin. If we cannot stand our own company, why should others want to be with us? If we know who we are and enjoy our solitude, we have a far greater chance of creating solid, give-and-take relationships with others.

One of the greatest fears many people have is the fear of loneliness. If we associate the lonely periods in our life with pain and struggle, we may think of loneliness only as a condition to be avoided as much as possible. Furthermore, we may identify being alone with being lonely and actively avoid having time by ourselves or else fill such time with distractions and diversions. Paradoxically, out of fear of rejection and loneliness, we may even make ourselves needlessly lonely by refusing to reach out to others or by holding back parts of ourselves in our intimate relationships.

In this chapter I encourage you to think of loneliness as a natural—and potentially valuable—part of human experience. I also encourage you to distinguish between being lonely and being alone. In a real sense, all of us are ultimately alone in the world, and appreciating our aloneness can actually enable us to enrich our experience of life. Moreover, we can use times of solitude to look within ourselves, renew our sense of ourselves as the center of choice and direction in our life, and learn to trust our inner resources instead of allowing circumstances or the expectations of others to determine the course of our life. Finally, if we fundamentally accept our aloneness and recognize that no one can take away *all* our loneliness, we can deal more effectively with our experiences of loneliness and give ourselves to our projects and relationships out of our freedom instead of running to them out of our fear.

OUR ULTIMATE ALONENESS

With the existentialist thinkers, I believe that, ultimately, we are alone. Although the presence of others can surely enhance our life, no one else can completely become us or share our unique world of feelings, thoughts, hopes, and memories. In addition, none of us knows when our loved ones may leave us or die, when we will no longer be able to involve ourselves in a cherished activity, or when the forest we love will be burned or cut down. We come into the world alone, and we will be alone again when the time comes to leave it.

This awareness of our ultimate aloneness—like the awareness of our freedom or of our mortality—can be frightening. Just as we may shrink from recognizing our freedom out of fear of the risks involved or resist thinking about our eventual death, so too we may avoid experiencing our ultimate aloneness. We may throw ourselves into relationships, activities, and diversions and depend on them to numb our sense of aloneness. Certainly, our society provides many distractions and escapes for those who choose to avoid the experience of aloneness. But we cannot deny something we deeply feel to be true without becoming alienated from ourselves.

To the extent that we accept responsibility for our life, we are alone. Responsibility implies that we are the author and designer of our life, which means that we forsake the idea that others will guard and direct us. In this sense, deep aloneness is inherent in the act of creating our destiny (Yalom, 1980).

Perhaps we fear our aloneness because we identify it with extreme loneliness. I think it's important to recognize that experiencing our aloneness is not the same as being without friends or loved ones or pondering something depressing or morbid. On the contrary, it can be an invaluable and positive experience. Throughout this book I have stressed the theme of choice and encouraged you to think about ways of directing your life according to *your own* inner standards, desires, values, and ethics. If you dare to experience your ultimate aloneness, you can strengthen your awareness of yourself as the true center of meaning and direction in your life. In times of solitude, we can restore our perspective on life and return to our projects and relationships refreshed and renewed. By experiencing our aloneness, we can become more fully aware that, although nothing we cherish is permanent, it is our free choice that makes it valuable and unique. In these ways, our freedom and aloneness come together as the twin sources of meaning in our life.

Escaping from Our Aloneness versus Confronting It

Just as we may look to others to make our choices for us, so we may become dependent on others for protection from fears of aloneness. Instead of confronting the fears we may have of being bored, empty, or lost, we can allow these fears to determine the choices we make. In so doing, we risk becoming alienated from our inner self and thus actually increasing our anxiety over aloneness.

Some of the ways in which we sometimes try to escape the experience of aloneness include the following:

- We busy ourselves in work and activities, so that we have little time to think or to reflect by ourselves.
- We schedule every moment and overstructure our life, so that we have no opportunity to think about ourselves and what we are doing with our life.
- We surround ourselves with people and become absorbed in social functions, in the hope that we won't have to feel alone.
- We try to numb ourselves with television, loud music, alcohol, or drugs.
- We immerse ourselves in helping others and in our "responsibilities."
- We eat compulsively, hoping that doing so will fill our inner emptiness and protect us from the pain of being alone.
- We make ourselves slaves to routine, becoming machines that don't feel much of anything.
- We find plenty of trivial things to occupy our attention, so that we never really have to focus on ourselves.
- We go to bars and other centers of activity, trying to lose ourselves in a crowd.

Most of us lead a hectic life in a crowded, noisy environment. We are surrounded by entertainments and escapes. Paradoxically, in the midst of our congested cities and with all the activities available to us, we are often lonely because we are alienated from ourselves. The predicament of many people in our society is that of the alienated person described by the Josephsons in their book *Man Alone: Alienation in Modern Society:* "The alienated man is everyman and no man, drifting in a world that has little meaning for him and over which he exercises no power, a stranger to himself and to others" (Josephson & Josephson, 1962, p. 11).

If we want to get back in touch with ourselves, we can begin by looking at the ways in which we have learned to escape being alone. We can examine the values of our society and question whether they are contributing to our estrangement from ourselves and to our sense of isolation. We can ask whether the activities that fill our time actually satisfy us or whether they leave us hungry and discontented. I believe that we can begin to feel connected with ourselves and with others, but it may take an active effort to resist the pressures of our life and take the time to be with ourselves.

THE VALUES OF LONELINESS AND SOLITUDE

Loneliness and solitude are different experiences, each of which has its own potential value. Loneliness generally results from certain events in our life—the death of someone we love, the decision of another person to leave us for someone else, a move to a new city, a long stay in a hospital. Loneliness can occur when we feel set apart in some way from everyone around us. And sometimes feelings of loneliness are simply an indication of the extent to which we've failed to listen to ourselves and our own feelings. However it occurs, loneliness is generally something that happens to us, rather than something we choose to experience; but we *can* choose the attitude we take toward it. If we allow ourselves to experience our loneliness, even if it is painful, we may be surprised to find within ourselves the sources of strength and creativity.

Unlike loneliness, solitude is something that we often choose for ourselves. In solitude, we make the time to be with ourselves, to discover who we are, and to renew ourselves. In her beautiful and poetic book *Gift from the Sea*, Anne Morrow Lindbergh (1975) describes her own need to get away by herself in order to find her center, simplify her life, and nourish herself so that she can give to others again. She describes how her busy life, with its many and conflicting demands, fragmented her, so that she felt "the spring is dry, and the well is empty" (p. 47).[1] Through solitude, she found replenishment and became reacquainted with herself:

> When one is a stranger to oneself, then one is estranged from others too. If one is out of touch with oneself, then one cannot touch others. . . . Only when one is connected to one's own core is one connected to others. . . . For me, the core, the inner spring, can best be refound through solitude [pp. 43–44].

[1]This and all other quotations from this source from *Gift from the Sea,* by A. M. Lindbergh. Copyright 1955 by Pantheon Books, a division of Random House, Inc.

If we don't take time for ourselves but instead fill our life with activities and projects, we run the risk of losing a sense of centeredness. As Lindbergh puts it, "Instead of stilling the center, the axis of the wheel, we add more centrifugal activities to our lives—which tend to throw us off balance" (1975, p. 51). Her own solitude taught her that she must remind herself to be alone each day, even for a few minutes, in order to keep a sense of herself and give of herself to others. I like the way she expressed this thought in words addressed to a seashell she took with her from an island where she had spent some time alone:

> You will remind me that I must try to be alone for part of each year, even a week or a few days; and for part of each day, even for an hour or for a few minutes, in order to keep my core, my center, my island-quality. You will remind me that unless I keep the island-quality intact somewhere within me, I will have little to give my husband, my children, my friends or the world at large [p. 57].

In much the same way as Lindbergh describes solitude as a way of discovering her core and putting her life in perspective, Clark Moustakas (1977) relates that a critical turning point in his life occurred when he discovered that loneliness could be the basis for a creative experience. He came to see that his personal growth and changed relationships with others were related to his feelings of loneliness. Accepting himself as a lonely person gave him the courage to face aspects of himself that he had never dared to face before and taught him the value of listening to his inner self. For him, solitude became an antidote to loneliness. He writes: "In times of loneliness, my way back to life with others required that I stop listening to others, that I cut myself off from others and deliberately go off alone, to a place of isolation" (p. 109). In doing so, Moustakas became aware of how he had forsaken himself and of the importance of returning to himself. This process of finding himself led him to find new ways of relating to others: "In solitude, silent awareness and self-dialogues often quickly re-

stored me to myself, and I was filled with new energy and the desire to renew my life with others in real ways" (p. 109).

Solitude can thus provide us with the opportunity to sort out our life and gain a sense of perspective. It can give us time to ask significant questions, such as: How much have I become a stranger to myself? Have I been listening to myself, or have I been distracted and overstimulated by a busy life? Am I aware of my sense experiences, or have I been too involved in doing things to be aware of them?

Many of us fail to experience solitude because we allow our life to become more and more frantic and complicated. Unless we make a conscious effort to be alone, we may find that days and weeks go by without our having the chance to be with ourselves. Moreover, we may fear that we will alienate others if we ask for private time, so we alienate ourselves instead. Perhaps we fear that others will think us odd if we express a need to be alone. Indeed, others may sometimes fail to understand our need for solitude and try to bring us into the crowd or "cheer us up." People who are close to us may feel vaguely threatened, as if our need for time alone somehow reflected on our affection for them. Perhaps their own fears of being left alone will lead them to try to keep us from taking time away from them. Thus, claiming what we need and want for ourselves can involve a certain risk; if we fail to take that risk, however, we give up the very thing solitude could provide—a sense of self-direction and autonomy.

I think that most of us need to remind ourselves that we can tolerate only so much intensity with others and that ignoring our need for distance can breed resentment. For instance, a mother and father who are constantly with each other and with their children may not be doing a service either to their children or to themselves. Eventually they are likely to resent their "obligations." Unless they take time out, they may be there bodily and yet not be fully present to each other or to their children.

In summary, I hope that you will welcome time alone. Once we fully accept it, our aloneness can become the source of our strength and the foundation of our relatedness to others. Taking time to *be* alone gives us the opportunity to think, plan, imagine, and dream. It allows us to listen to ourselves and to become sensitive to what we are experiencing. In solitude we can come to appreciate anew both our separateness from, and our relatedness to, the important people and projects in our lives.

CREATING OUR OWN LONELINESS THROUGH SHYNESS

Shyness is both a personality trait and a life-style that can lead to loneliness. Shy people tend to be easily frightened, timid, uncomfortable in social situations, and relatively unassertive. According to Phil Zimbardo (1978), a psychology professor at Stanford University and the founder of the Stanford Shyness Clinic, shyness is an almost universal experience. Eighty percent of those questioned reported that they had been shy at some point in their life. Of those, over 40 percent considered themselves shy at that time. This means that four out of every ten people you meet, or 84 million Americans, are shy. Shyness exists on a continuum. That is, some people see themselves as *chronically* shy, whereas others are shy with certain people or in certain situations.

Shyness often leads directly to feelings of loneliness. Zimbardo (1978) believes that shyness can be a social and a psychological handicap as crippling as many physical handicaps. He lists the following as some of the consequences of shyness:

- It prevents people from expressing their views and speaking up for their rights.
- It makes it difficult to think clearly and to communicate effectively.
- It holds people back from meeting new people, making friends, and getting involved in many social activities.
- It often results in feelings such as depression, anxiety, and loneliness.

You may be aware that shyness is a problem for you and that you are creating your own loneliness, at least in part. You might well be asking "What can I do about it?" For one thing, being shy is not necessarily only negative. I am surely not suggesting that you try to make yourself into an extraverted personality if this is not the person who you are. You can, however, challenge those personal fears that keep you unassertive. You can push yourself to make contact with people and to engage in social activities that interest you, even if you are intimidated. One way to begin is to keep track in your journal of those situations in which you are particularly shy. It is also helpful to write down the symptoms you experience and what you actually do in such situations. Pay attention to what you tell yourself when you are in difficult situations. For example, your "self-talk" might be negative, actually setting you up to fail. You might say silently to yourself: "I am ugly, so who would want anything to do with me?" "I'd better not try something new, because I might look like a fool." "I'm afraid of being rejected, so I won't even approach a person I'd like to get to know." These are the very statements that are likely to keep you a prisoner of your shyness and prevent you from making contact with others. You can do a lot by yourself to control how your shyness affects you by learning to challenge your self-defeating beliefs and by substituting constructive statements.

The purpose of this section is not to "cure" you of your shyness, if any. Rather, my aim is to ask you to monitor your own thoughts, feelings, and actions if shyness is a problem for you and if it is something that you'd like to change about yourself. One way to understand your own shyness and learn some ways of dealing with it would be to read Zimbardo's excellent book *Shyness* (1978).

TIME OUT FOR PERSONAL REFLECTION

1. *Do you try to escape from your aloneness? In what ways? Check any of the following statements that you think apply to you.*

_____   *I bury myself in work.*
_____   *I constantly seek to be with others.*
_____   *I drink excessively or take drugs.*
_____   *I schedule every moment so that I'll have very little time to think about myself.*
_____   *I attempt to avoid my troubles by watching television or listening to music.*
_____   *I eat compulsively.*
_____   *I sleep excessively to avoid the stresses in my life.*
_____   *I become overly concerned with helping others.*

_____ *I rarely think about anything if I can help it; I concentrate on playing and having fun.*

List other specific ways in which you sometimes try to avoid experiencing your aloneness:

_____

_____

_____

_____

2. *Would you like to change any of the patterns you've just identified? Is so, what are they? What might you do to change them?*

_____

_____

_____

_____

3. *Is shyness a problem for you? In what ways might you be creating your own loneliness through your shyness?*

_____

_____

_____

_____

4. *Do you agree or disagree with the idea that we are ultimately alone in the world? Why?*

_____

_____

_____

_____

5. *Do you see time spent alone as being valuable to you? If so, in what ways?*

_____

_____

_____

_____

6. Have you experienced periods of creative solitude? If so, what were some of the positive aspects of these experiences?

_____

_____

_____

_____

7. List a few of the major decisions you've made in your life. Did you make these decisions when you were alone or when you were with others?

_____

_____

_____

_____

A journal suggestion: If you find it difficult to be alone, without distractions, for more than a few minutes at a time, try being alone for a little longer than you're generally comfortable with. During this time you might simply let your thoughts wander freely, without hanging on to one line of thinking. In your journal, describe what this experience is like for you.

LONELINESS AND OUR LIFE STAGES

How we deal with feelings of loneliness can depend to a great extent on our lonely experiences in childhood and adolescence. Later in life we may feel that loneliness has no place or that we can and should be able to avoid it. It's important to reflect on our past experiences, because they are often the basis of our present feelings about loneliness. In addition, we may fear loneliness less if we recognize that it is a natural part of living in every stage of life. Once we have accepted our ultimate aloneness and the likelihood that we will feel lonely at many points in our life, we may be better able to take responsibility for our own loneliness and recognize ways in which we may be contributing to it.

Loneliness and Childhood

Reliving some of our childhood experiences of loneliness can help us come to grips with present fears about being alone or lonely. The following are some typical memories of lonely periods that people I've worked with in therapy have relived:

- A woman recalls the time her parents were fighting in the bedroom and she heard them screaming and yelling. She was sure that they would divorce, and in many ways she felt responsible. She remembers living in continual fear that she would be deserted.
- A man recalls attempting to give a speech in the sixth grade. He stuttered over certain words, and children in the class began to laugh at him. Afterwards, he developed extreme self-consciousness in regard to his speech, and he long remembered the hurt he had experienced.
- A Black man recalls how excluded he felt in his all-White elementary school and how the other children would talk about him in derisive ways. As an adult he can still cry over these memories.
- A woman recalls the fright she felt as a small child when her uncle made sexual advances toward her. Although she didn't really understand what was happening, she remembers the terrible loneliness of feeling that she couldn't tell her parents for fear of what they would do.
- A man recalls the boyhood loneliness of feeling that he was continually failing at everything he tried. To this day, he resists undertaking a task unless he is sure he can handle it, for fear of rekindling those old lonely feelings.
- A woman vividly remembers being in the hospital as a small child for an operation. She remembers the loneliness of not knowing what was going on or whether she would be able to leave the hospital. Since no one talked with her, she was all alone with her fears.

As we try to relive these experiences, we should remember that children do not live in a logical, well-ordered world. Our childhood fears may have been greatly exaggerated, and the feeling of fright may remain with us even though we may now think of it as irrational. Unfortunately, being told by adults that we were foolish for having such fears may only have increased our loneliness while doing nothing to lessen the fears themselves.

At this point you may wonder: "Why go back and recall childhood pain and loneliness? Why not just let it be a thing of the past?" I feel convinced that we need to reexperience some of the pain we felt as children to see whether we are still carrying it around with us now. We can also look at some of the decisions we made during these times of extreme loneliness and ask whether these decisions are still appropriate.

Frequently, strategies we adopted as children remain with us into adulthood, when they are no longer appropriate. For instance, suppose that your family moved to a strange city when you were 7 years old and that you had to go to a new school. Kids at the new school laughed at you, and you lived through several months of anguish. You felt desperately alone in the world. During this time you decided to keep your feelings to yourself and build a wall around yourself so that others couldn't hurt you. Although this experience is now long past, you still defend yourself in the same way, because you haven't *really* made a new decision to open up and trust some people. In this way, old fears of loneliness might contribute to a real loneliness in the present. If you allow yourself to experience your grief and work it through, emotionally as well as intellectually, you can overcome past pain and create new choices for yourself.

TIME OUT FOR PERSONAL REFLECTION

Take some time to decide whether you're willing to recall and relive a childhood experience of loneliness. If so, try to recapture the experience in as much detail as you can, reliving it in fantasy. Then reflect on the experience, using the following questions as a starting point.

1. Describe in a few words the most lonely experience you recall having as a child.

_____

_____

_____

_____

2. How do you think the experience affected you then?

_____

_____

_____

_____

3. How do you think the experience may still be affecting you now?

_____

_____

_____

_____

Journal suggestions: Consider elaborating on this exercise in your journal. Here are a few questions you might reflect on: How did you cope with your loneliness as a child? How has this influenced the way you deal with loneliness in your life now? If you could go back and put a new ending on your most lonely childhood experience, what would it be? You might also think about times in your childhood when you enjoyed being alone. Write some notes to yourself about what these experiences were like for you. Where did you like to spend time alone? What did you enjoy doing by yourself? What positive aspects of these times do you recall?

Loneliness and Adolescence

For many people, loneliness and adolescence are practically synonymous. Adolescents often feel that they are all alone in their world, that they are the first ones to have had the feelings they do, and that in some real way they are separated from others by some abnormality. Bodily changes and impulses are alone sufficient to bring about a sense of perplexity and loneliness, but there are other stresses to be undergone as well. Adolescents are developing a sense of identity. They strive to be successful yet fear failure. They want to be accepted and liked, but they fear rejection, ridicule, or exclusion by their peers. They are curious about sex yet often frightened to experiment or constrained from doing so. Most adolescents know the feeling of being lonely in a crowd or among friends, and many of the young people I've worked with report the loneliness they feel as a result of keeping their own convictions private and adopting the views and morals of their group, out of fear of being ostracized. Conformity can bring acceptance, and the price of nonconformity can be steep for those who have the courage to decide for themselves how they will think and behave.

As you recall your adolescent years—and, in particular, the areas of your life that were marked by loneliness—you might reflect on the following questions:

- Did I feel included in a social group? Or did I sit on the sidelines, afraid of being included and wishing for it at the same time?
- Was there at least one person whom I felt I could talk to—one who really heard me, so that I didn't feel desperately alone?
- What experience stands out as one of the most lonely times during these years? How did I cope with my loneliness?
- Did I experience a sense of confusion concerning who I was and what I wanted to be as a person? How did I deal with my confusion? Who or what helped me during this time?
- How did I feel about my own worth and value? Did I believe that I had anything of value to offer anyone or that anyone would find me worth being with?

As you reflect on your adolescence, add your own questions to the list I've suggested. Then try to discover some of the ways in which the person you now are is a result of your lonely experiences as an adolescent. Do you shrink from competition for fear of failure? In social situations are you afraid of being left out? Do you feel some of the isolation you did then? If so, how do you deal with it?

TIME OUT FOR PERSONAL REFLECTION

1. *Describe the most lonely experience of your adolescent years.*

_____

_____

_____

_____

2. *How did you cope with the loneliness you've just described?*

_____

_____

_____

_____

3. *What effect do you think the experience you've described has on you today?*

_____

_____

_____

_____

Loneliness and Young Adulthood

In our young-adult years we experiment with ways of being, and we establish life-styles that may remain with us for many years. We may be struggling with the question of what to do with our life, what intimate relationships we want to establish, and how we will chart our future. Dealing with all the choices that face us at this time of life can be a lonely process.

How we come to terms with our own aloneness at this time can have significant effects on the choices we make—choices that, in turn, may determine the course of our lives for years to come. For instance, if we

haven't learned to listen to ourselves and to depend on our own inner resources, we might succumb to the pressure to choose a relationship or a career before we're really prepared to do so, or we might look to our projects or partners for the sense of identity that we ultimately can find only in ourselves. Alternatively, we may feel lonely and establish patterns that only increase our loneliness. This last possibility is well illustrated by the case of Saul.

Saul was in his early twenties when he attended college. He claimed that his chief problem was his isolation, yet he rarely reached out to others. His general manner seemed to say "Keep away." Although he was enrolled in a small, informal class in self-awareness and personal growth, he quickly left after each session, depriving himself of the chance to make contact with anyone.

One day, as I was walking across the campus, I saw Saul sitting alone in a secluded spot, while many students were congregated on the lawn, enjoying the beautiful spring weather. Here was a chance for him to do something about his separation from others; instead, he chose to seclude himself. He continually told himself that others didn't like him and, sadly, made his prophecy self-fulfilling by his own behavior. He made himself unapproachable and, in many ways, the kind of person people would avoid.

In this time of life we have the chance to decide on ways of being toward ourselves and others as well as on our vocation and future plans. If you feel lonely on the campus, I'd like to challenge you to ask yourself what *you* are doing and can do about your own loneliness. Do you decide in advance that the other students and instructors want to keep to themselves? Do you assume that there already are well-established cliques to which you cannot belong? Do you expect others to reach out to you, even though you don't initiate contacts yourself? What fears might be holding you back? Where do they seem to come from? Are past experiences of loneliness or rejection determining the choices you make now?

Often we create unnecessary loneliness for ourselves by our own behavior. If we sit back and wait for others to come to us, we give them the power to make us lonely. As we learn to take responsibility for ourselves in young adulthood, one area we can work on is taking responsibility for our own loneliness and creating new choices for ourselves.

Loneliness and Middle Age

Many changes occur during middle age that may result in new feelings of loneliness. Although we may not be free to choose some of the things that occur at this time in our lives, we *are* free to choose how we relate to these events. Among the possible changes and crises of middle age are the following:

• Our spouse may grow tired of living with us and decide to leave. If so, we must decide how we will respond to this situation. Will we blame ourselves and become absorbed in self-hate? Will we refuse to see any of our own responsibility for the breakup and simply blame the other person? Will we decide never to trust anyone again? Will we mourn our loss and, after a period of grieving, actively look for another person to live with?

• Our life may not turn out the way we had planned. We may not have enjoyed the success we'd hoped for, we may feel disenchanted with our work, or we may feel that we passed up many fine opportunities earlier. But the key point is what we can do about our life *now*. What choices will we make in light of this reality? Will we slip into hopelessness and berate ourselves endlessly about what we could have done and should have done? Will we allow ourselves to stay trapped in meaningless work and empty relationships, or will we look for positive options for change?

• Our children may leave home, and with this change we may experience emptiness and a sense of loss. If so, what will we do about this transition? Will we attempt to hang on? Can we let go and create a new life with new meaning? When our children leave, will we lose our desire to live? Will we look back with regret at all that we could have done differently, or will we choose to look ahead to the kind of life we want to create for ourselves now that we don't have the responsibilities of parenthood?

These are just a few of the changes that many of us confront during the middle years of living. Although we may feel that events are not in our control, we can still choose the ways in which we respond to these life situations. To illustrate, I'd like to present a brief example that reflects the loneliness many people experience after a divorce and show how the two persons involved made different decisions about how to deal with their loneliness.

Amy and Gary were married for over 20 years before their recent divorce, and they have three children in their teens. Amy is 43; Gary is 41. Although they have both experienced a good deal of loneliness since their divorce, they have chosen different attitudes toward their loneliness. For his part, Gary felt resentful at first and believed that somehow they could have stayed together if only Amy had changed her attitude. He lives alone in a small apartment and sees his teenagers on weekends. He interprets the divorce as a personal failure, and he still feels a mixture of guilt and resentment. He hates to come home to an empty apartment, with no one to talk to and no one to share his life with. In some ways he has decided not to cultivate other relationships, because he still bears the scars of his "first failure." He wonders whether women would find him interesting, and he fears that it's too late to begin a new life with someone else.

Gary declines most of his friends' invitations, interpreting their concern as pity. He says that at times he feels like climbing the walls, that he sometimes wakes up at night in a cold sweat and feels real pangs of abandonment and loneliness. He attempts to numb his lonely feelings by burying himself in his work, but he cannot rid himself of the ache of loneliness. Gary seems to have decided on some level not to let go of his isolation. He has convinced himself that it isn't really possible for him to develop a new relationship. His own attitude limits his options, because he has set up a self-fulfilling prophecy: he convinces himself that another woman would not want to share time with him, and, as a consequence, others pick up the messages that he is sending out about himself.

For her part, Amy had many ambivalent feelings about divorcing. After the divorce, she experienced feelings of panic and aloneness as she faced the prospect of rearing her children and managing the home on her own. She wondered whether she could meet her responsibilities and still have time for any social life for herself. She wondered whether men would be interested in her, particularly in light of the fact that she had three teenagers. She anguished over such questions as "Will I be able to have another life with someone else? Do I want to live alone? Can I take care of my emotional needs and still provide for the family?" Unlike Gary, Amy decided to date several people—when she felt like it, and because she felt like it. At first she was pressured by her family to find a man and settle down. She decided, however, to resist this pressure, and she has chosen to remain single for the time being. She intends to develop a long-term relationship only if she feels it is what she wants after she has had time to live alone. Although she is lonely at times, she doesn't feel trapped and resists being a victim of her lonely feelings.

Experiences like those of Gary and Amy are very common among middle-aged people. Many find themselves having to cope with feelings of isolation and abandonment after a divorce. Some, like Gary, may feel panic and either retreat from people or quickly run into a new relationship to avoid the pain of separation. If they don't confront their fears and their pain, they may be controlled by their fear of being left alone for the rest of their lives. Others, like Amy, may go through a similar period of loneliness after a divorce, yet refuse to be controlled by a fear of living alone. Although they might want a long-term relationship again someday, they avoid rushing impulsively into a new relationship in order to avoid any feelings of pain or loneliness.

Loneliness and the Later Years

Our society emphasizes productivity, youth, beauty, power, and vitality. As we age, we may lose some of our vitality and sense of power or attractiveness. Many people face a real crisis when they reach retirement, for they feel that they're being put out to pasture—that they aren't needed anymore and that their life is really over. Loneliness and hopelessness are experienced by anyone who feels that there is little to look forward to or that he or she has no vital place in society, and such feelings are particularly common among older adults.

The loneliness of the later years can be accentuated by the losses that come with age. There can be some loss of sight, hearing, memory, and strength. Older people may lose their job, hobbies, friends, and loved ones. A particularly difficult loss is the loss of a spouse with whom one has been close for many years. In the face of such losses a person may ultimately ask what reason remains for living. It may be no coincidence that many old people die soon after their spouse dies or shortly after their retirement. However, the pangs of aloneness or the feelings that life is futile reflect a drastic loss of meaning rather than an essential part of growing old. Viktor Frankl (1969) has written about the "will to meaning" as a key determinant of a person's desire to live. He notes that many of the inmates in a Nazi concentration camp kept themselves alive by looking forward to the prospect of being released and reunited with their family. Many of those who lost hope simply gave up and died, regardless of their age.

At least until recently, our society has compounded the elderly person's loss of meaning by grossly neglecting the aged population. The number of institutions and convalescent homes in which old people are often left to vegetate testifies to this neglect. It's hard to imagine a more lonely existence than the one many of these people are compelled to suffer.

Despite this societal neglect, those who specialize in the study of aging often make the point that, if we have led a rich life in early adulthood, we have a good chance of finding richness in our later years. Certainly, if we have learned to find direction from within ourselves, we will be better

equipped to deal with the changes aging brings. A few years ago my wife and I had the good fortune to meet an exceptional man, Dr. Ewald Schnitzer, who retired from the University of California at Los Angeles in 1973 and moved to Idyllwild, California, a place that he considers his last and happiest home. For me, he provides an outstanding model of the way I hope I face my own old age.

Schnitzer lives alone by preference and continues to find excitement and meaning in his life in art, philosophy, music, history, hiking, writing, and traveling. He believes that his entire life has prepared him well for his later years. He has learned to be content when he is alone, he finds pleasure in the company of animals and nature, and he enjoys many memories of his rich experiences. I respect the way in which he can live fully now, without dreading the future. This spirit of being fully alive is well expressed in his book *Looking In:* "It would be painful should frailty prevent me from climbing mountains. Yet, when that time comes, I hope I find serenity in wandering through valleys, looking at the realm of distant summits not with ambition but with loving memories" (Schnitzer, 1977, p. 88).[2]

Schnitzer is an example of someone who can accept the fact of his aging yet recognize that each stage of life brings its unique challenges and

[2]This and all other quotations from this source from *Looking In,* by E. W. Schnitzer. Copyright 1977. Reprinted by permission.

potentialities for creating a meaningful existence. This is how he expresses this thought:

> I am writing this as I stand on the threshold of old age. Like everybody at this stage I have to face the fact of my bodily decline. I am saying this with a tinge of sadness but without a trace of despair. For it has always seemed to me that each age has its own possibilities and challenges, and I have often taken heart from this remark of Roger Fry's: "It is a wonderful thing to recognize the advanced age of a person less by the infirmity of his body than by the maturity of his soul" [p. 87].

I'd like to conclude this discussion of the later years—and, in a sense, this entire chapter on loneliness and solitude—by returning to the example of Anne Morrow Lindbergh. In her later years her lifelong courage in facing aloneness enabled her to find new and rich meaning in her life. I was extremely impressed with this woman when I first read her book *Gift from the Sea*, but my respect increased when I read the "Afterword" in the book's 20th-anniversary edition. There, she looks back at the time when she originally wrote the book and notes that she was then deeply involved in family life. Since that time, her children have left and established their own lives. She describes how a most uncomfortable stage followed her middle years—one that she hadn't anticipated when she wrote the book. She writes that she went from the "oyster-bed" stage of taking care of a family to the "abandoned-shell" stage of later life. This is how she describes the essence of the "abandoned-shell" stage:

> Plenty of solitude, and a sudden panic at how to fill it, characterized this period. With me, it was not a question of simply filling up the space or the time. I had many activities and even a well-established vocation to pursue. But when a mother is left, the lone hub of a wheel, with no other lives revolving around her, she faces a total reorientation. It takes time to re-find the center of gravity [Lindbergh, 1975, p. 134].

In this stage she did make choices to come to terms with herself and create a new role for herself. She points out that all the exploration she did earlier in life paid off when she reached the "abandoned-shell" stage. Here again, earlier choices affect current ones.

Before her husband, Charles, died in 1974, Lindbergh had looked forward to retiring with him on the Hawaiian island of Maui. His death changed her life abruptly but did not bring it to an end. Its continuity was preserved in part by the presence of her 5 children and 12 grandchildren; moreover, she continued to involve herself in her own writing and in the preparation of her husband's papers for publication. Here is a fine example of a woman who has encountered her share of loneliness and learned to renew herself by actively choosing a positive stance toward life.

TIME OUT FOR PERSONAL REFLECTION

Complete the following sentences by writing down the first response that comes to mind.

1. The most lonely time in my life was when _____

_____

2. I usually deal with my loneliness by _____

_____

3. I escape from loneliness by _____

_____

4. If I were to be left and abandoned by all those who love me, _____

_____

5. One value I see in experiencing loneliness is _____

_____

6. My greatest fear of loneliness is _____

_____

7. I have felt lonely in a crowd when _____

_____

8. When I'm with a person who is lonely, _____

_____

9. For me, being with others _____

_____

10. I feel most lonely when _____

_____

11. The thought of living alone the rest of my life _____

_____

CHAPTER SUMMARY

We have a need to be with others that is best satisfied through many forms of intimate relationships. Yet another essential dimension of the human experience is to be able to creatively function alone. Unless we can enjoy our own company, we will have difficulty finding real joy in being with others. Being with others and being with ourselves are two sides of the same coin.

Some people fail to reach out to others and make significant contact because they are timid in social situations and are relatively unassertive. Many people report that they are troubled by shyness or have had problems with being shy in the past. Shyness can lead to feelings of loneliness, yet shy people can challenge the fears that keep them unassertive. Shyness is not a disorder that needs to be "cured," nor are all aspects of being shy necessarily negative. What is important is to recognize that certain attitudes and behaviors can create much of the loneliness we sometimes experience.

As you will recall from earlier chapters on the developmental stages, each period of life presents unique tasks to be mastered. Loneliness can be best understood from a developmental perspective. There are particular circumstances that often result in loneliness as we pass through childhood, adolescence, young adulthood, middle age, and the later years. It helps to be able to recognize our feelings about events that are associated with each of these turning points.

In this chapter I've suggested that experiencing loneliness is part of being human. We can grow from such experiences if we understand them and use them to renew our sense of ourselves. Moreover, we don't have to remain victimized by early decisions that we made as a result of past loneliness. Some key points are:

1. Ultimately, we all are alone.
2. We can choose to face aloneness and deal with it creatively, or we can choose to try to escape from it.
3. Most of us have experienced loneliness during our childhood and adolescent years, and these experiences can have a significant influence on our present attitudes, behavior, and relationships.
4. Times of solitude can give us an invaluable opportunity to gain perspective on the direction and meaning of our life.
5. We have some choice concerning whether we will feel lonely or whether we will feel in touch with others. We can design our activities so that we reject others before they can reject us, or we can risk making contact with them.

List some other points from this chapter that were significant for you and that you would like to remember.

_____

_____

_____

_____

ACTIVITIES AND EXERCISES

1. Allocate some time each day in which to be alone and reflect on anything you wish. Note down in your journal the thoughts and feelings that occur to you during your time alone.
2. If you have feelings of loneliness when you think about a certain person who has been or is now significant to you, write a letter to that person expressing all the things you're feeling (you don't have to mail the letter). For instance, tell that person how you miss him or her or write about your sadness, your resentment, or your desire for more closeness.
3. Imagine that you are the person you've written your letter to, and write a reply to yourself. What do you imagine that person would say to you if he or she received your letter? What do you fear (and what do you wish) he or she would say?
4. If you sometimes feel lonely and left out, you might try some specific experiments for a week or so. For example, if you feel isolated in most of your classes, why not make it a point to get to class early and initiate contact with a fellow student? If you feel anxious about taking such a step, try doing it in fantasy. What are your fears? What is the worst thing you can imagine might happen? Record your impressions in your journal. If you decide to try reaching out to other people, record in your journal what the experience is like for you.
5. Think about the person who means the most to you. Now let yourself imagine that this person decides to leave you. Imagine what that would be like for you—what you might feel, say, and do. How do you think his or her leaving would affect you?
6. Recall some periods of loneliness in your life. Select important situations in which you experienced loneliness, and spend some time recalling the details of each situation and reflecting on the meaning each of these experiences has had for you. Now you might do two things:
   a. Write down your reflections in your journal. How do you think your past experiences of loneliness affect you now?
   b. Select a friend or a person you'd like to trust more, and share this experience of loneliness.
7. Many people rarely make time exclusively for themselves. If you'd like to have time to yourself but just haven't gotten around to arranging it, consider going to a place you haven't been to before or to the beach, desert, or mountains. Reserve a weekend just for yourself; if this seems too much, then spend a day completely alone. The important thing is to remove yourself from your everyday routine and just be with yourself without external distractions.

8. Try spending a day or part of a day in a place where you can observe and experience lonely people. You might spend some time near a busy downtown intersection, in a park where old people congregate, or in a large shopping center. Try to pay attention to expressions of loneliness, alienation, and isolation. How do people seem to be dealing with their loneliness? Later, you might discuss your observations in class.

9. Imagine yourself living in a typical rest home—without any of your possessions, cut off from your family and friends, and unable to do the things you now do. Reflect on what this experience would be like for you; then write down some of your reactions in your journal.

SUGGESTED READINGS

Lindbergh, A. M. (1955, 1975). *Gift from the Sea.* New York: Pantheon. Although this book is over 25 years old, it is still timely for both women and men as a catalyst for thinking about the need for solitude. It is a deep, simply written, and poetic book. The recent edition contains an afterword about the author's life during the ensuing 20 years.

Moustakas, C. (1961). *Loneliness.* Englewood Cliffs, N.J.: Prentice-Hall (Spectrum). In this classic book the central message is that loneliness is an experience that enables us to realize a deeper meaning in our life.

Moustakas, C. (1972). *Loneliness and Love.* Englewood Cliffs, N.J.: Prentice-Hall (Spectrum). This insightful book offers a unique approach to the positive dimensions of loneliness and emphasizes individuality, personal honesty, communication, and love in relation to oneself.

Moustakas, C. (1975). *The Touch of Loneliness.* Englewood Cliffs, N.J.: Prentice-Hall (Spectrum). This book contains many letters by the author and by people who have written accounts of their own loneliness.

Moustakas, C. (1977). *Turning Points.* Englewood Cliffs, N.J.: Prentice-Hall (Spectrum). In this book Moustakas deals with the uncertainty associated with the various transitions in our life. Its theme is that, by choosing to face these turning points, we can find strength within ourselves and reaffirm our existence.

Zimbardo, P. G. (1978). *Shyness.* New York: Jove. This highly readable book helps readers understand what shyness is, how it affects all aspects of our life, and what to do about it. There are many self-inventories and exercises and a rich bibliography.

WORK

PRECHAPTER SELF-INVENTORY

Use the following scale to respond: 4 = this statement is true of me *most* of the time; 3 = this statement is true of me *much* of the time; 2 = this statement is true of me *some* of the time; 1 = this statement is true of me *almost none* of the time.

_____ 1. I wouldn't work if I didn't need the money.
_____ 2. Work is one very important way in which I can express my creativity.
_____ 3. I expect to change jobs several times during my life.
_____ 4. It's more important to me to have a secure job than it is to have one that's exciting.
_____ 5. The thought of retirement petrifies me.
_____ 6. If I'm unhappy in my job, the cause for my unhappiness is most likely within me, not in the job itself.
_____ 7. I anticipate having to take some steps to prevent getting tired of my job.
_____ 8. I expect my work to fulfill many of my needs and to be an important source of meaning in my life.
_____ 9. My work allows me the leisure time that I want and require.
_____ 10. I enjoy my leisure time.

INTRODUCTION

Freud saw the goals of *lieben und arbeiten* as core characteristics of the healthy person; that is, to him the freedom "to love and to work" and to derive satisfaction from loving and working was of paramount importance. Work is intimately related to the topics discussed in earlier chapters. The quality of marriage and other intimate relationships, our ability to love ourselves and others, and our physical and psychological well-being are influenced by the level of satisfaction we derive from our work.

Most working people ignore the impact that work has on their life in general. Work is a good deal more than an activity that takes up a certain number of hours each week. If you feel creative and excited about your work, the quality of your life will be improved. If you hate your job and dread the hours you spend on it, your relationships and your feelings about yourself are bound to be affected.

If you have not yet begun a career, you can increase the relevance of this chapter by examining your expectations about work. You can talk to people in your immediate environment about their level of satisfaction in their work and use these observations to help you decide on your eventual career. If you let others' expectations or attitudes determine how you feel about your work, however, you'll surrender some sense of the autonomy and power to control your life that rightfully belong to you. Consequently, it's important to discover your own attitudes about work if you're to exercise real choice in this large part of your life.[1]

YOUR COLLEGE EDUCATION AS YOUR WORK

Most readers of this book are college students, ranging in age from their late teens to their sixties. You may have already made several vocational decisions and have held a number of different jobs, or you may now be in the process of exploring career options or preparing yourself for a career. If you are in the midst of considering what occupations might best suit you, it would be helpful to review the meaning that going to college has for you now. I believe that there is a direct relationship between how you approach your college experience and how you will someday approach your career. If my theory is correct, you can learn a good deal about your future attitudes toward work by reflecting on your attitudes and behavior as a student.

In a real way, school might be your present line of work. Ask yourself questions such as: Why am I in college? Is it my choice or someone else's choice for me? Do I enjoy most of my time as a student? Is my work as a student satisfying and meaningful? Would I rather be somewhere else or doing something other than being a student? If so, why am I staying in college?

In Chapter 1 you were asked to review the impact on you of your elementary and secondary school experience. You were asked what kind of learner you were, and if you saw yourself as a passive learner, you were encouraged to take steps to become an active and involved one. This would be a good time to review the goals that you set and determine how well you are progressing toward them. If you established a contract to take increased responsibility for your own learning and to get personally involved in this book and the course, I suggest that you check up on how pleased you are with the way you are now approaching this book and the course. Perhaps this is an ideal time to set new goals, to modify your original goals, and to try new behavior in reaching your goals.

Besides making this reassessment of the kind of student you are, I think it would be helpful to consider my hypothesis that there are parallels between the way you approach schooling and the way you will approach work. There are certain personality traits and attitudes that we transfer

---

[1]I wish to thank Dr. Jim Morrow, of Western Carolina University, who consulted with me on this chapter. I have incorporated many of his ideas.

from college to work. Let's consider some of these possible similarities of style between the two worlds. If you are taking responsibility for making your college experience meaningful, then you are likely to be the kind of person who will assume responsibility for making your job a satisfying experience. If you are doing more than the bare minimum as a student, you will probably go out of your way on the job to do more than just what is expected of you. If you are the kind of student who fears making mistakes and who will not risk saying what you think in class, then you may carry this same type of behavior to the job. You may be afraid of jeopardizing your grades by being assertive, and someday you may very well be unassertive in the work world out of fear of losing your job or not advancing. If you are taking on too many courses and other projects, planning poorly, procrastinating, getting behind, and then feeling utter frustration and exhaustion by a semester's end, might you not display this same behavior once you get involved in your occupation? Think of some of the ways in which you can learn about how you are likely to approach a career by making an honest inventory of your role as a student. If you decide that your present major is not what really interests you, then you are no more wedded to your course of study than you are to one particular job in the future. Determine for yourself why you are in college and what you are getting from it and giving to the project. The following case is an example of a student who did just this.

One of my students decided early in his high school career to major in business administration when he got to college. Jim also decided to follow in his father's footsteps and become a successful accountant. Eventually, he did graduate from college with high grades in his business administration major. Before graduating, however, he took a few electives in the human services program for his own enrichment and in the process discovered the difference between taking courses only because they were required and pursuing courses that excited him personally. As a result, he went on to earn a second bachelor's degree, this time in human services. As Jim put it, this second degree was for himself, whereas his first one had been for his father.

Today, Jim is struck by how unaware he initially was of why he was even in college and pursuing the kind of life he once did. It frightens him to think that he could have become an accountant simply because his father had an accounting firm and was pushing him in that direction. He realizes that his father had good intentions; after all, he would have had a natural place in his father's firm and wouldn't ever have had to worry about security. Nevertheless, he sees now that these plans were his father's and not his own. So he has made the choice to follow a less certain path and to explore an area that is exciting to him. In doing so he gives up the security of his father's clear design for his future, but he envisions other types of rewards.

I admire Jim's willingness to question his motivation for being in college and his courage in making a new decision that was his own. I think it was critically important that he realized first that he was being pushed too soon to make his career decision; with this awareness he was able to make his own choices.

TRENDS IN THE WORLD OF WORK

The information age and the explosion of high technology are transforming American society at least as radically as the Industrial Revolution did. This new revolution is based on microcomputers, robotics, gene splicing, microwaves, lasers, and satellite telecommunications (Toffler, 1981).

When we contemplate the vast increase in career choices open to both women and men in the future, the process of selecting and preparing for a vocation becomes more crucial than in less complex times. The most formidable challenge continues to be training people to work in the information society. In his best-seller *Megatrends*, John Naisbitt (1984) describes the following trends in society that will have a major impact on the world of work:

1. We have shifted from an industrial society to one based on the creation and distribution of information. In the late 1950s, 17 percent of Americans worked in information jobs; now, more than 60 percent work as programmers, teachers, clerks, accountants, secretaries, bankers, technicians, and the like. Of the 19,000 new job titles created in the 1970s, 90 percent were information related, whereas only 5 percent were in manufacturing. In the mid-1980s, 75 percent of all jobs involve computers in some way, and people who aren't familiar with their use are at a disadvantage.

2. As a society, we are moving in the dual direction of high technology and "high touch," matching each new technology with a compensatory human response. As technology advances, the challenge is to learn ways to balance the material wonders produced by it with the psychological, social, and spiritual demands of our human nature. The more technology that is introduced in society, the more people will gather together out of their need for human contact.

3. We will not continue to have the luxury of operating within an isolated, self-sufficient, national framework. It is becoming increasingly important to recognize that we are part of a global economy.

4. Lifelong learning will replace the notion of simply going to school and graduating. This long-term orientation may encourage the ideal of a generalist education, so that changing with the times is possible. People who narrowly specialize may find their specialty becoming obsolete.

5. There is a trend toward decentralization. As centralized structures crumble, people are rebuilding from the bottom up into a more balanced and diversified society. Decentralization means more opportunities and choices for people.

6. Americans are reclaiming their traditional sense of self-reliance, as seen in new health-care programs, the hospice movement, birth alternatives (such as natural childbirth), and community self-help programs. A transformation from a managerial to an entrepreneurial society is occurring.

7. Representative democracy is becoming obsolete in an era of instantaneously shared information. Individuals whose lives are affected by decisions must have a vital involvement in the decision-making process. This trend to a participatory democracy can be applied to the world of work. The assumption is that, if people are to enthusiastically support a project, they must feel a sense of "ownership" in it.

8. There is a trend away from a narrow society with a limited range of options, toward a multiple-option society. The increasing role of women in the world of work is but one example. Individuality in all phases of life is now more possible than in previous times.

Naisbitt maintains that it is only by understanding these larger patterns that individual events begin to make sense. Although his focus is on the broad outlines that will define the new society, he adds that we are not able to predict the shape of the new world. For him, the best and most reliable way to anticipate the future is to understand the present. As you think about the process of selecting a career, the evolution of your own career, or the possibility of changing careers at some point in your life, it would be well to consider these societal trends. Although I don't advocate letting your individual choices, including vocational decisions, be dominated by society, it is wise to be aware of the potential impact of such trends on your direction in life.

CHOOSING AN OCCUPATION OR CAREER

What do you expect from work? What factors do you give the most attention to in selecting a career or an occupation? In my work at a university counseling center I've discovered that many students haven't really thought seriously about why they are choosing a given vocation. For some, parental pressure or encouragement is the major reason for their choice. Others have idealized views of what it will be like to be a lawyer, engineer, or doctor. Many people I've counseled regarding career decisions haven't looked at what they value the most and whether these values can be attained in their chosen vocation. In choosing your vocation (or evaluating the choices you've made previously), you may want to consider which factors really mean the most to you.

Making vocational choices is a process that spans a considerable period of time, rather than an isolated event. Researchers in career development have found that most people go through a series of stages in choosing the occupation or, more typically, occupations that they will follow. As you recall from our discussion of the stages of the life span, various factors emerge or become influential during each phase of growth. The following factors have been shown to be important in determining a person's occupational decision-making process: self-concept, interests, abilities, values, occupational attitudes, socioeconomic level, parental influence, ethnic identity, gender, and physical, mental, emotional, and social handicaps.

Factors in Vocational Decision Making

Let's consider some of these factors related to career decision making, keeping in mind that vocational choice is a process, not an event. We'll look at the role of self-concept, occupational attitudes, abilities, interests, and values in choosing a career.

Self-Concept.   Some writers in career development contend that a vocational choice is an attempt to fulfill one's self-concept. People with a poor self-concept, for example, are not likely to envision themselves in a meaningful or important job. They are likely to keep their aspirations low, and thus their achievements will probably be low also. They may select and remain in a job that they do not enjoy or derive satisfaction from, based on their conviction that such a job is all they are worthy of. In this regard, choosing a vocation can be thought of as a public declaration of the kind of person we see ourselves as being.

Occupational Attitudes.   Research indicates that, among the factors that influence our attitudes toward occupational status or prestige, education is important (Pietrofesa & Splete, 1975). The higher the educational requirements for an occupation, the higher its status or prestige.

We develop our attitudes toward the status of occupations by learning from the people in our environment. Typical first-graders are not aware of the differential status of occupations (Gunn, 1964). Yet in a few years these children begin to rank occupations in a manner similar to that of adults. Other research has shown that positive attitudes toward most occupations are common among first-graders but that these preferences narrow steadily with each year of school (Nelson, 1963). As students advance to higher grades, they reject more and more occupations as unacceptable. Unfortunately, they rule out some of the very jobs from which

they may have to choose if they are to find employment as adults. It is difficult for people to feel positively about themselves or their occupation if they have to accept an occupation they perceive as low in status.

Abilities. Ability, or aptitude, has received as much attention as any of the factors deemed significant in the career decision-making process, and it is probably used more often than any other factor. There are both general and specific abilities. Scholastic aptitude, often called general intelligence or IQ, is a general ability typically considered to consist of both verbal and numerical aptitudes. Included among the specific abilities are mechanical, clerical, and spatial aptitudes, abstract reasoning ability, and eye/hand/foot coordination. Scholastic aptitude is particularly significant because it largely determines who will be able to obtain the levels of education required for entrance into the higher-status occupations.

Interestingly, most studies show little direct relationship between measured aptitudes and occupational performance and satisfaction (Herr & Cramer, 1984). This does not mean that ability is unimportant, but it does indicate that we must consider other factors in career planning.

Interests. Interest measurement has become popular and is used extensively in career planning. In Resource 10, Ways of Making Wise Vocational Choices, you will find a description of several personality and interest inventories that are used in occupational counseling.

Interests, unlike abilities, have been found to be moderately effective as predictors of vocational success, satisfaction, and persistence (Super & Bohn, 1970). Therefore, primary consideration should be given to interests in vocational planning. It is important to first determine your areas of vocational interest, then to identify occupations for which these interests are appropriate, and then to determine those occupations for which you have the abilities required for satisfactory job performance. Research evidence indicates only a slight relationship between interests and abilities (Tolbert, 1980). In other words, simply because we are interested in a job does not necessarily mean that we have the ability needed for it.

Values.   It is extremely important for you to identify, clarify, and assess your values so that you will be able to match them with your career. In Resource 10 the Allport-Vernon-Lindsey Study of Values is described. This inventory, which is available in most college counseling centers, helps pinpoint whether your central values are in the social area, the political area, or the economic area.

In counseling college students on vocational decision making I typically recommend that they follow their interests and values as reliable guides for a general occupational area. If your central values are economic, for example, your career decisions are likely to be based on a desire for some type of financial or psychological security. The security a job affords is a legitimate consideration for most people, but you may find that security alone is not enough to lead to vocational satisfaction. Your central values may be social, including working with people and helping people. There are many careers that would be appropriate for those with a social orientation.

Refer to Resource 11, Self-Assessment of Your Work-Related Values, for suggestions on how to inventory your life-style values.

Of course, the factors I've mentioned are only a few of the many considerations involved in selecting a vocation. Since so much time and energy are devoted to work, it's extremely important to decide for ourselves what weight each factor will have in our thinking. Too often, the motivating factor in choosing a job or a career is the money and status associated with it. I hope you'll ask yourself "Is the price of status and money worth the possible psychological distress of a job I don't like?" Thus, in considering a line of work, you might also ask yourself how much time you will have left over for leisure and for learning.

In short, *you* stand a greater chance of being satisfied with your work if you put time and thought into your choice and if you actively take steps toward finding a career or an occupation that will bring more enrichment to your life than it will disruption. Ultimately, *you* are the person who can best decide what you want in your work. In this regard, I like the suggestion given by Bolles (1978):

> You are in charge of your life. No matter how many forces there may be which seem to influence or even dictate part of your life, there is always that part over which you have control. You can increase that control. If you decide what it is that you want out of your Learning, and out of your Working, and out of your Playing, you will be infinitely less *powerless* and *"victimizable"* [p. 58].

Being Active in Career Planning

Perhaps one of the major factors that will prevent you from becoming active in the process of job planning is the temptation to put off doing what needs to be done to *choose* your work. If you merely "fall into a job," somewhat as you might "fall in love," you will probably be disappointed with the outcome.

One other consideration is worth mentioning in connection with career choices. One of the reviewers of this book called my attention to predictions that there will be five to seven occupational changes in a typical working lifetime during the last part of the century. It therefore seems that, if you're at the beginning of your working life, you can anticipate having a series of jobs. Thus, it could well be a mistake to think about selecting *one* occupation that will last a lifetime. Instead, it may be more fruitful to think about selecting a general type of work or a broad field of endeavor that appeals to you. With a broad goal in mind, you can consider your present job as a means of gaining experience and opening doors to new possibilities, and you can focus on what *you* want to learn from this experience. It can be liberating to realize that your decisions about work can be part of a developmental process and that your jobs can change as you change. If you see your job choices in this developmental way, you can remain open to making changes and integrating them with other changes in your life-style. Resource 10 provides some guidelines for making use of your career-development center.

The Dangers of Choosing an Occupation Too Soon

So much emphasis is placed on what we will do "for a living" that there is a real danger of feeling compelled to choose an occupation or a career before we're really ready to do so. The pressure to identify with some occupation begins in childhood with the often-heard question "What are you going to be when you grow up?" (Part of the implication of this question is that we're not grown up until we've decided to *be* something.) If freshman year in high school isn't too early to start worrying about acceptance to college, then no grade is too early to start worrying about acceptance to the right high school! Thus, the pressure is applied at a very early age to decide on what you basically intend to do with your life—before you've really had a chance to sample either the life out there in the world or the life within you.

One of the dangers in focusing on a particular occupation too soon is that interest patterns are often not sufficiently reliable or stable in late junior high and senior high or, sometimes, even the college years to be predictive of job success and satisfaction. Furthermore, the typical student does not have enough self-knowledge, as well as knowledge of educational offerings and vocational opportunities, to make realistic decisions. The pressure to make premature vocational decisions often results in choosing an occupation in which one does not have the interests and abilities that are required for success.

One of my daughters is graduating from high school this year. Heidi has changed her mind a number of times about specific college plans and is very unclear about what she'd like to pursue in college. It concerns her that she does not know exactly what she wants to be. Marianne and I consistently advise her not to burden herself with deciding on a particular path at this point. We see the first years of college as a time for general education and simply exploring interests and possibilities. Thus, we continue to encourage Heidi to remain open to a wide range of interests rather than narrowing down the field before she has adequately explored what is out there.

A few years ago I hired a young man of 22 to do some painting and carpentry work in my house. Paul went to a community college for a year in the Midwest, but he dropped out because he needed to work to support himself. Then he and a friend decided to travel and experiment with whatever jobs they could find. They traveled over 1000 miles by bicycle, doing odd jobs along the way. For a while they picked apples in the Northwest and really enjoyed that work. Afterwards, Paul wound up in my town to stay for a time.

Although Paul said that he wasn't really in a hurry to find a job, he found that he soon had plenty of work. He met a carpenter and became an apprentice, and he says that he has never enjoyed work as much as he does now. Previously, most of his jobs had been chores that he performed just to make money. Now he's doing something he likes while learning skills and making living money besides.

Paul has avoided committing himself to a vocation before he has a chance to experience life, the world of work, and his own interests and capabilities. Some people might see him as being aimless and as wasting valuable time, but I respect what he's doing, and I believe that he's really expanding his choices and eventually will find work that will be meaningful to him. Besides, he seems to be having an exciting time living right now, without worrying about preparation for the future.

Paul is a young man who ultimately resisted the pressure to select a vocation too early in life. Although different people may make appropriate career decisions at different times, I think it is generally a disservice to young people to pressure them to make crucial life decisions concerning what they want to be "when they grow up." I believe most of us need an opportunity to experiment with a diverse range of occupations, to clarify our interests, and to test our abilities. Although taking the time we need to make choices for ourselves can produce anxiety for all concerned, it can also lead to greater satisfaction in the long run.

TIME OUT FOR PERSONAL REFLECTION

This Time Out is a survey of your basic attitudes, values, abilities, and interests in regard to occupational choice.

1. Rate each item, using the following code: 1 = this is a most important consideration; 2 = this is important to me, but not a top priority; 3 = this is slightly important; 4 = this is of little or no importance to me.

————————   a. financial rewards
————————   b. security
————————   c. a job that would challenge me
————————   d. prestige and status
————————   e. the opportunity to express my creativity
————————   f. autonomy—freedom to direct my project
————————   g. opportunity for advancement
————————   h. variety within the job
————————   i. recognition
————————   j. friendship and relations with co-workers
————————   k. serving people
————————   l. a source of meaning
————————   m. the chance to continue learning
————————   n. structure and routine

Once you've finished making the above assessment, review the list to determine the three most important factors you associate with selecting a career or occupation.

—————————————————————————————

—————————————————————————————

—————————————————————————————

—————————————————————————————

2. How has your self-concept influenced your making of a vocational decision?

—————————————————————————————

—————————————————————————————

—————————————————————————————

3. What jobs do you associate with the lowest degree of prestige or status?

—————————————————————————————

—————————————————————————————

—————————————————————————————

4. *What jobs do you see as being the highest in prestige or status?*

_____

_____

_____

_____

5. *In what area(s) do you see your strongest abilities?*

_____

_____

_____

_____

6. *What are a few of your major interests?*

_____

_____

_____

_____

7. *Which one value of yours do you see as having some bearing on your choice of a vocation?*

_____

_____

_____

_____

8. *What pressure have you felt to decide on an occupation before you felt ready to make this decision, and from whom?*

_____

_____

_____

_____

9. *At this point, what jobs do you see as most suitable to your interests, abilities, and values?*

_____

_____

_____

_____

10. *Of Naisbitt's megatrends, which one has the most meaning for you, and why?*

_____

_____

_____

_____

11. *What are your reactions to the hypothesis that you will carry many of your attitudes and behaviors as a college student into your future career?*

_____

_____

_____

_____

12. *Most of the jobs I've had so far*
    a. have been very rewarding.
    b. have been unsatisfying.
    c. have primarily been a means to survival.
    d. have been of my own choosing.

    e. _____

13. *I would most like a job in which*
    a. I could be my own boss.
    b. I could work for others who would assume primary responsibility.
    c. I had a great deal of power and influence.
    d. I could work at my own pace.

    e. _____

14. *In regard to choosing my own occupation, I believe that*
    a. I can be whatever I choose to become.
    b. my choice is severely limited by the job market.
    c. fate will determine what kind of work I do.
    d. my choices, while limited, are nevertheless real and significant.

    e. _____

15. *I think that work satisfaction is related to satisfaction in other areas of my life*
    a. to a very high degree.
    b. to a considerable degree.
    c. to some degree.
    d. only to a very slight degree.

    e. _____

THE PLACE OF WORK AND LEISURE IN OUR LIFE

One way of looking at the place that work and leisure occupy in our life is to consider how we divide up our time. In an average day most people spend about eight hours sleeping, another eight hours working, and the other eight hours in chores and leisure. If our work is something that we enjoy, then at least half of our waking existence is spent in meaningful activities. Yet if we dread getting up and hate going to work, those eight hours can easily have a negative impact on the other eight hours that we are awake.

One way to increase the chances that we will find job satisfaction is to devote the time and effort required to make a career decision that will be congruent with our values, interests, and abilities. Further, it is useful to remind ourselves that the decisions we make concerning life-style should not be thought of as permanent. Mencke and Hummel (1984) underscore the point that even the term *career decision* is misleading, because it implies that we will make only one such decision that will bind us for the rest of our life. They emphasize that for most of us career choice is better seen as a sequential process of development—that is, a series of choices rather than a single choice we make and are then stuck with.

Work and the Meaning of Your Life

Whether or not you've already decided on an occupation or career, it's important to consider what you find or expect to find through work and how work can either contribute to or detract from the meaning and quality of your life. If you expect your work to provide you with a primary source of meaning and if your life isn't as rich with meaning as you'd like, you might begin to tell yourself "If only I had a job that I liked, *then* I'd be fulfilled." This "If only, then . . ." type of thinking can lead you to believe that somehow the secret of finding a purpose in your life depends on something outside yourself.

In his book *The Doctor and the Soul*, Frankl (1965) contends that "no one occupation is the sole road to salvation." He talks about people who try to deceive themselves by thinking that they *would* be fulfilled now *if only* they had gone into another occupation. Frankl notes that the fault may be in the person rather than in the work: "The work in itself does not make the person indispensable and irreplaceable; it only gives him the chance to be so" (p. 95). He describes a patient who found her life meaningless. He pointed out to her that her attitude toward her work and the manner in which she worked were more important than the job itself. He showed her that the way a person approaches a job and the special things he or she does in carrying it out are what make it meaningful.

If you decide that you must remain in a job that allows little scope for personal effort and satisfaction, you may need to accept the fact that you won't find much meaning in the hours you spend on the job. It's important, then, to be aware of the effects the time spent on the job has on the rest of your life and to minimize them. More positively, it's crucial to find something outside the job that fulfills your need for recognition, significance, productivity, and excitement. By doing so, you may develop a sense of your true work as something different from what you're paid to do; you may even come to think of your job as providing the means for the productive activities you engage in away from the job, whether they take the form of hobbies, creative pursuits, volunteer work, the spending of time with friends and family, or whatever the case may be. The point is to see whether things can be turned around so that you are the master rather than the victim of your job. Too many people are so negatively affected by their job that their frustration and sense of emptiness spoil their eating, leisure time, family life, sex life, and relationships with friends. If you can reassume control of your own attitudes toward your job and find dignity and pride elsewhere in your life, you may be able to do much to lessen these negative effects.

Leisure and the Meaning of Your Life

A work/leisure perspective offers a framework for understanding the healthy person and for living a balanced life. Work alone does not result in balance and fulfillment. Even rewarding work does take energy, and we need some break from it. Leisure is "free time," the time that we control and can use for ourselves. Freedom and autonomy are at the root of leisure. Whereas work requires a certain degree of perseverance and drive, play requires the ability to let go, to be spontaneous, and to avoid getting caught in the trap of being obsessed with what we "should" be doing. Compulsivity dampens the enjoyment of leisure time, and planned spontaneity is almost a contradiction in terms.

Many of us have difficulty getting the most from our leisure time. We may feel guilty having fun if our activities are not "productive." This feeling is rooted in the work ethic that views free time as wasteful. The Puritan admonition is that "the idle mind is the devil's workshop." Our acceptance of the work ethic makes it difficult for us to believe and act as though we have a right to leisure time. Even though I personally have much more difficulty with leisure time than I do with work time, I agree with Brennecke and Amick (1980), who make a strong case for a life of balance. They write: "The puritan attitude of work or sin should be replaced with a new ethic that calls for a healthy balance between work and leisure. The work-sin ethic denies humanness and makes workhorses or machines out of organisms that have the potential to be something more

than mere machines" (p. 181). The ancient Greeks viewed leisure time as essential for self-understanding, introspection, and personal growth. Within this framework leisure provides opportunities for achieving inner potential, for expressing ourselves, and for experiencing a rich and meaningful existence.

One of the challenges many of us face is how to find meaningful avocational activities and how to use leisure creatively. For some, leisure means doing nothing, which may mean escaping. Some escape by spending untold hours sitting passively in front of the television set. Others escape through drugs or alcohol. The challenge is to create a life-style that includes meaningful leisure pursuits as well as meaningful work. Of course, one person's leisure activity might well be another's work, or vice versa. There is a personal quality to defining leisure, and each of us must find activities that are personally meaningful. This may include activities that are very different from what we do in our work, or activities that are an extension of work.

Brennecke and Amick (1980) write about using leisure time for *re-creation*, which includes self-restoration, reenergizing, rebuilding, relaxing, and refreshing ourselves. They emphasize that re-creation and play, whether solitary or social, are basic elements in enriching human experience, for such activities replenish one physically, psychologically, socially, and spiritually. There are many routes to this re-creation of self, a few of which include engaging in sports, spending time with friends, getting out into nature, meditating, and being alone.

Leisure counseling, which has been getting increased attention, is a relatively new specialty (American Psychological Association, 1981). Psychologists who specialize in leisure counseling maintain that leisure can be viewed in much the same way that work is. The objectives of planning for a career and planning for creative use of leisure time are basically the same—to help us develop feelings of self-esteem, reach our potential, and improve the quality of our life. If we do not learn how to pursue interests apart from work, then we may well face a crisis when we retire. If we do plan for creative ways to use leisure, we can experience both joy and continued personal growth.

What follows are three examples of how work and leisure can be combined. I first discuss the effects that work has in my own life. Then I provide an example of a physician who relates to work differently. Also described are a couple, Judy and Frank, whom I see as having found a good balance. Although both Judy and Frank enjoy their work, they have also arranged their life to make time for leisure.

The Effects of Work in My Own Life

My professional life is varied, and these diverse work experiences provide me with excitement, stimulation, challenge, the chance to learn from others, and the inspiration to develop new projects.

I would find it very difficult to stay in a job simply because it provided financial security. I have made several career choices and at times given up tenured positions or security to get involved with programs that offered more meaning and challenge. When I assess my work activities, I become aware of how much energy I devote to them and how heavily I depend on them to structure my life. In many respects my life is my work, and my work is my life. At times it still frightens me to consider what my life would be like if I were not working as much as I am.

My work style has both positive and negative effects on my life. On the good side, I feel creative in my work, I derive a deep sense of personal satisfaction from my projects, and I'm doing them because I want to. I'm not writing books because of the pressure to "publish or perish" but because writing them is one way to express myself personally and professionally. Similarly, if I do additional consulting or teaching of graduate courses, it's not primarily because of the financial rewards but because I like being associated with counselor-education programs at this level. My work is generally fun and a source of vitality, and it gives me a sense of fulfillment and challenge.

Yet there are negative effects too. One disadvantage of my work style is that I tend to rely too heavily on work as a source of nourishment and to

W-O-R-K — W-O-O-R-R-K!
... I GOTTA HAVE W-O-R-K!!!

neglect other possible ways of giving and being nourished. I must be careful not to be consumed by my work. Too often I find myself missing the present moment because I'm busy thinking about some future project. Moreover, so much of my life is bound up with work that I find it difficult to really live when I'm not being "productive." During semester breaks or vacations I feel uneasy unless I'm accomplishing some form of significant work.

Other people are affected by my work style as well. Often I feel at a loss concerning what to say to someone when I don't talk about work. At times my family suffers from my investment in work, and I cheat myself out of contact with them and with many of the simple joys of life. While my family does share in my involvement with work, they are also willing to let me know when my overextension causes them pain. And our friends have pointed out to us that, while Marianne works very hard and enjoys her professional work, she seems much less driven than I. While I often say yes to an attractive offer for a workshop or a weekend conference (and then later find myself overextended), Marianne is more likely to say "It sounds exciting; let me think about it."

When all is said and done, however, I do feel fortunate in having work that I find meaningful, exciting, and fulfilling. I know that not everyone feels the way I do about work, so some of my struggles in this area may be different from yours. I know that I have choices to make about how I'll structure my life and that I must assess the price I pay for my investment in work. For me, the struggle comes in learning how to really *let go* and forget work at times and still feel that I'm alive and valuable.

A Man Who Is Not Wedded to His Work

Here's an example of a professional whose work style is different from mine. While this man does work to live, he is also able to get away from his profession of medicine by becoming fully involved in a number of unrelated hobbies.

Dr. Allan Abbott (whom I referred to earlier, in the chapter on "Your Body") has had a wide range of experiences as a physician, and he continues to be open to many different aspects of his profession. He practiced as an anesthesiologist until he decided that he wanted more contact with his patients than putting them to sleep. He worked with his wife, Katherine, a registered nurse, in the wilds of Peru. He went around the world as a ship's physician for a "floating high school." He conducted research on coronary-prone behavior that was stimulated by his observations of a primitive culture where heart disease was absent. He developed a family practice with his wife in the mountain community of Idyllwild, California, for three years. Later he accepted a position as an associate professor that entails supervising residents in the specialty of family practice in a hospital.

Although Abbott is very dedicated to his work, he devotes much time to diverse interests that could easily become careers in themselves. For example, one of his hobbies is the designing, building, and racing of aerodynamic bicycles. He has twice broken the world's speed record. His other talents and interests include painting, sculpturing, and home construction. Although his professional work could be all-consuming, he has chosen to provide time to cultivate his other areas of interest.

A Couple Who Are Able to Balance Work and Leisure

Judy and Frank were married when she was 16 and he was 20. They now have two grown sons and a couple of grandchildren. At 51 Frank works for an electrical company as a lineman, a job he has had for close to 30 years. Judy, who is 47, delivers meals to schools and helps serve them.

Judy went to work when her two sons were in elementary school. Although she felt no financial pressure to do so, she took the job because she liked the extras that their family could afford with her working. Because she was efficient as a homemaker, she felt that her days would not be filled with housework alone. She was interested in doing something away from home. She continues her work primarily because she likes the contact with both co-workers and the children and adolescents whom she meets daily. Judy has a good way with children, and they respond well to her. She values the impact that she is able to have on them and the affection she receives from them. If Judy had her preference, she'd work only three days a week instead the five she now does. She would like more time to enjoy her grandchildren and would like a longer weekend.

Frank is satisfied with his job, and he looks forward to going to work. He says that, inasmuch as he stopped his education at high school, he feels that he has a good job that both pays well and offers many fringe benefits. Although he is a bright person, he expresses no ambition to continue his formal education. A few of the things that he likes about his work are the companionship with his co-workers, the physical aspect, the security, and the routine. As a mechanically inclined person, he is both curious about and challenged by the way things work, why they malfunction, and how to repair them. He fixes things not only on his job but also at home and for his neighbors.

In terms of this couple's use of leisure, they each have their separate interests and hobbies, yet they also spend time together. Both of them are hardworking people, and they have achieved success financially and personally. They feel pleased about their success because they can see the fruits of their labor. They spend most of their weekends at their mountain cabin, which both of them helped build. He fishes, hikes, jogs, rides his motorcycle, cuts wood, fixes the house, visits with friends, and watches ballgames on TV. She is talented in working at arts and crafts, repairing the cars, housepainting, and preparing delicious meals. Together they enjoy their grandchildren, friends, and themselves.

Judy and Frank are a good example of people who enjoy their work life and their leisure life, both as individuals and as a couple. A challenge that many of us will face is to find ways of using our leisure well. As we have moved into a high-technology age, we are finding that we have more leisure. Now the question is how we can creatively use this time when we are not sleeping or working.

TIME OUT FOR PERSONAL REFLECTION

1. Mention a few of the most important benefits that you get (or expect to get) from work.

_____

_____

_____

_____

2. How do you typically spend your leisure time?

_____

_____

_____

_____

3. Are there any ways that you'd like to spend your leisure time differently?

_____

_____

_____

_____

4. What nonwork activities have you liked because in doing them you felt creative, happy, or energetic?

_____

_____

_____

_____

5. Could you obtain a job that would incorporate some of the activities you've just listed? Or does your job already account for them?

_____

_____

_____

_____

6. What do you think would happen to you if you couldn't work? Write what first comes to mind.

_____

_____

_____

_____

7. Some people experience a good deal of anxiety over making choices dealing with work. Check any of the following factors that create anxiety for you:

_____ I feel that I must make a career choice too quickly.
_____ I don't know what my abilities are.
_____ Once I make a choice, I think that I must stay with it.
_____ I fear that my choice will be wrong and that I'll be stuck with a miserable job.
_____ I'm afraid that I won't be able to find the kind of work I really want.
_____ I'm afraid that I'll become consumed by my work.

I'm concerned that I'll select a line of work because I've been influenced by others and that I'll be living up to their expectations rather than my own.

8. *Mention any other anxieties you are aware of concerning your decisions about work.*

_____

_____

_____

_____

9. *If you could quit your job and still have all your needs met, what would you do with your time?*

_____

_____

_____

_____

CHOICES AT WORK

We have discussed the process of choosing a vocation and the place that work and leisure occupy in our life. In this section the unifying theme is that we have choices *within* the careers we select. Just as choosing a career is a process, so is creating meaning in our work. If we grow stale in our job or do not find an avenue of self-expression through the work we do, we eventually lose our vitality. This section looks at ways to find meaning in work, ways of preventing burn-out, and approaches to keeping options open.

The Dynamics of Discontent in Work

It is certainly true that, if you're dissatisfied with your job, one recourse you have is to seek a new one. Change alone, however, might not produce different results. In general, I think it's a mistake to assume that change necessarily cures dissatisfactions, and this very much applies to changing jobs. To know whether a new job would be helpful, you need to understand as clearly as you can why your present job isn't satisfactory to you. Consequently, I'd like to talk about some of the external factors that can devitalize us in our job and the very real pressures and stresses our job often creates. Then I'd like to focus attention on the importance of looking *within ourselves* for the source of our discontent. The emphasis will be on what *you* can do about changing some of these factors in the job and in yourself. Often we blame external factors for our unhappiness and, in so doing, fail to look at how our own attitudes and expectations might be contributing to our discontent. The focus of much of the rest of the section is on what you can do *within* the job to lessen dissatisfaction, if not ensure thriving.

You may like your work and derive satisfaction from it yet at the same time feel drained because of irritations produced by factors that aren't intrinsic to the work itself. Such factors may include low morale among fellow workers or actual conflict and disharmony among them; authoritarian supervisors who make it difficult for you to feel any sense of freedom on the job; or organizational blocks to your creativity. There are also countless pressures and demands that can sap your energy and lead you to feel dissatisfied with your job. These include having to meet deadlines and quotas; having to compete with others instead of simply doing your best; facing the threat of losing your job; feeling stuck in a job that offers little opportunity for growth or that you deem dehumanizing; dealing with difficult customers or clients; and having to work long hours or perform exhausting or tedious work. A stress that is particularly insidious—because it can compound all the other dissatisfactions you might feel—is the threat of cutbacks or layoffs, an anxiety that becomes more acute when you think of your commitments and responsibilities. In addition to the strains you may experience on the job, there may also be the daily stress of commuting to and from work. You may be tense before you even get to work, and the trip home may only increase the level of tension or anxiety you bring home with you. One real problem for many of us is that our relationships with others are negatively affected by this kind of life-style. If our work drains and deenergizes us, we may have little to give to our children, spouse, and friends, and we may not be receptive to their efforts to give to us.

All the factors I've mentioned can contribute to a general discontent that robs our work of whatever positive benefits it might otherwise have. In the face of such discontent we might just plod along, hating our job and spoiling much of the rest of our life as well. The alternative is to look at the specific things that contribute to our unhappiness or tension and to ask ourselves what we can do about them. We can also ask what we should do about our own attitudes toward those pressures and sources.

Creating Meaning in Work

In *Working,* a fascinating report on the everyday lives of working people, Studs Terkel (1975) gives a penetrating inside view of the material and spiritual hardships that many workers experience in their struggle to make a living. He describes scores of interviews with people in many occupations, including a strip miner, a telephone operator, a bookbinder, a garbage man, a spot welder, a bus driver, a car salesman, a mail carrier, an interstate truck driver, a janitor, a waitress, and many others. Many of these first-person accounts testify to the meaninglessness of the worker's life.

Clearly, many, if not most, working people do not find their job personally meaningful or see it as an opportunity for self-expression and self-actualization. Thus, many of them do not identify themselves with their job, despite the time and energy they must devote to it. To these people, work must simply be made as tolerable as possible. No one can say what an enormous toll this attitude must take on the quality of their life and their sense of self-respect.

All of us will probably find certain aspects of our work to be boring, or at least unexciting. Every occupation has its tedious and routine chores. Apart from the boredom that might creep into any job, however, there are undoubtedly occupations in which most of the time on the job is merely endured. In *Working*, Terkel documents the quiet desperation experienced by many people in service occupations. He found certain themes running through his interviews: we need to be needed; we need to feel that our work (and we) are of some significance; we need and want to be remembered; we search for "daily meaning as well as daily bread"; we work for "recognition as well as cash." In Terkel's words, "To be remembered was the wish, spoken and unspoken, of the heroes and heroines in this book" (1975, p. xiii).[2] Terkel concludes that merely surviving the day is a victory for many who are among the "walking wounded" in the world of work. As he says, "The scars, psychic as well as physical, brought home to the supper table and the TV set, may have touched, malignantly, the soul of our society" (p. xiii).

In the automated age in which we live, many people feel as if their work could be done better by machines. Indeed, many of the people Terkel interviewed talk about feeling like robots, objects, or machines. They speak in their own way of being depersonalized—faceless, anonymous, interchangeable cogs in a gigantic machine. For example, an 18-year-old telephone operator complains that she is missing any personal touch in her work. People put coins in a machine, and she responds: "You're there to perform your service and go. You're kind of detached" (p. 65). Even though she'd like to be more personal in her job, and even though there are times when she'd like to engage callers in conversations or brief exchanges, she realizes that in her role she can't be much more than a programmed machine. "I'm a communications person," she says with elo-

[2]From *Working: People Talk about What They Do All Day and How They Feel about What They Do*, by S. Terkel. Copyright 1975 by Pantheon Books, a division of Random House, Inc. Reprinted by permission.

quent irony, "but I can't communicate" (p. 66). Instead, she is reduced to repeating a few acceptable and anonymous responses day after day, such as: "Good morning, may I help you?" "What number do you want?" "I have a collect call from Bill; will you accept the charges?" Apart from such standard phrases, she cannot interact with others in a human way without risking her supervisor's disapproval and perhaps her job itself.

If you find your work meaningless, what can you do about it? What can you do if, instead of energizing you, your job drains you physically and emotionally? What are your options if you feel stuck in a dead-end job? Are there some ways that you can constructively deal with the sources of dissatisfaction within your job?

One way of dealing with the issue of meaninglessness and dissatisfaction in work is to look at how you really spend your time. It would be useful to keep a running account for a week to a month of what you do and how you relate to each of your activities. Which of them are draining you, and which are energizing you? While you may not be able to change everything about your job that you don't like, by keeping a record of day-by-day activities within your job you might be surprised by the significant changes you can make to increase your satisfaction. People often adopt a passive and victimlike position in which they complain about everything and dwell on those aspects that they believe they cannot change. Instead, a more constructive approach is to focus on those factors within your job that you *can* change.

Perhaps, too, you can redefine the hopes you have for the job. Of course, you may also be able to think of the satisfactions you'd most like to aim for in a job and then consider whether there is a job that more nearly meets your needs and what steps you must take to obtain it. You might be able to find ways of advancing within your present job, making new contacts, or acquiring the skills that eventually will enable you to move on. The important thing is to look carefully at how much the initiative rests with *you*—your expectations, your attitudes, and your sense of purpose and perspective.

Job Burn-Out: Some Ways of Staying Alive

The phenomenon of job burn-out is receiving increasing attention. What is burn-out? What are some of its causes? What can be done to prevent it? How can it be overcome?

Burn-out is a state of physical, emotional, and mental exhaustion. It is the result of repeated emotional pressures, often associated with intense involvement with people over long periods of time. People who are burned out are characterized by physical depletion and by feelings of hopelessness and helplessness. They tend to develop negative attitudes toward themselves, others, work, and life (Pines, Aronson, & Kafry, 1981).

The problem of burn-out is especially critical for people working in the human-services field. With the emphasis in this kind of work on giving to others, there is often not enough focus on giving to oneself. According to Pines, Aronson, and Kafry (1981), people who perform human services share three basic characteristics: (1) they are involved in emotionally taxing work; (2) they tend to be sensitive to others' problems and have a desire to relieve suffering; and (3) they often see their work as a calling to be givers to those who need help. Unfortunately, some who enter the helping professions have high hopes that are never realized. If they meet with constant frustration, see almost no positive change in their clients, and encounter obstacles to meeting their goals of helping others, their hopes may eventually be replaced by a sense of hopelessness.

Burn-out is a problem for workers in other fields besides human services, and for students as well. I hear my students say that burn-out often catches them by surprise. They often do not recognize the general hurriedness of their life-style, nor do they always notice the warning signs that they have pushed themselves to the breaking point. Many students devote the majority of their life to school and work, while neglecting to maintain their friendships, to make quality time for their family, or to take time for their own leisure pursuits. Semester after semester they crowd in too many units, convincing themselves that they must push themselves so that they can graduate and then start making money. Sometimes they do not realize the price they are paying. Eventually they become apathetic, just waiting for a semester to end. They are physically and emotionally exhausted and often feel socially cut off.

Burn-out is a potential danger in any kind of job. Doing the same routine work and not enjoying it eventually exacts a toll. If we are giving and extending ourselves but getting very little in return for our investment, our energy eventually dries up. Unless we replenish the well that we dip into for others, we will have very little to offer them.

So what can we do if we feel a general sense of psychological and physical exhaustion? Christina Maslach (1982), a psychologist who has extensively studied the problem of burn-out, maintains that there are many constructive approaches. Once we recognize our state and seriously want to change it, the situation is not hopeless. Maslach provides many excellent suggestions: Instead of working harder, we can "work smarter," which means that we change the way we approach our job so that we suffer less stress. Setting realistic goals is another coping skill. We can also work at conquering feelings of helplessness, since such feelings lead to frustration and anger, which in turn result in our becoming exhausted and cynical. We can learn to relax, even if such breaks are short. Instead of taking all the problems we encounter personally, we can condition ourselves to assume a more objective perspective. Most important, we can learn that caring for ourselves is every bit as important as caring for others.

Although learning coping skills to deal with the effects of burn-out is helpful, I think that our energies are best directed toward preventing the condition. The real challenge is to learn ways of structuring our life so that we can stay alive as a person as well as a worker (or student). Maslach (1982) asserts that the key to prevention is early action. She stresses using solutions before there is a problem. This includes becoming sensitive to the first signs of burn-out creeping up on us. Finding ways to energize ourselves is critical as a preventive measure. This is where learning how to use leisure to nurture ourselves is so important. Each of us can find a different path to staying alive personally. The point is that we slow down and monitor the way we are living so that we will discover that path.

Women and Work Choices

Women work not only out of choice but also out of necessity. Some feel the pressure of taking care of the home and holding down an outside job to help support the family. And there are many single parents who must work. I am thinking of Deborah, who after her divorce said: "I know that I can survive, but it's scary for me to face the world alone. Before, my job was an additional source of income and something I did strictly out of choice. Now a job is my livelihood and a means to support my children."

One of the reviewers of this book reports that her young women students are very unrealistic about careers and that they limit their options in the world of work. She finds that they are unaware of how many women are in the work force or what the labor projections are for their lifetime. They tend to keep their job aspirations very low, thus cutting off options that could be open to them. In surveying her freshmen women students about their ideal and probable careers, this professor found, almost universally, that their dream career was to be either a model or a movie star. They tended to state their probable career as being a teacher, retail clerk, or secretary. Only one person, a Hispanic woman, gave becoming a lawyer as her ideal career.

Yet, according to Naisbitt's (1984) predictions, there is an explosion of occupational options for women. Women are now exploring a wide variety of choices besides those that have been viewed as appropriate for them. They are joining the labor force, going back to college, and entering professional schools. Women are studying medicine, business, and law. And by 1990 the number of women who attain a college degree in business will be eight times that of the 1960s. Women are also starting new businesses at a phenomenal rate.

The sharp distinction between a "man's job" and a "woman's job" is fading. In addition to assuming professional positions, women are moving into blue-collar jobs at an astonishing rate. Naisbitt (1984) cites statistics from the U.S. Bureau of Labor Statistics in 1981 revealing the following number of women in these trades: 10,600 brick masons, 51,000 truck driv-

ers, 15,000 butchers, 19,000 printing-press operators, 7,500 auto mechanics, and 170,000 bus drivers.

How is this widening of vocational options for women affecting men? Naisbitt (1984) observes that, as women continue to exercise personal options, choices also open up for men. Some men now have the freedom to become a full-time father or student or to share a job with their wife. Naisbitt writes that traditional family life, which depended on the woman's subordinating her individual interests and making her children and husband her priority, is not destined to return anytime soon.

Women in a Dual-Career Family.   We are increasingly seeing the dual-career marriage, which often imposes special burdens on the woman. Many women try to do their best both at home and at work, only to find that their energies are sapped and that they are fragmented from performing so many roles.

Following is a first-person account of some of the struggles that Marianne experiences in trying to combine her many roles—as a therapist, author, mother, homemaker, friend, consultant, community worker, lecturer, wife, teacher, traveler, and hostess, just to mention a few! Her struggle typifies those of other women who also juggle many roles.

> When I look at the list of my multiple roles it does not surprise me
> that I recently stuck my finger in the garbage disposal and absent-
> mindedly turned on the wrong switch. Although my hand was hurt, my

emotional pain was greater than the physical pain. This incident forced me to look at how many things I was attempting to do in one day.

Just to review that day! I got two daughters off to school beginning at 6:00 A.M. I straightened up the house. I had a cup of coffee and watched some news on the *Today* show. And I spent several hours writing and revising books with Jerry—which was interrupted by my doing laundry, answering phone calls, running errands in town, organizing and beginning to pack for my daughters' summer trip to Germany, and picking up the kids from school.

To top it off, I had three individual counseling sessions with clients in the afternoon. Immediately after the last one, I began to prepare the evening meal. I was still preoccupied with the last client, and I was thinking of all the details of making the arrangements for someone to stay with the girls while Jerry and I would be on a consulting trip/vacation out of the country. I was anticipating helping one of the girls with her homework—while Jerry was in the background asking "When is dinner ready?"

While this is not the way my typical day goes, there are times when it happens more than I would like. Looking at my activities, I find that I enjoy most of the things that I do, but their diversity often fragments me. Through my contact with women friends and clients, I find that I share a common struggle in combining many conflicting roles involved in having a career and also taking the role of mother and homemaker seriously.

The process of delicately balancing many different and sometimes conflicting roles has been a struggle for many years, and it seems to be a continuing one. I am very aware of my parental programming, which entailed the traditional conditioning of women. Growing up in a small German village for 19 years had a significant impact on me. It was not an easy task to break out of this traditional pattern, to risk my parents' disapproval, to pursue higher education, and eventually to become involved in a professional career. Over the years I have certainly modified many of my parents' designs for me, yet I have come to the realization that many of their values are ones that I have consciously chosen and am now choosing to live by. At this point in my life, I am not willing to give up my professional career. However, it is at least equally important for me to be a good wife, mother, and homemaker and above all to have a significant positive involvement in my children's lives.

I pride myself in being efficient in the many different things that I do. Yet this at times comes home to haunt me, because I am slow in learning to ask for help or to delegate work. I have conditioned Jerry, our children, and our friends to rely on my need to be efficient in all that I do, and they gladly let me be this way! I am aware that many of these tasks are self-appointed responsibilities; it is up to me to know my limits, to set them, and to let others know what I will and will not do. When I have worked myself into a panic, it is much easier for me to let off steam and complain about the people around me who make too many demands on me. When all is calm and I take time to reflect, I often come up with the reality that it is my responsibility to negotiate, to ask for what I want or need, and to directly and clearly specify my limits before I overextend myself—even if delegating certain routine tasks does not come easy to me.

I find that many women, and I am one of them, see it as unfair that their husband delights in their professional endeavors yet at the same times relies on them to perform the traditional role of homemaker. When I am not angry about this fact, I am able to recognize that there are changes taking place. Both men and women are slowly reconditioning themselves and not rigidly sticking to predefined roles. I realize that I must make the time to evaluate and arrange my priorities and that ultimately I am the one who chooses how I spend my days. Nevertheless, there are many times that I feel that I am performing a juggling act, and at times I get dizzy and feel overextended.

While women may be capable of doing any one of several tasks well, attempting to do *all* of them at the same time can be unrealistic. In her excellent book *Workaholics*, Marilyn Machlowitz (1980) discusses the ex-

pectations of the so-called "Superwoman" who attempts to live up to the roles of Supermom, Superwife, and Superworker. Of course, there is never enough time or energy to fulfill Superwoman's self-expectations, and thus she suffers from a sense of guilt. A woman like this needs to ask herself whether the physical and psychological price she is paying to maintain the Superwoman image is worth it.

In their book *Burnout: From Tedium to Personal Growth*, Pines, Aronson, and Kafry (1981) conclude that dual-career women need to accept the reality that they have two full-time jobs. A dual-career woman is often overburdened, harassed, guilt-ridden, and a likely candidate for burn-out. To combat these dangers, she needs to exercise her power of choice:

> She must be aware that she will face daily struggles for priorities of her time and energy. The home/career woman must define her goals in each of her different roles and distribute her mental, physical, and emotional energy accordingly. A decision to combine family and career means making compromises. The woman herself must decide how these compromises will be made, both between and within her roles [p. 98].

TIME OUT FOR PERSONAL REFLECTION

As you think about your choices at work, let yourself imagine what you would like to be different and how you might make these changes. If college is your primary work, you can apply these questions to your school experience.

1. A major dissatisfaction in my work is _____

_____

2. What I'd most like to have different in the future is _____

_____

3. A specific step I could take now to begin making these changes is ____

_____

4. One way that I have experienced burn-out is _____

_____

5. A main factor that could lead to burn-out for me is _____

_____

6. One way for me to prevent burn-out is _____

_____

7. One choice that I have as it applies to my work is _____

_____

CHANGING JOBS OR CAREERS

Certainly we have the option of changing jobs in order to increase our satisfaction with work, but changing jobs after a period of years can entail even more risk and uncertainty than making our first job selection. The key when we consider a vocational choice is to become clear about our own expectations and wants.

An illustration is provided by Ralph, a 34-year-old truck driver. Ralph tells me that he knows now that he became a truck driver because he always felt like a loner. He thought that truck driving was one occupation in which he could spend a lot of time alone and not have to deal with people. As he looks back on his decision, he sees that he took the job because he didn't feel that he had the confidence to interact with people. He felt inferior in most areas of his life, but he felt that he could handle trucking. And he adds that he gets some sense of power from driving a huge, noisy truck. However, things are changing within Ralph. He realizes now that he doesn't have to limit his life by staying in an occupation that he doesn't really *want* to stay in. He has resumed college, and he has begun to challenge his self-limiting notion that he is stupid and could never be anything else but a trucker. He says that what he really wants to do is work with adolescents who get themselves into trouble, because he feels a kinship with them. He still drives a truck in order to make a living, but at the same time he is taking steps to prepare himself for a change.

Even though Ralph had done well financially as a trucker, he no longer found his work satisfying. He realized that he had at least three alternatives: he could remain a trucker, he could do some kind of volunteer work in addition to his trucking, or he could prepare himself for another job while keeping his trucking job temporarily. Ultimately, Ralph chose the last option, but the first crucial step was his recognition of his motivations for choosing trucking in the first place. With this awareness he was able to see clearly that he did want a change and that he had the potential to be something different.

It's important to realize that we may be enthusiastic about some type of work for years and yet eventually become dissatisfied because of the changes that occur within us. With these changes comes the possibility that a once-fulfilling job will become monotonous and draining. If we outgrow our job, we can learn new skills and in other ways increase our options. Because our own attitudes are crucial, when a feeling of dissatisfaction sets in, it's wise to spend time rethinking what we want from a job and how we can most productively use our talents. If you want to pursue this subject further, I recommend reading Bolles' (1984) *What Color Is Your Parachute?*

CHAPTER SUMMARY

There are clear parallels between the way you approach your college education and the way you are likely to approach your work. Although some people treat college as a means to an end and eventually become very alive in their career, certain personality traits are likely to operate both at school and on the job.

Naisbitt has identified megatrends that have implications for the process of career development. The United States is moving from an industrial to an information society; in the direction of high technology/high touch; from a national economy to a world economy; from a short-term to a longer-term orientation; from centralization to decentralization; toward self-reliance; from a representative to a participatory democracy; and from a limited range of choices to a multiple-option society. Because predicting the future is shaky, perhaps the best way to anticipate the future is by understanding the present.

Choosing a career is best thought of as a process, not a one-time event. The term *career decision* is misleading, because it implies that we make one choice that we stay with permanently. Most of us will probably have several careers within a lifetime, which is a good argument for a general education. If we prepare too narrowly for a specialization, that job may become obsolete, as will our training. In selecting a career or occupation, it is important to first do a self-assessment of attitudes, abilities, interests, and values. The next step is to explore a wide range of occupational options to see what jobs would best fit our personality. There are clear dangers in choosing an occupation too soon, because our interests do change as we move into adulthood. Another danger is passively falling into a job, rather than carefully considering where we might best find meaning and satisfaction.

Because we devote about half of our waking hours to our work, it behooves us to actively choose a form of work that can express who we are as a person. Much of the other half of our waking time can be used for leisure. With the trend toward increased leisure time, cultivating interests apart from work becomes a real challenge. Just as our work can profoundly affect all aspects of our life, so too can leisure have a positive or negative influence on our existence. Our leisure time can be a source of boredom that drains us, or it can be a source of replenishment that energizes us and enrichens our life.

I've stressed that our job is important in part because our level of job satisfaction often carries over into the other areas of our life. I've also stressed that, although work can be an important source of meaning in our life, it is not the job itself that provides this meaning. The satisfaction we derive depends to a great extent on the way we relate to our job, the manner in which we do it, and the meaning that we ourselves attribute to it. Perhaps the most important idea in this chapter is that we must look to ourselves if we're dissatisfied with our work. It's easy to blame circumstances outside of ourselves when we feel a lack of purpose and meaning. Even if our circumstances are difficult, this kind of stance only victimizes us and keeps us helpless. We can increase our power to change our circumstances by accepting that we are the ones responsible for making our life and our work meaningful, instead of expecting our job to bring meaning to us.

Now write down some of the ideas you found especially significant in this chapter.

_____

_____

_____

_____

_____

ACTIVITIES AND EXERCISES

1. Interview a person you know who dislikes his or her career or occupation. You might ask questions such as the following:

   - If you don't find your job satisfying, why do you stay in it?
   - Do you feel that you have much of a choice about whether you'll stay with the job or take a new one?
   - What aspects of your job bother you the most?
   - How does your attitude toward your job affect the other areas of your life?

2. Interview a person you know who feels fulfilled and excited by his or her work. Some questions you might ask are:

   - What does your work do for you? What meaning does your work have for the other aspects of your life?
   - What are the main satisfactions for you in your work?
   - How do you think you would be affected if you could no longer pursue your career?

3. You might interview your parents and determine what meaning their work has for them. How satisfied are they with the work aspects of their life? How much choice do they feel they have in selecting their work? In what ways do they think the other aspects of their life are affected by their attitudes toward work? After you've talked with them, determine how your attitudes and beliefs about work have been influenced by your parents. Are you pursuing a career that your parents can understand and respect? Is their reaction to your career choice important to you? Are your attitudes and values concerning work like or unlike those of your parents?

4. If your college has a vocational-counseling program available to you, consider talking with a counselor about your plans. You might want to explore taking vocational-interest and aptitude tests. If you're deciding on a career, consider discussing how realistic your vocational plans are. For example, you can pursue such issues as:

   • What are your interests?
   • Do your interests match the career you're thinking about pursuing?
   • Do you have the knowledge you need to make a career choice?
   • Do you have the aptitude and skills for the career you have in mind?
   • What are the future possibilities for you in the work you're considering?

5. If you're considering a particular occupation or career, seek out a person who is actively engaged in that type of work and arrange for a time to talk with him or her. Ask questions concerning the chances of gaining employment, the experience necessary, the satisfactions and drawbacks of the position, and so on. In this way, you can make the process of deciding on a type of work more realistic and perhaps avoid disappointment if your expectations don't match reality.

SUGGESTED READINGS

Bolles, R. N. (1978). *The Three Boxes of Life*. Berkeley, Calif.: Ten Speed Press. This excellent book on life planning focuses on three areas: education, work, and leisure. It is a fine resource for lifelong learning, balanced working, and leisurely enjoying.

Bolles, R. N. (1984). *What Color Is Your Parachute?* Berkeley, Calif.: Ten Speed Press. If you were to select just one book as a guide for career planning, this would be my recommendation. The author's intent is to give job hunters or career changers a process they can use as many times as needed. Practical hints are given on how to decide on a vocation and then secure the job you want. This is an excellent resource guide to other books in the area, to securing professional help, and to keeping current in the job market.

Machlowitz, M. (1980). *Workaholics: Living with Them, Working with Them.* Reading, Mass.: Addison-Wesley. An interesting book that describes the personality characteristics of workaholics and the effects of their addiction on their families and on their own level of happiness. Some suggestions are given for maximizing the pleasures and minimizing the pressures of workaholism.

Maslach, C. (1982). *Burnout: The Cost of Caring.* Englewood Cliffs, N.J.: Prentice-Hall (Spectrum). This is my top recommendation for those who want to learn more about the burn-out syndrome—its causes and effects and ways to prevent it.

Mencke, R., & Hummel, C. L. (1984). *Career Planning for the 80's.* Monterey, Calif.: Brooks/Cole. Students will find this "how-to" book a useful introduction to career planning. Readers are given practical material for self-assessment, career exploration, and marketing their skills.

Naisbitt, J. (1984). *Megatrends.* New York: Warner Books. This best-seller discusses major societal trends that promise to transform our lives and outlines the challenges of the age of high technology.

Srebalus, D. J., Marinelli, R. P., & Messing, J. K. (1982). *Career Development: Concepts and Procedures.* Monterey, Calif.: Brooks/Cole. Though a bit on the technical side, this is a well-written, comprehensive textbook on career development. Particularly useful are the chapters on career assessment, career action, and career adjustment.

Terkel, S. (1975). *Working.* New York: Avon. This magnificent book gives penetrating views of what work means to many people in our society, how they deal with feelings of helplessness and meaninglessness, and how their job influences the rest of their life.

Toffler, A. (1981). *The Third Wave.* New York: Bantam. Toffler, also the author of *Future Shock,* attempts to make sense of the changes in our world. He offers a synthesis that casts a new light on marriage and family, business, and the world of work.

DEATH AND LOSS

PRECHAPTER SELF-INVENTORY

Use the following scale to respond: 4 = this statement is true of me *most* of the time; 3 = this statement is true of me *much* of the time; 2 = this statement is true of me *some* of the time; 1 = this statement is true of me *almost none* of the time.

_____ 1. The fact that I must die makes me take the present moment seriously.
_____ 2. I don't like funerals, because they make me dwell on a painful subject.
_____ 3. If I had a terminal illness, I'd want to know how much time I had left to live, so I could decide how to spend it.
_____ 4. Because of the possibility of losing those I love, I don't allow myself to get too close to others.
_____ 5. If I live with dignity, I'll be able to die with dignity.
_____ 6. One of my greatest fears of death is the fear of the unknown.
_____ 7. I've had losses in my life that in some ways were like the experience of dying.
_____ 8. There are some ways in which I'm not really alive emotionally.
_____ 9. I'm not especially afraid of dying.
_____ 10. I fear the deaths of those I love more than I do my own.

INTRODUCTION

In this chapter I encourage you to look at your attitudes and beliefs about your own death, the deaths of those you love, and other forms of significant loss. Although the topic of this chapter might seem to be morbid or depressing, I strongly believe that an honest understanding and acceptance of death and loss can be the groundwork of a rich and meaningful life. If we fully accept that we have only a limited time in which to live, we can make choices that will make the most of the time we have.

I also ask you to consider the notion of death in a broader perspective and to raise such questions as: What parts of me aren't as alive as they might be? In what emotional ways am I dead or dying? What will I do with my awareness of the ways in which I'm not fully alive? Finally, I discuss the importance of fully experiencing our grief when we suffer serious losses.

This discussion of death and loss has an important connection with the themes of the earlier chapter on loneliness and solitude. When we emotionally accept the reality of our eventual death, we experience our ultimate aloneness. I believe that this awareness of our mortality and aloneness helps us to realize that our actions do count, that we do have choices concerning how we live our life, and that we must accept the final responsibility for how well we are living.

This chapter is also a bridge to the next chapter, in which I discuss meaning and values. The awareness of death is a catalyst of the human search for meaning in life. Our knowledge that we will die can encourage us to take a careful and honest look at how we are living now. With a realistic awareness of death we can ask ourselves whether we're living by values that create a meaningful existence; if not, we have the time and opportunity to change our way of living.

OUR FEARS OF DEATH

Although a realistic fear of death seems to be a healthy and inevitable part of living, it's possible to become so obsessed with the fear of our own death or of the deaths of those we love that we can't really enjoy living. On the one hand, we may be afraid of really getting involved with life, of allowing ourselves to care for others, or of building hopes for the future. On the other hand, we may numb ourselves to the reality of death by telling ourselves there's no point in thinking about it—"When it comes, it comes." Neither of these attitudes permits us to realistically confront death and its meaning.

Young people often have the feeling that they will live forever. Death seems remote, and they are more likely to think of it as happening to others, rather than to them. Some young people adopt a reckless attitude,

almost daring death, as though they felt indestructible. They often blunt their anxieties over death with various defenses. Because of the awful finality of death they may deny this reality. It is only as they grow older that their finiteness becomes a reality to them. Indeed, years do go by, time does pass, and there is a greater urgency about living. These people who at one time did not seriously consider death for themselves may now realize that there is much they want to do before they die. There is a recognition that they don't have forever, and they acquire a deeper appreciation of life.

One of the reviewers of this book, who has taught personal-growth courses in college for years, observed that for the majority of young adults direct experience of death comes through the loss of a friend or a close family member. Young people may be more fearful of the death of others than of their own. They are often deeply affected by the death of someone close to them, which impels them to contemplate their own death. Based on years of reading freshman personal self-evaluation papers, this educator has found the one differentiating factor between superficiality and a degree of maturity to be experiencing a significant life crisis, usually a death. She has concluded that students who have not known death are often terrified of the death of a person close to them, because they are not sure how they will cope with the loss.

A fear of death often goes hand in hand with a fear of life. If we're excessively fearful of death, we'll probably be fearful of investing ourselves in life as well, because nothing we cherish seems permanent. By the same token, if we involve ourselves in the present moment as fully as possible, it's unlikely that we'll be obsessed with the thought of life's end.

We may fear many aspects of death, including leaving behind those we love, losing ourselves, encountering the unknown, coping with the humiliation and indignity of a painful or long dying, losing time in which we could be doing the things we most want to finish, and growing distant in the memories of others. For many people it's not so much death itself as it is the experience of dying that arouses fears. Here, too, it is well to ask what our fears are really about and to confront them honestly, as Schnitzer (1977) does in *Looking In:*

> Death is feared because it seems to condemn us to utter loneliness and to the loss of identity. But consciousness also vanishes, and what is there to be feared when it is totally gone? "To fear death means pretending to know what we don't know," Plato once said. What we are afraid of is not death but dying, the phase that confronts us with the loss of our world and its familiar beings—the only home we know. And that indeed must be painful. There may be agony, both physical and mental. At that last stage we will be much more in need of braveness [p. 89].

In his powerful book *Facing Death*, Kavanaugh (1972) describes the fears of a woman who was dying of cancer. She related that the fears she was actually experiencing were not nearly so terrible as the ones she had expected to feel and that any attempt to escape her fears was more painful than the fears themselves. She found that those friends who were not busy running from their own fears were the people who could be the most help and comfort to her as she neared death.

If we can honestly confront our fears of death, we have a chance to work on changing the quality of our life and to make real changes in our relationships with others and with ourselves. I agree with Gordon (1972) when he says that, if we could live with the idea that this very moment might be our last, "we would find that many problems and conflicts would evanesce, and life would be simplified and become more satisfying" (p. 17).

At this point, you might pause to reflect on your own fears of death and dying. What expectations seem to arouse the greatest fears in you? Do your fears concern death itself or the experience of dying? In what ways do you think your fears might be affecting how you choose to live now? Were you close to someone who died? If so, how did the experience of that person's death affect your feelings about death and dying?

If you consider yourself relatively young, you might ask: "Why should this topic interest me? I've got lots of time left, so why think about morbid subjects?" I've found that even the very young can be at least temporarily shocked into the realization that they could die at any time. This happens when a classmate dies from an automobile accident, drowning, suicide, cancer, or some act of violence. While I am obviously not suggesting that you should morbidly focus on your death, I am encouraging you to think of how you deal with your fears of it and to consider what death means to you in terms of *living fully* now.

DEATH AND THE MEANING OF LIFE

I accept the existentialist view that the acceptance of death is vitally related to the discovery of meaning and purpose in life. One of our distinguishing characteristics as human beings is our ability to grasp the concept of the future and thus the inevitability of death. Our ability to do so gives meaning to our existence, for it makes our every act and moment count.

The Stoics of ancient Greece had a dictum: "Contemplate death if you would learn how to live." Seneca commented: "No man enjoys the true taste of life but he who is willing and ready to quit it." And Saint Augustine said: "It is only in the face of death that man's self is born."

A sharply defined example of this basic theme is provided by those who are terminally ill. Their confrontation with death causes them to do much living in a relatively brief period of time. The pressure of time almost forces them to choose how they will spend their remaining days. Irvin Yalom (1980) found that cancer patients in group therapy had the capacity to view their crisis as an opportunity to instigate change in their life. Once they discovered that they had cancer, some of their inner changes included:

- a rearrangement of life's priorities—little attention to trivial matters
- a sense of liberation—the ability to choose to do those things they really wanted to do
- an increased sense of living in the moment—no postponement of living until some future time
- a vivid appreciation of the basic facts of life—for example, noticing changes in the seasons and other aspects of nature
- a deeper communication with loved ones than before the crisis
- fewer interpersonal fears, less concern over security, and more willingness to take risks (Yalom, 1980, p. 35)

The irony of the situation is well summed up by one of the patients: "What a tragedy that we had to wait till now, till our bodies were riddled with cancer, to learn these truths " (p. 165). This example serves to make a central point: it's only when we confront the reality that life does not go on forever that life becomes more precious.

In his book *Is There an Answer to Death?* Koestenbaum (1976) develops the idea that our awareness of death enables us to have a plan of life. It compels us to see our life in totality and to seek real and ultimate answers.

As Koestenbaum writes: "Many people think of death as unreal, as just beyond the horizon, as something they should postpone thinking about—in fact, as an event that is not to be mentioned. As a result, they are incapable of experiencing their lives as a whole, of forming any total life plan" (p. 32).

The awareness of death is also related to our ability to form a distinctive personal identity. By accepting our mortality, we enable ourselves to define the quality of life we want; as Koestenbaum says, our anticipation of death reveals to us who we are. This anticipation is both an intellectual awareness and an experiential understanding. It puts us in touch with our hopes and our anxieties and gives direction to our life.

The meaning of our life, then, depends on the fact that we are finite beings. What we do with our life counts. We can choose to become all that we are capable of becoming and make a conscious decision to fully affirm life, or we can passively let life slip by us. We can settle for letting events happen to us, or we can actively choose and create the kind of life we want. If we had forever to actualize our potentials, there would be no urgency about doing so. Our time is invaluable precisely because it is limited. Consequently, without living in constant fear of death, it is well for us to dwell on the unique importance of the present moment, for it is all we really have.

TIME OUT FOR PERSONAL REFLECTION

1. *What fears do you experience when you think about your own death? Check any of the following statements that apply to you:*

   I worry about what will happen to me after death.
   I'm anxious about the way I will die.
   I wonder whether I'll die with dignity.
   I fear the physical pain of dying.
   I worry most about my loved ones who will be left behind.
   I'm afraid that I won't be able to accomplish all that I want to accomplish before I die.
   I worry about my lack of control over how and when I will die.
   I fear ceasing to exist.
   I worry about being forgotten.
   I worry about all the things I'll miss after I die.

   List any other fears you have about death or dying.

   _____

   _____

   _____

   _____

2. *How well do you think you're living your life? List some specific things you aren't doing now that you'd like to be doing. List some things you think you'd be likely to do if you knew that you had only a short time to live.*

_____

_____

_____

_____

3. *In many of my courses I've asked students to write a brief description of what they might do if they knew they had only 24 hours left to live. If you're willing to, write down what occurs to you when you think about this possibility.*

_____

_____

_____

_____

4. *In what way does the fact that you will die give meaning to your life now?*

_____

_____

_____

_____

5. *For many people, it is not so much death itself as the experience of dying that arouses fears. Are you more anxious about dying than about death itself? If so, what is it about dying that you're most fearful of?*

_____

_____

_____

_____

6. *Are there ways in which you avoid facing the inevitability of your own death or the deaths of those you love? If so, in what ways do you try to deny this reality?*

_____

_____

_____

_____

7. *In what ways do you think your fears about death and dying might be affecting the choices you make now?*

_____

_____

_____

_____

8. *What have you learned from these exercises?*

_____

_____

_____

_____

SUICIDE: AN ULTIMATE CHOICE OR AN ULTIMATE COP-OUT?

Suicide is one of the leading causes of death in the United States, and it is on the increase. Kalish (1985) writes that adolescent suicide, in particular, is rapidly increasing. The rate for those between 15 and 24 years of age is three times higher than it was two decades ago.

In looking up the leading causes of death for a person my age, I found the following rank order: heart disease, stroke, cancer of the lung, cancer of the large intestine and rectum, bronchitis and emphysema, pneumonia, cancer of the prostate, cirrhosis, diseases of the arteries, suicide, motor-vehicle accidents, cancer of the stomach, cancer of the bladder, and leukemia. I am aware that many of these causes of death are related to choice. People may be engaging in some form of slow suicide by a chronic lack of exercise or by a variety of other ways of abusing their body. So the actual rate of suicide could be viewed as higher than is reported if we considered the multitude of ways in which we actually shorten our life. Furthermore, many people live in a "half-dead" state of depression, without joy and with many regrets. How alive are these people?

I strongly believe that people who attempt suicide simply do not want to go on in such deadening patterns, or they see life as unbearable. If they feel that they do not have any options, that the chances of change are slim, then they may decide that being dead is better than engaging in a futile struggle to find meaning when none exists.

Is suicide an ultimate choice or an ultimate cop-out? This question is a complex one, and I don't pretend to have an easy answer. I do see suicide as an ultimate choice in one respect; as I've mentioned, there are many ways that we can kill ourselves, whether by neglect or by certain acts.

What seems more critical to me is that we make conscious choices about how fully we are willing to live, realizing that we must pay a price for being alive. At the same time, for some people ending their life does seem like a cop-out—the result of not being willing to struggle or being too quick to decide to give up without exploring other possibilities. In thinking about how you would answer this question, ask yourself under what circumstances you think suicide is a choice, as opposed to simply giving up. Consider the following questions as a way of taking a position on this matter.

1. *What does your personal experience reveal?* At times you may have felt a deep sense of hopelessness, and you may have questioned whether it was worth it to continue living. Have you ever felt really suicidal? If so, what was going on in your life that contributed to your desire to end it? What factor or factors kept you from following through with taking your life? Would this act have been an authentic choice, or would it have been an act motivated by the feeling that you had no choices?

2. *What hidden meanings does suicide have?* Taking one's life is such a powerful act that we must look to some of its underlying messages and symbolic meanings:

- A cry for help: "I cried out, but nobody heard me!"
- A form of self-punishment: "I don't deserve to live."
- An act of hostility: "I'll get even with you; see what you made me do."
- An attempt to be noticed: "Maybe now people will talk about me and feel sorry for the way they treated me."
- A relief from hopelessness: "I see no way out of the despair I feel. Ending my life will be better than hating to wake up each morning."
- An end to pain: "I suffer extreme physical pain, which will not end. Suicide will put an end to this nightmare."

3. *Have you known anyone who committed suicide?* Typically, people who have been close to a person who committed suicide experience a range of feelings—including guilt, anger, and fear—that often are unexpressed. "Maybe if I had been more sensitive and caring," they might feel, "this terrible thing would not have happened. I wonder whether I did everything I could have done to prevent this?" If they were to put their anger into words, they might say, "I am angry with you for shutting me out, and for leaving me. Why didn't you let me know how desperate you were?" And they may feel fear: "If this happened to him, then maybe I am capable of doing the same thing." Have you known a person who decided that suicide was better than continuing to live? If so, what were your reactions?

4. *Can suicide be an act of mercy?* There have been victims of painful and terminal illnesses who decided *when* and *how* to end their life. Rather than wasting away with cancer and enduring extreme pain, some people

have actually called their family together and then taken some form of poison. What are your thoughts about a person's choice to end his or her life when it is certain that there is no chance for recovery?

These are simply a few issues on the important topic of suicide as a choice. See if you can come up with some other questions that will help you formulate your own opinions on the meanings of suicide, as well as alternatives to this final act.

FREEDOM IN DYING

The process of dying involves a gradual diminishing of the choices available to us. Even in dying, however, we still have choices concerning how we handle what is happening to us. The following account deals with my reactions to the dying of Jim Morelock, a student and close friend of mine. I don't know of anyone who showed better than Jim did how we remain free to choose our attitude toward life and toward life's ending.[1]

Jim is 25 years old. He is full of life—witty, bright, honest, and actively questioning. He had just graduated from college as a human services major and seemed to have a bright future when his illness was discovered.

About a year and a half ago, Jim developed a growth on his forehead and underwent surgery to have it removed. At that time, his doctors believed that the growth was a rare disorder that was not malignant. Later, more tumors erupted, and more surgery followed. Several months ago, Jim found out that the tumors had spread throughout his body and that, even with cobalt treatment, he would have a short life. Since that time, he has steadily grown weaker and has been able to do less and less; yet he has shown remarkable courage in the way he has faced this loss and his dying.

Some time ago Jim came to Idyllwild, California, and took part in the weekend seminar I had with the reviewers of this book. On this chapter, he commented that, although we may not have a choice concerning the losses we suffer in dying, we do retain the ability to choose our attitude toward our death and the way we relate to it.

Jim has taught me a lot during these past few months about this enduring capacity for choice, even in extreme circumstances. Jim has made many critical choices since being told of his illness. He chose to continue taking a course at the university, because he liked the contact with the people there. He worked hard at a boat dock to support himself, until he could no longer manage the physical exertion. He decided to undergo

---

[1] I am repeating this account as it appeared in this book's first edition. Many readers have commented to me about how touched they were as they read about Jim's life and his death, and in this way he seems to have lived on in one important respect.

cobalt treatment, even though he knew that it most likely would not result in his cure, because he hoped that it would reduce his pain. It did not, and Jim has suffered much agony during the past few months. He decided not to undergo chemotherapy, primarily because he didn't want to prolong his life if he couldn't really live fully. He made a choice to accept God in his life, which gave him a sense of peace and serenity. Before he became bedridden, he decided to go to Hawaii and enjoy his time in first-class style.

Jim has always had an aversion to hospitals—to most institutions, for that matter—so he chose to remain at home, in more personal surroundings. As long as he was able, he read widely and continued to write in his journal about his thoughts and feelings on living and dying. With his friends, he played his guitar and sang songs that he had written. He maintained an active interest in life and in the things around him, without denying the fact that he was dying.

More than anyone I have known or heard about, Jim has taken care of unfinished business. He made it a point to gather his family and tell them his wishes, he made contact with all his friends and said everything he wanted to say to them, and he asked Marianne to deliver the eulogy at his funeral services. He clearly stated his desire for cremation; he wants to burn those tumors and then have his ashes scattered over the sea—a wish that reflects his love of freedom and movement.

Jim has very little freedom and movement now, for he can do little except lie in his bed and wait for his death to come. To this day he is choosing to die with dignity, and, although his body is deteriorating, his spirit is still very much alive. He retains his mental sharpness, his ability to say a lot in a very few words, and his sense of humor. He has allowed himself to grieve over his losses. As he puts it, "I'd sure like to hang around to enjoy all those people that love me!" Realizing that this isn't possible, Jim is saying good-bye to all those who are close to him.

Throughout this ordeal, Jim's mother has been truly exceptional. When she told me how remarkable Jim has been in complaining so rarely despite his constant pain, I reminded her that I'd never heard her complain during her months on duty. I have been continually amazed by her strength and courage, and I have admired her willingness to honor Jim's wishes and accept his beliefs, even though at times they have differed from her own. She has demonstrated her care without smothering Jim or depriving him of his free spirit and independence. Her acceptance of Jim's dying and her willingness to be fully present to him have given him the opportunity to express openly whatever he feels. Jim has been able to grieve and mourn because she has not cut off this process.

This experience has taught me much about dying and about living. Through Jim, I have learned that I don't have to do that much for a person who is dying other than to be with him or her by being myself. So often I have felt a sense of helplessness, of not knowing what to say or how much to say, of not knowing what to ask or not to ask, of feeling stuck for words. Jim's imminent death seems such a loss, and it's very difficult for me to accept it. Gradually, however, I have learned not to be so concerned about what to say or to refrain from saying. In fact, in my last visit I said very little, but I feel that we made significant contact with each other. I've also learned to share with Jim the sadness I feel, but there is simply no easy way to say good-bye to a friend.

Jim was a group leader in several of my personal-growth courses, and I can recall some of the things he confronted others with and what he said to them. Now he is showing me that his style of dying will be no different from his style of living. By his example and by his words, Jim has been a catalyst for me to think about the things I say and do and to evaluate my own life.

TIME OUT FOR PERSONAL REFLECTION

1. *If you were close to someone during his or her dying, how did the experience affect your feelings about your life and about your own dying?*

_____

_____

_____

_____

2. *How would you like to be able to respond if a person who is close to you were dying?*

_____

_____

_____

_____

3. *If you were dying, what would you most want from the people who are closest to you?*

_____

_____

_____

_____

THE STAGES OF DYING

Death and dying have become topics of widespread discussion among psychologists, psychiatrists, physicians, sociologists, ministers, and researchers. Whereas these topics were once taboo for many people, they are now the focus of seminars, courses, and workshops. A number of recent books, some of which are described in the Suggested Readings section at the end of the chapter, give evidence of this growing interest.

Dr. Elisabeth Kübler-Ross is a pioneer in the contemporary study of death and dying. In her widely read books *On Death and Dying* and *Death: The Final Stage of Growth*, she treats the psychological and sociological aspects of death and the experience of dying. Thanks to her efforts, many people have become aware of the almost universal need the dying have to talk about their impending death and to complete their business with the important people in their life. She has shown how ignorance of the dying process and of the needs of dying people—as well as the fears of those around them—can rob the dying of the opportunity to fully experience their feelings and arrive at a resolution of them.

A greater understanding of dying can help us to come to an acceptance of death, as well as to be more helpful and present to those who are dying. For this reason, I'd like to describe the five stages of dying that Kübler-Ross (1969, 1975) has delineated, based on her research with terminally ill cancer patients. She emphasizes that these are not neat and compartmentalized stages that every person passes through in an orderly fashion. At times a person may experience a combination of these stages, perhaps skip one or more stages, or go back to an earlier stage he or she has already experienced. In general, however, Kübler-Ross found this sequence: denial, anger, bargaining, depression, and acceptance.

To make this discussion of the stages of dying more concrete, let me give the example of Ann, a 30-year-old woman who died of cancer. She was married and the mother of three children in elementary school. Before she discovered that she had terminal cancer, she felt that she had much to live for, and she enjoyed life.

The Stage of Denial

Ann's first reaction to being told that she had only about a year to live was shock. At first she refused to believe that the diagnosis was correct, and even after obtaining several other medical opinions she still refused to accept that she was dying. In other words, her initial reaction was one of *denial*.

Even though Ann was attempting to deny the full impact of reality, it would have been a mistake to assume that she didn't want to talk about her feelings. Her husband also denied her illness and was unwilling to talk to her about it. He felt that talking bluntly might only make her more depressed and lead her to lose all hope. He failed to recognize how important it would have been to Ann to feel that she *could* bring up the subject if she wished. On some level Ann knew that she could not talk about her death with her husband.

During the stage of denial the attitudes of a dying person's family and friends are critical. If these people cannot face the fact of their loved one's dying, they cannot help him or her move toward an acceptance of death. Their own fear will blind them to signs that the dying person wants to talk about his or her death and needs support. In the case of Ann it would not necessarily have been a wise idea to force her to talk, but she could have been greatly helped if those around her had been available and sensitive to her when *she* stopped denying her death and showed a need to be listened to.

The Stage of Anger

As Ann began to accept that her time was limited by an incurable disease, her denial was replaced by anger. Over and over she wondered why *she*—who had so much to live for—had to be afflicted with this dreadful disease. Her anger mounted as she thought of her children and realized that she would not be able to see them grow and develop. During her frequent visits to the hospital for radiation treatment, she directed some of her anger toward doctors "who didn't seem to know what they were doing," toward the "impersonal" nurses, and toward the red tape she had to endure.

During the stage of anger it's important that others recognize the need of dying people to express their anger, whether they direct it toward their doctors, the hospital staff, their friends, their children, or God. If this displaced anger is taken personally, any meaningful dialogue with the dying will be cut off. Moreover, people like Ann have every reason to be enraged over having to suffer in this way when they have so much to live for. Rather than withdrawing support or taking offense, the people who surround a dying person can help most by allowing the person to fully express the pent-up rage inside. In this way they help the person to ultimately come to terms with his or her death.

The Stage of Bargaining

Kübler-Ross (1969) sums up the essence of the bargaining stage as follows: "If God has decided to take us from this earth and he did not respond to any angry pleas, he may be more favorable if I ask nicely" (p. 72). Basically, the stage of bargaining is an attempt to postpone the inevitable end.

Ann's ambitions at this stage were to finish her college studies and graduate with her bachelor's degree, which she was close to obtaining. She also hoped to see her oldest daughter begin junior high school in a little over a year. During this time she tried any type of treatment that offered some hope of extending her life.

The Stage of Depression

Eventually Ann's bargaining time ran out. No possibility of remission of her cancer remained, and she could no longer deny the inevitability of her death. Having been subjected to radiation treatment, chemotherapy, and a series of operations, she was becoming weaker and thinner, and she was able to do less and less. Her primary feelings became a great sense of loss and a fear of the unknown. She wondered about who would take care of her children and about her husband's future. She felt guilty because she demanded so much attention and time and because the treatment of her illness was depleting the family income. She felt depressed over losing her hair and her beauty.

It would not have been helpful at this stage to try to cheer Ann up or to deny her real situation. Just as it had been important to allow her to fully vent her anger, it was important now to let her talk about her feelings and to make her final plans. Dying people are about to lose everyone they love, and only the freedom to grieve over these losses will enable them to find some peace and serenity in a final acceptance of death.

The Stage of Acceptance

Kübler-Ross found that, if patients have had enough time and support to work through the previous stages, most of them reach a stage at which they are neither depressed nor angry. Because they have expressed their anger and mourned the impending loss of those they love, they are able to become more accepting of their death. Kübler-Ross (1969) comments: "Acceptance should not be mistaken for a happy stage. It is almost a void of feelings. It is as if the pain has gone, the struggle is over, and there comes a time for 'the final rest before the long journey,' as one patient phrased it" (p. 100).

Of course, some people never achieve an acceptance of their death, and some have no desire to. Ann, for example, never truly reached a stage of acceptance. Her final attitude was more one of surrender, a realization that it was futile to fight any longer. Although she still felt unready to die, she did want an end to her suffering. It may be that if those close to her had been more open to her and accepting of her feelings, she would have been able to work through more of her anger and depression.

The Significance of Kübler-Ross's Stages

I want to reemphasize that Kübler-Ross's description of the dying process is not meant to be rigid and should not be interpreted as a natural progression that is expected in most cases. Just as people are unique in the way they live, they are unique in the way they die; it is a mistake to use these stages as the standard by which to judge whether a dying person's behavior is normal or right. The value of the stages is that they describe and summarize in a general way what many patients experience and therefore add to our understanding of dying.

Kalish (1985) comments that many doctors and nurses regard the stage progression as something that everyone will naturally follow. Patients who do not make it to the acceptance stage are sometimes viewed as failures. For example, some nurses get angry at patients who take steps "backwards" by going from depression to anger, or they question patients about why they have "stayed so long in the anger stage." Kalish emphasizes that people die in a variety of ways and have a variety of feelings during this process: hope, anger, depression, fear, envy, relief, and anticipation. Those who are dying move back and forth from mood to mood. Therefore, these stages should not be used as a method of categorizing, and thus dehumanizing, the dying; they are best used as a frame of reference for helping them.

The Hospice Movement

There is a trend toward more direct involvement of family members in caring for a dying person. An example of this is the hospice program, which was begun in England in 1967 and has rapidly spread through Europe and North America. The term *hospice* was originally used to describe a waiting place for travelers during the Middle Ages. Later, hospices were established for children without parents, the incurably ill, and the elderly. It was during the 19th and 20th centuries that a Catholic religious order developed hospices for dying persons (Kalish, 1985).

Kalish observes that the recent hospice movement has changed the attitude toward a dying person from "there is nothing more that we can do to help" to "we need to do what we can to provide the most humane care." This involves viewing patients and their family members as a unit. Caregivers do not separate the person who is dying from his or her family. Whenever possible, patients are kept at home as long as they wish. Both volunteers and a trained staff provide health-care aid, including helping the patient and the family members deal with psychological and social stresses. Although research on these programs is preliminary, hospice patients are more mobile and tend to report less general anxiety and fewer bodily symptoms than those being given traditional care. The spouse is able to spend more time in visiting and caring for the patient (Kalish, 1985).

GRIEVING OVER DEATH, SEPARATION, AND OTHER LOSSES

In a way that is similar to the stages of dying, people go through stages of grief in working through death and various other losses. Grief work refers to the exploration of feelings of sorrow, anger, and guilt over the experience of a significant loss. This process is often not an easy or simple one.

Allowing Yourself to Grieve

What major losses have you had, and how have you coped with them? Reflect on losses such as the following to determine how they could apply to you: a family member who died, a close friendship, a job that you valued, a spouse through divorce, a material object that had special meaning, a place where you once lived, a pet, and your faith in some person or group. Are there any similarities to how you responded to these different types of loss? Did you successfully work through your feelings about the losses? Did you shut off your feelings of grief because they were too intense? Or did you allow yourself to express your feelings with someone close to you? In recalling a particular loss, are the feelings still as intense as they were then?

Most writers on the psychological aspects of death and loss agree that grieving is necessary. A common denominator of all of these theories is that there is a general process of moving from a stage of depression to a recovery. Although people may successfully work through their feelings pertaining to loss, it can be expected that the loss may always be with them. In successful grieving, however, people are not immobilized by the loss, nor do they close themselves off from other involvements. Another commonality in all these theories is that not all people go through the grieving process at the same rate, nor do all people move neatly and predictably from one stage to another.

In counseling people I find that a chronic state of depression and a restricted range of feelings are often attributed to some unresolved reactions to a significant loss. Such individuals often fear that the pain will consume them and that it is better to shut off their feelings. What they fail to realize is that they pay a price for this denial in the long run. This price involves excluding feelings of closeness and joy. At times these people can go on for years without ever expressing emotions over their loss, being convinced that they have adequately dealt with it. Yet they might find

themselves being flooded with emotions for which they have no explanation. They may discover that another's loss opens up old wounds that they thought were successfully healed. I am reminded of a woman who reported that she could not stop crying and was overcome with emotions at the funeral of an acquaintance. What surprised her was the way her reaction contrasted with her "strength and composure" over the death of her husband. What she didn't realize was that she had not allowed herself to grieve over the loss of her husband and that years later she was having a delayed grief reaction.

A Young Woman's Denial of Grief.   Kelly is a 19-year-old community college student who recently enrolled in a course on death and dying. She let her instructor know privately that the course was touching her emotionally and confronting her with facing the death of her father five years before. She told him that, when her father died in an airplane crash, she simply refused to believe that he was actually dead. Kelly convinced herself that he had gone away on a long vacation and would someday return to her. Very few tears were shared in the family, his name was rarely mentioned, no reminiscing was done by any of the family members, and none of them visited his grave. With her peers, Kelly never acknowledged her father's death. Only a few close friends knew that she was without a father.

Kelly describes herself as never feeling extremely happy or very sad. She envies people whom she sees as spontaneous, joyous, and, as she puts it, "really able to laugh." Since she began the class on death and dying, she has surprised herself with occasional crying spells, and she notices that she is often angry at the slightest provocation. She gave her instructor some poetry that she had recently written pertaining to how much she was missing her father. She has a desire to go and visit his grave but says that she is afraid of doing so. Kelly is just now, years after her father's death, beginning to allow herself to grieve over her loss. As she permits herself to feel her pain, she will also be able to experience more joy in her life.

A Young Man's Acceptance of Grief.   Tony, who is 17 years old, recently told Marianne about the sudden death of his 57-year-old grandfather from a heart attack. He talked a lot about the kind of man his grandfather was and said he regretted their not having had more contact. He is experiencing much sadness over his recent loss. It was interesting to hear his description of and reaction to his grandfather's funeral. Because his grandfather was well known, a surprisingly large crowd attended the funeral. Many people eulogized and spoke about the man. As Tony put it, there were many tears, and it was extremely difficult for him to witness all this emotionality. He asserts that, when he dies, he does not want a funeral, because he wants to avoid putting people in such a painful position. What he does not realize is that, although it is indeed difficult for him to feel his own pain and observe the pain of others, it is this very process that will enable him to deal more effectively with the loss of his grandfather. Even though Tony reacted negatively to the funeral, unlike Kelly he is not denying his feelings of grief over his loss.

Most cultures have rituals that are designed to help people with this grieving process. Examples are the funeral practices of the Irish, the Jewish, the Russians, and others, whereby painful feelings are actually triggered and released. Many cultures have a formal mourning period (usually a year); other cultures provide rituals for assisting people with their emotions at the anniversary of a death. In all these cultures an obvious pattern is the direct involvement of people in the funeral process.

In the American culture those who suffer from a loss are typically "protected" from any direct involvement in the burial. People are praised for not displaying overt signs of grief. For example, Jacqueline Kennedy was admired for the strength and composure she displayed at her husband's funeral. Many of our rituals make it easy for us to deny our feelings of loss and therefore keep us from coming to terms with the reality of that loss. It has become clear that these practices are not genuinely helpful. The current trend is to provide ways of involving people directly in the dying process of their loved ones (such as the hospice movement) and the funeral process as well.

How My Family Dealt with a Death.   Earlier I talked about Jim More-lock's dying. Let me share some of the stages my family and I went through in dealing with Jim's loss. When Jim first told me that his cancer was terminal, it was difficult for me to believe. I had thoughts that some-how he would win the battle. It was hard for me to understand why he would have to die, since he had so much to live for and to offer others. Although at times I was able to accept the reality of his impending death, there were other times when I would ask "Why him?" Together we talked about his dying, even though that was difficult. I took the opportunity to say good-bye to him.

At a memorial service many of us had the opportunity to remember and share special times with Jim. About a year later some close friends of his came to our home, and we planted an apple tree in his memory. We again reminisced and shared the ways in which we were missing him. As the years go by the pain over his death becomes less intense. I find I bring him to my awareness in certain situations. He has now been dead for eight years, yet his memory is still with me.

Our daughters developed a very special relationship with Jim over the years, seeing him as their big brother. During some visits he was very frank with them about his cancer, including telling them that he might die. As he put it to them after one of his operations, "Well, I've won this battle, but that doesn't mean I've won the war yet." Cindy and Heidi were 9 and 10 at the time he was dying. They coped with his condition by talking to him, to us, to his mother, and to each other. Cindy wrote a detailed story with an unhappy ending. Heidi dreamed that she had "magic" ice cream that could cure anything. When she told us about her dream, she sadly added, "But there isn't any magic, is there?" Every doll that they had was operated on for cancer. These were the symbolic and direct ways in which our daughters dealt with the dying of a special friend. As parents we made ourselves available to them by listening to them and supporting them, yet we did not offer them false hope.

Heidi and Cindy went through different reactions to Jim's dying and death, many of which were described by Kübler-Ross. Because they genu-inely grieved and did not deny the reality of their friend's death, they were able to let his memory live on with them. Even though eight years have passed, they still bring Jim's name up spontaneously and recall humorous episodes with him. What follows is a poem that Cindy recently created in one of these spontaneous moments:

> Jim—
> I miss you very much
> I miss the songs we sang
> I miss the times we talked
> About our lives and our futures.
> You taught me an awful lot,
> You helped me also to grow.

It seems like you're not gone . . .
Just as if you're on a long trip.
Maybe someday I'll see you again?
I wish you could have stayed a while,
To enjoy all the love your friends and
   family had to give.
I miss you very much
And the times we had,
For they were all good
And never bad.
   Love Cindy,
   Your #1 Fan

Stages of Grief over a Divorce

The five stages of dying described by Kübler-Ross seem to have an application to separation and other losses—experiences that bear some similarity to dying. To illustrate, I'll discuss a divorce in terms of the five stages. Of course, you can broaden this concept and see whether it applies to separation from your parents, your children, or even from an old value system or way of being. Although not all people who divorce go through the stages in the same way, I've found that many people do experience similar questions and struggles.

The Stage of Denial.   Many people who are divorcing go through a process of denial and self-deception. They may try to convince themselves that the state of their marriage isn't all that bad, that nobody is perfect, and that things would be worse if they did separate. Even after the decision is made to divorce, they may feel a sense of disbelief that this could actually be happening to them. If it was the other person who initiated the divorce, the remaining partner might ask: "Where did things go wrong? Why is she (he) doing this to me? I really don't believe this is happening to me!"

The Stage of Anger.   Once people accept the reality that they are divorcing, they frequently experience anger and rage. They may say "Why did this have to happen? I gave a lot, and now I'm being deserted. I feel as if I've been used and then thrown away." Many people feel cheated and angry over the apparent injustice of what is happening to them. Just as it is very important for dying people to express any anger they feel over dying, it's also important for people who are going through the grief associated with a divorce or other loss to express any anger they feel. If they keep their anger bottled up inside, it is likely to be turned against themselves and may take the form of depression—a kind of self-punishment.

The Stage of Bargaining.   Sometimes people hope that a separation will give them the distance they need to reevaluate things and that they will soon get back together again. Although separations sometimes work this way, often it is futile to wish that matters can be worked out. Nevertheless, during the bargaining stage, one or both partners may try to make concessions and compromises that they hope will make a reconciliation possible.

The Stage of Depression.   In the aftermath of a decision to divorce, a sense of hopelessness may set in. As the partners realize that a reconciliation isn't likely, they may begin to dwell on the emptiness and loss they feel. They may find it very difficult to let go of the future they had envisioned together. They may spend time wondering what their lives would have been like if they had made their relationship work. It isn't uncommon for people who divorce to turn their anger away from their spouse and toward themselves. Thus, they may experience much self-blame and self-doubt. They may say to themselves: "Maybe I didn't give our relationship a fair chance. What could I have done differently? I wonder where I went wrong?" Depression can also be the result of the recognition that a real loss has been sustained. It is vitally important that people fully experience and express the grief they feel over their loss. Too often people deceive themselves into believing that they are finished with their sadness long before they have given vent to their grief. Unresolved grief tends to be carried around within a person, blocking the expression of many other feelings. For instance, if grief isn't worked through, it may be extremely difficult for a person to form new relationships, because in some ways he or she is still holding on to the past relationship.

The Stage of Acceptance.   If people allow themselves to mourn their losses, eventually the process of grief work usually leads to a stage of acceptance. In the case of divorce, once the two persons have finished their grieving, new possibilities begin to open up. They can begin to accept that they must make a life for themselves without the other person and that they cannot cling to resentments that will keep them from beginning to establish a new life. Although sadness may persist, there can be an acceptance that what has occurred is done with and that brooding won't change things. They can learn from their experience and apply that learning to future events.

In summary, these stages are experienced in different ways by each person who faces a significant loss. People do not pass through these stages in neat fashion, and not all people experience all the stages in working through their losses. Some, for example, express very little anger; others might not go through a bargaining stage. Nevertheless, the value of a model such as this one is that it provides some understanding of how we can learn to cope with the various types of loss in our life. Whatever the loss may be, and whatever stage of grieving we may be experiencing, it seems to be crucial that we freely express our feelings. Otherwise, we may not be able to achieve acceptance.

For me, the meaning of acceptance is well expressed in the prayer of Alcoholics Anonymous, and I'd like to close this section by quoting it here: "God, grant me serenity to accept the things I cannot change, courage to change the things I can change, and wisdom to know the difference."

BEING 'DEAD' IN PSYCHOLOGICAL AND SOCIAL WAYS

In talking about death in my university courses I've found it valuable to broaden the conception of death and dying to include being "dead" in a variety of psychological and social ways. What is dead or dying in us may be something we want to resurrect, or it may be something that *should* die in order to make way for new growth.

Sometimes growth requires that we be willing to let go of old and familiar ways of being, and we may need to mourn their loss before we can really move on. You may have experienced a letting go of the security of living with your parents, for example, in exchange for testing your independence by living alone and supporting yourself. In the process, you may have lost something that was valuable to you, even if it was incompatible with your further development and growth.

I'd like to focus now on some ways in which we commonly allow parts of ourselves to die that we might want to bring back into our life. I hope that the following questions will help you to decide whether you're living as fully as you'd like to be.

Can You Be Spontaneous and Playful?

Is the "child" part of you living, or have you buried it away inside? Can you be playful, fun, curious, explorative, spontaneous, inappropriate, silly? As adults, we sometimes begin to take ourselves too seriously and lose the ability to laugh at ourselves. If you find that you're typically realistic and objective to the point that it's difficult for you to be playful or light, you might ask what inner messages block your ability to let go. Are you inhibited by a fear of being wrong? Are you afraid of being called silly or of meeting with others' disapproval? If you want to, you can begin to challenge the messages that say: "Don't!" "You should!" "You shouldn't!" You can experiment with new behavior and run the risk of seeming silly or of "not acting your age." Then *you* can decide whether you like your new behavior and want to be like a child more often. Whatever your decision is, at least it will be your own instead of a command from your past.

Are You Alive to Your Feelings?

We can deaden ourselves to most of our feelings—the joyful ones as well as the painful ones. We can decide that feeling involves the risk of pain and that it's best to *think* our way through life. In choosing to cut off feelings of depression or sadness, we will most likely cut off feelings of joy. Closing ourselves to our lows usually seems to mean closing ourselves to our highs as well.

In my work with people I sometimes find it difficult to help them even to recognize their flat emotional state, so insulated have they made themselves. To begin assessing how alive you are emotionally, you might ask yourself such questions as the following:

- Do I let myself feel my sadness over a loss?
- Do I try hard to cheer people up when they're sad or depressed, instead of allowing them to experience their feelings?
- Do I let myself cry if I feel like crying?
- Do I ever feel ecstasy?
- Do I let myself feel close to another person?
- Are there some feelings that I particularly suppress? Do I hide my feelings of insecurity, fear, dependence, tenderness, anger, boredom?

Are You Caught Up in Deadening Roles?

Our roles and functions can eventually trap us. Instead of fulfilling certain roles while maintaining a separate sense of identity, we may get lost in our roles and in the patterns of thought, feeling, and behavior that go with them. As a result, we may neglect important parts of ourselves and thus limit our options of feeling and experiencing. Moreover, we may feel lost when we're unable to play a certain role. Thus, a supervisor may not know how to behave when he or she isn't in a superior position to others, an instructor may be at loose ends when he or she doesn't have students to teach, or a parent may find life empty when the children have grown.

Do you feel caught in certain roles? Do you depend on being able to identify with those roles in order to feel alive and valuable? Are you able to renew yourself by finding innovative ways of being and thinking? At this time in your life, you might find that you're so caught up in the student role that you have little time or energy left for other parts of your life. When our roles begin to deaden us, we can ask whether we've taken on a function or identity that others have defined, instead of listening to our own inner promptings.

Are Your Relationships Alive?

Our relationships with the significant people in our life have a way of becoming stale and deadening. It's easy to get stuck in habitual and routine ways of being with another person and to lose any sense of surprise and spontaneity. This kind of staleness is particularly common in long-term relationships such as marriage, but it can afflict our other relationships as well. As you look at the significant relationships in your life, think about how alive both you and the other person in each relationship feel with each other. Do you give each other enough space to grow? Does the relationship energize you, or does it sap you of life? Are you settling into a comfortable, undemanding relationship? If you recognize that you aren't getting what you want in your friendships or intimate relationships, you can ask what *you* can do to revitalize them. You can also consider what specific things you'd like to ask of the other person. Simply asking more from your relationships can do a lot to bring new life into them.

Are You Alive Intellectually?

Children typically display much curiosity about life, yet somehow they often lose this interest in figuring out problems as they grow older. By the time we reach adulthood we can easily become caught up in our activities, while devoting little time to considering *why* we're doing them and whether we even *want* to be doing them. It's also easy to allow our intellectual potential to shrivel up, either by limiting our exposure to the environment or by failing to follow our curiosity.

How might this apply to you as a student? Have you given up on asking any real and substantive questions that you'd like to explore? Have you settled for merely going to classes and collecting the units you need to obtain a degree? Are you indifferent to learning? Are you open to learning new things?

Are You Alive to Your Senses and Your Body?

Our body expresses to a large degree how alive we are. It shows signs of our vitality or reveals our tiredness with life. Since our body doesn't lie, we can use it as an indication of the degree to which we're affirming life. As you look at your body, you can ask: Do I like what I see? Am I taking good care of myself physically, or am I indifferent to my own bodily well-being? What does my facial expression communicate?

We can also become deadened to the input from our senses. We may become oblivious to fragrances or eat foods without tasting or savoring them. We may never stop to notice the details of our surroundings. In contrast, taking time to be alive to our senses can help us feel renewed and interested in life. You might ask yourself: What sensations have particularly struck me today? What have I experienced and observed? What sensory surprises have enlivened me?

TIME OUT FOR PERSONAL REFLECTION

1. *How alive do you feel psychologically and socially? Check any of the following statements that apply to you.*

   I feel alive and energetic most of the time.
   My body expresses aliveness and vitality.
   I feel intellectually curious and alive.
   I have significant friendships that are a source of nourishment for me.
   I can play and have fun.
   I allow myself to feel a wide range of emotions.
   I'm keenly aware of the things I see, smell, taste, and touch.
   I feel free to express who I am; I'm not trapped by my roles.

2. *When do you feel most alive?*

   _____

   _____

   _____

   _____

3. *When do you feel least alive?*

   _____

   _____

   _____

4. *What specific things would you most like to change about your life so that you could feel more alive? What can you do to make these changes?*

   _____

   _____

   _____

   _____

TAKING STOCK: HOW WELL ARE YOU LIVING LIFE?

It seems tragic to me that some people never really take the time to evaluate how well they are living life. Imagine for a moment that you're one of those people who get caught up in the routine of daily existence and never

assess the quality of their living. Now assume that you are told that you have only a limited time to live. You begin to look at what you've missed and how you wish things had been different; you begin to experience regrets over the opportunities that you let slip by; you review the significant turning points in your life. You may wish now that you had paused to take stock at many points in your life, instead of waiting until it was too late.

One way to take stock of your life is to imagine your own death, including the details of the funeral and the things people might say about you. As an extension of this exercise, you might try actually writing down your own eulogy or obituary. This can be a powerful way of summing up how you see your life and how you'd like it to be different. In fact, I suggest that you try writing three eulogies for yourself. First, write your "actual" eulogy—the one you would give at your own funeral, if that were possible. Second, write the eulogy that you *fear*—one that expresses some of the negative things someone could say of you. Third, write the eulogy that you would *hope* for—one that expresses the most positive aspects of your life so far. After you've written your three eulogies, seal them in an envelope and put them away for a year or so. Then do the exercise again, and compare the two sets of eulogies to see what changes have occurred in your view of your life.

This experience is not meant to be morbid; rather, it is a tool you can use in exploring the meaning of death and in creating a more meaningful life. For me, the exercise of writing my own eulogies was not an easy one. I found it difficult to separate my realistic view of myself from my hoped-for and feared assessments. At times when I was writing what I *feared* could be said about me, I wondered how much of what I was writing was actually true of me. I had much the same feeling as I wrote my hoped-for version—that some of what I wrote is true of me now. And no doubt my "actual" eulogy incorporated some of my hopes and fears as well as a truly objective assessment of my life. Nevertheless, the experience of writing my eulogies helped me to consider how fully I'm living life. It also challenged me to do something concrete about changing those aspects of my life that were reflected in the "feared" eulogy. For instance, in writing this eulogy I became aware of the great difficulty I have in living for the present moment. I tend to hurry about and put unnecessary pressure on myself, instead of allowing myself to be an experiencing, feeling, reflective human being. Of course, what you learn from writing your eulogies will be unique to you, but I believe that this exercise can help you see yourself and your life in a clearer perspective and challenge you to live more fully *now*.

POSTSCRIPT: TAKING TIME

Before he died, Jim Morelock gave me a poster showing a man walking in the forest with two small girls. At the top of the poster were the words "TAKE TIME." Jim knew me well enough to know how I tend to get caught up in so many activities that I sometimes forget to simply take the time to really experience and enjoy the simple things in life. As I write this, I'm also remembering what one student wrote to me as we were writing what we hoped and wished for each person in the class. On one of my slips of paper was written "I hope you will take the time to smell a rose." In another class one student gave each person an epitaph—what he thought could be written on that person's tombstone. Mine read "Here lies Jerry Corey—a man who all his life tried to do too many things at once." I promised myself that I'd make a poster with those words on it and place it on my office wall as a reminder for those times when I would begin to hurry and forget to take time to enjoy life. I think many of us could use reminders like these frequently—especially since it took me almost a semester to get around to putting that poster up! So I'd like to close this chapter with this simple message: *Take time.*

I wrote the preceding paragraph for the first edition of this book. Now, five years later, am I taking time to do fewer things at once and to enjoy life? In all honesty, I have to admit that I'm still a slow learner in this respect! Marianne and I were recently vacationing on the beach in Cancun, Mexico, and she asked me if the poster that Jim gave me had made any difference. My immediate response was "Sure, I'm taking time right now." "You could fool me," she replied. "It looks like you're working now!" She observed that we were sitting on the beach with *I Never Knew I Had a Choice* in hand and talking about what to revise. Even though I was doing what I wanted at that moment, I realized how difficult I find it to *really* take time. So this time I'd like to close the chapter with another simple message: Even if something is difficult, and even if you learn slowly, don't give up!

And the paragraph above I wrote for the second edition of this book. Have I made any progress in the last four years? Well, I still lead a very full professional life, yet I *do* make time for important things besides work. Most significant of all was a decision I made about four years ago to become more involved in both of my daughters' lives. We have taken time to talk and to be with one another in many ways, which has paid off for all of us. Interestingly, I made this decision to spend time with Cindy and Heidi while I was teaching and doing workshops in England and Germany for six weeks alone. This time apart from my family in foreign countries allowed me to take another perspective on what I wanted in life. In spite of a busy schedule I also *make* time each day to walk or ride my bicycle, because I enjoy this time. Although Marianne and I work together in writing and doing workshops, I value spending personal time with her alone, as well as with our family and friends. Yet I still have trouble in taking as much time as I would like. I become anxious as I experience the weeks and months passing too quickly. For me, it seems as though there is so much I want to do and simply not enough time to do it all.

CHAPTER SUMMARY

In this chapter I've encouraged you to devote some time to reflecting on your eventual death, because doing so can lead you to examine the quality and direction of your life and help you find your own meaning in living. The acceptance of death is closely related to the acceptance of life. Recognizing and accepting the fact of death gives us the impetus to search for our own answers to questions such as: What is the meaning of my life? What do I most want from life? How can I create the life I want to live? In addition, I've encouraged you to assess how much you are fully alive right now.

Although terminally ill people show great variability in the way they deal with their dying, a general pattern of stages has been identified, including denial, anger, bargaining, depression, and acceptance. These same stages have applicability to other types of loss, such as separation and divorce. People go through stages of grief in working through their losses. Grieving is necessary for people to recover from any significant loss. Unless people express and explore feelings of sorrow, anger, and guilt over their losses, they are likely to remain stuck with depression and a feeling of numbness.

Some of the key ideas presented in this chapter are listed below. As a way of stimulating your own reflections, you might think about each statement and decide how much you agree or disagree with it.

1. Many of us fear death, largely because of the uncertainty that surrounds it.
2. Life has meaning because we are finite beings; thus, death gives life meaning.
3. If we're afraid to die, we may be afraid to live.
4. Our culture makes it easy for us to deny the reality of death.
5. There are many ways of being "dead" psychologically, socially, and intellectually. By recognizing ways in which we're not fully alive, we can make decisions that will lead to richer living.
6. The way in which we view death has much to do with the way in which we view life.

Now list some other ideas from this chapter that you want to remember.

_____

_____

_____

_____

_____

ACTIVITIES AND EXERCISES

1. For a period of at least a week, take a few minutes each day to reflect on when you feel alive and when you feel "dead." Do you notice any trends in your observations? What can you do to feel more alive?
2. If you knew you were going to die within a short time, in what ways would you live your life differently? What might you give up? What might you be doing that you're not doing or experiencing now?
3. Imagine yourself on your deathbed. Write down whom you want to be there, what you want them to say to you, and what you want to say to them. Then write down your reactions to this experience.

4. For about a week write down specific things you see, read, or hear relating to the denial or avoidance of death in our culture.

5. Let yourself reflect on how the death of those you love might affect you. Consider each person separately, and try to imagine how your life today would be different if that person were not in it. In your journal, you might respond to such questions as: Do I now have the relationships with my loved ones that I want to have? What's missing? What changes do I most want to make in my relationships?

6. Consider making some time alone in which to write three eulogies for yourself: one that you think *actually* sums up your life, one that you *fear* could be written about you, and one that you *hope* could be written about you. Write the eulogies as if you had died today; then seal them in an envelope, and do the exercise again in the future—say, in about a year. At that time, you can compare your eulogies to see in what respects your assessment of your life and your hopes and fears have changed.

7. After you've written your three eulogies, you might write down in your journal what the experience was like for you and what you learned from it. Are there any specific steps you'd like to take *now* in order to begin living more fully?

8. Investigate what type of hospice program, if any, your community has. Who is on the staff? What services does it offer? You might write to the National Hospice Organization, 765 Prospect Street, New Haven, CT 06511.

SUGGESTED READINGS

DeSpelder, L., & Strickland, A. (1983). *The Last Dance: Encountering Death and Dying*. Palo Alto, Calif.: Mayfield. The authors present a comprehensive survey of death from many perspectives. They discuss the theoretical, practical, and personal aspects of death with the aim of helping readers become aware of their own attitudes and feelings about death and dying.

Friedman, M., & Rosenman, R. (1974). *Type A Behavior and Your Heart*. Greenwich, Conn.: Fawcett. This is an excellent book that deals with personality types and behavior associated with death from coronary diseases—and, more broadly, with learning to take time to enjoy life. Guidelines are given on how to recognize Type A behavior and what you can do about it.

Gordon, D. (1972). *Overcoming the Fear of Death*. Baltimore: Penguin. This is a very useful book dealing with the fear of death, the ways we avoid facing this fear, some aspects of dying, and the meaning of death.

Kalish, R. A. (1985). *Death, Grief, and Caring Relationships* (2nd ed.). Monterey, Calif.: Brooks/Cole. The author, who has been professionally interested in the themes of death and dying for over 20 years, has written an excellent and comprehensive textbook on the various aspects of death, the process of dying, and the grief process. If you had to select just one book for further reading on this topic, this would be my recommendation.

Kavanaugh, R. (1972). *Facing Death*. New York: Nash; Penguin edition, 1974. Kavanaugh discusses some unrealistic fears and attitudes toward dying and shows that a growing awareness of what we hope to achieve in life can bring about an accepting attitude toward death. Other topics include cultural expectations concerning dying, coping with tragic death, funerals, life after death, and grief work.

Koestenbaum, P. (1976). *Is There an Answer to Death?* Englewood Cliffs, N.J.: Prentice-Hall (Spectrum). This book discusses how a positive confrontation with death can be a liberating experience, how it can help us develop our individual identity and give us the security we need to live our lives courageously, and how an acceptance of death can bring greater meaning to life.

Kübler-Ross, E. (1969). *On Death and Dying*. New York: Macmillan. A thoughtful treatment of attitudes toward death and dying, this book is based primarily on interviews with terminal cancer patients. The author is one of the pioneers in the contemporary study of death and dying.

Kübler-Ross, E. (1975). *Death: The Final Stage of Growth*. Englewood Cliffs, N.J.: Prentice-Hall (Spectrum). This excellent book discusses such questions as: Why is it so hard to die? Are death and growth related? How is death the final stage of growth? What is the significance of death?

Kübler-Ross, E. (1981). *Living with Death and Dying*. New York: Macmillan. The author applies her knowledge of death to the dying child.

Kushner, H. (1981). *When Bad Things Happen to Good People*. New York: Schocken Books. Best-seller concerning the suffering of innocent people—in particular, the author's son—and how it can be reconciled with belief in a loving and all-powerful God.

Lund, D. (1975). *Eric*. New York: Dell. This touching book demonstrates how a person can live to the fullest even in the face of imminent death. After Eric finds out that he has leukemia, he continues to make life-oriented decisions, and he distinguishes himself in sports.

Shneidman, E. S. (Ed.). (1984). *Death: Current Perspectives*. Palo Alto, Calif.: Mayfield. The articles deal with the philosophical and ethical debates about death and dying. Perspectives are provided by historians, anthropologists, philosophers, sociologists, psychiatrists, and thanatologists. Some topics are the legal/ethical/moral aspects of death and suicide, the quality of life of the dying person, survivors of death, and the threat of death from nuclear holocaust.

Wilcox, S., & Sutton, M. (Eds.). (1984). *Understanding Death and Dying* (3rd ed.). Palo Alto, Calif.: Mayfield. Each section of this book includes an encounter with real-life issues that combine cognitive and affective learning. New topics include the presentation of death in the media and the impact of the nuclear threat on children.

12

MEANING AND VALUES: PUTTING LIFE IN PERSPECTIVE

Prechapter Self-Inventory

Introduction

Our Search for Identity

Our Quest for Meaning and Purpose

Reviewing Some Dimensions of Meaning and Values in Your Life

Where to Go from Here: Continuing Your Personal Growth

Chapter Summary

Activities and Exercises

Suggested Readings

PRECHAPTER SELF-INVENTORY

Use the following scale to respond: 4 = this statement is true of me *most* of the time; 3 = this statement is true of me *much* of the time; 2 = this statement is true of me *some* of the time; 1 = this statement is true of me *almost none* of the time.

_____ 1. At this time in my life I have a sense of meaning and purpose that gives me direction.

_____ 2. Most of my values are similar to those of my parents.

_____ 3. I have challenged and questioned most of the values I now hold.

_____ 4. Religion is an important source of meaning for me.

_____ 5. I generally live by the values I hold.

_____ 6. My values and my views about life's meaning have undergone much change over the years.

_____ 7. The meaning of my life is based in large part on my ability to have a significant impact on others.

_____ 8. I let others influence my values more than I'd like to admit.

_____ 9. I worry about the threat of nuclear annihilation.

_____ 10. I have a clear sense of who I am and what I want to become.

INTRODUCTION

In this chapter I encourage you to look critically at the *why* of your existence, to clarify the sources of your values, and to reflect on questions such as these: In what direction am I moving in my life? What steps can I take to make the changes in my life that I decide I want to make? What do I have to show for my years on this earth so far? Where have I been, where am I now, and where do I want to go?

Many who are fortunate enough to achieve power, fame, success, and material comfort nevertheless experience a sense of emptiness. Although they may not be able to articulate what is lacking in their life, they know that something is amiss. The astronomical number of pills and drugs produced to allay the symptoms of this "existential vacuum"—depression and anxiety—is evidence of our failure to find values that allow us to make sense out of our place in the world.

There are other signs of this need for a sense of meaning, including the popularity of many different religious groups and practices, the widespread interest in Eastern and other philosophies, the use of meditation, the number of self-help and inspirational books published each year, the experimentation with different life-styles, and even the college courses in personal adjustment! It seems fair to say that we are caught up in a crisis of meaning and values, and in this situation it's easy to look to some authoritative source for answers to our most deeply felt questions. As I have throughout this book, I want to suggest in this chapter that only the meaning and values we affirm from within ourselves, whatever form they may take, can guide us toward autonomy and freedom.

OUR SEARCH FOR IDENTITY

I believe that the discovery of meaning and values is essentially related to our achievement of identity as persons. The quest for identity involves a commitment to give birth to ourselves by exploring the meaning of our uniqueness and humanness. A major problem for many people is that they have lost a sense of self, because they have directed their search for identity outside themselves. In their attempt to be liked and accepted by everyone, they have become finely tuned to what *others* expect of them but alienated from their *own* inner desires and feelings. As Rollo May (1973) observes, they are able to *respond* but not to *choose*. Indeed, May sees inner emptiness as the chief problem in contemporary society; too many of us, he says, have become "hollow people" who have very little understanding of who we are and what we feel. May cites one person's succinct description of the experience of "hollow people": "I'm just a collection of mirrors, reflecting what everyone expects of me" (p. 15).

Moustakas (1975) describes the same type of alienation from self that May talks about. For Moustakas, alienation is "the developing of a life outlined and determined by others, rather than a life based on one's own inner experience" (p. 31). If we become alienated from ourselves, we don't trust our own feelings but respond automatically to others as we think they want us to respond. As a consequence, Moustakas writes, we live a world devoid of excitement, risk, and meaning.

In order to find out who we are, we may have to let parts of us die. We may need to shed old roles and identities that no longer give us vitality. Doing so may require a period of mourning for our old selves. Most people who have struggled with shedding immature and dependent roles and assuming a more active stance toward life know that such rebirth isn't easy and that it may entail pain as well as joy.

Jourard (1971) makes a point that I find exciting. He maintains that we begin to cease living when meaning vanishes from life. Yet too often we are encouraged to believe that we have only *one* identity, *one* role, *one* way to be, and *one* purpose to fulfill in a lifetime. This way of thinking can be figuratively deadly, for when our one ground for being alive is outgrown or lost, we may begin to die psychologically instead of accepting the challenge of reinventing ourselves anew. In order to keep ourselves from dying spiritually, we need to allow ourselves to imagine new ways of being, to invent new goals to live for, to search for new and more fulfilling meanings, to acquire new identities, and to reinvent our relationships with

LIFE MAY HAVE MANY DIFFERENT MEANINGS BETWEEN CHILDHOOD AND OLD AGE

others. In essence, we need to allow parts of us to die in order to experience the rebirth that is necessary for growth.

To me, then, achieving identity doesn't necessarily mean stubbornly clinging to a certain way of thinking or behaving. Instead, it may involve trusting ourselves enough to become open to new possibilities. Nor is an identity something we achieve for all time; rather, we need to be continually willing to reexamine our patterns and our priorities, our habits and our relationships. Above all, we need to develop the ability to listen to our inner selves and trust what we hear. To take just one example, I've known students for whom academic life has become stale and empty and who have chosen to leave it in response to their inner feelings. Some have opted to travel and live modestly for a time, taking in new cultures and even assimilating into them for a while. They may not be directly engaged in preparing for a career and, in that sense, "establishing" themselves, but I believe they are achieving their own identities by being open to new experiences and ways of being. For some of them, it may take real courage to resist the pressure to settle down in a career or "complete" their education.

Our search for identity involves asking three key existential questions, none of which has easy or definite answers: "Who am I?" "Where am I going?" "Why?"

The question "Who am I?" is never settled once and for all, for it can be answered differently at different times in our life. We need to revise our life, especially when old identities no longer seem to supply a meaning or give us direction. As we have seen, we must decide whether to let others tell us who we are or to take a stand and define ourselves.

"Where am I going?" This issue relates to our plans for a lifetime and the means we expect to use in attaining our goals. Like the previous question, this one demands periodic review. Our life goals are not set once and for all. Again, do we show the courage it takes to decide for ourselves where we are going, or do we look for a guru to show us where to go?

Asking the question "Why" and searching for reasons are characteristics of being human. We face a rapidly changing world in which old values give way to new ones or to none at all. Part of shaping an identity implies that we are actively searching for meaning, trying to make sense of the world in which we find ourselves.

At this point you might pause to assess how you experience your identity at this time in your life. The following Time Out may help you do so.

TIME OUT FOR PERSONAL REFLECTION

1. *In the space below list the things that you most like to do or the activities that have the most meaning for you.*

_____

_____

_____

_____

2. *How often do you do or experience each of the things you've just listed?*

_____

_____

_____

_____

3. *Does anything prevent you from doing the things you value as frequently as you'd like? If so, what?*

_____

_____

_____

_____

4. *What are some specific actions you can take to increase the amount of meaningful activity in your life?*

_____

_____

_____

_____

5. *Who are you? Try completing the sentence "I am . . ." 20 different ways by quickly writing down the words or phrases that immediately occur to you. Use the spaces provided below.*

   I am:

   _____   _____

   _____   _____

   _____   _____

   _____   _____

   _____   _____

   _____   _____

   _____   _____

   _____   _____

   _____   _____

   _____   _____

6. What does this list tell you about your view of yourself?

_____

_____

_____

_____

OUR QUEST FOR MEANING AND PURPOSE

Humans are the only creatures we know of who can reflect on their existence and, based on this capacity for self-awareness, exercise individual choice in defining their life. With this freedom, however, come responsibility and a degree of anxiety. If we truly accept that the meaning of our life is largely the product of our own choosing and the emptiness of our life the result of our failure to choose, our anxiety is increased. To avoid this anxiety, we may refuse to examine the values that govern our daily behavior or to accept that we are, to a large degree, what we have chosen to become. Instead, we may make other people or outside institutions responsible for the direction of our life. I believe that we pay a steep price for thus choosing a sense of security over our own freedom—the price of denying our basic humanness.

One obstacle in the way of finding meaning is that the world itself may appear meaningless. It's easy, when we look at the absurdity of the world in which we live, to give up the struggle or to seek some authoritative source of meaning. Yet creating our own meaning is, to me, precisely our challenge and task as human beings.

Creating meaning in our life isn't all a somber and serious business, however. We can also find meaning by allowing ourselves to play. It seems unfortunate to me that, as we "mature," so many of us lose the capacity we had as children to delight in the simple things in life. We busy ourselves in so many serious details that we really don't take the time to savor life or avail ourselves of its richness. Thus, we may work hard, maintaining all the while that we'll have time for fun when we retire. Then, when we do retire, we're bored and don't know what to do with ourselves. This kind of continued emphasis on the future can keep us from enjoying both our present and our future—when it, too, becomes present.

Yalom (1980) reviewed a number of empirical studies of the role of meaning in people's life and described results common to most of this research:

1. A person's lack of sense of meaning in life is related to the existence of emotional and behavioral disorders; the less sense of meaning, the greater the degree of personal disturbances.
2. A positive sense of meaning in life is associated with having a set of religious beliefs.
3. A positive sense of meaning is associated with possessing values relating to the betterment of humanity and an interest in the welfare of others.
4. A positive sense of meaning is associated with a dedication to some cause and with having a clear set of life goals.
5. Meaning in life is not to be seen as a static entity but should be viewed in a developmental perspective. The sources of meaning differ at various stages in life, and other developmental tasks must precede the development of meaning.

Viktor Frankl is a European psychiatrist who has dedicated his professional life to the study of meaning in life. The approach to therapy that he developed is known as *logotherapy,* which means "therapy through meaning," or "healing through meaning." According to Frankl (1963, 1965, 1969, 1978), what distinguishes us as humans is our search for meaning and purpose. The striving to find meaning in our lives is a primary motivational force. Humans are able to live and even die for the sake of their ideals and values. Frankl (1963) is fond of pointing out the wisdom of Nietzsche's words: "He who has a *why* to live for can bear with almost any *how*" (p. 164). Drawing on his experiences in the death camp at Auschwitz, Frankl asserts that inmates who had a vision of some goal, purpose, or task in life had a much greater chance of surviving than those who had no sense of mission.

Frankl (1978) talks about the unheard cry for meaning when he cites a follow-up study of 60 university students who attempted suicide. The reason given by 85 percent of these students was that "life seemed meaningless." Interestingly enough, 93 percent of these students who appeared to have a lack of meaning in their life were engaged in socially active ways, were doing well academically, and were on good terms with their family group. Even though people have the means to live, they often complain that they have no meaning to live for.

Yalom (1980) cites a number of psychotherapists who appear to agree on one major point: that many clients who enter psychotherapy do so because they lack a clear sense of meaning and purpose in life. Yalom states the crisis of meaninglessness in its most basic form: "How does a being who needs meaning find meaning in a universe that has no meaning?" (p. 423). Along with Frankl, Yalom concludes that humans require meaning to survive. To live without meaning and values provokes considerable distress, and in its severe form it may lead to the decision for

suicide. Humans apparently have a need for some absolutes in the form of clear ideals to which they can aspire and guidelines by which they can direct their actions.

Developing a Philosophy of Life

A philosophy of life is made up of the fundamental beliefs, attitudes, and values that govern a person's behavior. Many students I've taught, from high school to graduate school, have said that they hadn't really thought much about their philosophy of life. However, the fact that we've never explicitly defined the components of our philosophy doesn't mean that we are completely without one. All of us do operate on the basis of general assumptions about ourselves, others, and the world. Thus, the first step in actively developing a philosophy of life is to formulate a clearer picture of our present attitudes and beliefs.

We have all been developing an implicit philosophy of life since we first began, as children, to wonder about life and death, love and hate, joy and fear, and the nature of the universe. We probably didn't need to be taught to be curious about such questions; raising them seems to be a natural part of human development. If we were fortunate, adults took the time to engage in dialogue with us, instead of discouraging us from asking questions and deadening some of our innate curiosity.

During the adolescent years the process of questioning usually assumes new dimensions. Adolescents who have been allowed to question and think for themselves as children begin to get involved in a more advanced set of issues. Many of the adolescents I've encountered in my classes and workshops have at one time or another struggled with questions such as the following:

- Are the values that I've believed in for all these years the values I want to continue to live by?
- Where did I get my values? Are they still valid for me? Are there additional sources from which I can derive new values?
- Is there a God? What is the nature of the hereafter? What is my conception of a God? What does religion mean in my life? What kind of religion do I choose for myself? Does religion have any value for me?
- What do I base my ethical and moral decisions on? Peer-group standards? Parental standards? The normative values of my society?
- What explains the inhumanity I see in our world?
- What kind of future do I want? What can I do about actively creating this kind of future?

These are only a few of the questions that many adolescents think about and perhaps answer for themselves. However, I don't see a philosophy of life as something we arrive at once and for all during our adolescent years. The development of a philosophy of life continues as long as we live. As long as we remain curious and open to new learning, we can revise and rebuild our conceptions of the world. Life may have a particular meaning for us during adolescence, a new meaning during adulthood, and still another meaning as we reach old age. Indeed, if we don't remain open to basic changes in our views of life, we may find it difficult to adjust to changed circumstances.

I'm thinking now of a 37-year-old man who is facing a real crisis of meaning in his life, largely because he has been trying to structure his world and experiences the way he did as an adolescent. He has many fixed beliefs about how life should be, and, since his current life seems chaotic by these standards, he is really struggling to find a reason to continue living. What he hasn't realized is that he cannot force his experiences today into the value system he held as an adolescent, for his life has changed since that time.

Keeping in mind that developing a philosophy of life is a continuing activity of examining and modifying the values we live by, you may find the following suggestions helpful as you go about formulating and reforming your own philosophy:

- Frequently create time to be alone in reflective thought.
- Consider what meaning the fact of your eventual death has for the present moment.

- Make use of significant contacts with others who are willing to challenge your beliefs and the degree to which you live by them.
- Adopt an accepting attitude toward those whose belief systems differ from yours, and develop a willingness to test your own beliefs.

Religion and Meaning: A Personal View

Religious faith can be a powerful source of meaning and purpose. For many people religion helps to make sense out of the universe and the mystery of our purpose in living. Like any potential source of meaning, however, religious faith seems most authentic and valuable to me when it enables us to become as fully human as possible. By this I mean that it assists us to get in touch with our own powers of thinking, feeling, deciding, willing, and acting. The questions I would put to my religion in order to determine whether it is a constructive force in my life are the following:

- Does my religion help me to integrate my experience and make sense of the world?
- Does my religious faith grow out of my own experience?
- Do my religious beliefs assist me to live life fully and to treat others with respect?
- Does my religion encourage me to exercise my freedom and to assume the responsibility for my own life?
- Are my religious beliefs helping me to become more of the person I'd like to become?
- Does my religion encourage me to question life and keep myself open to new learning?

At the present time there appears to be a resurgence of interest in religion in our society. Increasing numbers of people seem to be deciding that some sort of religious faith is necessary if they are to find an order and purpose in life. At the same time, many others insist that religion only impedes the quest for meaning or that it is incompatible with contemporary beliefs in other areas of life. I've seen how religious faith has helped people endure great suffering. What seems essential to me is that our acceptance or rejection of religious faith come authentically from within ourselves and that we remain open to new experience and learning, whatever points of view we decide on.

It's perhaps worth emphasizing that a "religion" may take the form of a system of beliefs and values concerning the ultimate questions in life rather than (or in addition to) membership in a church. People who belong to a church may or may not be "religious" in this sense, and the same is true of those who don't follow an organized religion or even profess belief in God. Some of those whom I think of as religious don't believe in the existence of God or else say they simply don't know whether any higher being or force exists. Others who might claim to be religious find no incompatibility in using religious belief as a reason to be cruel, inhumane, or neglectful of others. For these reasons I don't believe that a profession of religious belief is, in itself, necessarily valuable or harmful. Like almost anything else in human life, religion (or irreligion) can be bent to worthwhile or base purposes.

In my own experience I've found religion most valuable when it is a challenge to broaden my choices and potential, rather than a restrictive influence. I find it hard to accept what seems to be the fairly common use of religion as a way of remaining dependent on external guidance or authority. I might add that I didn't always think this way; until I was about 30, I tended to think of my religion as a package of ready-made answers for all the crises of life and was willing to let my church make many key decisions for me. I now think that I was experiencing too much anxiety in many areas of life to take full responsibility for my choices; it was easier to lean on my religion for my answers. Besides, my religious training had taught me that I should look to the authority of the church for ultimate answers in the areas of morality, value, and purpose. Like many other people I was encouraged to learn the "correct" answers and conform my thinking to them. Now, when I think of religion as a positive force, I think of it as being *freeing*, in the sense that it encourages and even commands me to trust myself, to discover the sources of strength and integrity within myself, and to assume responsibility for my own choices.

Although as an adult I've questioned and altered many of the religious teachings with which I was raised, I haven't discarded many of my past moral and religious values. Many of them served a purpose earlier in my life and, with modification, are still meaningful for me. However, whether or not I continue to hold the beliefs and values I've been taught, it seems crucial to me that I be willing to subject them to scrutiny throughout my life. If they hold up under challenge, I can reincorporate them; by the same token, I can continue to examine the new beliefs and values I acquire.

Values for Our Children

In previous editions of this book I listed some of the values I hoped my daughters, Heidi and Cindy, would come to share. I found that thinking about what values I would like to see them choose helped me focus on the things that were (and are) most important to me. My list included these hopes for my daughters' futures:

- I hope that my children will be willing to dare and that they won't always choose caution over risk.
- I hope they form sets of values that are their own, not carbon copies of their parents'.

- I hope they always like and respect themselves and feel good about their abilities and talents.
- I'd like them to be open and trusting rather than fearful or suspicious.
- I hope they will respect and care for others.
- I like the way they can have fun, and I hope they don't lose this ability as they grow older.
- I'd like them to be able to express what they feel, and I hope they'll always feel free to come to Marianne and me and share meaningful aspects of their lives.
- I'd like them to be in touch with the power they have, and I hope they refuse to surrender it.
- I'd like them to be independent and to have the courage to be different from others if they want to be.
- I appreciate their interest in a religion that they freely chose.
- I'd like them to be proud of who and what they are, yet humble.
- I hope they will respect the differences in others.
- I hope they will not compromise their values and principles for material possessions.

My daughters are now facing the end of high school, and my hopes for them have materialized. I enjoy sharing in their lives and being with them. They like and respect themselves and are liked and respected by others. Although their lives are not problem free, my daughters have typically shown a willingness to face and deal with their struggles and have succeeded in making significant choices for themselves. I am delighted that they continue to feel free to come to Marianne and me to share their personal concerns. If you have children or expect to have children someday, you might pause to think about the values you would like them to develop.

Meaning in Life and the Nuclear Threat

The ever-present possibility of a nuclear holocaust affects all of us. This threat is so horrendous to contemplate that we often push it out of our awareness. Yet blocking out this potential reality is the very phenomenon that took place during the massacre of the Jews by the Nazis. Such an atrocity took place, in part, because most people did not allow themselves to believe that these horrors were happening. The outside world did little to stop the slaughter because of the incomprehensible scope of people's inhumanity. Jonathan Schell (1982) writes that insane crimes are not prevented from occurring simply because they are unthinkable; in fact, they may be more likely to occur for that reason. Perhaps the denial syndrome comes about as a mechanism of coping with destruction of such great magnitude. Simply blocking such devastating realities from our consciousness, however, does not mean that these threats do not have the power to profoundly affect the meaning and direction of our life.

In his provocative book *The Fate of the Earth*, Schell (1982) asserts that we do not allow ourselves to entertain thoughts of the extinction of the present and future generations because such thoughts are so contradictory to nature and to life's impulse. Rather than considering such a fate, we turn away in revulsion and disbelief. Schell warns us that we are profoundly affected by the continuous threat of nuclear annihilation: "But although we block out the awareness of this self-posed threat as best we can, engrossing ourselves in life's riches to blind ourselves to the jeopardy to life, ultimately there is no way that we can remain unaffected by it" (1982, p. 154). He further contends that we are living *as if* life were safe, yet living *as if* differs from just living. The problem of making denial a habit is that unresponsiveness then becomes a way of life. The danger is that we become cold and dull to all of the events of daily life. As Schell puts it, "The society that has accepted the threat of its utter destruction soon finds it hard to react to lesser ills, for a society cannot be at the same time asleep and awake, insane and sane, against life and for life" (p. 152).

In the previous chapter death was discussed as a factor that gives meaning to life. There are other ways in which death can confer meaning. We live on in the memory of others to whom we have made a difference; our projects may continue, serving as a memorial to our existence; and our impact is carried on through others. In a nuclear war, however, there is the threat of total extinction. Everything can cease to exist.

We cannot underestimate the impact that the threat of an all-out nuclear war has on all of us. Either we are very much preoccupied by this threat and engaged in preventing it, or we are operating from a state of denial and attempt to convince ourselves that there is nothing we can do about the situation. Schell writes that most of us have chosen to live on the edge of extinction by lunging toward the abyss, only to draw back from it before arriving at the point of no return. This leads to a situation of anxiety and uncertainty rather than one of absolute hopelessness.

As a society we have a choice between two ways of life, according to Schell. We can refuse to face the peril and continue piling up nuclear weapons until someday they are used. The other choice is to accept the peril, dismantle the weapons, and make sure that they will not be built again.

As individuals, it seems to me, we have choices, at least in terms of the attitude we assume toward the threat of total extermination as a civilization. We can become fatalistic and not allow ourselves to plan for our future, or we can continue living in the moment while designing a future, even if we do so with some anxiety. We can still find quality in life by doing what we can to bring as much meaning as possible to each day. It is also possible to fail to act or to plan on the ground that doing so makes utterly no difference. There is no solution that I am able to offer. Rather, what I aim to do is to encourage you to think about your personal response to the threats of the age in which we live.

TIME OUT FOR PERSONAL REFLECTION

1. *At this time, what are some of the principal sources of meaning and purpose in your life?*

   _____

   _____

   _____

   _____

2. *Sheldon Kopp (1972) contends that "a grown-up can be no man's disciple." Have you ever looked to some authority or guru to provide you with answers? What do you think of Kopp's contention?*

   _____

   _____

   _____

   _____

3. *Have there been occasions in your life when you've allowed other people or institutions to make key choices for you? If so, give a couple of examples.*

   _____

   _____

   _____

   _____

4. *What role, if any, has religion played in your life?*

   _____

   _____

   _____

   _____

5. *In your view, when is religion a constructive force in a person's life? a negative force?*

   _____

   _____

   _____

   _____

6. *If you were to create a new religion, what virtues and values would you include? What would be the vices and sins?*

_____

_____

_____

_____

7. *How is the quality of your present life (and your future) affected by the threat of a nuclear holocaust?*

_____

_____

_____

_____

8. *What are some of the choices you see open to you in finding meaning in life in the face of the nuclear threat?*

_____

_____

_____

_____

9. *What would you like to be able to say about the meaning in your life ten years from now? What do you hope will bring you meaning then?*

_____

_____

_____

_____

10. *What are some of the values you'd most like to see your children adopt?*

_____

_____

_____

_____

11. *The following is a list of some of the things different people value. Rate the importance of each one for you, using a 5-point scale, with 1 meaning* extremely important *and 5 meaning* very unimportant.

_____ *companionship*
_____ *family life*
_____ *security*
_____ *being financially and materially successful*
_____ *enjoying leisure time*
_____ *work*
_____ *learning and getting an education*
_____ *appreciation of nature*
_____ *competing and winning*
_____ *loving others and being loved*
_____ *a relationship with God*
_____ *self-respect and pride*
_____ *being productive and achieving*
_____ *enjoying an intimate relationship*
_____ *having solitude and private time to reflect*
_____ *having a good time and being with others*
_____ *laughter and a sense of humor*
_____ *intelligence and a sense of curiosity*
_____ *opening up to new experiences*
_____ *risk taking and personal growth*
_____ *being approved of and liked by others*
_____ *being challenged and meeting challenges well*
_____ *courage*
_____ *compassion*
_____ *being of service to others*

Now go back over your list, and circle the things you'd like to have more of in your life. You might think of what keeps you from having or doing the things that you value most.

REVIEWING SOME DIMENSIONS OF MEANING AND VALUE IN YOUR LIFE

There are many dimensions to a philosophy of life, and one of the best ways to clarify your own philosophy is to take a careful look at the specific things you value and find meaningful in your life now. In many ways, this entire book has dealt with the various sources of meaning in life, including learning, our autonomy as a person, the body, gender roles, sexuality, loving and being loved, intimate relationships, being alone, work, and death and dying. At this point I suggest that you review these areas in the light of these questions: What do I value? What values give meaning and substance to my life now? Do my actions reflect what I say I value?

Your Values and Learning

As you examine yourself as a learner, ask yourself whether you keep yourself open to new learning of all sorts—both in and out of school. You might consider what you've learned about yourself, about others, and about life during the past six months. You can look at what is blocking your learning and think about your fears and resistances toward being open to learning. Are your beliefs and values fixed, or are they open to revision? Do you welcome new ideas as a way of expanding the meaning life has for you, or do new ideas threaten you?

Your Values and Your Autonomy

As you look at your own development from early childhood to the present, you can probably find some significant patterns in your choices of values. Some questions you might ask in looking at your own autonomy are: Where did I get my values? Are my values open for modification as I grow toward maturity? Do I insist that the world remain the same for me now as it was during an earlier period of my development? Have I challenged the values I live by and really made them my own, or have I looked to someone else to define what I should value?

The struggle for autonomy is well illustrated by the experience of Carl Rogers, whose theory of personality is based on the idea that we must each trust ourselves and rely on our subjective experience as our ultimate guide in forming our values and making our choices. It's interesting that Rogers' emphasis on the value of autonomy seems to have grown, in part, out of his own struggles to become independent from his parents. As a college student he took the risk of writing a letter to his parents telling them that his views were changing from fundamentalist to liberal and that he was developing his own philosophy of life. Even though Rogers knew that his departure from the values of his parents would hurt them, he felt that such a move was necessary for his own intellectual and psychological freedom.

As you examine your own values, you might reflect on the value you place on your own autonomy. Is it important to you to feel that you are your own person? Are you satisfied with living by the expectations that others have for you? Do you want to become more independent, even though there are risks involved? Or do you prefer the security of being what others want you to be?

Your Values and Your Body

When you look at your body in the mirror, what does this reflection tell you about the degree to which you value that body? Your body presents an image, to both yourself and to others, of how you view yourself. Your ability to love others, to form nourishing sexual and emotional relationships with others, to work well, to play with joy, and to fully savor each day depends a great deal on your physical health. At this time you might think again about how well you are taking care of yourself physically, both through proper diet and regular physical exercise. Do you really value your body and your health, or are you choosing to neglect or abuse your body?

Your Values and Your Sex-Role Identity

Earlier in this book I encouraged you to look at your identity as a man or a woman and to ask whether there are ways in which you're trapped by others' standards of appropriate sex-role behavior. If you looked at yourself in this way, perhaps you discovered that you've been restricting yourself to the narrow range of feelings and behavior prescribed by a male or female stereotype. Deciding what it means for *you* to be a man or a woman is an important part of deciding what kind of person you want to be.

Your Values and Your Sexuality

Your sexuality can be an expression of your total self; it can enhance and vitalize you. But sex can also be a meaningless act or a way of avoiding intimacy with others. Your values will have much to do with how you experience sex and how you choose to act as a sexual person.

It does seem evident to me that being a sexual partner implies valuing one's own sexuality. Thus, one important "value" question is how much you respect your sexuality. What importance do you place on developing your sexuality? Do fears, shame, or guilt keep you from experiencing your sexuality and sensuality in the way you'd like to experience them?

Love and Meaning

Freud defined the healthy person as one who can work well and love well. Like work, love can make living worthwhile, even during bleak times. We can find meaning in actively caring for others and helping them to make their lives better. Because of our love for others or their love for us, we may be enabled to continue living, even in conditions of extreme hardship. Thus, Frankl (1963) noted that in the concentration camp some of those who kept alive the images of those they loved and retained some measure of hope survived the ordeal, while many who lost any memories of love perished. From his experiences Frankl concluded that "the salvation of man is through love and in love" (p. 59).

What place does love have in your life? How is your life different now because of those who love you or those whom you love? What meaning does love give to your life? What would your life be like if you didn't have love in it?

Your Values and Your Intimate Relationships

Do your friendships and other relationships contribute to the meaning in your life? Do you have friends with whom you can be completely yourself? Do they challenge or confront you concerning what you value and the degree to which you're living according to your beliefs? In these and many other ways, intimate relationships can be vitally related to our quest for meaning and values. I'm fond of Goethe's observation that, by taking people as they are, we make them worse, but by treating them as if they already were what they ought to be, we help make them better.

Your values have much to do with the relationships you choose. There are many ways of relating to another person, from a brief and casual encounter to a deep, long-term relationship. You may choose homosexual or heterosexual relationships, conventional marriage or your own variation of it, living with someone as an experiment, a group marriage, communal living, and so on. Whatever styles you choose, the important question is what values you find in them. What do your relationships bring to your life? Are you living in a certain life-style because parents, friends, or others expect you to, or have you selected a life-style that satisfies your own sense of values?

Your Values and Loneliness and Solitude

Loneliness is not a disease to be cured; rather, it is part of the human condition. Many people flee from loneliness because they experience anxiety over this condition. By reviewing times of loneliness in your life you may recognize significant choices you've made and thus acquire a new perspective on loneliness.

What value do you place on the experience of solitude? Have you found meaning in being alone with yourself? Is avoiding loneliness of overriding importance for you? Is it important to you to take time to be with your own thoughts, to see what you really care about, and to discover the things that most give your life meaning?

Your Values and Your Work

Work can be a major part of your quest for meaning, but it can also be a source of meaninglessness. Work can be an expression of yourself; it can be, as Gibran (1923) says, "love made visible" (p. 27). It can be a way for you to be productive and to find enjoyment in daily life. Through your work you may be making a significant difference in the quality of your life or the lives of others, and this may give you real satisfaction. But work can also be devoid of any self-expressive value. It can be merely a means to survival and a drain on your energy. Instead of giving life value and meaning, it can actually be a destructive force that contributes to an early death. I encourage you to ask yourself: Is my work life-giving? Does it bring meaning to my life? If not, what can I do about it? Is my most meaningful activity—my true work—something I do away from the job?

Death and Meaning

In the preceding chapter I stressed the idea that our awareness of death enables us to give meaning to our life. The reality of our finiteness compels us to look at our priorities and to ask what we value most. In this way, coming to terms with death can teach us how to really live. To run from death is to run from life, for as Gibran (1923) wrote, "Life and death are one, even as the river and the sea are one" (p. 71). Are you living *now* the way you want? Do you have goals you have yet to meet? What do you most want to be able to say that you have experienced or accomplished before you die?

TIME OUT FOR PERSONAL REFLECTION

Complete the following sentences by writing down the first responses that come to mind.

1. *My parents have influenced my values by* _____

   _____

2. *Life would hardly be worth living if it weren't for* _____

   _____

3. *One thing that I most want to say about my life at this point is* _____

   _____

4. *If I could change one thing about my life at this point, it would be*

_____

5. *If I had to answer the question "Who am I?" in a sentence, I'd say*

_____

6. *What I like best about me is* _____

_____

7. *I keep myself alive and vital by* _____

_____

8. *I'm unique, in that* _____

_____

9. *When I think of my future, I* _____

_____

10. *I feel discouraged about life when* _____

_____

11. *My friends have influenced my values by* _____

_____

12. *My beliefs have been most influenced by* _____

_____

13. *I feel most powerful when* _____

_____

14. *If I don't change,* _____

_____

15. *I feel good about myself when* _____

_____

16. *To me, the essence of a meaningful life is* _____

_____

17. *I suffer from a sense of meaninglessness when* ____

_____

WHERE TO GO FROM HERE: CONTINUING YOUR PERSONAL GROWTH

In this final section I ask you to consider the personal meaning this book and this course have held for you. Throughout the book you've been continually invited to look at some new choices you'd like to make. One of the final challenges is to determine where you will go from here. Now that you've finished this book and are completing this course, will this be a place where you stop? Will this be a commencement, a new beginning in the best sense? If you've invested yourself in the process of questioning your life and devising ways to change it, this is a prime time to make a commitment to yourself to actively put to use what you've been learning about yourself.

As you consider what avenues for continued personal growth you are likely to choose at this time, be aware that your meaning in life is not cast in concrete. As you change, you can expect that what brings meaning to your life will also change. The projects that you were deeply absorbed in as an adolescent may hold little meaning for you today. And where and how you discover meaning today may not be the pattern for some future period in your life.

You can deliberately choose experiences that will help you actualize your potentials. Perhaps you remember reading a book or seeing a film

that had a profound impact on you and really seemed to put things in perspective. Certainly, reading books that deal with significant issues in your life can be a growth experience in itself, as well as an encouragement to try new things.

Often, we make all sorts of resolutions about what we'd like to be doing in our life or about experiences we want to share with others, and then we fail to carry them out. Is this true of you? Are there activities you value yet rarely get around to doing? Perhaps you tell yourself that you prize making new friendships; yet you find that you do very little to actually initiate any contacts. Or perhaps you derive satisfaction from growing vegetables or puttering in your garden and yet find many reasons to neglect this activity. You might tell yourself that you'd love to take a day or two just to be alone and yet never get around to arranging it. When you stop to think about it, aren't there choices you could be making right now that would make your life a richer one? How would you really like to be spending your time? What changes are you willing to make today, this week, this month, this year?

In addition to activities that you enjoy but don't engage in as often as you'd like, there are undoubtedly many new things you might consider trying out as ways of adding meaning to your life and developing your potentials. You might consider making a contract with yourself to start now on a definite plan of action, instead of putting it off until next week or next year. Some of the ways in which many people choose to challenge themselves to grow include the following:

- finding hobbies that develop new sides of themselves
- going to plays, concerts, and museums
- taking courses in pottery making, wine tasting, guitar playing, and innumerable other special interests
- getting involved in exciting work projects or actively pursuing forms of work that will lead to the development of hidden talents
- spending time alone to reflect on the quality of their life
- initiating contacts with others and perhaps developing an intimate relationship
- enrolling in continuing-education courses or earning a degree primarily for the satisfaction of learning
- doing volunteer work and helping to make others' lives better
- experiencing the mountains, the desert, and the ocean—by hiking, sailing, and so on
- becoming involved in religious activities
- traveling to new places, especially to experience different cultures
- keeping a journal

Any list of ways of growing is only a sample, of course; the avenues to personal growth are as various as the people who choose them. What I want to suggest is that growth can occur in small ways and that there are many things that you can do on your own (or with friends or family) to continue your personal development. Perhaps the greatest hindrance to our growth as a person is our failure to allow ourselves to imagine all the possibilities that are open to us. What follow are a few resources for continued personal growth.

Reading Program

One excellent way to keep alive your motivation for self-exploration is by reading good books, including selected self-help books. I caution you to beware of those self-help books that offer quick and sure solutions, that promise a prescription for eternal happiness, or that give you steps to follow to find guaranteed success in any and all of your personal endeavors. I've provided a variety of self-help references in the Suggested Readings sections that should give you a fine start for developing a personal reading program. Many students and clients tell me how meaningful selected books have been for them in putting into perspective some of the themes they have struggled with.

Writing Program

Along with setting up a reading and reflection program for yourself, another way to build on the gains that you have made up to this point is to continue the practice of journal writing. If you have begun a process of personal writing in this book or in a separate notebook, I'd urge you to keep up with this practice. Even devoting a short period a few times each week to reflecting on how your life is going and then recording some of your thoughts and feelings is most useful in providing you with an awareness of patterns in your behavior. Without being self-critical you can learn to observe what you are feeling, thinking, and doing; then you have a basis for determining the degree to which you are successfully changing some old patterns that might not be working for you.

Self-Directed Behavioral Change

Now that you have finished this book, there are probably a few specific areas that you have identified where you could do further work. If you recognize that you are not as assertive as you'd like to be in various social situations, for example, you can begin by doing some reading on the topic of assertion training. You can go further by setting up a program of self-directed change by following the guidelines given in Resource 7. Of course there are other areas you can target. If you decide that you are frequently tense and that you do not generally react well to stress, you can construct a self-change program that will involve practicing relaxation methods and breathing exercises, all of which are described in Resource 5. The main point is that you identify some target areas for change, that you set realistic goals, that you develop some specific techniques for carrying out your goals, and that you practice selected behaviors that will help you make those changes that you want to make.

Support Groups

You can keep your programs of reading, writing, and self-directed change going by yourself. In addition to these avenues that you can pursue alone, I hope you'll consider how you can reach out to others as a source of continued challenge and support. Assume that you are having a difficult time in working through the loss of a loved one. Doing selected reading on death and loss as well as writing down your feelings in your journal can be of some help, yet if you interact with a small group of others who have experienced loss, you can receive the empathy and support necessary to assist you in mourning and expressing your grief.

Most colleges and community mental-health centers offer a variety of self-help groups that are facilitated by a person who has coped or is coping with a particular life issue. A good support group will help you see that you are not alone in your struggle. The experience can also provide you with alternatives that you may not be considering. Other examples of support groups include those that deal with rape or incest, consciousness-raising groups for women and for men, groups for reentry students, groups for people concerned about gay and lesbian issues, and medical self-help groups. As is the case with self-help books, you are advised to proceed with some caution in joining a support group. These groups do have the potential for negative outcomes, especially if you get in a group where people are quick to give you ready-made advice and tell you what you should do. Beware of "support" groups in which people have an axe to grind and tell you how you should feel, think, and behave.

Counseling

I hope you'll keep the options open for yourself to seek professional counseling as an avenue of personal growth. You don't have to be in a crisis to benefit from either individual or group counseling. You may find that you can only do so much by yourself in effectively making the changes you desire. Resource 13 provides very specific information about when it is advisable to seek counseling. It also offers you a consumer's guide for selecting a counselor and guidelines on how to evaluate professional help.

TIME OUT FOR PERSONAL REFLECTION

1. *Check any of the following activities that you think you might like to pursue in the near future as a way of continuing your personal development:*

   _____ *take another psychology course*
   _____ *take a class in Eastern philosophies*
   _____ *learn to practice yoga*
   _____ *join a consciousness-raising group*
   _____ *get involved in some type of self-control program (for example, to lose weight or stop smoking)*
   _____ *attend a massage workshop*
   _____ *learn relaxation exercises*

2. *What are some of the reasons that you haven't previously done the things you've listed? Check any of the following responses that fit you.*

   _____ *I haven't known about some of the available resources.*
   _____ *I haven't been able to afford some of the activities I've listed.*
   _____ *I'm afraid of failing.*
   _____ *I'm hesitant about trying new things.*
   _____ *I haven't had the time.*

3. *What are some things you'd like to do more often, or begin doing, that would not demand the use of professional resources? Check any of the following that fit you.*

   _____ *play more often*
   _____ *spend more time alone*
   _____ *exercise more frequently*
   _____ *do more reading*
   _____ *keep a detailed daily journal*
   _____ *attend church more often*
   _____ *be more open in my intimate relationships*
   _____ *take better care of my body*
   _____ *increase my enjoyment of sex and sensuality*
   _____ *do things for other people*
   _____ *cultivate more hobbies*
   _____ *develop the practice of meditation*

4. *List any other things that you'd like to do, either by yourself or with others:*

   _____

   _____

   _____

   _____

5. What are some of the reasons that you haven't done more often the things you've listed?

_____

_____

_____

_____

6. How open are you to seeking professional help, either in times of personal crisis or as a way to expand your self-understanding? When might you make use of counseling?

_____

_____

_____

_____

CHAPTER SUMMARY

Seeking meaning and purpose in life is an important part of being human. In this chapter I've suggested that meaning is not automatically bestowed on us but instead is the result of our active thinking and choosing. I've encouraged you to recognize your own present values and to ask both how you acquired them and whether you can affirm them for yourself out of your own experience and reflection. This task of examining our values and purposes is, to me, one that lasts a lifetime.

You can take a number of steps on your own if you are interested in actualizing your potentials. A few of these activities include meditation, keeping a journal, reading, travel, finding hobbies, and setting up a program of self-directed behavioral change. You can also reach out to others by establishing meaningful relationships with them. Many people find value in getting involved in a support group composed of peers who are struggling with a particular issue in their life. This can be done in conjunction with setting up a program for self-change.

The following are some of the key ideas in this chapter. I encourage you to think about each idea and to take your own position regarding it.

- We need to have a sense of hope and a reason for living.
- Many people who appear to have achieved success lead an empty and unfulfilling life.
- When meaning is absent in our life, we begin to die psychologically.
- We create meaning by our own choices.

- Only if we challenge our values and make them truly our own can they give us direction in living.
- Developing a philosophy of life is a lifelong endeavor.

List some additional ideas from this chapter that you'd most like to remember:

_____

_____

_____

_____

_____

ACTIVITIES AND EXERCISES

1. Refer to Resource 12, Writing Your Philosophy of Life. If you attempted to write at least a part of your philosophy of life at the outset of reading this book, you have a basis for comparison if you now revise your philosophy. The outline provided is very detailed and comprehensive, and writing such a paper can be a major project in a course. As you review the outline, you might select only one or two of the major topics and use them as a focus of your paper. If you take this project seriously, the assignment can help you clarify your goals for the future and the means to obtain them.

2. Ask a few close friends what gives their life meaning. How do they find their identity as persons? What projects give them meaning and purpose in life?

3. Again, ask a few close friends how their sense of meaning in life is affected by living in an age when nuclear extermination is possible. To what degree do they recognize the peril, or do they deny such a possible fate as "unthinkable"? How does this threat affect the quality of their life, both in terms of what they are doing now and in terms of their future plans? You might ask people of various age groups the same questions. Interviewing children, adolescents, younger adults, and older adults could be an interesting project, especially if you bring the results to class and share them. A further project, as a class, is to pool ideas of what you and your fellow students think you can do as individuals to prevent such an unthinkable fate.

4. Think about the hopes you have for your own children or what you'd most want for your children if you should someday have them. What values would you want to see them acquire and live by? In what ways would you like them to be like you? And in what ways do you hope they

differ from you? Doing this exercise in class in small groups can be enlightening and fun.

5. Now that the course is coming to an end, review each of the broad topics explored in this book and in your class. Discuss with other students which topics meant the most to you. What did you learn about yourself from reading the book and taking the course? What do you think you will do with what you have learned? Do you see any specific behavioral changes you intend to make? What questions were raised that are still open for you? Do you have some ideas on ways that you might follow through with your plans aimed at continued personal growth? What are some ideas and plans your fellow students have in this regard?

SUGGESTED READINGS

Frankl, V. (1963). *Man's Search for Meaning*. New York: Washington Square Press; Pocket Books edition, 1975. In describing his experiences in a concentration camp, Frankl shows how it is possible to find meaning in life through suffering. His thesis is that we all have a need to discover meaning.

Gibran, K. (1923). *The Prophet*. New York: Knopf. A famous book of poetic essays on such topics as religion, death, friendship, self-knowledge, joy and sorrow, and prayer.

Kopp, S. (1972). *If You Meet the Buddha on the Road, Kill Him!* New York: Bantam. The message of this powerful book is that no meaning that comes from outside ourselves is real. The book deals with the theme of finding meaning in life by accepting freedom and responsibility.

Powell, J. (1969). *Why Am I Afraid to Tell You Who I Am?* Niles, Ill.: Argus Communications. An easy-to-read and popular book of insights concerning self-awareness, personal growth, and the meaning of life. Powell discusses the human condition, interpersonal relationships, dealing with emotions, and methods of ego defense.

Schell, J. (1982). *The Fate of the Earth*. New York: Knopf. In this provocative book the author describes what would happen to our planet should there be a full-scale nuclear holocaust. In the second part of his book he explores personal and individual death and then discusses the meaning of human extinction. He asserts that the prospect of annihilation has resulted in a mood of coldness, bitterness, and hopelessness.

Toffler, A. (1981). *The Third Wave*. New York: Bantam. The author takes a look at the major changes in contemporary society and offers an optimistic look at our new potentials. He explores future prospects for various aspects of living and suggests a synthesis of new forms for the 21st century.

Walsh, R. (1984). *Staying Alive: The Psychology of Human Survival*. Boulder, Colo.: New Science Library. Deals with the global threats to human survival and well-being. Walsh's thesis is that global extinction is not inevitable. Individual and collective efforts to change certain beliefs can lead to a reduction of fear and defensiveness and can lead to a global psychology.

Yalom, I. D. (1980). *Existential Psychotherapy.* New York: Basic Books. Chapters 2–5 contain excellent resources for an in-depth analysis of the relationship of death to meaning in life. Written from an existential viewpoint, these chapters treat the interrelationships among life, death, and anxiety. Also discussed are children's concepts of death and the implications of death for the practice of psychotherapy. Chapters 6 and 7 deal with freedom and responsibility as crucial factors in creating meaning in one's life. Chapters 10 and 11 consider the problem of finding meaning in life and the implications of meaninglessness for psychotherapy. These chapters contain rich clinical material and interesting case examples.

As I mentioned in Chapter 1, this section contains a variety of tools you can use to make changes in your life. This guide is not intended to be read as a chapter; rather, you are meant to refer to a specific resource when you deal with the relevant topic in one of the chapters. Some of these resources will help you make an assessment of your behaviors, and others will provide you with some guidance as you begin a self-change program. You may want to consider professional counseling as a resource for change, especially if you have tried self-help procedures and you have not met with success. Refer to Resource 13 for a more detailed discussion of *when, where,* and *how* to seek counseling.

RESOURCE 1: IMPROVING READING AND STUDY HABITS

In keeping with the spirit of developing active learning habits, I suggest that you tackle your reading assignments systematically. A useful approach is Robinson's (1970) SQ3R technique (survey, question, read, recite, review). It is intended to get you actively involved with what you are reading. The technique does not have to be applied rigidly; in fact, you can develop your own way of carrying it out. This five-step method involves breaking a reading assignment down into manageable units and checking your understanding of what you are reading. The steps are as follows:

Step 1: Survey. Rather than simply reading a chapter, begin by skimming it to get a general overview of the material. Look for ways in which the topics are interrelated, strive to understand the organization of the chapter, and give some preliminary thought to the information you are about to read.

Step 2: Question. Once you get the general plan of the chapter, look at the main chapter headings. What questions do they raise that your reading of the chapter should answer? Formulate in your own words the questions that you would like to explore as you read.

Step 3: Read. After skimming the chapter and raising key questions, proceed to read one section at a time with the goal of answering your questions. After you've finished a section, pause for a few moments and reflect upon what you've read to determine if you can address clearly the questions you've raised.

Step 4: Recite. In your own words, recite (preferably out loud) the answers to your questions. Avoid rote memorization. Attempt to give meaning to factual material. Make sure that you understand the basic ideas in a section before you go on to the next section. Writing down a few key notes is a good way to have a record for your review later. Then go on to the next section of the chapter, repeating steps 3 and 4.

Step 5: Review. After you finish reading the chapter, spend some time reviewing the main points. Test your understanding of the material by putting the major ideas into your own words. Repeat the questions, and attempt to answer them without looking at the book. If there is a chapter summary or listing of key terms, be sure to study this carefully. A good summary will help you put the chapter into context. Attempt to add to the summary by listing some of the points that seem particularly important or interesting to you.

RESOURCE 2: SUGGESTIONS FOR GETTING THE MOST FROM YOUR COURSES

I find that many college students fail to plan ahead and budget time wisely. The following hints are designed to help you think about how to manage your time more effectively, how to prevent yourself from becoming overwhelmed and then discouraged, and ultimately how to derive the maximum benefit from your educational experience.

1. First of all, take a realistic number of courses. Some students work full time, have family obligations, desire at least a minimum social life, and then attempt to carry 18 units! Consider taking fewer units, even if it means stretching out the number of years it will take to complete your degree.

2. Before you enroll in a class, check out the instructor. You are making an investment, so it pays to select an instructor who is knowledgeable, excited about the subject, and can communicate with students. Don't just pick easy teachers, but search out those who will inspire you to learn.

3. Keep up to date in your reading and writing assignments. Begin early, and don't wait until the night before all the assignments are due. Putting off projects does not make things easier; it only contributes to your feeling hopelessly bogged down toward the end of a semester.

4. Work out a schedule for the entire semester, and then develop a weekly schedule. Allocate a certain time for studying. Establish some priorities rather than trying to do everything at once.

5. Find a place that is conducive to thinking and reflecting. See if you can find ways to cut down on distractions for the time you've allocated to study.

6. Go over your notes from lectures fairly soon after the class. Spend some time organizing the lecture material and thinking about what you have heard.

7. You'll get more out of lectures if you come to class prepared. At a minimum this means completing the assigned reading and bringing questions to class. Challenge yourself to raise questions to help you clarify the material. If the structure of the class permits, get involved in the discussions and other activities.

R E S O U R C E   G U I D E

RESOURCE 3: ASSESSMENT AND CONTROL OF YOUR WEIGHT

Self-Assessment

You will need to determine whether you are willing to exert the consistent effort that it takes to keep physically fit, as well as whether this is the right time for you to lose weight. Williams and Long (1983) have a few questions that help people make these determinations.

- Are you at least 10 percent overweight?
- Do you have problems interpersonally because of your weight?
- Does your present weight pose a health problem?
- Are you getting negative feedback because of your weight?
- Are you experiencing other problems that you consider more important than losing weight at this time?
- Are you able to find a support system that will help you stay with your weight-reducing program?

Some questions that I find useful to add to the list of Williams and Long in determining whether you're ready to do what is needed to lose weight are:

- Do *you* see yourself as having a weight problem?
- Are your self-image and self-respect suffering?
- Are you willing to look in the mirror and really experience your body?
- Do you like what you see? If not, are you willing to do anything to change it?
- Can you learn to reinforce yourself, even if you do not receive positive feedback and support from others in your environment?
- To what degree do you value your health, and what priority do you place on physical appearance?

Strategies in Weight Control

The following are some practical suggestions if you decide that losing weight and then maintaining an appropriate weight is a priority for you. If you are serious about this issue, review these suggestions and see which of them make the most sense to you. Also, you will probably want to do some additional reading, especially in applying behavioral methods as a part of your self-directed program. With this in mind, consider the following strategies as a way of carrying out your choice.

1. Are you really overweight? Some thin people perceive themselves as being fat, while some people who are overweight by most objective standards may see themselves as just fine. In deciding if you are overweight you could ask yourself: Are there things you'd like to do but that you are prevented from doing because of your condition? Can you participate in

sports? Can you exert yourself physically? Can you participate in satisfactory sex? Do you get overly tired?

2. If you are overweight, are you blaming yourself and putting yourself down? Are you accepting personal responsibility for your condition and what you are doing now to contribute to that condition? What are you willing to do to change?

3. Are you paying attention to your *behavior* and not just to what you *say* you want to do or how you'd like to be different? (While some people say that they hate being fat and resolve to change, they also continue to eat fattening foods or large portions, and they fail to exercise. I tend to believe what people actually do rather than what they say.)

4. Have you had a thorough physical examination, and did you consult your physician about your plans to develop a weight-control program? If you are overweight, did you check first to see if there are some medical causes for the problem?

5. Are you familiar with some reading on diet, nutrition, and exercise? In addition to watching your diet, develop an exercise program that will work for you. In this way you are not only being calorie conscious but are also doing something to keep your body physically fit and burn off excess calories.

6. Beware of common methods of sabotage, including self-sabotage and others' attempts to thwart your plans. You might overeat when you feel depressed, have fattening food within reach, or decide to reward your progress by going on an eating binge. Others can sabotage your efforts with statements such as: "Forget the calories. You've worked hard so enjoy your dessert." "Oh hell, you can start dieting after this vacation." "Have a chocolate malt with me. I don't like to drink alone."

7. Apply some behavioral principles and procedures in your attempt to lose weight: Develop specific and realistic goals. Monitor your eating habits and keep records of what you eat, when you eat, how much you eat, and how you feel during and afterwards. Keep a record of your weight. And develop a system of reinforcements as an incentive to keep on your program.

8. Make a list of target foods that add to your weight problem. Eliminate one type of food at a time. For example, perhaps you can avoid dessert. As you make progress, then you can avoid other foods on your list.

9. Avoid eating fattening food as much as possible. Avoid snacking on candy and potato chips. Substitute fruits or raw vegetables.

10. Develop alternatives to overeating, such as physical activity. This form of substitution has obvious benefits.

11. Recognize that simply taking weight off, as difficult as it may be, does not mean that you have your problem solved. If you don't understand what your overeating and being overweight mean and the reasons

for these behaviors, you could easily revert to self-defeating practices. Accept the reality that maintaining a healthy weight will entail continued work and commitment on your part.

12. After taking off the weight you wanted to remove, take another look at yourself standing naked in that full-length mirror. Let yourself go through the exercise of "becoming your body and speaking." What does it say? How do you feel as you see a new reflection in that mirror?

Group Weight-Control Programs

If you are thinking about supplementing your self-directed weight-control program with some type of group program that makes use of the "buddy system" for support and guidance, a word of caution is in order. There are far too many programs designed strictly for making money; some of them are dangerous to your health; and some of them foster dependency on others to the extent that you are likely to revert to old ways if you leave the program. Ideally, you should be able to make it on your own if something happens to the program. In general, the programs that seem to be the most successful have some of the following characteristics in common:

- Support groups are a part of the program.
- Attention is given to the psychological dynamics of being overweight and to why you put weight on in the first place.
- The program is well structured, and there is a form of observation and accountability.
- Attention is devoted to good nutritional habits and exercise.
- The program helps you become aware of what, when, how, how much, where, and why you eat.
- There is an encouragement for you to develop life-long proper eating habits, rather than fostering a crash diet.
- The program teaches you to develop responsibility and self-direction and to create a self-management program based on a system of positive reinforcement.

Note: Before you embark on any weight-control program, be sure to check with a physician. Develop a realistic plan with medical guidance.

RESOURCE 4: MONITORING STRESS IN YOUR LIFE

The *Social Readjustment Rating Scale* was developed by Holmes and his colleagues (1967, 1970) as an objective method of measuring the stress resulting from life events. Stress is measured in terms of life change units (LCUs). Each life change is given a numerical value. For example, pregnancy is assigned 40, change in school is given 20, change in sleeping habits is given 16, and so on. To determine the severity of stress that you have experienced, total up the LCUs. Keep in mind that it is the demand to adjust that a life change places on you that is important, rather than the type of life change alone.

Social Readjustment Rating Scale

Life Change	Scale of Impact (LCUs)
Death of spouse	100
Divorce	73
Marital separation	65
Jail term	63
Death of close family member	63
Personal injury or illness	53
Marriage	50
Dismissal from job	47
Marital reconciliation	45
Retirement	45
Change in health of family member	44
Pregnancy	40
Sexual difficulties	39
Gain of a new family member	39
Business readjustment	39
Change in financial state	38
Death of a close friend	37
Change to a different line of work	36
Change in number of arguments with spouse	35
Mortgage or loan for major purchase	31
Foreclosure of mortgage or loan	30
Change in responsibilities at work	29
Son or daughter's leaving home	29
Trouble with in-laws	29
Outstanding personal achievement	28
Wife's beginning or quitting work	26
Starting or completing school	26
Change in living conditions	25
Revision of personal habits	24
Trouble with boss	23
Change in work hours or conditions	20
Change in residence	20
Change in school	20
Change in recreation	19
Change in church activities	19

R E S O U R C E   G U I D E

Social Readjustment Rating Scale *(continued)*

Life Change	Scale of Impact (LCUs)
Change in social activities	18
Mortgage or loan for lesser purchase	17
Change in sleeping habits	16
Change in number of family get-togethers	15
Change in eating habits	15
Vacation	13
Christmas	12
Minor violation of the law	11
Total LCUs	_____

Holmes and his colleagues found a strong relationship between the likelihood of physical illness and the total LCU score. Their results suggested that a score in the 200s was associated with about a 50 percent chance of illness and that a score above 300 was associated with about an 80 percent chance of illness.

It is important that you interpret your score in the context of a rough estimate of the stresses you have experienced by changing life situations, rather than using your score as an exact measure. There is a great deal of individual variability with respect to the impact of specific life events. If your score indicates that you have been subjected to a high degree of stress, it is well to consider ways in which you can reduce your exposure to stress and more effectively deal with the stress that is inevitable in your life.

R
E
S
O
U
R
C
E

G
U
I
D
E

RESOURCE 5: RELAXATION EXERCISE

Let me describe an exercise in self-relaxation that you can do by yourself. You can practice relaxation in many situations, and doing so can help you assume control of your own behavior, instead of being controlled by situations that produce tension within you. For a period of at least a week (and preferably much longer), engage in relaxation training for approximately 20 to 30 minutes daily. The purpose of the exercise is to teach you to become more aware of the distinction between tension states and relaxation states. A further objective is to reduce unnecessary anxiety and tension. The strategy for achieving muscular relaxation is to repeatedly tense and relax various muscle groups. To deepen your relaxation, auxiliary techniques such as concentrating on your breathing and imagining yourself in peaceful situations can eventually be added.

Here are some guidelines for your relaxation exercise. Make sure that you're in a peaceful setting and in a relaxed position. Tighten and relax the various parts of your body, beginning with your upper extremities and progressing downward to your lower extremities.

- Clench your fists tightly—so tightly that it hurts. Let go of the tension and relax.
- Stiffen the lower part of one arm. Tense it. Feel the tension. Let go of the tension.
- Tense the upper part of the arm. Tighten it until it begins to hurt. Relax it.
- Repeat the last two steps for your other arm.
- Wrinkle up your forehead. Wrinkle it tighter and tighter. Then relax and smooth it out. Picture your entire forehead and scalp becoming smoother and more relaxed.
- Raise your eyebrows as high as you can. Hold this position. Relax.
- Close your eyes as tightly as you can. Feel the tension. Close them even tighter, and feel that tension. Let go, and feel the relaxation around your eyes.
- Wrinkle your nose as tightly as you can. Relax.
- Clench your jaw, and bite your teeth together hard. Feel the pressure. Increase the tension in your jaw. Let your jaw and mouth become increasingly relaxed. Enjoy this relaxation.
- Smile in an exaggerated way, and hold it. Let go. Purse your lips as tightly as you can. Tighten your mouth muscles, and feel the tension in your entire face. Let go of the tension. Relax.
- The exercise progresses with the neck, shoulders, and upper back; then the chest, abdomen, and lower back; then the rest of the body, down to the toes; and finally the entire body. During the entire exercise, keep your eyes gently closed. Cover all the major muscle groups. For each group, tense the muscles for several seconds and then relax them. Note

the difference between the tension and relaxation states, and repeat the tension/release cycles at least once or twice for each muscle group.

With practice, you can become aware of tension in every part of your body, and you can learn to relax all the areas of your body, separately or together, without first having to tense them. Ultimately, the goal is to teach you to control your tension states by choosing to switch to a deep muscular-relaxation state.

I recommend that you review this relaxation exercise and practice it twice daily. It takes only about 20 minutes once you have learned the procedure, and you can call on it at those times in the day when you are under particular stress. Even closing your eyes for a few moments, concentrating on your breathing and the tension within your body, and telling yourself to "let go" are valuable tools in dealing with stress when you feel its effects on your body.

If you are like most people, you may not be consciously aware of the tension that you are carrying around in your body. People will sometimes give up too quickly as they are learning progressive-relaxation procedures, because they are not seeing immediate results. It may take several weeks of practice to really feel the tension in your body and to release it. However, once you master some skills of progressive relaxation, it will be possible to relax your entire body in a few moments.

Proper breathing is another antidote to stress, and it is essential to learning how to relax fully. Many of us busy ourselves so much that we literally forget to breathe. If you have developed poor breathing habits, one way to begin improving is simply to pay attention to how you breathe at any given moment. At times during the day you can actually stop and become aware of your breathing and spend a few minutes taking deep breaths. Breathing exercises can help reduce anxiety, irritability, muscular tension, depression, and fatigue.

RESOURCE 6: ARE YOU A PROBLEM DRINKER?

To answer this question, ask yourself the following questions and answer them as honestly as you can with a *Yes* or a *No*.

_____	1. Do you lose time from work or school because of drinking?
_____	2. Is drinking making your home life unhappy?
_____	3. Do you drink because you're shy with other people?
_____	4. Is drinking affecting your reputation?
_____	5. Have you ever felt remorse after drinking?
_____	6. Have you ever gotten into financial difficulties as a result of drinking?
_____	7. Do you turn to lower companions and an inferior environment when drinking?
_____	8. Does your drinking make you careless of your family's welfare?
_____	9. Do you have less ambition because of drinking?
_____	10. Do you crave a drink at a definite time every day?
_____	11. Do you want a drink the next morning?
_____	12. Does drinking cause you to have difficulty in sleeping?
_____	13. Has your efficiency declined because of drinking?
_____	14. Is drinking jeopardizing your job or business?
_____	15. Do you drink to escape from worries or trouble?
_____	16. Do you drink alone?
_____	17. Have you ever had a complete loss of memory as a result of drinking?
_____	18. Has your physician ever treated you for drinking?
_____	19. Do you drink to build up your self-confidence?
_____	20. Have you ever been to a hospital or institution on account of drinking?

The above questions are used by Johns Hopkins University Hospital in Baltimore in deciding whether a patient is alcoholic. According to Alcoholics Anonymous, if you have answered yes to any one of these questions, there is a definite warning that you may be an alcoholic. If you answered yes to any two, the chances are that you are an alcoholic. If you have answered yes to three or more, you are definitely an alcoholic.

I think that the above interpretations should be made with caution. Rather than using your responses to categorize yourself as an alcoholic or a nonalcoholic, I would suggest using them to determine whether you have a problem in using alcohol. If you answered yes to several questions, it would be well to seriously consider that you might be using alcohol as a method of escape from dealing directly with stress. It might be wise to attend an Alcoholics Anonymous meeting in your community, simply to learn more about recognizing how drinking can be problematic for you and what you can do about it.

RESOURCE 7: A MODEL FOR SELF-DIRECTED CHANGE

Two books that I find especially helpful in teaching people how to take increasing charge of their own life are *Self-Directed Behavior: Self-Modification for Personal Adjustment*, by Watson and Tharp (1985), and *Toward a Self-Managed Life Style*, by Williams and Long (1983). If you want to undertake a self-modification program, you'll find these two books most helpful in outlining specific steps leading to behavioral change. What follows is an adaptation and modification of the systematic model for self-directed change presented by Watson and Tharp (1985):

1. *Select your goals.* (In counseling applications, the client, not the counselor, selects the goals.) What do *you* want for yourself? How do you want to be different?
2. *Translate your goals into target behaviors*—that is, the behaviors you need to change or acquire in order to reach your goal. What specific behaviors would you like to increase? What behaviors do you want to decrease? How might you reach your goal?
3. *Observe your behavior* by focusing your awareness on what you're doing. Keep a record of your behavior. You might carry in your pocket a small notebook to keep track of behaviors (and feelings associated with them) that you want to change.
4. *Develop a contract.* After you've increased your awareness of a particular behavior pattern, you can devise a plan for change. This involves, first, negotiating a working contract with yourself, your counselor, or another person and, second, actually doing things to change. These two steps make up the action phase of the program.
5. *Arrange to get information and feedback.* If you want to know how effective your new behavior is, it's essential to get reactions from others and think about it. Is your changed behavior working for you?
6. *Revise your plan of action as needed.* The more you learn about yourself and the impact you have on others, the more you can refine your plans to change.

R E S O U R C E   G U I D E

RESOURCE 8: SEX-ROLE INVENTORY*

Here is a sample of a sex-role inventory used by therapists to assess the degree of masculinity, femininity, or androgyny of their clients. The inventory is taken by writing in the box following each descriptive word or phrase a number according to the following scale: 7 = I *always or almost always* display this trait; 6 = I *usually* display this trait; 5 = I *often* display this trait; 4 = I *occasionally* display this trait; 3 = I *sometimes but infrequently* display this trait; 2 = I *usually don't* display this trait; 1 = I *never or almost never* display this trait. Certain traits, such as self-reliance, are considered highly masculine; others, such as cheerfulness, highly feminine; and others, such as moodiness, neither highly masculine nor highly feminine. Extremely high masculine or feminine scores need to be explored.

self-reliant		cheerful		conscientious	
yielding		moody		athletic	
helpful		independent		affectionate	
defends own beliefs		shy		theatrical	

R
E
S
O
U
R
C
E

G
U
I
D
E

RESOURCE 9: HOW MUCH DO YOU KNOW ABOUT SEXUALITY?

The following true/false test is given in Barry and Emily McCarthy's (1984) book *Sexual Awareness: Enhancing Sexual Pleasure.* To assess your knowledge about sexuality and sexual functioning, take a few moments to take this test.

T F   1. Sexual expression is purely natural, not a function of learning.

T F   2. Foreplay is for the woman; intercourse is for the man.

T F   3. Once a couple establishes a good sexual relationship, they don't need to set aside time for intimacy together.

T F   4. If you love each other and communicate, everything will go fine sexually.

T F   5. Sex and love are two sides of the same coin.

T F   6. Technique is more important than intimacy in achieving a satisfying sexual relationship.

T F   7. Casual sex is more exciting than intimate sex.

T F   8. If you have a good sexual relationship, you will have a fulfilling experience each time you have sex.

T F   9. After age 25 your sex drive dramatically decreases, and most people stop being sexual by 65.

T F   10. It is primarily the man's role to initiate sex.

T F   11. If one or both partners become aroused, intercourse must follow or there will be frustration.

T F   12. Men are more sexual than women.

T F   13. Having "G" spot and multiple orgasms is a sign you are a sexually liberated woman.

T F   14. Since men don't have spontaneous erections after age 50, they are less able to have intercourse.

T F   15. When you lose sexual desire, the best remedy is to seek another partner.

T F   16. The most common female sexual problem is pain during intercourse.

T F   17. The most common male sexual problem is not having enough sex.

T F   18. Penis size is crucial for female sexual satisfaction.

T F   19. Oral/genital sex is an exciting but perverse sexual behavior.

T F   20. Simultaneous orgasms provide the most erotic pleasure.

T F   21. Married people do not masturbate.

T F   22. Using sexual fantasies during intercourse indicates dissatisfaction with your partner.

T F   23. Clitoral orgasms are superior to vaginal orgasms.

T F   24. Male-on-top is the most natural position for intercourse.

T   F   25. People of today are doing much better sexually than the previous generation.

The McCarthys provide the following directions for scoring and interpreting this test: Add the number of *trues* you've checked. This will tell you the number of sex myths you believe. What you took was a sex-myth test, so all the answers are false. Don't be surprised if you believed several of these myths; the average person thinks nine of these statements are true. Sexual myths are rampant in our culture, and they die hard. Even among college students taking a human sexual-behavior course, the average number of myths believed is seven.

If you discovered that your knowledge about sexuality is lacking and you'd like to increase it, consider reading the McCarthys' book. They have chapters devoted to sexual comfort and pleasure, exercises designed to enhance sexual satisfaction, and solving sexual problems.

RESOURCE GUIDE

RESOURCE 10: WAYS OF MAKING WISE VOCATIONAL CHOICES

The question you may be asking yourself now is "How can I go about deciding what will be a meaningful line of work?" A good place to begin is the counseling center or career-development center on your campus. A career counselor can be a great help to you in starting the process of your life and work planning. Other resources typically available at the center include interest inventories and personality assessments. Tests and inventories do not give answers, but they can provide guidelines in helping you to look at how your interests, personality traits, and values might be related to various career options. Ultimately, you still have to make choices, but these inventories may show you some alternatives that you hadn't considered before. Rather than relying on one test alone, I typically suggest several, including some of the following:

The Edwards Personal Preference Schedule. The questions in this inventory are designed to identify 15 dimensions of a person's personality: the needs for achievement, deference, order, exhibition, autonomy, affiliation, intraception, succorance, dominance, abasement, nurturance, change, endurance, heterosexuality, and aggression. This device can help us to see more clearly how these needs are related to vocational choices, and it can also help us understand why we are drawn to certain types of people and not to others.

The Myers-Briggs Personality Type Indicator. This personality-assessment device gives us some indication of a variety of personality orientations (such as extraversion and introversion). While the results, which yield a certain "personality type," may not be significant in themselves, this information could be useful background for a discussion of what kinds of personality might fit various careers and occupations.

The Strong-Campbell Interest Inventory. Designed as an objective measurement of interest patterns, this inventory gives clues to whether a person would be most satisfied working with data, things, or people. It is not an assessment of abilities or aptitudes but rather a measurement of likes and preferences as compared with those of people in many different occupations. It usually points to several possible occupations that the person could consider.

The Kuder Occupational Interest Survey. This is an alternative to the Strong-Campbell interest inventory, geared mainly to the same objectives.

The Allport-Vernon-Lindsey Study of Values. This is a useful device designed to clarify value orientations. For example, it will show whether your central values are in the social area, the political area, or the economic area. Considering your values and how they are related to various occupations is an important part of career counseling.

In addition to making use of the counseling and testing center on your campus, here are some other things you might do to aid your work planning.

• Talk to people in the career or occupation that you think you want to pursue. What is it like for them to be in this type of work? What advice could they offer you? Would they make the same choice again? What are the advantages and disadvantages of their job? What do they get from their work? What specific skills are needed? What does the job market look like in the near future? Talking with a number of people in the same line of work could be one of your best resources. Again, as with interest and personality inventories, these people will not give you an answer concerning the "right" decision for you, but they can give you valuable data to use in making a better choice for yourself.

• If you have several careers in mind, try to get involved with them in some way as soon as possible. Part-time jobs during the school year that are related to a job that interests you, or a full-time job in the summer, could shed some realistic light on your situation.

• Read *What Color Is Your Parachute?* by Richard Bolles (1984). This book is a practical manual for job hunters and career changers. It is the distillation of the experience of millions of successful job hunters of all ages in all types of work. It provides a wealth of practical information that should give you some clear direction in choosing jobs. Bolles stresses that career and life planning is a continuous process, not a single event that is finished for all time. He also makes the point that only you can decide what you want to do. He encourages readers to adopt an active stance toward selecting and getting a job.

RESOURCE 11: SELF-ASSESSMENT OF YOUR WORK-RELATED VALUES

If you are in the process of selecting a career, you can give time to evaluating your values to determine how you can best match them to some form of work that will be satisfying for you. The process of career decision making best begins with a comprehensive *self-assessment*. This assessment involves several factors discussed by Mencke and Hummel (1984).

1. Make an inventory of your life-style values. How important is having time for your personal life to you? What priority do you place on money and advancement? Are you more attracted by taking risks for possible advancement or by job security? How will your preferences for geographic location fit your career choices?

2. Assess your values with regard to other people. What value do you place on interaction with co-workers? What kind of stimulation is important for you? Is support essential? Do you enjoy working with people? What do you receive from helping others?

3. Assess your values with respect to level of responsibility. Are you the kind of person who enjoys being in charge? Do you prefer being a leader or a follower? In defining your work-related values, how important is achievement? money? recognition? degree of influence? promoting a cause? contributing to society? autonomy? structure? freedom?

4. Make an assessment of your intellectual values. Are you primarily interested in thinking and in solving problems? Do you like to acquire new skills? Is it important for you to continue to learn? Do you like intellectual challenges? Do you have a talent for organizing events, people, activities, or academic material? Do you like to plan, organize, and translate ideas into action? Do you expect to see measurable outcomes of your efforts? Would you describe yourself as a practical person who is interested in seeing a product?

Review your priorities, looking for a pattern in your values. You can then use the value summary to evaluate some of the career options you are considering. One way of doing this is by listing your career possibilities on a sheet of paper. On this same sheet list the values you hold to be most central to your future satisfaction. Then evaluate the degree to which each of the careers you have listed is likely to satisfy the values you have identified.

RESOURCE 12: WRITING YOUR PHILOSOPHY OF LIFE

To integrate your thoughts and reflections on the topics raised in this chapter and throughout this book, I encourage you to develop, in writing, your philosophy of life. Your paper should represent a critical analysis of who you are now and of the factors that have been most influential in contributing to that person. You should also discuss the person you'd like to become; include your goals for the future and the means by which you think you'll be able to achieve them.

The following outline may be a helpful guide as you write your paper. Feel free to use or omit any part of the outline, and modify it in any way that will help you to write a paper that is personally significant. You might also consider adding poetry, excerpts from other writers, and pictures or works of art to supplement your writing, if they will contribute to the meaningfulness of your paper.

I. Who are you now? What influences have contributed to the person you are now?
  A. Influences during childhood:
    1. your relationship with your parents
    2. your relationship with your siblings
    3. important turning points
    4. successes and failures
    5. personal conflicts
    6. family expectations
    7. impact of school and early learning experiences
    8. your relationships with friends
    9. experiences of loneliness
    10. other
  B. Influences during adolescence:
    1. impact of your family and your relationship with your parents
    2. school experiences
    3. personal struggles
    4. critical turning points
    5. influence of your peer group
    6. experiences of loneliness
    7. successes and failures, and their impact on you
    8. influential adults other than parents
    9. your principal values
    10. other
  C. Love and sex:
    1. your need for love
    2. your fear of love
    3. the meaning of love for you

    4. dating experiences and their effect on you

    5. your view of sex roles

    6. expectations of others and their influence on your sex role

    7. attitudes toward the opposite sex

    8. meaning of sexuality in your life

    9. your values concerning love and sex

    10. other

  D. Intimate relationships and family life:

    1. the value you place on marriage

    2. how children fit in your life

    3. the meaning of intimacy for you

    4. the kind of intimate relationships you want

    5. areas of struggle for you in relating to others

    6. your views of marriage

    7. your values concerning family life

    8. how social expectations have influenced your views

    9. sex roles in intimate relationships

    10. other

  E. Death and meaning:

    1. your view of an afterlife

    2. religious views and your view of death

    3. the way death affects you

    4. sources of meaning in your life

    5. the things you most value in your life

    6. your struggles in finding meaning and purpose

    7. religion and the meaning of life

    8. critical turning points in finding meaning

    9. influential people in your life

    10. other

II. Whom do you want to become?

  A. Summary of your present position:

    1. how you see yourself now (strengths and weaknesses)

    2. how others perceive you now

    3. what makes you unique

    4. your relationships with others

    5. present struggles

  B. Your future plans for an occupation:

    1. nature of your work plans and their chances for success

    2. kind of work that is meaningful to you

    3. how you chose or will choose your work

    4. what work means to you

    5. what you expect from work

  C. Your future with others:

    1. the kind of relationships you want

   2. what you need to do to achieve the relationships you want
   3. plans for marriage or an alternative
   4. place of children in your future plans
D. Future plans for yourself:
   1. how you would like to be ten years from now
      a. what you need to do to achieve your goals
      b. what you can do now
   2. your values for the future
   3. your view of the good life
      a. ways to achieve it
      b. how your view of the good life relates to all aspects of your life
   4. choices you see as being open to you now
      a. choices in work
      b. choices in school
      c. value choices
      d. other areas of choice in your life

R
E
S
O
U
R
C
E

G
U
I
D
E

RESOURCE 13: INDIVIDUAL AND GROUP COUNSELING AS AVENUES TO PERSONAL GROWTH

A psychologist can often help us gain insight into our early decisions and learn to make new choices for more effective living. Counseling refers to the process whereby people explore personal concerns with a trained professional. Generally speaking, counseling is short term, focuses on problems, and helps people remove blocks to their personal growth and discover their inner resources.

When to Seek Professional Counseling

People are often unclear about whether they need or want to get involved in psychological counseling. How can you know whether you have a need for psychological services? This is an extremely difficult question to answer in general, but I'll give as examples some reasons that clients typically seek professional assistance. *Some* people initiate personal therapy because:

- They are facing a situational crisis in which they feel their subjective world (or some part of it) is collapsing.
- They have been unable to get free from a prolonged period of depression, anxiety, or guilt.
- They find that their work is no longer meaningful and that they want to explore other options.
- They are hurting over a situation and want help in understanding how to deal with their hurt.
- They find their marriage intolerable and want to resolve their conflicts by discovering more constructive ways of living together.
- They feel a deadness and lack of meaning in their lives.
- They have certain symptoms that interfere with their functioning, such as being overweight, frequently getting sick, having exaggerated fears, and so forth.

It takes courage to acknowledge that you have a particular problem, and it takes even more courage to actually take steps to cope with the problem. Professional counseling could be a valuable resource for you. I hope you will not stop yourself from using this resource because of fears of asking for professional help. I'd like to emphasize that you do not have to be seriously disturbed before you consider getting professional assistance. In fact, counseling can be viewed as preventive, much like a regular medical examination or dental checkup.

The Experience of Individual and Group Counseling

Most clients enter counseling with definite expectations, although these will be different for each client. Some expect relief from disabling symptoms. Some are searching for an answer to their conflicts from the counselor; others hope that the counselor will help them find their own answers. In addition to their hopes or expectations, most clients have some fears about what counseling will be like or about what they might discover about themselves. During the initial stages one of the best ways for a client to establish a trusting relationship with the counselor is to talk about these expectations and fears. Rapport is a prerequisite of any real progress.

As counseling progresses, clients usually begin to express feelings and thoughts that they formerly kept out of awareness. They become able to talk about themselves in a deeply personal way and to trust that their feelings are being accepted. Because of the care and acceptance they receive from the counselor, they are increasingly able to accept themselves. They feel less need to be defensive, and they move in the direction of being open to all the facets of themselves. This openness enables them to achieve a clarity about themselves that they did not have before.

It isn't unusual for clients to feel worse before they feel better, however. As people open up to another human being (and to themselves), they become more vulnerable and exposed. As they shed the defenses that have been shielding them from threat, they experience some anxiety before they develop new resources with which to replace these defenses. Some people may say: "Sometimes I wonder whether it was wise to begin counseling, because I *feel* my sadness and fear more now than I ever did before. Maybe I should have stayed less aware and more comfortable." Fortunately, if they have the courage to stay with the counseling process for a time, they generally discover resources within themselves that they can draw on in making changes.

The expression of feelings, the reliving of past experiences, and the discussion of current struggles are all a part of counseling, but they are not the whole story. As clients express themselves, they begin to see connections between their past and their present, they come to see their own role in creating their own unhappiness or dissatisfaction, and they generally gain new insight into themselves. For most counselors, this achievement of self-awareness is not the end of the counseling but merely the beginning. The crucial issue is what clients choose to do with the awareness they acquire. For this reason, most approaches emphasize that it's very important for clients to work on actively changing their behavior outside of the counseling sessions in ways that accord with their new insights. As they make specific changes in their behavior, they generally feel more in control of their own life. When a client and counselor decide to discontinue their sessions together, the client takes an important step

R
E
S
O
U
R
C
E

G
U
I
D
E

toward greater autonomy. Ideally, by the time clients come to the end of the counseling process, they have acquired some of the tools they need to continue their own growth and to challenge themselves. They aren't "finished products," any more than anyone else, but they have become able to make clearer, more authentic choices.

This general description of psychological counseling is applicable to both individual and group counseling. Although these two broad types of counseling have much in common, each has its unique features and strengths.

Individual counseling provides an opportunity for an in-depth involvement between clients and counselors. The one-to-one relationship can provide the continuity and trust that enable clients to explore highly personal material. Further, it can give them the opportunity to relive past and present conflicts with the significant individuals in their life. Through the counseling relationship, clients can come to understand how their other relationships affect them.

In therapeutic groups, the one-to-one relationship is not the primary focus. Generally, a group is a microcosm of society. Group members, in relating to one another, can begin to appreciate how others perceive them. They can use the group situation to try out new behavior among people who are responsive and accepting. Through this process of experimentation, they can make decisions about what changes they want to make in their everyday behavior. Groups also give people the chance to learn interpersonal skills. The members open themselves to certain risks; they confront others and are confronted by others; they give and receive support; and they have an opportunity to get a clearer picture of themselves.

Risks in Individual and Group Counseling

When considering counseling, you should be aware of some of the hazards involved and of what you can do to protect yourself from them. The following are a few important guidelines.

1. Keep in mind that either individual or group counseling may lead to a disruption in your life-style. For example, you may have a style of asking for very little for yourself and so tolerate a mediocre marriage. As a result of counseling, you may begin an intense process of searching and questioning that leads to drastic changes in your values and behavior. Of course, these changes may be constructive and lead to a revitalization of your personal life, but the process may also involve crisis and turmoil. Your spouse, for instance, may not welcome or be ready for changes, and this can create a difficulty for you.

2. Be aware of your rights as a client. You can choose whether to enter into individual counseling or try a group. You have the right to disagree with or question the therapist or group leader, as well as the right to

terminate your counseling. If you don't feel satisfied with a therapist, you can select another one.

3. There is a risk that you will be turned off to counseling because of a single negative experience with a counselor. Consequently, it's important to recognize that counselors don't all function in the same way and that personality differences among counselors are also significant.

4. It's important not to quit counseling prematurely. There is a danger of opening up vulnerable areas and then terminating counseling before they are really dealt with.

5. Keep in mind that you are the one who should decide on the goals of your counseling. Remember that counseling is a tool to help you clarify your own issues and provide you with resources for making choices; it's not a way of having your decisions made for you.

Misconceptions Concerning Individual and Group Counseling

Some common myths and misconceptions may lead you to conclude that the disadvantages of counseling far outweigh the advantages. For this reason, I want to comment briefly on some of these misconceptions.

1. *Counseling is a form of brainwashing.* On the contrary: counseling should assist you to look within yourself for your own answers to present and future problems in your life. Counseling is not synonymous with advice giving; nor does it involve the indoctrination of a "correct" philosophy of life.

2. *Only sick people seek individual or group counseling.* Although some forms of counseling are specifically aimed at helping people in crises or assisting people who are psychologically disturbed, many people utilize individual and group counseling to come to a fuller recognition of their potential and to remove blocks to personal growth.

3. *People in counseling become more unhappy, because their problems come to the surface.* There is some truth to this statement. Conflict *can* arise if you face painful truths about yourself, but it's important to realize that this increased awareness can lead to decisive steps toward change. Once you accept that you are contributing to your own unhappiness or dissatisfaction, you have the choice of doing something to change your life.

4. *Counseling leaves a person defenseless.* People frequently express the fear that counseling will only rob them of defenses and that they won't have the resources to cope successfully without them. In fact, many people learn through counseling that rigid defenses aren't always necessary and that they can decide to shed unnecessary defenses that seal them off from others.

5. *Fear of counseling isn't normal.* On the contrary: most people who enter individual counseling or join a group do experience some anxiety.

The important thing is how we deal with the fears we experience as we confront ourselves.

6. *Counselors will make you dependent on them, and they will keep you coming to them for longer than is necessary.* Both the client and the counselor should be involved in determining the length of the counseling program. If you have any doubts, you should bring them up and discuss them.

7. *Counseling provides an instant cure.* It is not uncommon, when people begin to experience immediate relief (mainly because someone is listening to them), for them to have the illusion that "all is well." They may quit prematurely after the first or second session, believing that they have effectively dealt with the problem that brought them to the counselor. It is important to realize that counselors are not magicians and that people change only through difficult and sustained work.

Where to Go for Professional Assistance

If you decide that you want to use professional resources, where can you go for help, and how can you find out what resources are available? In most communities, there are mental-health centers and free clinics that offer a variety of services. These agencies can also give you leads on where to go for assistance with particular problems. You can check with friends to see whether any of them have been involved in counseling and, if so, what their impression of the counselor was. The university or college counseling center is another place to look. If you're enrolled in the college, the services may be free or available on an ability-to-pay basis. If you aren't enrolled, the center can probably give you a list of professionals in private practice or in community clinics. Ministers and physicians can also refer you to counseling professionals.

You should also have some understanding of the major types of mental-health professional. Each type has its own strengths, but they all have much in common. Members of the helping professions generally try to minimize or eliminate the environmental conditions that may be causing and maintaining behavioral problems. They all are concerned with developing therapeutic (growth-producing) relationships with clients, and many of them use similar techniques.

Major Providers of Counseling Services

Clinical psychologists. Clinical psychologists have a Ph.D. in psychology and have had two years of supervised clinical practice (internship). They deal with psychological testing, psychotherapy, and research. Clinical psychologists are usually trained in both individual and group therapy; in most states, they must also have a license to engage in private practice.

R E S O U R C E G U I D E

Counseling psychologists.   Counseling psychologists hold a doctoral degree, either a Ph.D. or an Ed.D., from a counseling program at a university. They have had essentially the same kind of training as clinical psychologists, although their internships are with clients who have problems related to educational, vocational, and personal/social matters. Counseling psychologists often work in college counseling centers or for community mental-health agencies. They might also have a private practice in which they perform individual and group counseling or therapy, in which case they must be licensed by the state.

Clinical social workers.   Clinical social workers have a master's degree in social work and have had supervised internships in psychiatric settings. They may work in clinics, in private practice as psychotherapists, or in social-service agencies. Their training makes them especially qualified to work with families of clients in treatment, with social and cultural realities that cause personal stress, with community groups, and with individuals.

Marriage and family counselors.   Marriage and family counselors hold master's or doctoral degrees in a behavioral-science field (usually counseling or psychology) or in marriage, family, and child counseling. They specialize in problems in relationships and often help couples with their sexual conflicts.

Paraprofessionals.   In addition to the professionals who work in the mental-health field, there are increasing numbers of paraprofessionals who perform many of the same psychological services. Paraprofessionals usually have A.A. degrees in human services from a community college or B.A. degrees in human services from a college or university. There are also paraprofessionals who are serving internships as part of their master's degree programs; these people work under supervision and have an opportunity to meet with their supervisors and other interns. Many paraprofessionals are both talented and qualified for the work they do with clients—a fact that may not be appreciated by clients who are disappointed when they have their first session with an intern or a paraprofessional. Sometimes clients ask to see the "real doctor" or have reservations about trusting a person who has not had advanced professional training. You should know that much more than training goes into the making of a sensitive and helpful counselor, and many paraprofessionals have had life experiences that are most advantageous to them in their work with clients.

Some Consumer Guidelines for Selecting a Counselor or a Group

With the range of professional services available, the consumer is sometimes at a loss in making a decision and knowing what to look for. Although there are no assurances that the group or counselor you pick will be the right one for you, the following suggestions may be helpful in making your selection.

1. Try to check with others who know the counselor or group leader before you make your decision. Although some reports may be biased (either positively or negatively), information from people who have worked with a counselor or group leader can be valuable.

2. Before you begin, interview the counselor or group leader. If the counselor resists such a request, you should probably avoid him or her. When you do speak with a counselor, try to decide the degree to which he or she inspires trust in you.

3. Learn to be an intelligent consumer of psychological services. In making your selection, consider some of the following questions:

- What are the responsibilities of the counselor and of the client?
- What are the expectations of the counselor or group leader?
- What are some of the psychological risks involved in participating in this type of counseling?
- What are the desired outcomes, and what measures are taken to achieve them? What techniques does the counselor use?
- What are the fees? Will insurance cover a portion of them?
- What background, training, and experience does the counselor have?
- What is his or her specialty? What degrees and licenses does he or she possess?

4. Be very cautious about responding to advertisements or to brochures and pamphlets circulated in the mail. Referrals from agencies, from professionals, and most of all from clients who have worked with a counselor can more appropriately guide you in your selection.

5. Check with your college or university counseling center to find out what professional services it offers. These counseling services are generally offered free to students and are designed especially for the needs of college students of all ages.

6. Look into the continuing-education or extension programs and summer sessions of the community colleges and other colleges and universities in your area. Increasingly, departments of psychology, education, and counseling are offering many types of experiential courses, personal-growth groups, weekend workshops, and special-interest programs. For instance, most college-extension programs offer several types of workshops or groups, such as groups for the divorced, assertiveness-training groups, groups for professionals, couples' workshops, and consciousness-raising groups for both men and women.

7. Check out the resources for individual counseling, marriage and family counseling, and groups available at community mental-health centers. Many local agencies provide counseling services on an ability-to-pay basis.

In evaluating different counselors, a crucial issue is how to determine their competence. Degrees and licenses ensure a minimum level of competence, but there are qualitative differences among those who hold these credentials. Moreover, many qualified persons who work in institutions such as schools and churches are not required to have licenses yet may be very effective counselors. Ultimately, after you have consulted others and considered a counselor's qualifications, you still need to trust your own feelings and judgment concerning whether to work with a particular person.

R
E
S
O
U
R
C
E

G
U
I
D
E

The writing of this book has been a source of excitement, joy, and pain. It was a difficult and challenging book to write, because it provided a stimulus for me (as well as for Marianne and our daughters) to look at the choices we make and to examine the quality of our life. The personal challenge that I continue to face through my writing, teaching, consulting, and practice as a psychologist is: To what degree am I attempting to live by the values that I espouse? What choices do I make each day, and what do these choices say about what I really value in life?

In the courses I teach I can converse with my students and get their reactions to what I say. But in a book the conversation is decidedly one-way. Nevertheless, Marianne and I would very much like to know how you are affected by *I Never Knew I Had a Choice*, and we hope that, if you want to, you'll write and tell us your impressions and reactions. We'd be very interested in finding out how you'd like to see this book changed, as well as knowing the topics that affected you the most (and the least). At the end of the book is a form for your convenience, which you could send to us in care of Brooks/Cole Publishing Company, Monterey, California 93940.

Albrecht, K. (1979). *Stress and the manager.* Englewood Cliffs, N.J.: Prentice-Hall.

American Psychological Association (1981). Leisure counseling [Special issue]. *The Counseling Psychologist, 9*(3).

Axline, V. (1976). *Dibs: In search of self.* New York: Ballantine.

Baruch, D. (1964). *One little boy.* New York: Dell (Delta).

Basow, S. A. (1980). *Sex-role stereotypes: Traditions and alternatives.* Monterey, Calif.: Brooks/Cole.

Berne, E. (1975). *What do you say after you say hello?* New York: Bantam.

Bettelheim, B. (1967). *The empty fortress: Infantile autism and the birth of self.* New York: Free Press.

Bloomfield, H. H., with Felder, L. (1983). *Making peace with your parents.* New York: Ballantine.

Bobrow, R. (1983, June). The choice to die. *Psychology Today,* pp. 70–72.

Bolles, R. N. (1978). *The three boxes of life.* Berkeley, Calif.: Ten Speed Press.

Bolles, R. N. (1984). *What color is your parachute?* Berkeley, Calif.: Ten Speed Press.

Brammer, L. M. (1984). Counseling theory and the older adult. *The Counseling Psychologist, 12*(2), 29–37.

Breggin, P. R. (1983). *Psychiatric drugs: Hazards to the brain.* New York: Springer.

Brennecke, J. H., & Amick, R. G. (1980). *The struggle for significance* (3rd ed.). Encino, Calif.: Glencoe.

Brooks-Gunn, J., & Matthews, W. S. (1979). *He and she: How children develop their sex-role identity.* Englewood Cliffs, N.J.: Prentice-Hall (Spectrum).

Browne, H. (1973). *How I found freedom in an unfree world.* New York: Avon.

Burns, D. D. (1981). *Feeling good: The new mood therapy.* New York: New American Library (Signet).

Buscaglia, L. (1972). *Love.* Thorofare, N.J.: Charles B. Slack.

Coleman, J. C., & Glaros, A. G. (1983). *Contemporary psychology and effective behavior* (5th ed.). Palo Alto, Calif.: Scott, Foresman.

Daniels, V., & Horowitz, L. J. (1984). *Being and caring: A psychology for living* (2nd ed.). Palo Alto, Calif.: Mayfield.

Davis, K. E. (1985, February). Near and dear: Friendship and love compared. *Psychology Today,* pp. 22–30.

Davis, M., Eshelman, E. R., & McKay, M. (1980). *The relaxation and stress reduction workbook*. Richmond, Calif.: New Harbinger Publications.

Deaux, K. (1976). *The behavior of women and men*. Monterey, Calif.: Brooks/Cole.

Dienstfrey, H. (1983, January). Homosexual America. *Psychology Today*, p. 14.

Dowling, C. (1981). *The Cinderella complex*. New York: Pocket Books.

Dusek, D., & Girdano, D. A. (1980). *Drugs: A factual account*. Reading, Mass.: Addison-Wesley.

Eastman, P. (1984, January). Elders under seige. *Psychology Today*, p. 30.

Ellis, A. (1984). The essence of RET. *Journal of Rational-Emotive Therapy, 2*, 19–25.

Ellis, A., & Harper, R. A. (1975). *A new guide to rational living*. Englewood Cliffs, N.J.: Prentice-Hall.

Ellis, A., & Whiteley, J. M. (Eds.). (1979). *Theoretical and empirical foundations of rational-emotive therapy*. Monterey, Calif.: Brooks/Cole.

Emery, G. (1981). *A new beginning: How you can change your life through cognitive therapy*. New York: Simon & Schuster.

Erikson, E. (1963). *Childhood and society* (2nd ed.). New York: Norton.

Erikson, E. (1982). *The life cycle completed*. New York: Norton.

Farrell, W. (1975). *The liberated male*. New York: Bantam.

Frankl, V. (1963). *Man's search for meaning*. New York: Washington Square Press.

Frankl, V. (1965). *The doctor and the soul*. New York: Bantam.

Frankl, V. (1969). *The will to meaning: Foundation and applications of logotherapy*. New York: New American Library.

Frankl, V. (1978). *The unheard cry for meaning*. New York: Bantam.

Freud, S. (1949). *An outline of psychoanalysis*. New York: Norton.

Freud, S. (1955). *The interpretation of dreams*. London: Hogarth Press.

Friedman, M., & Rosenman, R. H. (1974). *Type A behavior and your heart*. Greenwich, Conn.: Fawcett.

Fromm, E. (1956). *The art of loving*. New York: Harper & Row (Colophon).

Gibran, K. (1923). *The prophet*. New York: Knopf.

Glasser, W. (1984). *Take effective control of your life*. New York: Harper & Row.

Goldberg, H. (1976). *The hazards of being male*. New York: Nash.

Goldberg, H. (1979). *The new male*. New York: New American Library (Signet).

Gordon, D. (1972). *Overcoming the fear of death*. New York: Penguin.

Gould, R. L. (1978). *Transformations: Growth and change in adult life*. New York: Simon & Schuster (Touchstone).

Goulding, M., & Goulding, R. (1979). *Changing lives through redecision therapy*. New York: Brunner/Mazel.

Goulding, R., & Goulding, M. (1978). *The power is in the patient*. San Francisco: TA Press.

Gunn, B. (1964). Children's conceptions of occupational prestige. *Personnel and Guidance Journal, 44*, 558–563.

Hall, C. (1954). *A primer of Freudian psychology*. New York: New American Library (Mentor).

Hall, C. S., & Nordby, V. J. (1973). *A primer of Jungian psychology*. New York: New American Library (Mentor).

Havighurst, R. (1972). *Developmental tasks and education* (3rd ed.). New York: David McKay.

Herr, E. L., & Cramer, S. H. (1984). *Career guidance and counseling through the life span* (3rd ed.). Boston: Little, Brown.

Hodge, M. (1967). *Your fear of love*. Garden City, N.Y.: Doubleday.

Holmes, T. H., & Rahe, R. H. (1967). The social readjustment rating scale. *Journal of Psychosomatic Research, 11*, 213–218.

Holmes, T. S., & Holmes, T. H. (1970). Short-term intrusions into the life-style routine. *Journal of Psychosomatic Research, 14*, 121–132.

Hunt, M. (1984, January). Sex never ages. *Psychology Today,* pp. 16–17.

Josephson, E., & Josephson, M. (Eds). (1962). *Man alone: Alienation in modern society.* New York: Dell.

Jourard, S. (1971). *The transparent self* (rev. ed.). New York: Van Nostrand Reinhold.

Joyce, C. (1984, November). A time for grieving. *Psychology Today,* pp. 42–46.

Kaiser, R. B. (1981, March). The way of the journal. *Psychology Today,* pp. 64–76.

Kalish, R. A. (1985). *Death, grief, and caring relationships* (2nd ed.). Monterey, Calif.: Brooks/Cole.

Kavanaugh, R. (1972). *Facing death.* New York: Nash.

Kiley, D. (1983). *The Peter Pan syndrome.* New York: Avon.

Koestenbaum, P. (1976). *Is there an answer to death?* Englewood Cliffs, N.J.: Prentice-Hall (Spectrum).

Kopp, S. (1972). *If you meet the Buddha on the road, kill him!* New York: Bantam.

Kübler-Ross, E. (1969). *On death and dying.* New York: Macmillan.

Kübler-Ross, E. (1975). *Death: The final stage of growth.* Englewood Cliffs, N.J.: Prentice-Hall (Spectrum).

Levin, J., & Levin, W. C. (1980). *Ageism: Prejudice and discrimination against the elderly.* Belmont, Calif.: Wadsworth.

Lindbergh, A. (1975). *Gift from the sea.* New York: Pantheon.

Lyon, W. (1975). *Let me live!* (rev. ed.). North Quincy, Mass.: Christopher.

Machlowitz, M. (1980). *Workaholics: Living with them, working with them.* Reading, Mass.: Addison-Wesley.

Marin, P. (1983, July). A revolution's broken promises. *Psychology Today,* pp. 50–57.

Maslach, C. (1982). *Burnout: The cost of caring.* Englewood Cliffs, N.J.: Prentice-Hall (Spectrum).

Maslow, A. (1968). *Toward a psychology of being.* New York: Van Nostrand.

Maslow, A. (1970). *Motivation and personality* (2nd ed.). New York: Harper & Row.

Maslow, A. (1971). *The farther reaches of human nature.* New York: Viking.

Masters, W. H., & Johnson, V. E. (1974). *The pleasure bond.* New York: Bantam.

Masters, W. H., & Johnson, V. E. (1980). *Human sexual inadequacy.* New York: Bantam.

May, R. (1973). *Man's search for himself.* New York: Dell (Delta).

May, R. (1981). *Freedom and destiny.* New York: Norton.

Mayeroff, M. (1971). *On caring.* New York: Harper & Row.

McCarthy, B., & McCarthy, E. (1984). *Sexual awareness: Enhancing sexual pleasure.* New York: Carroll & Graf.

McLeod, B. (1984, December). Saying the right thing to the bereaved. *Psychology Today,* p. 17.

Meiselman, K. C. (1978). *Incest: A psychological study of causes and effects with treatment recommendations.* San Francisco: Jossey-Bass.

Mencke, R., & Hummel, R. L. (1984). *Career planning for the 80's.* Monterey, Calif.: Brooks/Cole.

Meredith, N. (1984, January). The gay dilemma. *Psychology Today,* pp. 56–62.

Mornell, P. (1979). *Passive men, wild women.* New York: Ballantine.

Moses, A. E., & Hawkins, R. O. (1982). *Counseling lesbian women and gay men: A life issues approach.* St. Louis: C. V. Mosby.

Moustakas, C. (1975). *Finding yourself, finding others.* Englewood Cliffs, N.J.: Prentice-Hall (Spectrum).

Moustakas, C. (1977). *Turning points.* Englewood Cliffs, N.J.: Prentice-Hall (Spectrum).

Naisbitt, J. (1984). *Megatrends.* New York: Warner Books.

Nass, G. D., Libby, R. W., & Fisher, M. P. (1984). *Sexual choices: An introduction to human sexuality* (2nd ed.). Monterey, Calif.: Wadsworth.

Nelson, R. C. (1963). Knowledge and interests concerning sixteen occupations among elementary and secondary school students. *Educational and Psychological Measurement, 23,* 741–754.

Nissenson, M. (1984, January). Therapy after sixty. *Psychology Today,* pp. 22–26.

Okun, B. F. (1984). *Working with adults: Individual, family, and career development.* Monterey, Calif.: Brooks/Cole.

Palmore, E. (1982). Facts on aging. In S. Zarit (Ed.), *Readings in aging and death* (2nd ed.). New York: Harper & Row.

Peplau, L. A. (1981, March). What homosexuals want in relationships. *Psychology Today,* pp. 28–38.

Pietrofesa, J. J., & Splete, H. (1975). *Career development: Theory and research.* New York: Grune & Stratton.

Pines, A. M., & Aronson, E. (with Kafry, D.). (1981). *Burnout: From tedium to personal growth.* New York: Free Press.

Pleck, J., & Sawyer, J. (Eds.). (1974). *Men and masculinity.* Englewood Cliffs, N.J.: Prentice-Hall (Spectrum).

Robinson, F. P. (1970). *Effective study* (4th ed.). New York: Harper & Row.

Rogers, C. R. (1961). *On becoming a person: A therapist's view of psychotherapy.* Boston: Houghton Mifflin.

Rogers, C. R. (1980). *A way of being.* Boston: Houghton Mifflin.

Rogers, C. R. (1984). One alternative to nuclear planetary suicide. *The Counseling Psychologist, 12*(2), 3–12.

Rubenstein, C. (1983, July). The modern art of courtly love. *Psychology Today,* pp. 40–49.

Rubin, Z. (1983, May). Are working wives hazardous to their husbands' mental health? *Psychology Today,* pp. 70–72.

Schell, J. (1982). *The fate of the earth.* New York: Knopf.

Schiff, N. R. (1984, January). The art of aging. *Psychology Today,* pp. 32–41.

Schnitzer, E. (1977). *Looking in.* Idyllwild, Calif.: Strawberry Valley Press.

Schwartz, J. (1982). *Letting go of stress.* New York: Pinnacle.

Sheehy, G. (1976). *Passages: Predictable crises of adult life.* New York: Dutton.

Sheehy, G. (1981). *Pathfinders.* New York: William Morrow.

Smyer, M. A. (1984). Life transitions and aging: Implications for counseling older adults. *The Counseling Psychologist, 12*(2), 17–28.

Srebalus, D. J., Marinelli, R. P., & Messing, J. K. (1982). *Career development: Concepts and procedures.* Monterey, Calif.: Brooks/Cole.

Steiner, C. (1975). *Scripts people live: Transactional analysis of life scripts.* New York: Bantam.

Sterns, H. L., Weis, D. M., & Perkins, S. E. (1984). A conceptual approach to counseling older adults and their families. *The Counseling Psychologist, 12*(2), 55–61.

Stress: Can we cope? (1983, June 6). *Time,* pp. 48–54.

Super, D. E., & Bohn, M. J. (1970). *Occupational psychology.* Belmont, Calif.: Wadsworth.

Terkel, S. (1975). *Working.* New York: Avon.

Toffler, A. (1981). *The third wave.* New York: Bantam.

Tolbert, E. L. (1980). *Counseling for career development* (2nd ed.). Boston: Houghton Mifflin.

Waters, E. B. (1984). Building on what you know: Techniques for individual and group counseling with older people. *The Counseling Psychologist, 12*(2), 63–74.

Watson, D. L., & Tharp, R. G. (1985). *Self-directed behavior: Self-modification for personal adjustment* (4th ed.). Monterey, Calif.: Brooks/Cole.

Weiten, W. (1983). *Psychology applied to modern life: Adjustment in the 80s.* Monterey, Calif.: Brooks/Cole.

Wellman, F. E., & McCormack, J. (1984). Counseling with older persons: A review of outcome research. *The Counseling Psychologist, 12*(2), 81–96.

Williams, R. L., & Long, J. D. (1983). *Toward a self-managed life style* (3rd ed.). Boston: Houghton Mifflin.

Woodman, N. J., & Lenna, H. R. (1980). *Counseling with gay men and women: A guide for facilitating positive lifestyles.* San Francisco: Jossey-Bass.

Yalom, I. D. (1980). *Existential psychotherapy.* New York: Basic Books.

Yudkin, M. (1984, April). When kids think the unthinkable. *Psychology Today,* pp. 18–25.

Zimbardo, P. G. (1978). *Shyness.* New York: Jove.

PHOTO CREDITS

p. 4, Michael Hayman, Stock Boston, Inc.; **p. 6,** Anne McQueen, Stock Boston, Inc.; **p. 11,** George Bellerose, Stock Boston, Inc.; **p. 12,** Owen Franken, Stock Boston, Inc.; **p. 21,** Owen Franken, Stock Boston, Inc.; **p. 45** (top right), Peter Menzel, Stock Boston; **p. 45** (top left), Peter Menzel, Stock Boston, Inc.; **p. 45** (bottom right), George Malave, Stock Boston, Inc.; **p. 45** (bottom left), Fredrik D. Bodin, Stock Boston, Inc.; **p. 55,** Erika Stone; **p. 66,** Mike Mazzaschi, Stock Boston, Inc.; **p. 82,** Erika Stone; **p. 92,** Addison Geary, Stock Boston, Inc.; **p. 103,** Jerry Howard, Stock Boston, Inc.; **p. 107,** Jerry Burndt, Stock Boston, Inc.; **p. 120,** Roger Mallock, Magnum Photos, Inc.; **p. 121,** Arthur Grace, Stock Boston, Inc.; **p. 139,** Jean Claude Lejune, Stock Boston, Inc.; **p. 143,** Peter Soutwick, Stock Boston, Inc.; **p. 149,** Erika Stone; **p. 169** (left), Barbara Alper, Stock Boston, Inc.; **p. 169** (right), Peter Simon, Stock Boston, Inc.; **p. 178,** Greg Mancuso, Stock Boston, Inc.; **p. 187,** Erika Stone; **p. 220,** Miro Vintoniv, Stock Boston, Inc.; **p. 227,** Erika Stone; **p. 248,** Bill Binzen; **p. 262,** Judy Canty, Stock Boston, Inc.; **p. 275** (left), Christopher Morrow, Stock Boston, Inc.; **p. 275** (right), Stuart Rosner, Cooking School, Providence, RI, Stock Boston, Inc.; **p. 284,** George Bellerose, Stock Boston, Inc.; **p. 296,** Erika Stone; **p. 308,** Peter Menzel, Stock Boston, Inc.; **p. 323,** Robert Eckert, Stock Boston, Inc.; **p. 342,** Mark Antman, Stock Boston, Inc.; **p. 346,** Gabor Demjem, Stock Boston, Inc.

To the owner of this book:

We hope that you have been significantly influenced by reading *I Never Knew I Had a Choice* (3rd edition). We'd like to know as much about your experiences with the book as you care to offer. Your comments can help us make it a better book for future readers.

School: _____ Instructor's name: _____

1. What I like most about this book is _____

   _____

2. What I like least about this book is _____

   _____

3. How much personal value did you find in the Time Out for Personal Reflection sections?

   _____

   _____

4. Of how much interest and value were the end-of-the-chapter Activities and Exercises?

   _____

5. Specific topics in the book I thought were most relevant and important are _____

   _____

6. Specific suggestions for improving the book: _____

   _____

   _____

7. Some ways I used this book in class: _____

   _____

8. Some ways I used this book out of class: _____

   _____

9. The name of the course in which I used this book: _____

   _____

10. How much use did you make of the Resource Guide? _____

    _____

11. In the space below—or in a separate letter, if you care to write one—please let us know what other comments about the book you'd like to make. We welcome your suggestions!

Optional:

Your name: _____ Date: _____

May Brooks/Cole quote you, either in promotion for *I Never Knew I Had a Choice* or in future publishing ventures?

Yes _____ No _____

Sincerely,

Gerald Corey

CUT PAGE OUT AND
FOLD HERE

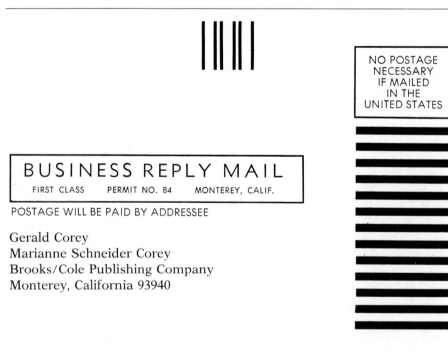

NO POSTAGE
NECESSARY
IF MAILED
IN THE
UNITED STATES

BUSINESS REPLY MAIL

FIRST CLASS   PERMIT NO. 84   MONTEREY, CALIF.

POSTAGE WILL BE PAID BY ADDRESSEE

Gerald Corey
Marianne Schneider Corey
Brooks/Cole Publishing Company
Monterey, California 93940